Liminality in Tourism

Liminality is not typically associated with tourism, even though it can be viewed as an intrinsic element of the social/cultural experiences of tourism. *Liminality in Tourism*: *Spatial and Temporal Considerations* aims to build upon the tradition of liminality as expounded in social and anthropological disciplines, elaborating on the theoretical principles and concepts found within certain aspects of the tourist journey and tourist product. The emergence of post-modern society has impelled a change in the tourist gaze towards a more experiential and adventuresome globalised experience. An important aspect of the tourist phenomenon of liminality is where a transformative experience is triggered by entering a liminoid tourist space, leaving the tourist permanently psychologically transformed, before returning to normalised society.

The narrative provides a new perspective on the tourist experience with a provocative examination into the multidimensional aspects of tourism, by exploring tourism within the spatial and temporal aspects of liminal landscapes. Covid-19 has further changed the rubric of tourism. Until the current pandemic, tourism has basically been a fun experience. In a post pandemic world, however, the tourist is now facing an unknown future which will almost certainly affect tourism liminality.

This book presents the reader with a wealth of examples and case studies closely illustrating the association between tourism and liminal experiences. The geographical perspectives explore the more subconscious outcomes of destination and tourist product consumption. The book should be a useful reader to tourism geography where the theory of liminality can be synthesised into tourist experiences.

The chapters in this book were originally published as a special issue of the journal *Tourism Geographies*.

Robert S. Bristow is Professor in the Department of Geography, Planning and Sustainability at Westfield State University, Massachusetts, USA. His research interests include cultural resource management in parks and protected areas and fright tourism.

Ian S. Jenkins was Associate Professor at the Department of Geography and Tourism, University of Iceland and is currently a visiting Associate Professor there. Published research includes the areas of festivals, sustainable tourism, literary tourism, adventure tourism, together with risk and safety management.

Liminality in Tourism

Spatial and Temporal Considerations

Edited by
Robert S. Bristow and Ian S. Jenkins

Routledge
Taylor & Francis Group

LONDON AND NEW YORK

First published 2022
by Routledge
2 Park Square, Milton Park, Abingdon, Oxon OX14 4RN

and by Routledge
605 Third Avenue, New York, NY 10158

Routledge is an imprint of the Taylor & Francis Group, an informa business
Chapters 1–3, 5–10 and 12 © 2022 Taylor & Francis
Chapter 4 © 2020 Nitasha Sharma. Originally published as Open Access.
Chapter 11 © 2019 Eugenio Conti and Susanna Heldt Cassel. Originally published as Open Access.

British Library Cataloguing in Publication Data
A catalogue record for this book is available from the British Library

ISBN: 978-0-367-77117-1 (hbk)
ISBN: 978-0-367-77118-8 (pbk)
ISBN: 978-1-003-16985-7 (ebk)

Typeset in Myriad Pro
by Newgen Publishing UK

Publisher's Note
The publisher accepts responsibility for any inconsistencies that may have arisen during the conversion of this book from journal articles to book chapters, namely the inclusion of journal terminology.

Disclaimer
Every effort has been made to contact copyright holders for their permission to reprint material in this book. The publishers would be grateful to hear from any copyright holder who is not here acknowledged and will undertake to rectify any errors or omissions in future editions of this book.

Contents

Citation Information   vii

Notes on Contributors   ix

1   Spatial and temporal tourism considerations in liminal landscapes   1
    Robert S. Bristow and Ian S. Jenkins

2   The liminality in popular festivals: identity, belonging and hedonism as
    values of tourist satisfaction   11
    Lorena Rodríguez-Campo, Fátima Braña-Rey, Elisa Alén-González and
    José Antonio Fraiz-Brea

3   Transformative landscapes: liminality and visitors' emotional experiences at
    German memorial sites   32
    Doreen Pastor and Alexander J. Kent

4   Dark tourism and moral disengagement in liminal spaces   55
    Nitasha Sharma

5   Liminality and difficult heritage in tourism   80
    Velvet Nelson

6   Communitas in fright tourism   101
    Robert S. Bristow

7   South African township residents describe the liminal potentialities of tourism   120
    Meghan L. Muldoon

8   Between space and place in mountaineering: navigating risk, death,
    and power   136
    Maggie C. Miller and Heather Mair

9   Change within the change: pregnancy, liminality and adventure
    tourism in Mexico   152
    Isis Arlene Díaz-Carrión, Paola Vizcaino-Suárez and Hugo Gaggiotti

10   Liminality at-sea: cruises to nowhere and their metaworlds   174
     Bradley Rink

11   Liminality in nature-based tourism experiences as mediated through
     social media   195
     Eugenio Conti and Susanna Heldt Cassel

12   Liminality Wanted. Liminal landscapes and literary spaces: The Way of St. James   215
     Rubén C. Lois González and Lucrezia Lopez

     Index   236

Citation Information

The chapters in this book were originally published in the journal *Tourism Geographies*, volume 22, issue 2 (2020). When citing this material, please use the original page numbering for each article, as follows:

Chapter 1
Spatial and temporal tourism considerations in liminal landscapes
Robert S. Bristow and Ian S. Jenkins
Tourism Geographies, volume 22, issue 2 (2020), pp. 219–228

Chapter 2
The liminality in popular festivals: identity, belonging and hedonism as values of tourist satisfaction
Lorena Rodríguez-Campo, Fátima Braña-Rey, Elisa Alén-González and José Antonio Fraiz-Brea
Tourism Geographies, volume 22, issue 2 (2020), pp. 229–249

Chapter 3
Transformative landscapes: liminality and visitors' emotional experiences at German memorial sites
Doreen Pastor and Alexander J. Kent
Tourism Geographies, volume 22, issue 2 (2020), pp. 250–272

Chapter 4
Dark tourism and moral disengagement in liminal spaces
Nitasha Sharma
Tourism Geographies, volume 22, issue 2 (2020), pp. 273–297

Chapter 5
Liminality and difficult heritage in tourism
Velvet Nelson
Tourism Geographies, volume 22, issue 2 (2020), pp. 298–318

Chapter 6
Communitas in fright tourism
Robert S. Bristow
Tourism Geographies, volume 22, issue 2 (2020), pp. 319–337

Chapter 7
South African township residents describe the liminal potentialities of tourism
Meghan L. Muldoon
Tourism Geographies, volume 22, issue 2 (2020), pp. 338–353

Chapter 8
Between space and place in mountaineering: navigating risk, death, and power
Maggie C. Miller and Heather Mair
Tourism Geographies, volume 22, issue 2 (2020), pp. 354–369

Chapter 9
Change within the change: pregnancy, liminality and adventure tourism in Mexico
Isis Arlene Díaz-Carrión, Paola Vizcaino-Suárez and Hugo Gaggiotti
Tourism Geographies, volume 22, issue 2 (2020), pp. 370–391

Chapter 10
Liminality at-sea: cruises to nowhere and their metaworlds
Bradley Rink
Tourism Geographies, volume 22, issue 2 (2020), pp. 392–412

Chapter 11
Liminality in nature-based tourism experiences as mediated through social media
Eugenio Conti and Susanna Heldt Cassel
Tourism Geographies, volume 22, issue 2 (2020), pp. 413–432

Chapter 12
Liminality Wanted. Liminal landscapes and literary spaces: The Way of St. James
Rubén C. Lois González and Lucrezia Lopez
Tourism Geographies, volume 22, issue 2 (2020), pp. 433–453

For any permission-related enquiries please visit:
www.tandfonline.com/page/help/permissions

Notes on Contributors

Elisa Alén-González is Associate Professor of Marketing specializing in tourism marketing at the University of Vigo. Her research work lines focused in the area of tourist behaviour.

Fátima Braña-Rey holds a PhD in Applied Social Anthropology (University of Santiago de Compostela) and is Associate Professor at University of Vigo. Her research is focused on cultural heritage and territory.

Robert S. Bristow is Professor in the Department of Geography, Planning and Sustainability at Westfield State University, Massachusetts, USA. His research interests include cultural resource management in parks and protected areas and fright tourism.

Susanna Heldt Cassel is Professor of Cultural Geography at Dalarna University, Sweden, Head of CeTLeR, and supervisor of master and PhD students at Dalarna University, Mid Sweden University and Uppsala University. Cassel's areas of research are rural tourism, mobility and destination development in peripheral areas, with a focus on social sustainability, identity and cultural heritage.

Eugenio Conti is PhD candidate in Tourism Studies at Mid Sweden University, and research assistant at Dalarna University, Sweden. He is a member of CeTLeR. Conti's current areas of research are tourism experience, experience value, tourism social media, and nature based tourism.

Isis Arlene Díaz-Carrión is Associate Professor on Tourism Geography and Sustainable Development in the Facultad de Turismo y Mercadotecnia at the Universidad Autonoma de Baja California. She is interested in tourism, sustainability, and gender.

José Antonio Fraiz-Brea is Professor of Marketing and Market Research and Coordinator of master's degree in Inland and Health Tourism Management and Planning at the University of Vigo.

Hugo Gaggiotti is Associate Professor in the Faculty of Business and Law, University of the West of England, Bristol, UK. His research focuses on nomadic work, professional liminality, stigma, and the meaning of employability.

Ian S. Jenkins was Associate Professor at the Department of Geography and Tourism, University of Iceland and is currently a visiting Associate Professor there. Published research includes the areas of festivals, sustainable tourism, literary tourism, adventure tourism, together with risk and safety management.

Alexander J. Kent is Reader in Cartography and Geographic Information Science at Canterbury Christ Church University in the UK, where he lectures on map design, GIS, remote sensing, and on European and political geography. His research explores the relationship between maps and society, and in particular, the intercultural aspects of topographic map design and the aesthetics of cartography.

Rubén C. Lois González is Full Professor of Geography in the Department of Geography at the University of Santiago de Compostela. He is the former General Director for Tourism of the Autonomous Government of Galicia (2005–2009). He is the author of more than two hundred publications and has published a considerable number of articles in scientific reviews, such as *Geographical Research, Tourism Management Perspective, Die Erde, Journal of Tourism and Cultural Change, Tourism and Hospitality Research*.

Lucrezia Lopez is Lecturer of Geography at the Department of Geography of the University of Santiago de Compostela. She holds a PhD in Geography from the University of Santiago de Compostela. Her main research lines include: Human and Cultural Geography; Tourism Geography; Heritage and Heritage Management; Geography of Pilgrimages and Geography of Sacred Spaces (Cultural itineraries and the Way of St. James); Geo-Humanities.

Heather Mair is Professor in the Recreation and Leisure Studies Department at the University of Waterloo. Her work concentrates on critical explorations of the role of leisure, tourism, and sport in the development of communities.

Maggie C. Miller is a senior lecturer in tourism at Swansea University, and holds a PhD in Recreation and Leisure Studies. Much of her work concentrates on critical explorations of the role of tourism and leisure in the development of communities. In particular, she takes up research to understand and enhance social justice and equity within these contexts.

Meghan L. Muldoon is Assistant Professor with the School of Community Resources and Development at Arizona State University, based at the newly-established HNU-ASU Joint International Tourism College in Hainan, China. Her areas of research interest include tourist–host encounters, postcolonialism, representations of Indigeneity, feminisms, digital discourses, arts-based methodologies, and critical pedagogies.

Velvet Nelson is Professor in the Department of Geography and Geology at Sam Houston State University in Huntsville, Texas, USA. She is a human geographer with a specialization in the geography of tourism.

Doreen Pastor completed her PhD in German Studies at the University of Bristol and is currently a lecturer in German Society and Politics at the University of Bath. Her research is focused on the politics of memorialisation of the Nazi and Communist past in Germany, in particular the visitor response to exhibitions and memorials.

Bradley Rink is human geographer and Associate Professor in the Department of Geography, Environmental Studies and Tourism at the University of the Western Cape (UWC). His research and teaching focuses on mobilities, tourism, and urban place-making.

Lorena Rodríguez-Campo is PhD in Management and Business Administration and Associate Professor at University of Vigo. Her research is focused on destination management, marketing, festivals, and emotions.

Nitasha Sharma is Research Fellow at the Faculty of Spatial Sciences, University of Groningen, Netherlands. Her research broadly examines the multiple and contested representations of South Asia through projects situated in critical tourism studies and global environmental change.

Paola Vizcaino-Suárez is Lecturer in the Faculty of Management, Bournemouth University, UK. Her research focuses on the gender dimensions of tourism, hospitality and events, with a particular interest in the Latin American context.

Spatial and temporal tourism considerations in liminal landscapes

Robert S. Bristow (iD) and Ian S. Jenkins

ABSTRACT

Anthropogenic geographic studies in tourism should consider the liminality of the experience. Tourism by definition means a temporal and/or spatial movement takes place. How the tourist interacts and behaves during this transitory experience is a logical progression into human leisure behaviour. Several recent international gatherings of geographers provide the foundation to explore liminality in tourism and we build on those papers in this special issue. The papers are varied in geographies, yet have a central theoretical basis in all things liminal. Invited papers in this special issue are founded on the research presented at two international geography conferences in sessions devoted to tourism. The American Association of Geographers meeting in Boston, Massachusetts in 2017 and the Royal Geographic Society with the Institute of British Geographers in Cardiff, Wales in 2018 gathered geographers from around the world to study this theme. The following papers give the most comprehensive geographic review in tourism to date and we encourage additional dialogue.

摘要

旅游地理研究应该考虑到经验的阈限。旅游的定义是指一种时间和/或空间的移动。游客在这种短暂的体验中如何互动和行为表现是人类休闲行为的逻辑发展。最近几次国际地理学家会议为探索旅游业中的阈限提供了基础,本期特刊中的论文以这些会议论文为基础发展而来。这些论文涉及到的地理区域各不相同,但所有主题都以阈限为核心理论基础。本期特刊的特邀论文是基于两个国际地理会议旅游论坛的研究成果。2017年,美国地理学家协会(American Association of geo)在马萨诸塞州的波士顿召开;2018年,英国皇家地理学会(Royal Geographic Society)在威尔士的加的夫(Cardiff)与英国地理学家协会(Institute of British geo)在威尔士召开会议。本期论文提供了迄今为止最全面的旅游地理评论,我们鼓励开展更多的对话。

Introduction

Liminality has recently grown in importance for a number of tourism scholars and the tourism discipline (Andrews & Roberts, 2012; Brooker & Joppe, 2014; Crouch, 2000; Mulcahy, 2017; Preston-Whyte, 2004; Pritchard & Morgan, 2006; Wu, Li, Wood, Senaux, & Dai, 2020). The transitional time and space for the tourist experience is an important one to understand since it has a great impact on the overall encounter and experience. Yet the sheer nature of liminality is generally so abstract (Preston-Whyte, 2004) that only recently has research attempted to explore the relationship in tourism. The concept is so fluid that scholars across the disciplines have applied the term to any transition that may occur, permitting an explanation for something that the author may or may not be able to explain. And this of course may mean a digression from the initial theory of liminality, and the notion of threshold created in the late 19th century from the Latin 'limen or Limin'.

In other words, authors sometimes use the term liminal because they really do not know how to explain something. But this fluidity is useful. Downey, Kinane, and Parker (2016) suggests this 'malleability' permits a broader explanation in an imprecise world. Further its use in humanities and social sciences are commonly threaded by spatiality. This blends nicely with geography and our exploration in this issue.

Andrews and Roberts (2012) identify the inherent spatio-temporal link of liminality noting the threshold denotes spatiality and sequential elements alluding to temporal. Without this foundation, liminality just becomes the catch-all phrase to explain the unexplainable. And while these authors suggest liminal landscapes can be explored in a multidisciplinary approach, tourism by definition has this spatio-temporal groundwork.

Liminality is anthropologically associated with Rites of Passage (van Gennep, 1909/1960). Van Gennep suggests three stages in the experience, a separation, the liminal threshold and aggregation. The first phase occurs with the detachment from the social norms. The transition of the second phase fuses preconceived and future unknowns and are set aside permitting an immersive experience. The final phase elevates the person to a higher plane, fed by their personal journey and the liminal encounter.

Turner (1974) and Shields (2013) broadened liminality as the temporal and/or spatial transition from one stage to another. It is this extrapolation that permits the additional use, and misuse of liminality to explain behaviour.

Thomassen (2012) cautions us about using Turner's 'liminoid' to explain liminal space in today's world. And this is wise, considering the miss use and abuse to explain an unknown or threshold. If we remain true to van Gennep's writings, only a few of the papers that address pilgrimages in tourism in this special issue would apply. Yet we would argue that Turner's expansion of the original theory is most relevant in a tourist experience once we view the entirety of the trip, both in space and time. Are these not characteristic of Thomassen (2012) fear of transformative events and those celebrations that follow?

For the tourist experience, the chance to break away from the norms of daily life is an important aspect of tourism. Liminality is a logical transition for tourists since they are leaving the comfort of home to travel across time and space and some threshold or boundary to various unknown experiences. This reflects the period and space during the early phases of the experience (Clawson & Knetsch, 1966; Lew, 2012; Light, 2009; Nelson, 2017; White & White, 2004).

The Clawson and Knetsch (1966) model is simple yet frequently forgotten in our desire to understand the tourist. Beginning with the anticipation phase, the tourist begins to ponder the trip. During this planning phase the traveler begins to review guidebooks, travel review sites, Google Earth and other resources needed to actually take the trip. Next, the travel phase occurs where some mode of movement is aided by transport. It could be a car, bus, train, or plane. This transition is part of the experience and the traveler is typically excited about the anticipated experience. On-site, opportunities for experiences take place. Something new and unexpected is found at the destination, and this is a primary reason to take the trip in the first place. Returning home perhaps exhausted and broke, the excitement winds down as we re-enter our life, be it the work place, or home responsibilities. We next recollect the trip. Good times and bad are remembered. For many, even the bad experiences (e.g., sun burned) are quickly forgotten although others may not be so easy (e.g., dropped cell phone in ocean). But in any case this post-travel opportunity fuels the next anticipation phase (i.e., remember to take sun screen, and don't take cell phone on the fishing boat).

As noted earlier, liminality as a subject in tourism has never been a main focus of interest, but recently there has been a resurgence in its importance with current literature reflecting this view. A quick evaluation of previous texts relating to tourism and liminality, reveals some research in this area, with certain publications discussing features of a tourist's 'rite of passage'. For example Disney and aspects of liminality can be found in Moore's paper (1980). Typically this paper reflects the more religious aspects of liminality and its relationship to one of the biggest players in the tourism industry that is the Disney Corporation.

Perhaps the revival of liminality in tourism mirrors some major cultural shifts that have taken place in tourism for example the tourist gaze and its link to postmodernist theory. Some influential seminal texts, such as Urry's 'The Tourist Gaze' (2002) have given a new meaning to experiential aspects of tourism, to the extent that a more behavourist and reflective approach has developed in the way that tourism is viewed and researched. Post-modernism has in one sense identified significant changes in tourist experiences, in particular reflecting a hyper-reality product, more closely linked to liminality (Urry, 2002; Wang, 2000). Transformative personal experiences are a common theme to be found in many products of the current tourist market. Numerous tourism products are developed which exploit the human need for novel experiences, whereby the consumer is transported out of the everyday and mundane into more novel, hedonistic, ritualized and new experiential dimensions; reflective of unreal or hyper-normal frames. Many of these themes are to be found in the papers presented in this special issue.

Experiential is a key word in many tourism products that people wish to consume. Perhaps the exponential growth of festivals is symptomatic of this need for more liminal experiences by tourists? Certainly some festivals have a very specific aura relating to its integrity, providing a sense of communitas. To fully commune with the festival one must participate in its ambiance and rituals, leading to a feeling of communitas.

Although spatially defined, some festivals are clearly temporal and otherworldly, where following the actual event its tangible elements have completely disappeared; a good example of this is the Hay Festival in Wales (Jenkins, 2019). Within days of the Festival's end there is no material evidence of a tourist presence or what might have been experienced. The product, as with most tourism products, is intangible; all that remains is the memory of the experience, the unbounded liminal space that has been consumed. For example do we remain the same person following attendance at a major music/arts festival such as Glastonbury or Hay?

It seems evident that van Gennep (1909/1960) and Turner's (1974) original understanding of a liminal experience has changed to encompass commercialisation, as noted earlier with the Disney example. Attendance at Disney has been likened to a liminal experience and has similarities with the 'rite of passage' journey for all children and parents, (predominantly from the developed world) who purchase and consume this transformative experience.

Certainly the collected papers in this special issue, illustrate how the boundaries of liminality are changing and evolving to encompass the needs and wants of both global tourists and markets. It appears that the singularity of the tourist product has transformed into a multi-dimensional mix which offers, in some products, a new liminoid experience.

History of special issue

So how did this volume come about? Recent tourism papers presented during the American Association of Geographers (Boston 2017) and Royal Geographic Society with the Institute of British Geographers (Cardiff 2018) illustrate the growing body of literature on the theme of liminality and tourism. The theme of the Boston conference was an exploration of dark(er) liminal spaces in tourism. Dark(er) tourist attractions may range from the lighter end (e.g., fright tourism for entertainment) to the darker side (e.g., sites of genocide). Further some sites may have 'darker' reputation due to one's perception of fear and safety. So people can be expected to have different motivations or reasons to visit (educational, pilgrimage, entertainment). Studies reference the transition in liminal space from one's ordinary life into a spatial and temporal one found at the destination, from either the tourist's viewpoint and/ or the site's management. Several ideas from Boston are found in the new papers here.

A year later, Cardiff hosted the broader session of liminality and tourism. And unlike the Boston meeting, this broader approach includes other topics of tourism. The work of van Gennep and Turner continue to serve as the stepping stones toward our understanding of liminal, and yet we are able to explore space on the fringe as illustrated by Iceland and Nepal. Dark tourism continues to support liminality as we gaze into our difficult heritage. We are also fortunate to have submissions from that conference in this volume.

This special issue of *Tourism Geographies* builds on this research and presents an overview of how liminality is experienced by the tourist and is based on invited papers that address liminality in tourism landscapes. It is our intent that the papers will provide a more holistic insight into the tourist experience.

Organizing the papers in this special issue is as problematic as the concept of liminality. In general we attempted to provide a broad collection of papers dealing temporal and/or spatial considerations in tourism landscapes around the world. The discovered new and revised terms of tourism are introduced in this collection and illustrate the depth and breadth of the studies. In some cases the research questions are based on quantitative or qualitative survey instruments, and others explore the role of social media or travel review websites to assess the liminal experience. In all cases, human's interaction in a tourism environment involves a temporal and spatial component.

Themes from the special issue

If we are to categorize our papers, four main ideas are found. Pilgrimages are a classic theme in tourism and we start with this theme. From that the papers blend into topics of the dark tourism arena, where tourists may be seeking to understand a darker element of our world. Peripheral areas offer some liminal landscape experienced in adventure tourism. And we conclude with papers emphasizing virtual geographies of tourists.

A traditional approach to liminality is highlighted by a paper on a religious festival; here the observations imply visitors are brought together for a shared liminal experience based upon becoming part of the ritual. Rodríguez-Campo and her colleagues bridge the gap between the ritualized experience and present day hedonism; they research an 800 year old festival using quantitative methods to examine participant experience. They are able to identify and show a two dimension liminal experience with an emphasis on hedonism, which given the context of a religious festival seems somewhat of a paradox. The tourists bond through the ritual of the festival and this creates a form of communitas, leading to a liminal experience based upon a sense of hedonism for the individual. The liminoid experience creates a need to repeat this and hence the event has a large number of repeat tourists to the festival. As a result of the repeat visitors the phenomenon of novelty is rarely part of the liminoid experience felt by the tourists. The nine day festival clearly lifts the guests from the mundane into a liminoid experience which must be repeated each year. This example is clearly different from more conservative rites of passage where the experienced rite or event is singular and the participant is supposedly permanently changed (e.g., Christian confirmation, Jewish Mitzvah and perhaps the university graduation ceremony).

Sites of the horrific history of Europe are sought by tourists in an attempt to understand and give some meaning to the events in the middle of the 20th century. The transformation of German concentration camps to tourist attractions has not been an easy one. The local government is challenged with educating the public about the atrocities via an educational format, while the air of the history remains on the minds of local citizens. The tourists must view a sanitized version of Ravensbrück and Flossenbürg. Ravensbrück was the largest women's concentration camp in Germany and 'processed' 130,000 inmates until 1945. Flossenbürg processed over 100,000 inmates. Both sites are dark tourist destinations that have a lingered history that the visitors must grasp. For instance, how does someone accept the reality that their hostel was formerly a SS female guard building?

Elements of Southern Asia's liminality is explored by Sharma where tourists gaze the cremation rituals, disregarding the somber occasion and photographing the Aghoris at the cremation grounds in Varanasi. The visitors are outside of the experience, looking in and do not realize the intrusive nature of the photograph that pierce the liminal threshold in this transgressive behaviour. Perhaps desensitized by the macabre yet personally important experience, the fleeting visit of the tourist is shoved into the extreme liminal ritual. Perhaps the visitor has little time to grasp the significance of the ceremony. Are the tourists really desensitized or are they engrossed in the extreme experience of a cremation ritual? Not for the faint of heart, this form of tourism fuses the historic culture with present day interest. Dark tourism in particular is often viewed as an exploitive experience and the cremation rituals is an excellent example.

Cruise tourists are attracted to Bonaire known for scuba diving and coral reefs. Nelson takes this tropical paradise with a checkered history to reflect on tourist's perception of that history. During their visit, they encounter restored slave huts characteristic of a darker time. The encounter is frequently unexpected since these restored structures are found along the beaches that are popular for diving. TripAdvisor becomes the travel diary for the visitors and the banter between the writers reflects the insensitivity toward Caribbean slavery and the disgust toward by others that reflect on this difficult heritage in the paper. Some visitors reflect on the somber occasion while others use the huts to change into their swim suit oblivious to the significance. The recollection phase of the experience allows the authors to reflect on what they saw and felt when faced with the difficult heritage.

In North America, the lighter form of dark tourism, called fright tourism is found for a haunted attraction (Bristow). Built on the work by Bristow and Newman (2005), fright tourism occurs when a tourist seeks a scary opportunity for pleasure at a destination that may have a sinister history or may be promoted to have one. Popular haunted houses enable the visitor to experience liminality knowing that it will be a safe and orchestrated experience that still offers a fright or two. The travel from the safety of home and the anticipation of the frightful experience is heightened while the tourists are in the queue. The guests do not know what to expect but the unexpected is part of the fun. The fright tourist party is made up of family and/or friends and is shown to contribute to the fears we all share. The bonds of these communitas are defined by the measures of fear and yield some insight on the relationship of our fears and fun in a liminal dark attraction.

Cape Town, South Africa, is the locale for a paper which explores the legacy of, apartheid and slum tourism. Muldoon discovers the human side of liminality through examining the narratives of local people who continue to live under horrific conditions and reflect on the gawking of tourist strangers to their home environment. Perhaps this paper echoes how 'real tourism' was originally envisaged and could achieve, not just a monetary exchange but a substantial social and cultural understanding of different human worlds. The use of CAP (Creative Analytical Practice) is a challenging but exciting methodology in which research is contained in an 'inventive/imaginary' narrative, based upon discourse methods. Using stories to illustrate reality by vicarious characters creates aspects of liminal experience and space. CAP is a means of recreating the real through reconstructing the known into an imaginary story. Visiting the homes of locals by tourists is a sensitive and delicate tourist product but can be transformative for both guest and host bringing a transformation in terms of understanding the economic, social and cultural differences that are perpetuated by the media. Furthermore our own understanding of countries and the locales that people inhabit can be changed by unbounded experiences. Township tourism or slum tourism is not new but is clearly open to much criticism. In this paper the discourse analysis tries to identify the liminal aspects of having predominantly white tourists visit predominantly black townships, illustrating aspects of how black communities may begin to actually have some respect for who they are and what they stand for.

A liminal approach to our peripheral landscapes is reflected by Miller and Mair, who explore the risky adventure tourism employees that cater to the tourists seeking to summit the mountains in Nepal. The Sherpas responsible for this opportunity risk their lives to earn a living and attempt to balance this economic need in the high mountains. Living and working in the high mountains is the norm for Sherpas, yet a threshold experience for the mountaineer. Like Clawson and Knetsch's model of the recreation experience the adventure tourist must make the arduous hike, gaining elevation to acclimatize in extreme conditions. What is temporary and fleeting for the tourist is the norm for the Sherpa. Liminality in the mountains drives the Sherpas to reflect on their role in this dangerous adventure tourism enterprise. And summiting the mountains is not without deadly risk.

In the paper by Díaz-Carrión an explanation of the liminal nature of womanhood and tourism is questioned. Add to this, the entry in a formerly male dominated world of adventure tourism, how do these women embrace the internal and external changes during the experience? Due to this emphasis, there is little research into women and adventure tourism. And what studies are found provide just basic participation data. Interviews of the adventure tourism enthusiasts offer an understanding of the changes that may occur through a qualitative review. For example, advance stages of pregnancy may drive participation away from some activities, as in activity substitution, while others may feel empowered by the opportunity. The narratives provide an insight on the liminal nature of the women's growth and the interest in adventure tourism in Mexico.

Debauchery tourism (Rink) serves as a reminder that human tourist behavior is frequently atypical, permitting an escape from the norms of home. A floating party boat is fueled by alcohol and non-stop entertainment transforms the tourist from a sane human toward a hedonistic state. Once the long weekend has passed, they can return home knowing that what happens on *Oh Ship*, stays on *Oh Ship*. This paper identifies a number of issues relating to liminality and tourism. Little has been written on cruise tourism and how liminality affects the cruise tourist, so this paper explores the idea of destination. Furthermore exploring liminality in the context of 'debauchery tourism' is somewhat challenging and although much has been written relating to other aspects of debauchery tourism such as sex tourism, the context of drug induced liminality is a somewhat innovative approach. Can liminoid states be engendered by drug fueled tourism? The paper seeks to explore this sensitive area in a subtle and empathetic way. In many respects, cruise companies are just satisfying a gap in cruise sales (while ships wait for scheduled cruises) and having a cruise to nowhere (spatially non-destination specific) is an essential part of this product. A lack of destination can induce a change in reality, as guests don't know where they are, which seems to play an important part in the transforming experience, so that 'the space of the cruise ship has the potential to serve as a 'liminoid playground' (Selänniemi, 2003).

Nature viewed through social media provides another gaze for exploring liminality of tourists. Conti & Heldt Cassel's article evaluates social media and travel narratives which reflect the experiences of nature tourists. The method they use is based on a netnographic study of nature based experiences. Netnography is an emerging methodology exploring meaning and understanding of social and cultural experiences through on-line resources and platforms. This in essence is a 'post-holiday' experience based upon the presentation and narration of their visual images on-line. The authors found the use of social media, was able to allow the users to create a liminal experience based upon a created virtual space. The popular social media platform Instagram was used for the study to source data 'posters' (the person posting pictures and texts) and establish whether a liminal experiences had occurred. Conti and Heldt Cassel demonstrate the individual experiential changes that take place while posters are using Instagram. As discussed earlier in this chapter the postmodernist developments of tourism can be seen in the tourism markets and this particular paper seems to be an exemplar of it. This paper identifies a new way of understanding liminoid experience through virtual on-line forms of communitas. The 'posters' (individuals active on Instagram) can be seen to engage and remove themselves from the mundane and social norms of society. Some of the posters even create their own alter egos which are clearly seen as a transformative and liminal experience.

The famous pilgrimage of The Way of St. James is studied by González and Lopez and report on the travel narratives that evolve during the trek. Pilgrimages are a classic example exhibited by van Gennep's thesis. Truly a ritualized experience, The Way has also become a popular hike for pilgrims world-wide. In this case, as the tourist experiences the walk, both temporally and spatially, the narrative changes illustrative of the spiritual growth of the traveler. A liminal literary landscape evolves illustrating the nature of the landscape. The pilgrimage embraces the liminality of the landscape along The Way, transforming the individual. The shear act of writing is a way of communicating the thoughts of and reflects the journey of the authors.

Concluding thoughts

Across the spectrum of place and activities, tourists encounter liminal landscapes by the shear act of time and movement. Our collection of papers is founded on a mix of geographic and tourism theory which are clearly linked to Liminality but we do acknowledged the caution of Downey et al. (2016, p.3) who have called liminality the 'catch-all expression for an ambiguous, transitional, or interstitial spatio-temporal dimensions', and we have tried to ensure that these papers do reflect liminality rather than a catch-all. That said the papers do cover a wide variety of different subjects.

It seems evident from the articles collated here that liminality has evolved from its roots in van Gennep's and Turner's addendum into a theory allowing a much wider understanding and multi-disciplinary acceptance of liminality. As with the notion of globalization, liminality is itself a reflected form of globalization, especially when viewed through the tourist product and the tourist experience. What is exciting about this special issue is the number of authors that have used different methodologies to explore the transformative experience and ideas of liminality and communitas. Many areas of current tourist markets have been researched by the authors, including those of virtual worlds, with tourists creating, through social media and digital technology, meta-realities outside the mundane and every day. It is anticipated that this special edition will stimulate further research into the tourism topics that have been presented, in particular, the use and exploration of innovative research methods such as CAP and Netnography. It is also heartening to see more 'traditional' aspects of liminality, such as religious festivals and pilgrimages, featuring in the submissions; these are more aligned with the original foundations of liminality. From a geographical perspective it is pleasing to see new understandings of destinations featuring, such as 'moving space', 'digital space' and even 'imaginative' spatial locations, all of which still identify the transformative and communitas experience which are key to liminality. It is self-evident that the novel, spiritual and hedonistic nature of many tourism products allow the tourist to experience these feelings. Liminality is not a new phenomenon (it has always existed) of the authors van Gennep and Turner, but they have given us a theoretical premise to more fully understand how tourism can be used to transform the tourist.

Liminality is not the goal of tourism; it merely is something that we get through during the experience. In most cases, it is probably just a hurdle that we must jump to get to the fun. But in some cases liminality provides a life changing event. Tourists want the thrill of a good time, but also desire the shudder of the bad (Eco, 1986). And isn't that what many tourists' seek?

Disclosure statement

No potential conflict of interest was reported by the author(s).

ORCID

Robert S. Bristow (iD) http://orcid.org/0000-0001-7927-794X

References

Andrews, H., & Roberts, L. (Eds.). (2012). *Liminal landscapes: Travel, experience and spaces in-between*. London: Routledge.

Bristow, R. S., & Newman, M. (2005). Myth vs. fact: An exploration of fright tourism. In Bricker, Kelly (Comp., Ed.), *Proceedings of the 2004 Northeastern Recreation Research Symposium. Gen. Tech. Rep. NE*-326 (pp. 215–221). Newtown Square, PA: US Department of Agriculture, Forest Service, Northeastern Research Station.

Brooker, E., & Joppe, M. (2014). Developing a tourism innovation typology: Leveraging liminal insights. *Journal of Travel Research, 53*(4), 500–508. doi:10.1177/0047287513497839

Clawson, M., & Knetsch, J. L. (1966). *Economics of outdoor recreation*. Washington, DC: Resources for the Future.

Crouch, D. (2000). Places around us: Embodied geographies in leisure and tourism. *Leisure Studies, 19* (2), 63–76. doi:10.1080/026143600374752

Downey, D., Kinane, I., & Parker, E. (2016). *Landscapes of liminality: Between space and place*. London: Rowman & Littlefield International.

Eco, U. (1986). *Travels in hyper reality: Essays*. San Diego, CA: Houghton Mifflin Harcourt.

Jenkins, I.S. (2019). The Hay festival: A longitudinal study on its attributes and the sustainable impacts on a small Welsh Town. In I. S. Jenkins & and K. A. Lund (Ed.), *Literary tourism theories, practices and case studies* (pp. 120–132). Wallingford: CABI.

Lew, A. A. (2012). Tourism incognita: Experiencing the liminal edge of destination places. *Études Caribéennes, 19*, 1–12. doi:10.4000/etudescaribeennes.5232

Light, D. (2009). Performing Transylvania: Tourism, fantasy and play in a liminal place. *Tourist Studies, 9* (3), 240–258. doi:10.1177/1468797610382707

Moore, A. (1980). Walt Disney World: Bounded ritual space and the playful pilgrimage center. *Anthropological Quarterly, 53*(4), 207–218.

Mulcahy, D. (2017). The salience of liminal spaces of learning: Assembling affects, bodies and objects at the museum. *Geographica Helvetica, 72*(1), 109–118. doi:10.5194/gh-72-109-2017

Nelson, V. (2017). *An introduction to the geography of tourism*. Lanham, MD: Rowman & Littlefield.

Preston-Whyte, R. (2004). The beach as a liminal space. In A. Lew, C. M. Hall, & A. Williams (Eds.), *The Blackwell's tourism companion* (pp. 249–259). Oxford: Blackwell.

Pritchard, A., & Morgan, N. (2006). Hotel Babylon? Exploring hotels as liminal sites of transition and transgression. *Tourism Management, 27*(5), 762–772. doi:10.1016/j.tourman.2005.05.015

Shields, R. (2013). *Places on the margin: Alternative geographies of modernity*. London: Routledge.

Selänniemi, T. (2003). On holiday in the liminoid playground: Place, time and self in tourism. In T. G. Bauer & B. McKercher (Eds.), *Sex and tourism: Journeys of romance, love, and lust* (pp. 19–31). New York: Haworth Hospitality Press.

Thomassen, B. (2012). Revisiting liminality. In H. Andrews & L. Roberts, L. (Eds.), *Liminal landscapes: Travel, experience and spaces in-between* (pp. 21–35). New York: Routledge.

Turner, V. (1974). *Liminal to liminoid, in play, flow, and ritual: An essay in comparative symbology*. Rice Institute Pamphlet-Rice University Studies, 60(3), 53–92.

Urry, J. (2002). *The tourist gaze*. London: SAGE.

van Gennep, A. (1909/1960). *The rites of passage*. Chicago: University of Chicago Press.

Wang, N. (2000). *Tourism and modernity: A sociological analysis*. Oxford: Pergamon.

White, N. R., & White, P. B. (2004). Travel as transition: Identity and place. *Annals of Tourism Research, 31*(1), 200–218. doi:10.1016/j.annals.2003.10.005

Wu, S., Li, Y., Wood, E. H., Senaux, B., & Dai, G. (2020). Liminality and festivals—Insights from the East. *Annals of Tourism Research, 80*, 102810. doi:10.1016/j.annals.2019.102810

The liminality in popular festivals: identity, belonging and hedonism as values of tourist satisfaction

Lorena Rodríguez-Campo (iD), Fátima Braña-Rey (iD), Elisa Alén-González (iD) and José Antonio Fraiz-Brea (iD)

ABSTRACT

A Festa do Boi is a festive celebration linked to the Catholic liturgical calendar, which is celebrated in Allariz (Galicia-Spain). This festival reappears in the 1980s and like other popular festivals, it collects traditional elements and re-builds them into a new festive ritual, more in line with the new temporal and spatial configuration of the late 20th century. They are festivals in which tradition is combined, in representation of the local community, and the tourist approach (Prats, 1997). This event can be analysed as a spontaneous communitas (Turner, 1974a), a happening between hosts and guests (Smith, 1992), where the liminal space can be occupied by tourists as 'others' necessary for the identification of 'ourselves'. The participation of tourists in the festive ritual is carried out from two liminal positions: an unstable state because their daily life has been broken by the movement and involvement required in the festivals with the role of equals, but different. Both actors are required for the exaltation of collective identity. The level of satisfaction of tourists with the liminal experience based on the feeling of belonging and identification with the host community and the hedonistic perception, to provide a more holistic view of the festive ritual. A self-administered on-site survey was conducted on 393 tourists attending the 700th edition of *A Festa do Boi* in Allariz (Spain). The results suggest that hedonism acts as a precedent for satisfaction evaluation, and satisfaction evaluation for the attendees' future intentions. In addition, the liminal experience has a two-dimensional structure composed of the individual changes experienced and of the festive ritual.

摘要

亚马逊复活牛节是一个与天主教礼拜日历相联系的节日庆典, 在西班牙西北部的加利西亚阿拉兹庆祝。这个节日重新出现在80年代, 和其他流行节日一样, 它汇集传统元素, 重新建构成一个新的节日仪式, 以更符合20世纪末新的时空格局。这些节日与传统相结合, 代表了当地社区和发展旅游方式(Prats, 1997)。这个节事可以作为一个自发的共同体(Turner, 1974a)、一个发生在主人和客人之间的事件(Smith, 1992)进行分析, 在这里, 游客作为'他人'占据了有限的空间, 以表明'我们自己'所必需的身份。游客参与节日仪式有两种阈限立场:一种不稳定的状态, 因为他们的日常生活已经被节日所要求的移动和节日所要求的参与打破了, 它们扮演着同等但不同的角色。这两个行动者都是提高集体身份所必需的。游客阈限

体验的的满意程度以他们对当地社区的归属感、认同感还有对享
乐主义的感知为基础, 这为节日仪式提供了更全面的视角。本研究
对393名参加第700届西班牙阿拉力兹国际亚马逊复活牛节的游客
进行了现场调查。研究结果表明, 享乐主义是满意度评估的一个先
因, 也是对参与者未来意向的满意度评估。此外, 阈限体验具有由
个体经历的变化和节日仪式构成的二维结构。

Introduction

In recent years, liminality has gained interest among tourism specialists (Andrew & Roberts, 2012; Brooker & Joppe, 2014; Carnicelli, 2014; Duignan, Everett, Walsh, & Cade, 2017; Lança, Marques & Pinto, 2017; Mulcahy, 2017; Povilanskas & Armaitienė, 2014). The tourist trip, as a liminal period, provides a space-time totally different from that of production and work. This facilitates the possibilities of liberation, in the sense of physical and psychological passage, from everyday life (Bauer & McKercher, 2003) towards a leisure break. The anthropological concept of liminality (Turner, 1974a; Van Gennep, 1909) personifies the tourist's experience of voluntarily escaping from his usual routine to live in a new place temporarily, where he can relax, enjoy himself and rejuvenate. The interval 'betwixt and between' leaving home and eventual returning is a threshold during which existing standards can be replaced by disorder, anti-structure and experimental behaviour (Brooker & Joppe, 2014). Turner (1974a, p. 47) defined liminality as 'any condition outside or on the peripheries of everyday life', a counter to daily living that potentially allows people to discover their true self (selves) (Graburn, 2001; Preston-Whyte, 2004; Wickens, 2002).

Efforts have been made from different academic disciplines such as anthropology, sociology, psychology, education or marketing to try to conceptualize and contextualize the liminality applied to the tourist field and understand the time of transition and space, where the tourist experiences it. However, tourism literature has increased the need to expand studies on consumer behaviour. Liminal experiences are boosted and generated through human interaction and collective participation, on the one hand, collective meanings and on the other hand, a sense of communitas within the group, that is, a strong social bond between strangers, that for Turner (1974a) are favoured, mainly, in the calendrical rites.

Given that festivals are periodic rituals that organise the social calendar by interrupting the linear succession of time, forming cycles and periods (Velasco, 1982) and favouring a liminal atmosphere for tourists, this present study has the purpose of incorporating indicators that measure liminal learning and the individual changes that occur during these rites of passage that involve a kind of ritual process and that provoke individual transformative experiences, and thus, address the need for new research approaches that provide a more holistic view of the tourist experience. Therefore, the aim of this research is to analyse the level of satisfaction with the liminal experience of tourists participating in the 700th edition *of A Festa do Boi* of Allariz (Galicia-Spain) based on the feeling of belonging and identification with the host community and the hedonist perception, in order to know their future intentions. Festivalgoers have not generally been viewed as producers who actively and subjectively interpret the festival to create their own unique festival experiences (Lee et al., 2019; Manthiou et al., 2014). The current understanding of festivals does not sufficiently explain their significant role as unique opportunities away from everyday life, in which intense extraordinary experiences can be shared (Morgan, 2008). In this regard, Getz (2012) argued that research should concentrate on concepts such as liminality, communitas and authenticity, in order to holistically understand peoplés experiences in the special framework of festivals because they are events that suspend time and remove the normal restrictions of everyday life.

Literature review

Rituals of passage, community and liminality

This paper shows an analysis of the processes that take place at individual and group level in tourism attracted by traditional festivals. In particular, festivals have been offered as prime examples of a popular organizational form for creating experience spaces (Johansson & Kociatkiewicz, 2011). In this type of festival, the contemporary processes of exalting the tradition are combined in order to promote local identities and also tourist resources. In addition, it is necessary to count on the traces of Christian religiosity that recalls not only the tradition but also the social origin. These characteristics enable to know more about the liminal phenomenon and the tourist time/space of traditional festivals incorporating the communitas concept into liminality.

Chambers (2012) suggested that all tourism is a secular ritual and thus, a liminal experience. Turner (1988) develops these concepts by taking as a reference point 'the outline of rites of passage includes a sequence of pre-liminal rites (separation), liminal rites (transition) and post-liminal rites (incorporation)' (Van Gennep, 1909, p. 33). In the face of the universality of the social ritual, Turner (1974b, 1988, 1990) provides a procedural vision between the individual and society, between the moment and the period (Thomassen, 2009). Liminality appears as 'necessarily ambiguous attributes which remain outside the system of classifications that normally establish the situations and positions of the cultural space. Liminal entities are neither in one place nor in the other' (Turner, 1988, p. 56).

Liminality involves a break from everyday life and, therefore, a release of state and associated discipline (Meethan, 2012; Pritchard & Morgan, 2006; Shields, 1991). This break has been linked to refreshment (Howard, Tinsley, Tinsley, & Holt, 1993), meaningfulness (Wilson & Harris, 2006) and novelty (Duman & Mattila, 2005).

The concept of liminality goes hand in hand with communitas (Turner, 1974b). This refers to the communion of individuals as humans, to an essential link, a state opposed to the social structure according to Turner (1988, 1990). Communitas is the social link, which through the ritual process joins individuals in new forms and status, it is communion, the sense of being with others (Mackay Yarnal & Kerstetter, 2005; Pritchard & Morgan, 2006). In this aspect, the concept refers us to the social identity because the festive and ritual process leads individuals to feel part of a group, to develop a sense of belonging and identify (Rickly-Boyd, 2012). This identification can occur between the community, boosting a deeply rooted sense to the place (De Bres

& Davis, 2001), or otherwise, through the ritual experience to which tourists gain access to the participation in the festive event (Ducros, 2018). Identification through ritual participation could be an element to consider in hedonism, satisfaction and behaviour intention.

Based on Turner's liminal state typology (1974b), in which social time and space are crossed, Thomassen (2009) establishes a bidirectional model that allows to understand the different aspects by which a traditional festival can have meaning for the agents participating in it. In the former, the liminality state could take place as an individual moment in which there is a transformation of status, similar to what occurs in the rites of passage described by Van Gennep (1909), and which has been detected by other actors in their role of tourists (Carnicelli, 2014; Lança, Marques & Pinto, 2017). Secondly, as part of a group, through the social identification that takes place in the ritual participation 'being part of', which would take place during the festival period, before and after it, provided that the social interaction is focused on the festive ritual (De Bres & Davis, 2001). That is, the festive event is a ritual process and therefore social, of importance for what is individual.

On the other hand, Bourdieu (1982) indicates that the concepts of liminality and communitas do not refer to homogeneity, but to a structural separation as such. Liminality would be understood as a separation of groups of individuals in their relationship with access to resources, and rites would be actions that enable to see what is arbitrary as something natural. Based on this argument, the liminal experience would be linked to subjectivation, which implies interpersonal ways of doing and thinking (Mendiola, 2001; Turner, 1979) and therefore, what is liminal also leads us to the determination in power relationships and to obtaining subjects.

In short, liminal is an ambiguous concept that is related to the border, with the separation of states and the transit between them in a rhizomatic way (Mendiola, 2001; Mulcahy, 2017). It indicates a potential position; thus, it does not specify a place without space. According to the theoretical review carried out, it is established that the concept of liminality has been incorporated into the tourist experience in that it implies placing oneself outside the ordinary and implies a change of state (Graburn, 1992). In this context, different authors talk about experiences between the duality of tourist transit (Carnicelli, 2014; Lança, Marques & Pinto, 2017), or how the state of liminality breaks the routine and allows for the subversion of order (Farris, 2017).

The role of communitas in tourism has been examined extensively (Di Giovine, 2011) but more commonly with regard to the interaction of hosts and guests (Pearce et al., 1998) than to the role of tourists in influencing each other (Yagi & Pearce, 2007). Regarding this, existing literature suggests that tourist-to-tourist interactions, that generate feelings of communitas, enhance tourists' experiences (Huang & Hsu, 2010; Wu, 2007).

Festival spaces are both liminal and carnivalesque places (Chapman & Light, 2017; Pielichaty, 2015), that must be examined within a matrix that understands local identity, uniqueness, authenticity and liminality (Ma & Lew, 2012). In festive contexts, there is a sense of communitas within the group (for example, Halloween in Light, 2009), through a strong social bond between strangers, who regardless of their individual backgrounds, find they have something in common temporarily (Franklin, 2003; Kim &

Jamal, 2007; Wallace, 2006). Other tourists make our experience more enjoyable because they both reify communitas and ensure our safety in a strange place via the obligations communitas entails (Bauman, 1996). Fry (2014) found that visitors to a festival moved beyond the role of mere spectators and became a vital part of it, thereby coming to experience community. Giovanardi et al. (2014) recently found that festivals were further enriched and diversified by the interactions, mutual experiences and cooperation between tourists.

According to the concepts of liminality and communitas as realities of the social sense, constituent and constituted of a sense of belonging, the first hypothesis is shown:

Hypothesis 1: Communitas has a positive influence on the liminal experience

Hedonism, satisfaction and behavioural intentions

Picard and Robinson (2006) argue that festivals are liminal areas in which the transformation of social space gives way to non-traditional behaviour. The true nature of tourism, as a liminal period, is to represent a break in daily life, which facilitates the predisposition to enjoyment. In addition, festivals allow for the exploration of limits as part of individuation (Tucker, 2005), as it is possible to experience a sense of freedom (Farris, 2017), being able to reveal what is repressed (Lança et al., 2017). In this way, festivals provide freedom from the institutional obligations of work and also freedom to engage with entertainment and diversions (Turner, 1974b). Leisure of this sort is not out of obligation of legality or morality, it is engaged with at a voluntary level (Moss, 2018).

All this facilitates the feelings of refreshment (Howard, Tinsley, Tinsley, & Holt, 1993; Hull & Michael, 1995; Samdahl, 1991), meaningfulness (Jamal & Hollinshead, 2001; Noy, 2004; Wilson & Harris; 2006) and novelty (Duman & Mattila, 2005; Farber & Hall, 2007) to emerge in the liminal subject during the festive process. Kim, Ritchie, & McCormick (2012) discover that learning more about oneself and about new things is one of the ways in which the individual finds meaning through tourism experiences. In the case of visits to museums, Mulcahy (2017) denominates it liminal learning. Finally, as the level of social contact of the individual increases with different individuals and groups of people, both tourists and residents, with whom he interacts, the possibility of understanding oneself should also increase (Kim, Ritchie, & McCormick, 2012) and during this dialectical process, progress in the group is made (Paladino, 2011). Following this line, the second hypothesis of this investigation is shown:

Hypothesis 2: The liminal experience has a positive influence on hedonism

Consumers mainly want a sense of pleasure from a service experience (Carbone and Haeckel, 1994). Most studies suggested that the degree to which tourists experience local culture significantly affected how they evaluate tourism products (Lee et al., 2019; Lin & Wang, 2012). These studies have suggested that the festival experience impacts satisfaction positively and directly. Consequently, for some festival tourism researchers, understanding pleasure is necessary because it is the main benefit that the consumer obtains (Hirschman & Holbrook, 1982; Holbrook & Hirschman, 1982). In addition, hedonic benefits should be among the main drivers of perceived satisfaction (Duman & Mattila, 2005). In this sense, different investigations have confirmed that customer satisfaction is affected by the hedonic level perceived by consumers during the consumer experience (Babin, Lee, Kim, & Griffin, 2005; Caruana, Money, & Berthon, 2000; Hume, 2008).

Hypothesis 3: Hedonism has a positive influence on satisfaction

Finally, the finding that satisfaction serves as a precursor to behavioural intentions has also been acknowledged in the literature on festivals (Baker & Crompton, 2000; Choo et al., 2016; Lee et al., 2011; Mason & Paggiaro, 2012; Yoon et al., 2010). For example, Baker and Crompton (2000) have shown that satisfaction is the strongest predictor of repeated attendance intentions for participants in an annual festival, while Mason and Nassivera (2013) found that the satisfaction of the festival-goers signifi- cantly influenced, in this case, their intention to revisit the festival and to spread word-of-mouth advertising about it. More recently, it was shown that there was direct causality between satisfaction and behavioural intentions of festival-goers in Wales (Jung et al., 2015) and South Korea (Sohn et al., 2016).

Hypothesis 4: Satisfaction has a positive influence on behavioural intentions

Methodology

Research context. A Festa do Boi as a festive ritual

A Festa do Boi has been celebrated annually since 1982 in the Concello de Allariz Ourense - Galicia - Spain. The festivals that are introduced in the community are linked to tradition and in many cases include the changes that took place during that decade with the transition from an agrarian economy to a services economy that was consoli- dated in those years (Braña-Rey & Fernández-Silva, 2008). The new work calendar allows for leisure, and it is concentrated in the summer. These new festive phenomena are characterized, on the one hand, as a reencounter with tradition extolling the value of the community through the encounter between generations and on the other hand, with a tourist purpose in which we show ourselves to others (Prats, 1997).

In its original discourse, A Festa do Boi is linked to the procession of Corpus Christi. This procession emerged in the 12th century and was consolidated for the entire Christian territory under the papacy of John XXII in 1316. In the Iberian Peninsula, the celebration of this procession took place in different localities associated with the fig- ure of the bull (González-Casarrubios & Timón-Tiemblo, 1982; Porras-Arboledas, 2010).

In a very brief way, the argument of A Festa do Boi is based on the figure of Xan de Arzúa, who in 1317, in order to take revenge for the mockery of the Jewish com- munity towards the procession of Corpus Christi, led the procession on ox-back guided by six servants, in order to charge at the Jews who made fun of the event (Puga-Brau, 1996). Since then, in Allariz, the feast of Corpus Christi is linked to the fig- ure of Xan de Arzúa and the ox. The passage of time modified the festive elements and their characteristics and since the 1960s, the ox stopped going out through the streets of Allariz (Gil & Prol, 2009; Puga-Brau, 1996). The process of recovery of the presence of the ox and the secularization of the festival was made from the 1980s in which the young generation is involved to 'take out the ox again' (Gil & Prol, 2009).

The route of an ox tied and guided through the streets of Allariz begins to become a symbol of the recovery of the life of the town, regeneration that wants to be seen as the heir to tradition and of previous generations. Resorting to tradition is a form of authority, which encourages the participation and supports desires regarding the festivity. The tradition is re-invented to adapt it to new demands (Hobsbawm & Ranger, 2002), adding new elements that cooperate with future expectations.

The festival lasts nine days and on this occasion it took place between 10 and 18 June. The following are included as the main activities developed in the different geographical areas: a picnic and traditional games in San Salvador dos Penedos, the recreation of the treatment of the animal in Paicordeiro, medieval ox races for both adults and children, the medieval market, the procession and dramatization of the origin of the festival, the costume show of the medieval procession, the performance of the guilds and the troubadour contest, and the medieval neighbourhood lunch and dinners.

The Festa do Boi is a festive process that allows us to know the liminal positions that are formed in tourist time/space. Its constituent elements -such as its long duration, animal participation, occupation of urban space, corporate and symbolic activities in relation to what is represented as common and recreational, together with the proposal to assume a break with time, indicate that it is an exceptional space/time to analyse liminal processes. The Festa do Boi represents a break in the annual calendar, according to the ideology of traditional festivals whose analysis allows to identify liminal practices. At the same time, this unique event demonstrates the relationship of liminality with elements of communitas from the historical and religious imagery. These imageries build in the festive development a peculiar us, between what is individual and collective, which contributes to the configuration of varied identity positions.

Data collection and sample

The field work was carried out throughout the nine-day period of the 700th edition of *A Festa do Boi*. A self-administered questionnaire was selected, since it has a high level of accuracy and limited cost, and the responses are anonymous (Malhotra, 2004). They were distributed at different points and times of the day to ensure that the sample was unbiased. It can be ensured that each unit of the sample represents an equal portion of the total population through systematic random sampling (Jawale, 2012). Therefore, every three people participating in the main activities were asked to complete the survey. A total of 393 usable questionnaires were collected during the event.

Theoretical model development

The proposed theoretical model (Figure 1) arises from the integration of research hypotheses based on the review of the literature and the different liminal components of the tourism experience of this research: the Allariz Area – Reserve of the Biosphere

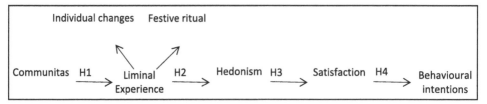

Figure 1. Theoretical model.

as the public liminal space (for example, the beach in Maciel, 2017); the transition time (nine days of duration); the liminal groups through the different participating medieval guilds (for example, the artists in Povilanskas & Armaitienė, 2014); the liminal atmosphere of the festival (for example, the slumber party in Farris, 2017); the restructuring of power, as it is the neighbours, who through the Cultural Association Xan de Arzúa organise and maintain *A Festa do Boi* and the accompanying events (Thomassen, 2016); and the costumes, both in the medieval procession and in the dramatization of the origin of the festival (for example, the dance costume in Jaimangal-Jones, Pritchard, & Morgan, 2006).

Measures

An extensive review of the literature was conducted in order to generate the items, which produced 25 items that match the variables of our model (see Figure 1): communitas (4 items), liminal experience (10 items), hedonism (4 items), satisfaction (3 items) and behavioural intentions (4 items). A 5-point Likert scale was used to measure all of them (1 = not at all and 5 = extremely much).

Regarding the communitas dimension, or feeling of belonging, this study uses the scales used by Bagozzi and Dholakia (2006) and Grappi and Montanari (2011) to measure social identification. A four-item scale was developed and included the following: *I have a feeling of belonging to the group of participants, I have an identity similar to the participants', I feel strongly attached to the group of participants, and I feel close to the regular participant.*

A ten-item scale was developed to measure the liminal experience, inspired mainly by the research of Kim et al. (2012), Lança et al. (2017), Lett (1983), Paladino (2011) and Turner (1998), and included the following items divided into two dimensions: (1) Individual changes: *I have experienced something new with A Festa do Boi, I consider that my participation in A Festa do Boi has been significant for me, I consider that my participation has been important for me, It has been a liberating experience to participate in A Festa do Boi, I enjoyed a feeling of freedom during my visit, It has been a reviving experience and It has been a revitalizing experience, and* (2) Festive ritual: *I think Boi is a festive ritual, I feel part of the people of Allariz in A Festa do Boi, and A Festa de Boi promotes a sense of identity and continuity.*

Regarding the hedonism dimension, this study is inspired by the scales used by Babin, Darden, and Griffin (1994) and Grappi and Montanari (2011), and included a four-item scale: *A Festa do Boi experience was truly enjoyable, I really feel that A Festa*

Table 1. Sociodemographic characteristics of the respondents.

Variables	(%)	X̄
Age		37
18–25	13.74	
26–35	39.95	
36–45	23.41	
46–55	12.47	
56–65	8.91	
+65	1.53	
Gender		
Male	47.1	
Female	52.9	
Education		
None	1	
Primary school	13.5	
High school	40.5	
University degree	45	
Origin		
Galicia	87.5	
Rest of Spain	11.2	
France	1.3	
Companion		
Alone	2.03	
Partner	10.18	
In a group (family and/or friends)	87.79	

do Boi is like a getaway, It represents an experience of personal enjoyment for me, and I was truly delighted.

A three-item scale was developed to measure satisfaction (Grappi & Montanari, 2011; Lee et al., 2011): *I believe that I did the right thing in attending A Festa do Boi, On the whole, I am happy with A Festa do Boi, and consider that the overall experience of the trip is satisfactory.*

Finally, behavioural intentions were measured by a four-item scale selected from previous research (Grappi & Montanari, 2011; Lee et al., 2011): *I would like to visit A Festa do Boi again next time, I will prioritise A Festa do Boi over other Festivals of Tourist Interest when deciding whether to attend, I will recommend A Festa do Boi to other people, and I will encourage friends and relatives to visit A Festa do Boi again next time.*

Findings

First, the sociodemographic profile of the interviewees is shown. As shown in Table 1, of the total number of individuals (n = 393), 47.1% were women. The average age of the respondents was 37, with the youngest being 18 and the oldest being 81. The segment aged between 18 and 45 represents 77.10% of the total. Of these, a large majority has some educational qualifications, mainly university (45%) and secondary studies (40.5%). Regarding the origin of the respondents, we can observe a great weight of proximity tourism (87.5%), either from the same province (58%) or from the rest of the provinces of the Autonomous Community (29.5%). A vast majority attend the event accompanied.

For most of the respondents, it was not the first time they attended the festival (82.95%). While some had attended two or three times before (26.21%), a high proportion of the sample said they had been there between 4 and 10 times (40.71%) and 16.03% said they had attended more than 10 times before. On the other hand, short break tourists (2–3 days) represent slightly more than half of those interviewed (52.67%), followed by those who are in the destination between 4 and 6 days (22.9%) and visitors (15.52%). Only a small proportion (8.9%) extend the length of their stay to between 7 and 9 days.

To test the hypotheses proposed in the theoretical model, Structural Equation Modelling (SEM) will be used. SEM provides simultaneous testing for the whole set of variables in a hypothesized model. For the configuration of the complete structural model, we start from the following premises: (1) the causal relationships raised are those shown in the diagram, and (2) the causal relationships are considered linear. According to Anderson and Gerbing (1988), a two-phased approach should be established. The first step involves using maximum likelihood confirmatory analysis to confirm the measurement model and formally assess its construct validity. In the measurement model, the liminal experience was specified as a second-order factor determining two first-order factors, individual changes and festive ritual. Figure 2 shows the sequence diagram with all the variables: latent variables of first-order, second-order and observable variables.

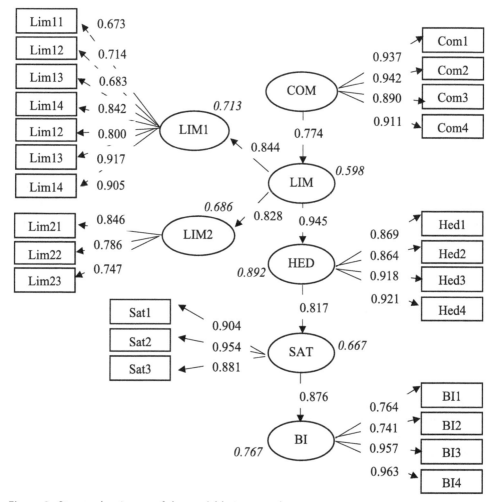

Figure 2. Structural estimates of the model being tested.

Table 2. Reliability and validity of the measurement model.

Construct	Cronbach's alpha	Composite reliability	Extracted variance	Factor loadings[a]	R^2
Communitas (COM)	0.924	0.977	0.913		
I have a feeling of belonging to the group of participants (Com1)				0.937	0.877
I have an identity similar to the participants (Com2)				0.943	0.889
I feel strongly attached to the group of participants (Com3)				0.889	0.790
I feel close to the regular participant (Com4)				0.911	0.830
Liminal experience (LIM)	0.921				
Individual changes (LIM1)	0.927	0.954	0.751	0.800	0.712
I have experienced something new with A Festa do Boi (Lim11)				0.671	0.450
I consider that my participation in A Festa do Boi has been significant for me (Lim12)				0.714	0.510
I consider that my participation has been important for me (Lim13)				0.683	0.466
It has been a liberating experience to participate in *A Festa do Boi* (Lim14)				0.841	0.707
I enjoyed a sense of freedom during my visit (Lim15)				0.800	0.64
It has been a reviving experience (Lim16)				0.916	0.839
It has been a revitalizing experience (Lim17)				0.905	0.819
Festive ritual (LIM2)	0.827	0.900	0.752	0.834	0.686
I think Boi is a festive ritual (Lim21)				0.841	0.707
I feel part of the people of Allariz *in A Festa do Boi* (Lim22)				0.789	0.622
A Festa do Boi promotes a sense of identity and continuity (Lim23)				0.748	0.559
Hedonism (HED)	0.940	0.968	0.884		
A Festa do Boi experience was truly enjoyable (Hed1)				0.869	0.755
I really feel that *A Festa do Boi* is like a getaway (Hed2)				0.865	0.748
It represents an experience of personal enjoyment for me (Hed3)				0.923	0.852
I truly felt delighted (Hed4)				0.923	0.852
Satisfaction (SAT)	0.937	0.967	0.907		
I believe that I did the right thing in attending *A Festa do Boi* (Sat1)				0.903	0.815
On the whole, I am happy with *A Festa do Boi* (Sat2)				0.958	0.917
I consider that the overall experience of the trip is satisfactory (Sat3)				0.882	0.778
Behavioural intentions (BI)	0.918	0.954	0.839		
I would like to visit *A Festa do Boi* again next time (BI1)				0.766	0.586
I will prioritise *A Festa do Boi* over other Festivities when deciding whether to attend (BI2)				0.745	0.555
I will recommend *A Festa do Boi* to other people (BI3)				0.956	0.914
I will encourage friends and relatives to visit *A Festa do Boi* again next time (BI4)				0.963	0.927

[a]Every factor loading is significant at 1% level.

The first confirmatory factor analysis includes all the indicators available to measure each of the constructs and included covariances between all pairs of latent factors. In order to validate the measurement model, the standardized factor loading, the composite reliability (CR), the average variance extracted (AVE), and Cronbach's alpha were examined. According to Hair et al. (1999), factor loading and AVE should be totally larger than 0.5. Meanwhile, the CR for all the factors from the measurement model should be above 0.6 (Fornell & Larcker, 1981).

The results included in Table 2, confirmed that all items load substantially and significantly on their respective constructs confirming the existence of convergent validity, reaching the lowest standardized load a value of 0.671 (>0.5) and the value of R^2 0.452 (>0.3). Regarding the reliability analysis, it can be observed that the CR indexes are always higher than 0.9, while the AVE is above 0.75 for all the constructs considered, reaching in both cases values always above the recommended minimum. The internal consistency of the different scales measured by Cronbach's Alpha is high, every coefficient is above the recommended 0.80 level (Bagozzi & Yi, 1988; Bollen, 1989). Therefore, the results of the measurement model indicate that the model fits the data well and shows adequate construct validity.

Table 3. Structural model results.

	Estimated path coefficient	Standard error	Critical ratio	Hypotheses
Communitas ➔ Liminal experience	0.774	0.043	11.801	H_1: Accepted
Liminal Experience ➔ Hedonism	0.945	0.094	13.372	H_2: Accepted
Hedonism ➔ Satisfaction	0.817	0.035	19.258	H_3: Accepted
Satisfaction ➔ Behavioural intentions	0.876	0.044	23.233	H_4: Accepted

After confirming the measurement model, the second step is to validate the structural model (Anderson & Gerbing, 1988). Figure 2 presents the estimated standardized factor loading and the squared multiple correlation coefficients (R^2). The structural model provided the following rating values: GFI $= 0.858$; RMSEA $= 0.072$; CFI $= 0.958$; NNFI$= 0.952$; RMR $= 0.08$; $\chi^2/df = 3.04$. The coefficients reached by these measures make us consider the model as adequate, since the indexes are all close or above to the recommended levels with the exception of the probability ($p = 0.000$). The probability associated with the Chi-square statistic is less than 0.05, and this may be due to the influence of the sample size (Chin, Paterson & Brown, 2008) and also to the high number of parameters estimated in the global model that increase the random error (Hair et al., 1999), so we take into account the rest of the adjustment indicators.

Del Barrio and Luque (2000) recommend paying attention to the structural model, regardless of whether the global adjustment measures indicate acceptable values. Thus, the first thing that must be evaluated is the significance achieved by the estimated coefficients ($t > 2.58$, $p = 0.01$) (Steenkamp & Van Trijp, 1991). Then, it is tested that the standardized loads reach values higher than 0.5 in all cases (Hildebrandt, 1987) and later, that the contribution of each item to the explanation of the construct is significant (at least $R^2 > 0.3$) (Blesa, 2000). The standardized path coefficients in Figure 2 were all significant at $p < 0.01$ and were in the hypothesized direction.

The acceptance of the proposed model allows for contrasting the hypotheses proposed. The model explained 60% variance in liminality, 94% variance in hedonism, 67% variance in satisfaction and 77% variance in behavioural intentions (Figure 2).

Examining the hypotheses was based on the t-value (Table 3). A value which is greater than 2.58 represents a significant path at a 1% level. In the first place, it has been found that communitas has a positive influence on liminality ($\beta = 0.774$; $t = 11.801$; $p < 0.01$). Hence, H1 was accepted. On the other hand, it was found that liminality has a two-dimensional structure, and has a positive effect on hedonism ($\beta = 0.945$; $t = 13.372$). We can explain a very high proportion of its variability through the observable variables and also the relationship of hedonism directly with liminality and indirectly with communitas. In turn, a positive and significant relationship can also be observed for the cases of the relationship between hedonism and satisfaction ($\beta = 0.817$; $t = 19.258$), and satisfaction with behavioural intentions ($\beta = 0.876$; $t = 23.233$). Hence H2, H3 and H4 were supported

Discussion

This study analyses the level of satisfaction of the tourists who participate in the 700th edition of *A Festa do Boi* of Allariz (Galicia-Spain), with the aim of deepening the holistic understanding of the festival experience. In addition, the role played by communitas, liminality, hedonism and satisfaction in the participants' future intentions is identified. Finally, indicators that measure the liminal experience both through transformative individual changes and the festive ritual are established.

Firstly, this research demonstrates the importance of satisfaction ($\beta = 0.876$) in the behavioural intentions of the participants of A Festa do Boi. In line with other research (for example, Baker & Crompton, 2000; Grappi & Montanari, 2011; Lee, Lee, Lee, & Babin, 2008; Mason & Paggiaro, 2012; Yoon et al., 2010), the more consumers are satisfied with the festival experience, the more willing they are to participate again. In particular, in our case, the effect on the intentions of recommending it, is noteworthy ($\beta = 0.957$ and $\beta = 0.963$).

Second, and as Grappi and Montanari (2011) announced, given the predominantly experiential nature of festival consumption, hedonism plays a key role in increasing visitor satisfaction ($\beta = 0.817$). Moreover, it is possible to explain a very high proportion of its variability through the direct relationship of satisfaction with hedonism ($\beta = 0.945$), and indirectly with communitas. This connection is built on a sense of communitas among attendees (Getz, 2012), which is perhaps best exemplified through the large number of loyal repeat visitors and by the fact that the uniqueness of this event contributes to the memorability of the liminal experience (Westwood et al., 2018). On the other hand, the item that contributes most to the satisfaction construct is 'On the whole, I am happy with A Festa do Boi' ($\beta = 0.954$). For the case of hedonism, the feeling of being delighted ($\beta = 0.921$) and the festival being an experience of personal enjoyment ($\beta = 0.918$), is what facilitates pleasure.

Third, it was found that the liminal experience has a two-dimensional structure. On the one hand, the first dimension includes the individual changes that occur during the consumption of the tourist experience ($\beta = 0.844$). The items that contribute most to this dimension are those related to the feelings of refreshment that are brought about in festivals, and which emerge due to the experience being reviving ($\beta = 0.917$) and revitalizing ($\beta = 0.905$), as well as those that reflect a sense of freedom ($\beta = 0.800$) and define the tourist experience as liberating ($\beta = 0.842$). The item that contributes least is the one that shows a feeling of novelty ($\beta = 0.673$), probably because almost 83% of the sample has participated in this event on other occasions. Regarding the second dimension that is called festive ritual ($\beta = 0.828$), it is emphasised that the ox can be considered a festive ritual ($\beta = 0.846$). As in other cases, the festival theme arose from community members' desire to celebrate their community's unique identity (Morgan, 2008; Simeon & Buonincontri, 2011). So, the festive ritual has included the goal of preserving and promoting the region's unique cultural heritage.

Fourthly, the results show that the satisfaction with the liminal experience of tourists also depends on the identification with the host community ($\beta = 0.942$) and on the feeling of belonging to the group of participants ($\beta = 0.937$), which are the items that contribute most to the sense of belonging. As indicated by Jaimangal-Jones et al. (2010), in dance music festivals, the trip encourages interpersonal bonding, which is further reinforced by the experience of the event itself. Forging closer links with certain individuals and becoming accustomed to communitas and the type of interaction facilitated by such social formations can lead to repeated attendance to calendric events. The findings show that this festival offers opportunities for social interaction in a traditional and distinctive setting, together with a range of experiences that are not easily replicated elsewhere.

The results of this study contribute to the existing literature in several ways. On the one hand, the proposed model allows for contrasting the hypotheses that arise from the theoretical framework and the different liminal components of the tourism experience analysed. The relationship between the five constructs was tested: communitas, liminality, hedonism, satisfaction and future behavioural intentions. On the other hand, this tourist trip is a liminal (Lett, 1983, p. 45) and non-liminal experience (as in the case of the festival #EATCambridge, Duignan et al., 2017), since *A Festa do Boi* is a performative ritual process and a calendrical ritual linked to the Catholic liturgical calendar, with mechanical solidarity by similar characteristics (Durkheim, 1982). That is, the festival is based on the similarity of social feelings that are shared by all the individuals that make up the social system. In addition, it is promoted by the rural and sustainable context (Allariz Area - Biosphere Reserve), whose festive activities involve group participation through the Xan Arzúa Association and where meanings are generated collectively (Turner, 1974b).

In addition, the individual change of the tourist is verified as a result of the experimental behaviour with oneself and with the others (hosts and guests, Smith, 1992), encouraged by the liminal space of learning. According to Mulcahy (2017) and Zembylas (2017), the festive environment facilitates learning experiences and liminality co-produced by and beyond humans. These liminal environments cause one to explore boundaries as part of individuation (Farris, 2017). The same as the tourists staying in hotels (Pritchard & Morgan, 2006) or those going to nudist beaches (Monterrubio, 2013), the tourists of *A Festa do Boi*, reconfigure their personal identities with the participants, even if only temporarily. The festive activities that take place during the nine days of the event seem to be a representation of freedom and an escape from normal, social and cultural limitations (Preston-Whyte, 2004),due to encouraging to adopt behaviours radically different from those of everyday life. In the destination, during the celebration, tourists can express aspects of themselves that are repressed by social restrictions in everyday situations. Participating in the festivity, provides anonymity and escaping from social control, duty and obligations, which also implies a freedom of fantasy, imagination and adventure (Ryan & Hall, 2001). The individual can feel free to act in any way he/she wants, since he/she is far from the society of belonging (Pritchard & Morgan, 2000) and the spirit of communitas and mutual acceptance (Light, 2009) is also promoted.

Conclusion

This research has used concepts which are usually presented in qualitative lines of work and within the scope of symbolic and cognitive anthropology. Based on the texts by Van Gennep and Víctor Turner, the concepts of rites of passage, liminality and communitas have been used as a theoretical basis to analyse a contemporary and recurrent phenomenon of the participation of tourists in local festive rituals. It was verified that these festive events include specific proposals for the recognition of belonging between the members of the community itself and at the same time, they invite tourists to be part of that ritual. It seems that there is an explosion of sensations that are found between the different positions of the actors: from the transition between routine and festivity, between the local and the foreign, between 'I' and 'us'. In this way, the peculiar articulation of the different elements observed in A Festa do Boi of Allariz (Ourense) as a festive and touristic process has enabled to carry out an analysis that connects the individual agency to the festive social processes. Based on this work, the satisfaction of the tourist experience in ethnographic celebrations cannot be taken into account only as a result of the characteristics of the offer, but also in relation to the link between the collective formulation, the services offered and the position of the actors. in a symbiotic relationship that allows for less biased analyses than those that have been carried out so far on A Festa do Boi.

In short, this research has contributed to the development of knowledge about liminality in tourism landscapes, specifically in the field of ethnographic festivals. The organizers of this event now have a more holistic view of the liminal tourist experience that the attendees to A Festa do Boi experience.

It is verified that place-specific festivals promote the sense of communitas, transform spaces and identities, and offer opportunities for tourism revenue generation (Getz, 2012), with direct effects for the (re) structuring power (Thomassen, 2016) during their duration. In addition, it was found that the liminal experience has a two-dimensional structure constituted by the individual changes experienced and by the festive ritual.

However, certain limitations to the study are recognised. On the one hand, the limits between the personal and social, that is, the internal and the external, oneself and others are not analysed specifically (Lewiecki-Wilson & Cellio, 2011) in order to deepen the knowledge of transformative liminal experiences. In addition, the contribution of evolutionary psychology to the analysis of this individual change at a cognitive, social and emotional level would be interesting. On the other hand, an analysis of the behaviour and ethical codes of this festival with the animal is necessary, given that they can enter into conflict with the norms of common society, faced by the criticism from ecological groups due to the stress and anxiety that the oxen suffer, as they are tied and suffer the screaming of the neighbours and visitors.

Finally, for future studies, the aim is to investigate other types of events. At the same time, it is proposed to analyse the creativity and spontaneity in individuals that tend to emerge in liminal spaces (Povilanskas & Armaitienė, 2014). In addition, we want to confirm the evidence concerning the two-dimensional structure of the liminal experience in the local community.

Disclosure statement

No potential conflict of interest was reported by the authors.

ORCID

Lorena Rodríguez-Campo ⓘ http://orcid.org/0000-0001-8149-3836
Fátima Braña-Rey ⓘ http://orcid.org/0000-0001-6770-537X
Elisa Alén-González ⓘ http://orcid.org/0000-0002-6304-7805
José Antonio Fraiz-Brea ⓘ http://orcid.org/0000-0002-3190-6942

References

Anderson, J. C., & Gerbing, D. W. (1988). Structural equation modelling in practice. A review and recommended two-step approach. *Psychological Bulletin, 103*(3), 411–423. doi:10.1037//0033-2909.103.3.411

H. Andrew, & L. Roberts (Eds.). (2012). *Liminal landscapes: Travel, experience and spaces in-between.* London: Routledge.

Babin, B. J., Darden, W. R., & Griffin, M. (1994). Work and/or fun: Measuring hedonic and utilitarian shopping value. *Journal of Consumer Research, 20*(4), 644–656. doi:10.1086/209376

Babin, B. J., Lee, Y. K., Kim, E. J., & Griffin, M. (2005). Modeling consumer satisfaction and word-of-mouth: Restaurant patronage in Korea. *Journal of Services Marketing, 19*(3), 133–139. doi:10.1108/08876040510596803

Bagozzi, R. P., & Yi, Y. (1988). On the evaluation of structural equation models. *Journal of the Academy of Marketing Science, 16*(1), 74–94.

Bagozzi, R. P., & Dholakia, U. (2006). Antecedents and purchase consequences of customer participation in small group brand communities. *International Journal of Research in Marketing, 23*(1), 45–61. doi:10.1016/j.ijresmar.2006.01.005

Baker, D. A., & Crompton, J. L. (2000). Quality, satisfaction and behavioral intentions. *Annals of Tourism Research, 27*(3), 785–804. doi:10.1016/S0160-7383(99)00108-5

Bauer, T., & McKercher, B. (Eds.) (2003). *Sex and tourism: Journeys of romance, love and lust.* New York: The Haworth Hospitality Press.

Bauman, Z. (1996). From pilgrim to tourist – Or a short history of identity. In S. Hall, & P. duGay (Eds.), *Questions of cultural identity* (pp. 18–36). London: Sage.

Blesa, A. (2000). *Influencia de la Orientación al Mercado del Fabricante en las Relaciones en el Canal de Distribución* (Doctoral dissertation). Universidad de Valencia, Spain.

Bollen, K. A. (1989). *Structural equations with latent variables.* New York: Wiley.

Bourdieu, P. (1982). Les rites comme actes d'institution. In *Actes de la Recherche En Sciences Sociales* (vol. 43(1), pp. 58–63). https://www.persee.fr/doc/arss_0335-5322_1982_num_43_1_2159

Braña-Rey, F., & Fernández-Silva, C. (2008). Tradición e modernidade: Análisis de elementos e funcionalidade da festa da maruxaina. In *Actas Do II Congreso de Patrimonio Etnográfico Galego: O Patrimonio No Século XXI*, Ourense, Spain (pp. 41–48).

Brooker, E., & Joppe, M. (2014). Developing a tourism innovation typology: Leveraging liminal insights. *Journal of Travel Research, 53*(4), 500–508. doi:10.1177/0047287513497839

Carbone, L. P., & Haeckel, S. H. (1994). Engineering customer experiences. *Marketing Management, 3*, 9–19.

Caruana, A., Money, A. H., & Berthon, P. R. (2000). Service quality and satisfaction: The moderating role of value. *European Journal of Marketing*, *34*(11/12), 1338–1352. doi:10.1108/03090560010764432

Carnicelli, S. (2014). White-water rafting guides, leisure behaviour and liminality. *Tourism & Management Studies*, *10*(1), 82–86.

Chambers, E. (2012). *Native tours: The anthropology of travel and tourism*. Long Grove, IL: Waveland Press.

Chapman, A., & Light, D. (2017). Working with the carnivalesque at the seaside: Transgression and misbehaviour in a tourism workplace. *Tourist Studies*, *17*(2), 182–199. doi:10.1177/1468797616665768

Chin, W. W., Peterson, R. A., & Brown, S. P. (2008). Structural equation modeling in marketing: Some practical reminders. *Journal of Marketing Theory and Practice*, *16*(4), 287–298. doi:10.2753/MTP1069-6679160402.

Choo, H., Ahn, K., & Petrick, J. F. (2016). An integrated model of festival revisit intentions: Theory of planned behaviour and festival quality/satisfaction. *International Journal of Contemporary Hospitality Management*, *28*(4), 818–838. doi:10.1108/IJCHM-09-2014-0448

De Bres, K., & Davis, J. (2001). Celebrating group and place identity: A case study of a new regional festival. *Tourism Geographies*, *3*(3), 326–337. doi:10.1080/14616680110055439

Di Giovine, M. A. (2011). Pilgrimage: Communitas and contestation, unity and difference – An introduction. *Tourism Review*, *59*, 247–268.

Ducros, H. B. (2018). "Fête de la Soupe": Rural identity, self-representation, and the (re)-making of the village in France. *Journal of Place Management and Development*, *11*(3), 296–314. doi:10.1108/JPMD-07-2017-0068

Duignan, M., Everett, S., Walsh, L., & Cade, N. (2017). Leveraging physical and digital liminoidal spaces: The case of the #EATCambridge festival. *Tourism Geographies*, doi:10.1080/14616688.2017.1417472

Duman, T., & Mattila, A. S. (2005). The role of affective factors on perceived cruise vacation value. *Tourism Management*, *26*(3), 311–323. doi:10.1016/j.tourman.2003.11.014

Durkheim, E. (1982). *La división del trabajo social*. Madrid: Akal Universitaria. doi:10.2307/40184406

Farber, M. E., & Hall, T. E. (2007). Emotion and environment: Visitors' extraordinary experiences along the Dalton Highway in Alaska. *Journal of Leisure Research*, *39*(2), 248–270. doi:10.1080/00222216.2007.11950107

Farris, A. (2017). Experimenting with the occult: The role of liminality in slumber party rituals. *Preternature: Critical and Historical Studies on the Preternatural*, *6*(1), 154–179.

Fornell, C., & Larcker, D. F. (1981). Evaluating structural equation models with unobserved variables and measurement error. *Journal of Marketing Research*, *18*(1), 39–50. doi:10.2307/3151312

Franklin, A. (2003). *Tourism: An introduction*. London: Sage.

Fry, R. W. (2014). Becoming a "True Blues Fan": Blues tourism and performances of the King Biscuit Blues Festival. *Tourist Studies*, *14*(1), 66–85. doi:10.1177/1468797613511686

Getz, D. (2012). *Event studies: Theory research and policy for planned event*. Oxford: Routledge.

Gil, M., & Prol, P. (2009). *Allariz, 1989. Crónica dunha revolta*. Ourense: Difusora de letras, artes e ideas.

Giovanardi, M., Lucarelli, A., & Decosta, P. L. E. (2014). Co-performing tourism places: The "Pink Night" festival. *Annals of Tourism Research*, *44*, 102–115. doi:10.1016/j.annals.2013.09.004

González-Casarrubios, C., & Timón-Tiemblo, P. M. (1982). Fiesta del Corpus Christi en Badajoz. *Narria: Estudios de Artes y Costumbres Populares*, *25-26*, 47–51.

Graburn, N. (1992). Turismo: El viaje sagrado. In V. L. Smith (Eds.), *Anfitriones e invitados. (Turismo y sociedad)*. Madrid: Endymion.

Graburn, N. (2001). Secular ritual: A general theory of tourism. In V. Smith, & M. Brent (Eds.), *Hosts and guests revisited: Tourism issues of the 21st century* (pp. 42–52). New York: Cognizant Communication.

Grappi, S., & Montanari, F. (2011). The role of social identification and hedonism in affecting tourist re-patronizing behaviours: The case of an Italian festival. *Tourism Management, 32*(5), 1128–1140. doi:10.1016/j.tourman.2010.10.001

Hair, J. F., Anderson, R. E., Tatham, R. L., & Black, W. C. (1999). *Análisis multivariante* (Vol. 491). Madrid: Prentice Hall.

Hildebrandt, L. (1987). Consumer retail satisfaction in rural areas: A reanalysis of survey data. *Journal of Economic Psychology, 8*(1), 19–42. doi:10.1016/0167-4870(87)90004-3

Hirschman, E. C., & Holbrook, M. B. (1982). Hedonic consumption: Emerging concepts, methods and propositions. *Journal of Marketing, 46*(3), 92–101. doi:10.2307/1251707

Hobsbawm, E., & Ranger, T. (2002). Introducción: La invención de la tradición. *La invención de la tradición* (pp. 7–21). Barcelona: Crítica.

Holbrook, M. B., & Hirschman, E. C. (1982). The experiential aspects of consumption: Consumer fantasies, feelings, and fun. *Journal of Consumer Research, 9*(2), 132–140. doi:10.1086/208906

Howard, E. A., Tinsley, J. A. H., Tinsley, D. J., & Holt, M. S. (1993). Attributes of leisure and work experiences. *Journal of Counselling Psychology, 40*(4), 447–455. doi:10.1037//0022-0167.40.4.447

Huang, J., & Hsu, C. H. C. (2010). The impact of customer-to-customer interaction on cruise experience and vacation satisfaction. *Journal of Travel Research, 49*(1), 79–92. doi:10.1177/0047287509336466

Hull, R. B., & Michael, S. E. (1995). Nature-based recreation, mood change, and stress reduction. *Leisure Sciences, 18*, 1–14. doi:10.1080/01490409509513239

Hume, M. M. (2008). Developing a conceptual model for repurchase intention in the performing arts: The role of emotion, core service and service delivery. *International Journal on Arts Management, 10*, 40–55.

Jaimangal-Jones, D., Pritchard, A., & Morgan, N. (2010). Going the distance: Locating journey, liminality and rites of passage in dance music experiences. *Leisure Studies, 29*(3), 253–268. doi:10.1080/02614361003749793

Jamal, T., & Hollinshead, K. (2001). Tourism and the forbidden zone: The underserved power of qualitative inquiry. *Tourism Management, 22*(1), 63–82. doi:10.1016/S0261-5177(00)00020-0

Jawale, K. V. (2012). Methods of sampling design in the legal research: Advantages and disadvantages. *Online International Interdisciplinary Research Journal, 2*(6), 183–190.

Johansson, M., & Kociatkiewicz, J. (2011). City festivals: Creativity and control in staged urban experiences. *European Urban and Regional Studies, 18*(4), 392–405. doi:10.1177/0969776411407810

Jung, T., Ineson, E. M., Kim, M., & Yap, M. H. (2015). Influence of festival attribute qualities on slow food tourists' experience, satisfaction level and revisit intention: The case of the mold food and drink festival. *Journal of Vacation Marketing, 21*(3), 277–288. doi:10.1177/1356766715571389

Kim, H., & Jamal, T. (2007). Touristic quest for existential authenticity. *Annals of Tourism Research, 34*(1), 181–207. doi:10.1016/j.annals.2006.07.009

Kim, J.-H., Ritchie, J. R. B., & McCormick, B. (2012). Development of a scale to measure memorable tourism experiences. *Journal of Travel Research, 51*(1), 12–25. doi:10.1177/0047287510385467

Lança, M., Marques, J. F., & Pinto, P. (2017). Liminality and the possibilities for sex and romance at an international bike meeting: A structural modelling approach. *Tourism & Management Studies, 13*(1), 18–26. doi:10.18089/tms.2017.13103

Lee, Y.-K., Lee, C.-K., Lee, S.-K., & Babin, B. J. (2008). Festivalscapes and patrons' emotions, satisfaction, and loyalty. *Journal of Business Research, 61*(1), 56–64. doi:10.1016/j.jbusres.2006.05.009.

Lee, H., Hwang, H., & Shim, C. (2019). Experiential festival attributes, perceived value, satisfaction, and behavioural intention for Korean festival-goers. *Tourism and Hospitality Research, 19*(2), 199–212. doi:10.1177/1467358417738308

Lee, J. S., Lee, C. K., & Choi, Y. (2011). Examining the role of emotional and functional values in festival evaluation. *Journal of Travel Research, 50*(6), 685–696. doi:10.1177/0047287510385465

Lett, J. (1983). Ludic and liminoid aspects of charter yacht tourism in the Caribbean. *Annals of Tourism Research*, *10*(1), 35–56. doi:10.1016/0160-7383(83)90114-7

Lewiecki-Wilson, C., & Cellio, J. (2011). *Disability and mothering. Liminal spaces of embodied knowledge.* New York: Syracuse University Press.

Light, D. (2009). Performing Transylvania: Tourism, fantasy and play in a liminal place. *Tourist Studies*, *9*(3), 240–258. doi:10.1177/1468797610382707

Lin, C. H., & Wang, W. C. (2012). Effects of authenticity perception, hedonics, and perceived value on ceramic souvenir-repurchasing intention. *Journal of Travel and Tourism Marketing*, *29*(8), 779–795. doi:10.1080/10548408.2012.730941

Luque, T. (2000). *Técnicas de análisis de datos en investigación de mercados.* Madrid: Pirámide.

Maciel, W. (2017). Fronteiras sociais e simbólicas no espaço público liminar: Um estudo de caso. *Revista Crítica de Ciências Sociais*, *114*, 47–68. doi:10.4000/rccs.6766

Mackay Yarnal, C., & Kerstetter, D. (2005). Casting off an exploration of cruise ship space, group tour behavior, and social interaction. *Journal of Travel Research*, *43*(4), 368–379. doi:10.1177/0047287505274650

Ma, L., & Lew, A. A. (2012). Historical and geographical context in festival tourism development. *Journal of Heritage Tourism*, *7*(1), 13–31. doi:10.1080/1743873X.2011.611595

Malhotra, N. K. (2004). *Marketing research: An applied orientation* (4th ed.). Upper Saddle River, NJ: Prentice Hall.

Manthiou, A., (Ally) Lee, S., (Rebecca) Tang, L., & Chiang, L. (2014). The experience economy approach to festival marketing: Vivid memory and attendee loyalty. *Journal of Services Marketing*, *28*(1), 22–35. doi:10.1108/JSM-06-2012-0105

Mason, M. C., & Nassivera, F. (2013). A conceptualization of the relationships between quality, satisfaction, behavioral intention, and awareness of a festival. *Journal of Hospitality Marketing and Management*, *22*(2), 162–182. doi:10.1080/19368623.2011.643449

Mason, M. C., & Paggiaro, A. (2012). Investigating the role of festivalscape in culinary tourism: The case of food and wine events. *Tourism Management*, *33*(6), 1329–1336. doi:10.1016/j.tourman.2011.12.016

Meethan, K. (2012). Walking the edges: Towards a visual ethnography of beachscapes. In H. Andrews, & K. Roberts (Eds.), *Liminal landscapes: Travel, experience and scapes in-between* (pp. 69–86). London: Routledge.

Mendiola, I. (2001). Cartografías liminales: El (des)pliegue topológico de la práctica identitaria. *Política y Sociedad*, *36*, 205–221.

Morgan, M. (2008). What makes a good festival? Understanding the event experience. *Event Management*, *12*(2), 81–93. doi:10.3727/152599509787992562

Moss, J. M. H. (2018). *A phenomenological exploration of music festival experience* (Doctoral). UK: Sheffield Hallam University.

Mulcahy, D. (2017). The salience of liminal spaces of learning: Assembling affects, bodies and objects at the museum. *Geographica Helvetica*, *72*(1), 109–118. doi:10.5194/gh-72-109-2017

Noy, C. (2004). This trip really changed me: Backpackers' narratives of self-change. *Annals of Tourism Research*, *31*(1), 78–102. doi:10.1016/j.annals.2003.08.004

Paladino, F. J. (2011). Sociedad y comunidad: Dialéctica entre totalidad e interrupción. Un esbozo de articulación a contramano del sentido común sociológico. *Nomadas. Critical Journal of Social and Juridical Sciences. Recuperado de, 30*(2), 1–21. http://www.redalyc.org/articulo.oa?id=18120143008

Pearce, P. L., Kim, E., & Lussa, S. (1998). Facilitating tourist-host social interaction: An overview and assessment of the culture assimilator. In E. Laws, B. Faulkner, & G. Moscardo (Eds.), *Embracing and managing change in tourism: International case studies* (pp. 347–364). London & New York, NY: Routledge.

Picard, D. & Robinson, M. (Eds.) (2006). *Festivals, tourism and social change: Remaking worlds.* Clevedon: Channel View.

Pielichaty, H. (2015). Festival space: Gender, liminality and the carnivalesque. *International Journal of Event and Festival Management*, *6*(3), 235–250. doi:10.1108/IJEFM-02-2015-0009

Porras-Arboledas, P. A. (2010). Fiestas y diversiones en Ocaña a comienzos del siglo XVI *Cuadernos de Historia del Derecho. Extraordinario*, extra *2*, 507–567.

Povilanskas, R., & Armaitienė, A. (2014). Marketing of coastal barrier spits as liminal spaces of creativity. *Procedia - Social and Behavioral Sciences, 148*, 397–403. doi:10.1016/j.sbspro.2014.07.058

Prats, L. L. (1997). *Antropología y patrimonio.* Madrid: Alianza.

Preston-Whyte, R. (2004). The beach as a liminal space. In A. Lew, M. Hall, & A. Williams (Eds.), *Companion to tourism* (pp. 349–359). Malden, MA: Blackwell.

Pritchard, A., & Morgan, N. (2000). Privileging the male gaze: Gendered. *Tourism Landscapes. Annals of Tourism Research, 27*(4), 884–905. doi:10.1016/S0160-7383(99)00113-9

Pritchard, A., & Morgan, N. (2006). Hotel Babylon? Exploring hotels as liminal sites of transition and transgression. *Tourism Management, 27*(5), 762–772. doi:10.1016/j.tourman.2005.05.015

Puga-Brau, X. (1996). *Os Xudeos de Allariz O boi do Corpus e as danzas gremiais.* Ourense: Concello de Allariz.

Ryan, C., & Hall, M. (2001). *Sex tourism: Marginal people and liminalities.* London: Routledge.

Rickly-Boyd, J. M. (2012). Lifestyle climbing: Toward existential authenticity. *Journal of Sport & Tourism, 17*(2), 85–104. doi:10.1080/14775085.2012.729898

Samdahl, D. M. (1991). Issues in the measurement of leisure: A comparison of theoretical and connotative meanings. *Leisure Sciences, 13*(1), 33–50. doi:10.1080/01490409109513123

Shields, R. (1991). *Places on the margin: Alternative geographies of modernity.* London: Routledge.

Simeon, M. I., & Buonincontri, P. (2011). Cultural event as a territorial marketing tool: The case of the Ravello Festival on the Italian Amalfi Coast. *Journal of Hospitality Marketing and Management, 20*(3-4), 385–406. doi:10.1080/19368623.2011.562425

Smith, V. L. (1992). *Anfitriones e invitados (Turismo y sociedad).* Madrid: Endymion.

Sohn, H. K., Lee, T. J., & Yoon, Y. S. (2016). Relationship between perceived risk, evaluation, satisfaction, and behavioral intention: A case of local-festival visitors. *Journal of Travel & Tourism Marketing, 33*(1), 28–45. doi:10.1080/10548408.2015.1024912

Steenkamp, J. E. M., & Van Trijp, H. C. M. (1991). The use of LISREL in validating marketing constructs. *International Journal of Research in Marketing, 8*(4), 283–299. doi:10.1016/0167-8116(91)90027-5

Thomassen, B. (2009). The uses and meanings of liminality. *International Political Anthropology, 2*(1), 5–28.

Thomassen, B. (2016). *Liminality and the modern: Living through the in-between.* London: Routledge.

Tucker, E. (2005). Ghosts in Mirrors: Reflections of the Self. *Journal of American Folklore, 118*(468), 186–203. doi:10.1353/jaf.2005.0028

Turner, V. (1974a). *Dramas, fields and metaphors.* New York: Cornell University Press.

Turner, V. (1974b). *Liminal to liminoid, in Play, flow, and ritual: An essay in comparative symbology* (Vol. 60, pp. 53–92). Houston, TX: Rice University Studies.

Turner, V. (1988). *El proceso ritual. Estructura y antiestructura.* Madrid: Taurus.

Turner, V. (1990). *La selva de los símbolos* (Vol. XXI). Madrid: Siglo.

Van Gennep, A. (1909). *Les rites de passage.* Paris: Emile Nourry.

Velasco, H. (Ed.). (1982). *Tiempo de fiesta.* Madrid: Tres-catorce-diecisiete.

Wallace, T. (2006). Working of the train gang: Alienation, liminality and communitas in the UK preserved railway sector. *International Journal of Heritage Studies, 12*(3), 218–233. doi:10.1080/13527250600604167

Westwood, C., Schofield, P., & Berridge, G. C. (2018). Agricultural shows: Visitor motivation, experience and behavioural intention. *International Journal of Event and Festival Management, 9*(2), 147–165. doi:10.1108/IJEFM-09-2017-0050

Wickens, E. (2002). The Sacred and the Profane. *Annals of Tourism Research, 29*(3), 122–834. doi:10.1016/S0160-7383(01)00088-3

Wilson, E., & Harris, C. (2006). Meaningful Travel: Women, Independent Travel and the Search for Self and Meaning. *Tourism, 54*(2), 161–172.

Wu, C. H.-J. (2007). The impact of customer-to-customer interaction and customer homogeneity on customer satisfaction in tourism service: The service encounter perspective. *Tourism Management, 28*(6), 1518–1528. doi:10.1016/j.tourman.2007.02.002

Yagi, C., & Pearce, P. L. (2007). The influence of appearance and the number of people viewed on tourists' preferences for seeing other tourists. *Journal of Sustainable Tourism, 15*(1), 28–43. doi:10.2167/jost528.0

Yoon, Y. S., Lee, J. S., & Lee, C. K. (2010). Measuring festival quality and value affecting visitors' satisfaction and loyalty using a structural consumer loyalty. *International Journal of Hospitality Management, 29*(2), 335–342. doi:10.1016/j.ijhm.2009.10.002

Zembylas, M. (2017). The contribution of non-representational theories in education: Some affective, ethical and political implications. *Studies in Philosophy and Education, 36*(4), 393–407. doi:10.1007/s11217-016-9535-2

Transformative landscapes: liminality and visitors' emotional experiences at German memorial sites

Doreen Pastor and Alexander J. Kent

ABSTRACT

The atrocities of Nazi Germany included the radical transformation of natural landscapes. At Ravensbrück (Brandenburg), a lakeside setting became the site of the largest women's concentration camp in Germany, processing approximately 159,000 inmates until 1945. Similarly, at Flossenbürg (Bavaria), a picturesque valley in the *Oberpfälzer Wald* housed a large concentration camp with approximately 100,000 inmates over seven years and a granite quarry to support Hitler's extensive construction programme. After the war, part of Ravensbrück became a Soviet Army base, while large sections of Flossenbürg were removed to make way for a new housing and industrial development. Along with other former camps (particularly Auschwitz-Birkenau), parts of these landscapes were developed into memorial sites that aim to provide a liminal experience for visitors – a 'rite of passage'. In attempting to regain a sense of place that evokes the trauma of the past, the landscapes of the memorial sites of Ravensbrück and Flossenbürg were recently altered to resemble their appearance in 1945. For visitors, however, the aesthetic experience of these landscapes lies in stark contrast to the narrative they encounter at both sites; they are surprised to see signs of life, objecting to modernisation at Ravensbrück or the existence of a supermarket next to the memorial site in Flossenbürg. This paper examines the transformative processes of these landscapes and explores how their liminality is constructed, experienced and challenged. Through empirical visitor research conducted at both sites, it provides a critical evaluation of the narrative given to visitors and suggests how these important sites can offer a more engaging 'rite of passage'.

摘要

纳粹德国的暴行包括对自然景观的彻底改造。在拉文斯布吕克（勃兰登堡），一个湖滨环境成为了德国最大的女性集中营，在1945年之前大约有159,000名囚犯被关押。类似地，在弗罗森堡（巴伐利亚），奥伯法尔泽瓦尔德的一个风景如画的山谷里，有一个大集中营，7年里关押了大约10万名囚犯，还有一个花岗岩采石场，用来支持希特勒的大规模建设计划。战后，拉文斯布吕克的一部分变成了苏联的军事基地，而弗罗森堡的大部分被拆除，为新的住房和工业发展让路。和其他以前的集中营(尤其是奥斯威辛-比克瑙集中营)一样，这些景观的一部分被开发成纪念场所，旨在为游客提供一种短暂的阀限体验———一种"通过仪式"。为了试图重新获得一种唤起过去创伤的地方感, 勃兰登堡和弗罗森堡纪念馆的景观最近被改造成类似于1945年的样子。然而, 对于游客来说, 这些景观的审美体验与他们在这两个地方遇到的叙述形成了鲜明的对比;他们惊讶地看到了生命的迹象, 反对拉文斯布吕克的现代化, 也反对在弗罗森堡的纪念遗址旁建超市。本文考察了这些景观的改造过程, 并探讨了它们的阈限是如何被建构、体验和挑战的。通过在这两个场所进行的实证游客研究, 它给游客的叙事提供了一个批判性的评价, 并建议这些重要的场所如何可以提供一个更有吸引力的"通过仪式"。

Introduction

Lennon and Foley (2000) first recognised the phenomenon of rising visitor numbers to sites associated with death and disaster, and coined the term 'dark tourism'. A range of research projects have since attempted to shine a light on tourists' experiences and understand their motivations for visiting these sites (e.g., Dunkley, Morgan, & Westwood, 2011; Nawijn and Fricke, 2015). More recently, Stone (2018) asserts that societies' inability to deal with death in the public sphere encourages tourists to seek such encounters at memorials and 'death-related' museums. However, such explanations neglect the cultural and social factors that influence tourist activities and ignore the multi-faceted nature of visitor experiences at German memorial sites such as Buchenwald. For instance, Volkhard Knigge (2004), Head of the Buchenwald concentration camp memorial site near Weimar, explains that he met a visitor who sought a spiritual experience by praying on the site while another wanted to step into the shoes of former victims by enduring a strenuous nine-kilometre walk from Weimar instead of taking the bus. Reynolds (2018) argues that when tourists travel to a memorial site they seek immediacy through actually being in the space. The transformation from space to place, as a complex of physical, social, cultural, and emotional qualities that is a part of the tourism experience (Rickly-Boyd, 2013, p.684), crosses a threshold that epitomises the concept of liminality. Thus, if memorial sites are to be regarded as liminal landscapes, it is necessary to apply empirical methods of visitor research to understand how such landscapes are constructed.

As an anthropological concept, liminality was introduced by van Gennep (1960) in *Rites of passage*, which focused on the sacred rites of transition from one socially sanctioned stage to another. The concept was developed further by Turner (1969), who identified the ambiguous status of the individual in their transition between cultural realms of experience. Since tourism inherently involves a process of transition in moving from a space of everyday life to a space of new experiences and encounters, the emerging position of liminality within tourism studies has focused on mobility between spaces (e.g., Beckstead, 2010; Shields, 1991). Hence, there is scope for tourism research to explore anthropological perspectives towards the individual tourist at a memorial site, who is influenced by their own cultural and educational background as well as by their own thoughts, emotions and feelings. While Downey, Kinane, and Parker (2016) define liminality as an in-between space of potentiality, Beckstead (2010) concludes that a liminal tourist experience occurs at the boundary between an inner construction of meaning and an external confrontation with symbolic objects and landscapes.

Furthermore, Prosise (2003) argues that the concept of liminality is particularly relevant in museum environments, as visitors step out of their daily routine and encounter a highly symbolic environment through a guided experience. A case in point is Ravensbrück concentration camp memorial site. Located in Germany's picturesque lake district of *Mecklenburger Seenplatte*, the local tourism campaign promises *Endlich Ruhe* (finally peace and quiet). Stepping onto the grounds of the Ravensbrück memorial site is, however, no longer an experience of calmness. Within a couple of minutes, the tourist is confronted with remnants of the atrocities committed there. In addition, the visitor has to negotiate between different layers of commemorative design and Ravensbrück's past as a Soviet Army base for almost 50 years. As such, memorial landscapes present societies' commemorative attitude at the time (Violi, 2012). The physical remnants, however, provide visitors with an indexical link between the past and the present.

Malpass (2011, p.14) asserts that 'understanding landscapes means understanding the forms of actions out of which they arise', hence emphasising the performative aspect of landscapes. This complexity is evident in a sentence projected onto a wall at the museum in Flossenbürg: 'the landscape is not responsible for what happened here'. It highlights the anxiety of the local community who fear that the landscape is permanently tainted by the memorial site. Indeed, the proposal for the first memorial emphasised that 'traumatic memories' should be contained in the natural valley to avoid spilling over to the surrounding area (Skriebeleit, 2016). Hence, the desire was to create a liminal space - a landscape with a defined boundary that would not disturb the local community. As such, the landscape was set aside as a liminal setting that would invite visitors to take part in the ritual process of grieving and commemoration. Yet, visitors to the landscape, be they survivors, or, increasingly, tourists, establish an ambiguous boundary (Casey, 2011) as memories of past traumas travel with them and cannot be contained exclusively within a liminal space.

Tourists within these spaces, however, also experience liminality within themselves. Their external senses attempt to comprehend a landscape that bears little resemblance to past atrocities while simultaneously their mind imagines the past (Popescu, 2016). Indeed, Popescu argues that this is a hallucinatory experience as the visitor tries to bridge the gap between the past and the present by using his/her own emotions.

This process is complicated further by the dynamic multi-layered nature of landscapes, particularly memorial sites that have witnessed changes in ownership as well as physical transformation. Landscapes may be regarded as palimpsests that evidence many successive transformations by human intervention, changing land-use and management, natural succession of vegetation, and also climatological and geological factors (Nijhuis, 2019). The traces or 'scars' left by history can enhance the sense of place and allow a multi-faceted experience of landscape that may evoke different emotional responses in the visitor.

Memorial sites therefore present unique challenges in how their landscapes are managed and reinterpreted for the visitor. This includes the maintenance of the material landscape and its aesthetics to construct a particular sense of place. The development of the landscapes of Ravensbrück and Flossenbürg from their liberation in 1945 to the memorial sites of today, each hosting thousands of visitors per year, has involved their material transformation and reinterpretation (and to some extent, their reconstruction). Recent landscape design initiatives have aimed to create a sense of place that evokes the trauma of the past and encourages the visitor to re-imagine the camp at the point of liberation. This aim is also reflected in the designs of visitor maps of both sites, which incorporate wartime aerial reconnaissance photographs. Far from providing passive guides to wayfinding, these maps are designed to actively con-tribute to the re-imagining of the site. If affective experiences shape our identities (Attfield, 2000), it will serve the interests of site management to construct and portray these landscapes in ways that recognise liminality as part of their function.

This paper explores how visitors to two concentration camp memorial sites in Germany, Flossenbürg and Ravensbrück, experience a 'rite of passage' from their 'ordinary' lives to the depths of human atrocity. It examines how the development and portrayal of these memorial sites serves to enhance their role as liminal land-scapes, thereby supporting the transition of individual visitors and their response to the changing identity of these memorial sites.

Liminality in Ravensbrück and Flossenbürg

Ravensbrück concentration camp memorial site

The construction and use of Ravensbrück concentration camp until 1990

Initially built to process female prisoners, Ravensbrück concentration camp was con-structed near the town of Fürstenberg, 50 miles north of Berlin, and gained its name from the local village. The area covered by the camp was mostly uninhabited, agricul-tural land in the 1930s, while the lake nearby and its beaches attracted bathers in the summer (Köhler and Plewe, 2001).

Construction began in 1938 using male prisoners from the nearby camp at Sachsenhausen. New buildings were required in 1940 to accommodate an increase in the number of inmates, for which extensive earthworks were carried out on marshland near the lake. Köhler and Plewe (2001) remark that the erection of the camp must have been a major eyesore for the local community, yet local newspapers did not include reports about the construction, neither does there appear to have been any local opposition.

In the later stages of Ravensbrück's operation, the camp changed its status as a forced labour camp to an extermination camp with the construction of a gas chamber. A shortage of building materials meant that the gas chamber was not completed before the Red Army arrived, and, consequently, a barracks near the crematorium was used from February to April 1945. By the time of its liberation in 1945, some 159,000 prisoners (139,000 women and children and 20,000 men) had passed through the camp, of which tens of thousands had died during their internment (Eschebach, 2014).

After the liberation of Ravensbrück, the Soviet Army turned the site into a large military base within the German Democratic Republic (GDR). The former SS (Schutzstaffel) guard houses were reused for accommodating military personnel. The barracks were carefully dismantled and re-erected at different locations to house ethnic German refugees from *Sudetenland* (Czechoslovakia) and Silesia (Poland). The Soviet Army built additional housing for military staff in the typical communist-era style on the edge of the camp boundary, including local amenities such as shops. Although the official narrative was one of friendship between the Soviet military and East German civilians, the base was strictly off-limits for local Germans (Jacobeit & Stegemann, 2004). Thus, the area never regained the recreational character it had enjoyed prior to the construction of the camp. The Soviet Army was also less concerned about the site's historical importance. Buildings were significantly altered and adapted for military purposes. The former Youth Protection Camp Uckermark (located two miles north of Ravensbrück main camp) was flattened and used as an exercise area for tanks. Consequently, only a small part of the site was available for the development of a memorial, following intense negotiations between the GDR government and Soviet military officials.

The development of Ravensbrück concentration camp memorial until 1990

In April 1948, a delegation of the VVN (the Trust for Victims of the Nazi regime), travelled to Ravensbrück and observed that the camp was in a desolate condition (Schwarz & Steppan, 1999). The only building considered to be in a reasonable state was the crematorium and it was agreed that the first memorial should be erected adjacent to this building. Consequently, the first memorial consisted of a simple wooden pillar and a 'fire bowl', and opened on 14th September 1948. With the founding of the GDR on 7th October 1949, the potential for developing a permanent memorial arose again. A new committee was formed in the GDR (the committee of the anti-fascist fighters), which set the tone for the future development of the memorial; the focus now was on the communist victims.

Subsequently in June 1956, Will Lammert, an East German artist, was asked to design the sculptures. He proposed two statues. One statue, *The Burdened*, representing a female prisoner carrying another, was erected by the lake and placed upon a seven-metre-high plinth in order to be visible from the surrounding landscape (Lammert, 1965). This statue was intended to be supported by a group of mothers, which was, however, not completed due to the premature death of the artist, and was later added at the entrance to the concentration camp (Marchetta, 2001). The other statue, *Group of Women*, was erected near the crematorium. In addition, the former solitary confinement block was transformed into a museum and the former mass grave became a rose bed. Hence, the first GDR memorial was designed to take the visitor on a path 'from darkness to light', symbolising the journey from fascist rule to the GDR. The 'dark' was represented by the crematorium, the execution path and the mass grave; *The Burdened,* overlooking the lake with one step forward towards the future, signified the 'light'.

The development of the current Ravensbrück memorial site

After the reunification of Germany, an expert commission formed in the federal state of Brandenburg recommended that the GDR exhibition should be replaced by a new exhibition called 'History and Memory of the Women's Concentration Camp' (Ministerium für Wissenschaft und Kultur Brandenburg, 2009). There were additional plans for the former Youth Protection Camp Uckermark, the nearby Siemens factory, the former SS guard houses, and the actual grounds of the camp to be incorporated into the memorial. However, during its occupation by the Soviet Army, the land was contaminated by chemicals (such as kerosene) and the former camp structures had been significantly altered.

A landscape architecture competition was launched in 1998 with the aim of transforming the site closer to its 1945 appearance without reconstructing its buildings. The architectural collaborative Oswalt and Tischer won with a proposal that included covering the former *Appellplatz* with an 'artificial' surface made from clinker, thereby creating raised areas where the barracks once stood. Trees that were planted during the camp's operation remained as 'natural eyewitnesses' (Tischer, *pers. comm.*), while any other vegetation that had grown since 1945 was to be removed. The original landscape design envisaged that significant Soviet Army buildings were to be retained, yet this was rejected by the memorial site management team, the local conservation authority and the survivors (Tischer, *pers. comm.*). Consequently, most Soviet buildings were demolished, including a building which housed an exhibition about the Soviet Army. As no physical evidence remained of the former Uckermark camp, the architects' vision was to set aside the area as a meadow, sewn with wild flowers to symbolise the fragility of life (Oswalt & Tischer, 1998).

The first stage of the landscape design (laying the clinker surface) has been completed, creating a vast and bleak open space with no formal pathways to encourage visitors to explore the site without restrictions. Although the landscape designers were open to a rewilding of the area, weeds are frequently removed by the memorial groundsmen, ensuring that the traces of the former camp remain visible. Nevertheless, returning the site to its 1945 appearance has removed almost all evidence of the former Soviet Army base, thus almost erasing a 49-year history (between 1945 and 1994). Although Soviet soldiers did not suffer in the same way as per the Nazi victims, the site's post-war history is a significant part of the wider history of the GDR, and its impact on the local community is undeniable.

Furthermore, not all aspects of the former concentration camp are integrated within the current memorial landscape. These include the locations of severe suffering, e.g., the area covered by the tent (erected to house large numbers of prisoners in the most appalling living conditions and also known as the 'zone of misery'), the Siemens

Figure 1. Two views of the landscape design model for Ravensbrück proposed by Oswalt and Tischer (1998) (reproduced courtesy of Oswalt and Tischer).

Figure 2. The former SS female guard house at Ravensbrück, now a youth hostel (Source: Authors).

factory, and the Uckermark camp. None of these locations appear on the official visitor map either. The current memorial therefore represents a fragmented version of the former camp. Indeed, Ravensbrück's memorial landscape is characterised by constant change and absence. For the victims, the barracks, the medical block in which the SS performed medical experiments, and the areas of forced labour were the spaces of intense suffering; for the visitor, however, these are not recognisable. The former SS female guard buildings, an integral part of the concentration camp landscape, have been converted into a youth hostel and staff offices (Figure 2), while the SS officers' buildings, previously used by the Soviet Army as officers' accommodation, are in a state of controlled decay, with the exception of the *Führerhaus*.

The visitor map of Ravensbrück, designed by the German company unit-design in 2007 and currently available on-site as a leaflet, incorporates a wartime aerial reconnaissance photograph of the camp taken by the Royal Air Force in 1945 (Figure 3). Although the map serves to list and indicate the locations of various buildings around the camp using the established method of a numbered key, the use of the aerial photograph as the base for the map is significant as a device for supporting the affective role of the site's landscape design. It allows visitors to embody the experience of co-location across time; to orientate and to align their bodies to perceive and imagine the camp at the point of liberation. Far from being a passive tool for wayfinding, the map of Ravensbrück is an active agent for influencing the experience of the visitor towards liminality. The map allows the visitor's own imagination and the site's unique sense of place to combine, transporting the visitor to a reality of 1945 and creating a personal experience for each individual.

Figure 3. Ravensbrück visitor map, 2007 (reproduced courtesy of unit-design).

Flossenbürg concentration camp memorial site

Historical development of Flossenbürg concentration camp

Flossenbürg is located in North Bavaria in the *Oberpfälzer Wald* region, very close to the border of the former Czechoslovakia. As Hitler's extensive building programme in the 1930s increased the demand for stone, Flossenbürg, with its extensive granite quarry, became the ideal location for a forced labour camp. The construction of the camp began in 1938 near the existing village. On 12th April the first barracks were erected and on 21st April 'Flossenbürg Labour Camp' opened. Until its liberation in April 1945, approximately 100,000 prisoners were processed at Flossenbürg, of which one third had died as inmates (Benz, Diestel, & Königseder, 2007).

Flossenbürg concentration camp played a significant role within the whole concentration camp system. It was at the centre of an extensive network of 90 subcamps reaching as far as Saxony and Czechoslovakia. Flossenbürg was also the model for subsequent forced labour camps and is thought to have been the first site where the slogan *Arbeit macht frei* (Work sets you free) was displayed (Stier, 2015). Yet, after its liberation, it vanished from public memory and became known as the 'forgotten concentration camp' (Skriebeleit, 2011).

The development of the first memorial and the deliberate destruction of historical evidence

After the liberation of Flossenbürg concentration camp, the US Army established a Prisoner of War (POW) camp for 4,000 German soldiers that was maintained by 800 US guards from July 1945 to April 1946 (Heigl, 1989). With the closure of the POW camp, the UNRRA (United Nations Relief and Rehabilitation Administration) used the barracks as a 'Displaced Persons' (DP) camp. By the time of the camp's closure at the end of

1947, between 1,500 and 2,000 DPs, predominantly of Polish origin, were living in Flossenbürg.

Whilst the camp was in use as a DP camp, an executive committee for erecting the monument and chapel at Flossenbürg concentration camp had been formed, consisting mainly of Polish DPs who had not been imprisoned at Flossenbürg (Skriebeleit, 2009). Polish Catholics dominated the committee to the exclusion of Jewish members who had little influence on the development of the first memorial. A local architect was tasked with the design of a Christian chapel, which was supposed to commemorate the victims of different nations who had suffered at the hands of the Nazis. He proposed a 'memory landscape' that would include the crematorium and the mass grave located in a valley which avoided compromising the significance of the existing landscape (Skriebeleit, 2009). Thus, the 'valley of death', designed as the way of the cross with a descent into hell (crematorium) and an ascent upto salvation (chapel), provided the natural backdrop for the memorialisation process (Skriebeleit, 2016). It also functioned as a container, with the dense surrounding woodland creating a barrier between village life and the memorial itself.

The construction of the chapel commenced on 1st September 1946, near the former mass shooting area and the crematorium, and opened on 25th May 1947. The chapel's name Jesus im Kerker (Jesus in prison) shifted the focus away from the individual victim to the Christian symbolism of Jesus as victim. Hence, the early commemoration at Flossenbürg was centred around the Catholic influence of the Polish group at the UNRRA camp and completely ignored the other victim groups.

In 1947, American Property Control (the owner of the site), decided to lease the quarry and the surrounding factory buildings for five years (Skriebeleit, 2009). According to the parish council, this provided vital employment opportunities and much-needed accommodation for the new refugees from Sudetenland who had settled in the area (32% of the local population were now Sudetendeutsche). The decision to lease the quarry formed the basis for the 'deliberate forgetting' of the atrocities on site. It also suited the parish council, who had adopted the stance of the victim, i.e., the concentration camp was forced upon them and they had to live side-by-side with criminals and anti-socials.

By November 1948, 93 families were living in the former camp, most of whom were refugees from Sudetenland. The desolate condition of the buildings was no longer considered to be appropriate housing for these refugees and the council began to formulate a house-building programme (Skriebeleit, 2009). It was convenient on two levels: the ugly reminders of the concentration camp (the barracks), would finally be removed and erase the traces of the atrocities, while the refugees, although ethnic Germans, were considered to be foreigners and could be housed on the edge of the village. The former SS accommodation was much more luxurious and was built to blend in with the landscape, thus it was not regarded as part of the concentration camp landscape and had already been sold off as private residences.

In 1958, the house-building programme finally commenced and all barracks were removed. In the meantime, control of the first memorial (the chapel and the cemetery), was transferred to the new Staatliche Schlösser, Gärten und Seen (the government department responsible for maintaining castles, gardens and lakes), which was administered by the Bavarian Finance Ministry. This transfer set the precedent for the future development of the chapel and cemetery; the focus being the beautification of the area, largely through the removal of derelict buildings.

In 1962, a proposal to remove the camp prison was objected by the Lutheran Church, as it was thought to erase the legacy of the theologian Dietrich Bonhoeffer. A compromise was reached in 1964 to preserve the place where Bonhoeffer was hanged in 1945 and to erect a small exhibition commemorating his life, but resulted in the removal of up to 80% of the historical fabric of the former camp. Bonhoeffer's increasing popularity led subsequently to an increase in international visitors. Whilst the memorial had previously been regarded as an eyesore it now became an important part of Flossenbürg's tourism landscape.

The development and integration of a new memorial, 1970-2007

In 1979, the veil of silence over Flossenbürg began to lift as the first historical study of the camp was published by Toni Siegert, a local journalist (Siegert, 1979). The project coincided with the broadcasting of the US TV series *Holocaust* in West Germany. Slowly, West Germany's attitude towards the Nazi period and its legacy began to change. Finally, in 1984, it was decided to develop a new exhibition, and whilst it offered a considerable improvement on the site of the 1960s, it did not involve any specific pedagogical intervention by the museum.

In 1999, the opportunity arose to re-establish the camp outline and provide a new permanent memorial in situ. Building work commenced in 2004 by demolishing the old factory buildings and returning the site to its 1945 appearance as closely as possible. Figure 4 demonstrates how the *Appellplatz* was reinstated by removing buildings and trees to create a barren landscape. The locations of the former barracks were indicated by white lines and the camp boundary was reinstated by using white concrete fence posts (Figure 5(a,b)). There is, however, one issue that Flossenbürg will always find difficult to resolve: the housing development on the foundations of the former barracks.

Due to the removal of buildings and the re-use of the Flossenbürg concentration camp for industrial purposes after 1945, there is little evidence of the conditions at the camp during the Nazi period. As such, the current memorial does not reflect the typical atmosphere a visitor might expect. Indeed, one could say that the beautification process of the 1960s and 1970s was successful, as it created a 'sanitised' version of a concentration camp. Whilst the current memorial site attempts to present the former camp and its history, even winning the Museum of the Year Award of 2014 for its brave exhibition on Flossenbürg after 1945, it is, in its current form, a fragmented site. The quarry, where prisoners experienced daily hardship, is not integrated into the memorial site as it is still in use. Although visitors can see the quarry from a viewing platform, hardly anyone does. Much like Ravensbrück, the visitor at Flossenbürg only gets a glimpse of the sheer scale of operation at a concentration camp.

The visitor maps at the memorial site of Flossenbürg also include a black-and-white wartime aerial reconnaissance photograph (Figure 6), which is wall-mounted separately from the map of the site. The use of black-and-white photography brings a sense of continuity to images taken at the time of the camps' operation (Charlesworth &

Figure 4. The redevelopment phases of Flossenbürg Concentration Camp memorial after 2003 (Flossenbürg Concentration Camp memorial, 2015; reproduced courtesy of Flossenbürg memorial site).

Figure 5. (a) Former camp boundary wall prior to site development in 2003 (Flossenbürg Concentration Camp memorial, 2015; reproduced courtesy of Flossenbürg memorial site); (b) reinstatement of former camp boundary after 2003.

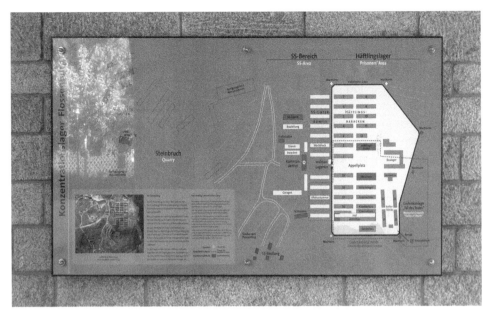

Figure 6. Visitor sign in Flossenbürg Concentration Camp memorial incorporating a map and wartime aerial image (Source: Authors).

Addis, 2002) and the aerial photograph introduces a sense of objectivity and authority in portraying how the camp looked at the point of liberation. Unlike the leaflet available at Ravensbrück, however, the photograph does not serve as the base for the visitor map for Flossenbürg and is not portable. Consequently, the map and the photograph here act more as reference points for the visitor and less as agents that reinforce their perception and re-imagining as they explore the site.

Investigating the emotional experiences of visitors to memorial sites

Method

Buchenwald memorial's manager, Volkhart Knigge, pleaded for caution in 2004 with regard to visitor research at memorial sites. He argued that standard museum research methodologies cannot be transferred to a concentration camp memorial. The smallest physical intervention, e.g., a sign, can cause serious upset, which is unheard of at 'normal' museums. He recalls, for instance, the visitor who screamed at him for using gaseous pesticides at the memorial site. Equally, Küblböck (2012) explains that researching visitors at memorial sites is beyond the skill set of most social scientists. The complex interplay of cultural and personal backgrounds, collective memory narratives and emotions are, according to him, difficult to capture through the standard repertoire of qualitative and quantitative research methods, and requires an interdisciplinary approach.

Pereiro (2010) highlights that anthropological research can reveal the complex social realities of tourism activities, and Light (2017) emphasises that researchers need to get close to tourists in order to develop an understanding of how they experience 'dark' sites. In particular, ethnographic research is able to highlight the meaning-making processes which are essential when investigating tourism at memorial sites. For example, Sumartojo (2019) demonstrates the importance of sensory experiences at memorial sites by asking tourists at a concentration camp memorial in France to take photographs of locations that resonate with them. The subsequent video-taped interviews reveal the meaning of these sites and how they are understood by the visitor.

Thus, in order to gain an understanding of the visitor experience in situ, ethnographic research in the form of open participant observation (Herbert, 2000) was conducted at each location over a four-week period in June and July 2016. The visitor research undertaken at Flossenbürg and Ravensbrück formed part of a wider project to investigate visitor responses at German memorial sites. Including school visits, in 2018 Ravensbrück memorial site received approximately 100,000 visitors while Flossenbürg recorded 90,500 (Das Gupta & Sandkuhl, 2019). This paper focuses on the interaction between the visitor and the landscape, and discusses the results of the qualitative research.

During open participant observation, the researcher can 'join in', allowing him/her to record visitor behaviour as and when it happens (Dewalt and Dewalt, 2010). As such, the researcher is able to record activities in their natural setting, gaining an understanding of social phenomena (Kawulich, 2005). Whilst participant observation is an established method within anthropological research, often studying cultural groups in their 'original' settings over extensive periods of time, it is not usually adopted for research at memorial sites. Hence, the relatively short stay of visitors on-site (on average two hours) required trust to be established quickly in order to gain insights into the visitors' reactions.

Open participant observations may also be disadvantaged in that the research subject can alter their behaviour in the presence of the researcher. Nightingale (2008, p.107), however, emphasises that 'to produce good qualitative research, accurate observation has to be combined with communication and exchange of information and ideas'. Indeed, how visitors respond to a landscape, especially emotionally, can only be established through conversation. Hence, despite the disadvantages of open participant observation, it was considered to be the most appropriate research methodology in this case.

Individual visitors were approached at random on arrival at each memorial site (n = 52). At Ravensbrück (n = 25), most visitors were German (19), while others originated from the United States (2), Belgium (1), Poland (1), Switzerland (1) and the United Kingdom (1). Similarly, at Flossenbürg (n = 27), most visitors were from Germany (20), in particular from the local federal state of Bavaria, followed by visitors from the United States (4), often stationed at the nearby US Army base, and visitors from Sweden (2) and Belgium (1). At Ravensbrück, the most common age groups were 50 to 60 years old and over 70 years old, with only two visitors in the 20 to 30 age group. By contrast, at Flossenbürg, most participants were in the age groups of 20 to 30 and of 60 to 70 years old, although the age groups of 30 to 40 and of 50 to 60 years were also represented. Conversations with visitors were conducted in either German or English, thus excluding those whose language ability provided a barrier. As the research took place at the height of summer, weather conditions were often sunny and very hot which, could have affected visitors' perceptions of the wider memorial landscapes more positively.

Since there is no prescribed route at either memorial site, visitors are free to choose which locations they visit and in which order. Visitors were therefore accompanied (but were not guided) across the memorial landscape, although historical questions were answered, e.g., to explain what happened in the crematorium. During these observations, the visitors' comments, their emotional reactions and the locations they visited were all recorded in field notes and were subsequently analysed using NVivo software. This provided a sufficient distance from the data to develop a reflective interpretation (Berger, 2015).

Results and interpretation

At the Ravensbrück memorial site, a German male visitor commented: 'It is perverse; this morning I had a great breakfast in my hotel, then I look at this [Ravensbrück], then you forget everything and carry on with your cycling tour'. Most individual visitors at both memorial sites engaged with what could be described as tourist activities; they were either on holiday in the area or were on a day trip. Thus, they were in a transitional stage, away from ordinary day-to-day life to one marked by new experiences. These experiences are usually characterised by positivity, e.g., Sun, beach, relaxation. Yet in the case of memorial sites, it is a transition into negativity, into the depths of the human psyche. Often within a space of minutes, the visitor suddenly encounters a world of destruction and mass murder. Once s/he leaves these areas of violence, however, s/he is re-entering an ordinary space that subsequently feels inappropriate. The visitor's remark above stresses the importance of those transitional periods that are either hindered or supported by the landscape itself. Yet these landscapes are often characterised, as shown previously, by absence. The murder and violence that had taken place is no longer visible; a feeling often expressed by survivors.

'Nature has overgrown all suffering; I only found the area where Siemens docked their ships on the River Havel and some remains of the *Sonderblock* that my daughter unearthed' (Gedenkort KZ Uckermark Online, 2018). This comment is from Maria Potrzeba, a survivor of the Youth Protection Camp Uckermark. Maria describes what so many survivors experience when they return to Ravensbrück: a feeling of alienation on encountering a picturesque lakeside setting at a site where the most horrific atrocities had taken place and where their lives had been changed for good. The landscapes themselves, however, appear to be indifferent to the former suffering (Rapson, 2015).

For some visitors, the landscapes remain contaminated. One female German visitor commented at Ravensbrück: 'These places have a dark and mystical atmosphere that will always hang over them' and a German male visitor concluded that 'The longer one stays in these places, the more depressing they become'. Such sentiments are also evident in buildings that symbolise the Nazis' industrial management of death, i.e., crematoria. Some visitors at both Ravensbrück and Flossenbürg were hesitant in walking into these buildings or started to tremble. It was almost as if the visitor attempted to take on the emotions of the victim, which of course they cannot. A female German visitor commented on encountering the crematorium at Ravensbrück: 'I've had enough now, this industrial processing unnerves me', whilst a German teenager suggested when viewing the 'execution path' that 'This is too sad for me'. These reactions highlight the performative aspect of traumatic landscapes. Although suffering and death are no longer visible, the meaning of the landscape evokes a sense of place in visitors that goes beyond the material evidence.

It is, however, not only the buildings of mass murder that are tainted. At Flossenbürg, visitors frequently remarked that the residential houses built on the foundations of the barracks 'looked sad' and they could not understand how anyone could possibly live there. One German visitor at Ravensbrück complained about the modern addition of the visitor centre which 'does not fit into the landscape'; whilst another visitor encountering the clinker surface argued that 'These places should not be cleaned up'. In this case, the visitor did not realise that the surface had only been installed recently, yet for her the 'bleakness' symbolised historical evidence. Hence, pathemic restoration (Violi, 2012), designed to engender emotions in visitors, can affect their overall experience of the site. However, signs of life, such as residential homes or new buildings, appear to disrupt the visitors' expectation (or need) to encounter a bleak atmosphere. Indeed, the aesthetically pleasing elements of the landscape, like the lake at Ravensbrück or the valley in Flossenbürg, work against the visitors' experience, as the serenity of the landscape stands in contrast to the atrocities that happened.

Keats (2005) notes during his visitor research at Auschwitz-Birkenau (Poland) and at Sachsenhausen Concentration Camp memorial site (near Berlin) that visitors 'filter their experiences through a cultural lens' (p.180), i.e., they will interpret the site according to their own frame of reference. For example, one Swedish visitor admired the natural landscape of Flossenbürg, enjoying the birdsong and commented 'Every nation has done something bad'. Clearly, this visitor was less disturbed by the site than the German visitors mentioned above, and could therefore approach the memorial in a more emotionally detached way. This supports Violi's (2012) claim that emotional reactions at memorial sites are influenced by the positioning of the visitor. The more knowledge visitors have about associated historical events, the deeper the emotions they are likely to experience. As Klüger (2003, p.94) suggests about journeys to Auschwitz, 'He who thinks something could be found there, has brought it with him in his luggage'.

It was not just buildings of mass murder that provoked feelings of unease. At Ravensbrück, some visitors who had stayed overnight in the youth hostel in the former SS female guard houses experienced sleepless nights. One German visitor stated, 'I slept well the first night, but not anymore afterwards'. Another German visitor noted that 'One cannot shake off the fact that one sleeps in a former SS building'. Furthermore, the contrast between the SS houses, the lake, and then the camp, brought the malicious nature of the Nazi system to the fore, as one German visitor concluded. Hence, not only the atrocities are projected onto the landscape; the entire Nazi system is palpable.

Aspects of nature, such as trees, inspired visitors to reflect on the victims' experience. One visitor from the US remarked 'It is so calm here, when one considers the atrocities that have taken place', while a German visitor said that for him, 'Every stone is a destiny'. Even the trees were transformed into witnesses of violence, as one German visitor pondered 'The trees would have been here' (referring to Flossenbürg's time as a concentration camp).

At times, the memorial landscape functioned as the backdrop for dealing with one's own traumatic memories. A German male visitor stated at the beginning of his visit to Flossenbürg 'I know what a concentration camp is like, I had one at home'. He was referring to his abusive father who had been an avid supporter of the Nazi regime. A female German visitor at Ravensbrück was flooded with memories as she walked across the landscape: 'When I walk around here, all these memories are coming back. My grandfather dying after he was released from Neuengamme concentration camp and my father returning disabled from World War II'. Another German (but having grown up in Australia) female visitor at Flossenbürg explained on arrival that her father had survived Mauthausen concentration camp and subsequently emigrated to Australia. He had never talked about his experiences. For her, the visit to Flossenbürg was marked by a commemoration of the victims and by coming to terms with her father's silence. She concluded the visit by saying 'I have to emotionally distance myself from the visit, otherwise I won't cope'. Feelings of emotional distancing in order to cope were frequently expressed by visitors and also amongst those who had no direct connection to the concentration camp system. In addition, a recurrent theme amongst German visitors was 'My relatives never talked'. Hence, the memorial site can also be a form of individual German *Vergangenheitsbewältigung* (coming to terms with the past).

While tourists in other contexts desire an emotional bond, especially at museum and heritage sites (Biran, Poria, & Oren, 2011; McIntosh, 1999), German memorial sites appear to promote the opposite; a safe distance, so that one does not get emotionally overwhelmed (Yair, 2014). Moreover, these findings reveal that visitor experiences at concentration camp memorial sites are highly subjective and influenced by a number of factors, including their cultural background and the physical environment. This supports Light's (2017) view that only by getting close to the visitor can one understand the visitor experience at 'dark' sites.

Other visitor comments suggest that these landscapes seem to become almost sacred spaces. When one German female visitor overheard a tour guide explaining to another group that the GDR had to flatten the ashes to build the first memorial at Ravensbrück, she reacted in horror: 'I can't believe I'm walking on ashes now'. The sacredness of the site was also mirrored in another situation observed during fieldwork. Some canoeists who had anchored their boats next to the Ravensbrück memorial statue (having paddled across the lake from the nearby town of Fürstenberg) were immediately reprimanded by the water police and were asked to leave in their canoes. Eschebach (2011) explains that since 1945, there is a common belief that human ashes were dumped into the lake, thus for survivors it is a grave. The lake's dual function as a graveyard and as a water sports area resulted in a division into a 'sacralised' space (marked by buoys) and a 'leisure' space. Although canoeists have long been demanding a landing stage, this is rejected by survivors and by the management team as a 'profanation of the site' (p.140). It nevertheless appears to be somewhat paradoxical, given that the Ravensbrück site houses a youth hostel where visitors can enjoy barbeques and parties.

The landscape also functions as evidence for the crimes committed. Visitors are increasingly influenced by either the representation of the Holocaust in films, such as

Schindler's List or *The Boy in the Striped Pyjamas* (Alexander, 2002; Cole, 1999), or by previous visits to other memorial sites, particularly Auschwitz. Some visitors therefore suggested that they did not get the gruesome feeling they had experienced when visiting Auschwitz or Dachau. This was mainly due to the absence of former camp structures and by the overwhelming feeling that 'Auschwitz had been much worse'. For instance, one German female at Flossenbürg said 'I could not eat anything after a visit to Auschwitz, while here I quite happily go to the cafe'. Another German visitor argued that Auschwitz was more emotional, as 'You could still see the electric fences which you are confronted with immediately after arrival'. Indeed, four young German visitors suggested that 'Auschwitz was more interesting because one could still see the scratch marks on the wall'. Whilst this is an extreme example, it emphasises the power of the media which clouds visitors' perceptions of what a concentration camp memorial ought to look like. Zelizer (1998) poignantly argues that we are on our way 'to remember to forget'. The results of this research support her argument, as visitors tended to recall the artefact rather than the historical facts.

Tourists at memorial sites are often criticised for their shallow behaviour which manifests itself, for instance, in taking inappropriate photographs (including 'selfies'). However, this research found that German visitors did not tend to take photographs at memorial sites, and those who did usually took panoramic pictures. In contrast, visitors from the US specifically focused on the material evidence of the site, e.g., by taking photographs at Flossenbürg of the watchtowers, barbed-wire fence posts and the memorial plaque of the US Infantry Division who had liberated the camp in 1945. Thus, tourists to concentration camp memorial sites cannot simply be described (e.g., by Cole, 1999; Pollock, 2003) as shallow or voyeuristic. German visitors appeared to experience a psycho-cultural barrier that prevents them from taking photographs. For US visitors, capturing these physical remnants operated as proof for preconceived or stereotypical images; in a sense 'seeing is believing' and even comforting.

Rapson (2015) noted that curatorial decisions on memorial landscape design are rarely considered in academic research and that research on visitor responses is even rarer. These findings reveal the complex interplay between visitors' identity, the memorial space, cultural memory and emotions. Crucially, tourists are not distant spectators (Knudsen, 2011). The memorial landscape is more than just a backdrop, since visitors actively engage with tangible and intangible aspects of the site. In fact, it is their own imagination and interpretation that often creates the meaning. Thus, as Crouch, Aronsson, and Wahlström (2001) suggest, tourism needs to be considered as an active encounter rather than a passive activity. Visitors to memorial sites can be secondary witnesses to the trauma they take with them when they leave (Reynolds, 2018). The visit is therefore a transitional, liminal process and although this visitor research has cast light on the transition phase, knowing precisely how such visits 'transform' the individual before they re-enter ordinary life remains elusive.

More generally, visitor experiences of these memorial sites indicate how the sites' sense of place is embodied. The immateriality that characterises these experiences appears to enhance the effect on the visitors' bodies; sleepless nights in the on-site youth hostel or trembling when engaging with near-empty spaces in this context. The gaps are filled by the visitors' imaginations in their perceptions of bleak, dehumanised landscapes. That the sites' visitor maps (and most of the on-site signage) are devoid of colour provides a sense of continuity with wartime imagery (Charlesworth & Addis, 2002), but also reinforces these re-imaginings and perceptions, that in turn evoke a sense of place that creates liminality.

This construction of liminality is further complicated by the multi-layered history and function of memorial sites such as Ravensbrück and Flossenbürg. The changing owners of the landscape have each left their mark and so the sites in effect become palimpsests that bear witness to the different phases in their development. The recent active landscaping of these memorial sites in an attempt to revert to their 1945 appearance, and thereby attempting to erase different layers of their past, raises serious questions regarding the preservation of the historical integrity of these sites. How this process affects the sense of place is potentially a subject of future visitor research.

Conclusion: Connecting visitors to transformative landscapes

The changing political narratives of memorialisation are inscribed into the landscapes at the memorial sites of Ravensbrück and Flossenbürg. Hence, these landscapes have had to adapt to Germany's changing attitudes towards its Nazi past, especially after 1990 as a re-unified country. At Flossenbürg, this required a reinstatement of the original camp structure by demolishing factory buildings that had been built after 1945 and indicating the location of former barracks by white concrete lines. At Ravensbrück, Soviet Army buildings were demolished in order to recover traces of the former camp.

However, returning the landscapes to their former appearance is not without its shortcomings. At Ravensbrück, the process almost erased a fifty-year history of the Soviet Army which had a significant impact on the local community and their perception of the site. At Flossenbürg, the removal of the factory buildings opened up the view to the housing development, which is now considered to be inappropriate.

These findings have demonstrated that being in the space of former suffering is an integral part of the visit to such an extent that signs of new life are experienced as disturbing. The spaces that caused the strongest emotional reactions were those locations where death was processed (e.g., the execution areas and crematoria). However, visitors overlooked the fact that suffering did not just occur in these places; the real suffering was the daily struggle for survival in the appalling working and living conditions at both camps.

Landscapes are palimpsests of memory which 'go beyond individual experience; [combining] memory and history, objective and subjective, in a blend of perception and meaning-making' (Manning, 2010, p. 237). Yet, visitors at both concentration camp memorials remain largely unaware of the changing nature of these landscapes. A better way to introduce this for visitors may be to embrace the landscape as a palimpsest that brings the visitor closer to experiencing the different layers. One example of this approach is adopted at the Gusen subcamp memorial site of the former Mauthausen concentration camp. Apart from a memorial erected in the 1960s and a visitor centre which opened in 2004, nothing remains. Much like Flossenbürg, the former barracks were removed and replaced by an Austrian housing development.

Through an audio tour, however, visitors are guided through the village where the voices of survivors, residents, and actors representing SS staff and guards interplay with specially designed soundtracks. The visitor only hears fragments of those voices; hence it is not a complete historical analysis of the Gusen subcamp. However, by featuring those different perspectives, the visitor gains a sense of the complexity of how a memorial site comprises a multi-layered landscape.

The use of maps at memorial sites can actively encourage visitors to re-imagine past landscapes as palimpsests, whilst also supporting the aim of evoking a sense of place and enhancing liminality. The potential of other methods to encourage exploration of the sites' history and to allow visitors to discover otherwise hidden aspects should be an integral way of memorial site management. After all, a space cannot just be read as a fixed point in time, but one must be aware of its transformation (Massey, 2005).

Giordano and Cole (2018) suggest the introduction of a place-based GIS (geographical information system) that combines qualitative with quantitative data, e.g., the visitor would either see past images or historical documents that are connected to a specific location. The creation of a 'soundscape' at concentration camp memorial sites would be a sensory method for engaging visitors at sites where there are few visible remains. Whilst such developments must be sensitive to ethical boundaries, audio tours have the ability to create a form of 'embodied listening', forcing people to negotiate the current landscape while also engaging with the 'memoryscape' (High, 2013). Thus, memory is able to 'cut through the layers' and show how time-bound places are (Klüger, 2001).

The management at both memorial sites envisages the re-integration of areas which formed part of the concentration camp landscape (the 'zone of misery' at Ravensbrück and the quarry at Flossenbürg). At Ravensbrück the 'zone' is merely a grassland as there is no physical evidence remaining, while the quarry at Flossenbürg is still in operation. Ironically, this expansion mirrors that of the sites' original growth and physical transformation of natural landscapes. Yet, in regressing these spaces to landscapes of trauma, defined solely by one layer of their history, they become liminal for visitors. Curatorial decisions regarding memorial sites should therefore not only focus on their museum spaces, but also on the management and design of their wider landscapes and the associated ethical considerations.

Disclosure statement

No potential conflict of interest was reported by the author(s).

References

Alexander, J. C. (2002). On the social construction of moral universals: The 'Holocaust' from war crime to trauma drama. *European Journal of Social Theory*, *5*(1), 5–85. doi:10.1177/1368431002005001001

Attfield, J. (2000). *Wild things: The material culture of everyday life*. Oxford: Berg.

Beckstead, Z. (2010). Commentary: Liminality in acculturation and pilgrimage: When movement becomes meaningful. *Culture & Psychology*, *16*(3), 383–393. doi:10.1177/1354067X10371142

Benz, W., Diestel, B., & Königseder, A. (2007). *Flossenbürg: Das Konzentrationslager Flossenbürg und seine Außenlager. [Flossenbürg: The concentration camp Flossenbürg and its subcamps]* Munich: C.H. Beck.

Berger, R. (2015). Now I see it, now I don't: Researcher's position and reflexivity in qualitative research. *Qualitative Research*, *15*(2), 219–234. doi:10.1177/1468794112468475

Biran, A., Poria, Y., & Oren, G. (2011). Sought experiences at (Dark) heritage sites. *Annals of Tourism Research*, *38*(3), 820–841. doi:10.1016/j.annals.2010.12.001

Casey, E. S. (2011). The edge(s) of landscape: A study in liminology. In J. Malpass (Ed.), *The place of landscape: Concepts, contexts, studies* (pp. 91–110). Cambridge: MIT Press.

Charlesworth, A., & Addis, M. (2002). Memorialization and the ecological landscapes of Holocaust sites: The cases of Plaszow and Auschwitz-Birkenau. *Landscape Research*, *27*(3), 229–251. doi: 10.1080/01426390220149502

Cole, T. (1999). *Selling the Holocaust: From Auschwitz to Schindler: How history is bought. Packaged, and sold*. New York: Psychology Press.

Crouch, D., Aronsson, L., & Wahlström, L. (2001). Tourist encounters. *Tourist Studies*, *1*(3), 253–270. doi:10.1177/146879760100100303

Das Gupta, O., & Sandkuhl, I. (2019). Politischer Rechtsruck beschäftigt Besucher von KZ-Gedenkstätten [Political shift to the right occupies visitors to concentration camp memorials]. Süddeutsche Zeitung. [online] 27 Jan. Retrieved from https://www.sueddeutsche.de/politik/kz-gedenkstaetten-besucher-holocaust-1.4305186

Dewalt, K. M., & Dewalt, B. R. (2010). *Participant observation - A guide for fieldworkers*. Plymouth: Altamira Press.

Downey, D., Kinane, I., & Parker, E. (Eds.). (2016). *Landscapes of liminality: Between space and place*. London: Rowman & Littlefield International.

Dunkley, R., Morgan, N., & Westwood, S. (2011). Visiting the trenches: Exploring meanings and motivations in battlefield tourism. *Tourism Management*, *32*(4), 860–868. doi:10.1016/j.tourman.2010.07.011

Eschebach, I. (2011). Soil, ashes, commemoration: Processes of sacralization at the former Ravensbrück Concentration Camp. *History and Memory*, *23*(1), 131–156. doi:10.2979/histmemo.23.1.131

Eschebach, I. (2014). *Das Frauen-Konzentrationslager Ravensbrück: Neue Beiträge zur Geschichte und Nachgeschichte. [The women's concentration camp Ravensbrück. New contributions to history and post-history]*. Berlin: Metropol-Verlag.

Gedenkort KZ Uckermark Online, 2018. *Portraits von Überlebenden* [Portraits from survivors], [Accessed 30 June 2018].

Giordano, A., & Cole, T. (2018). The limits of GIS: Towards a GIS of place. *Transactions in GIS*, *22*(3), 664–676. doi:10.1111/tgis.12342

Heigl, P. (1989). *Flossenbürg in Geschichte und Gegenwart: Bilder und Dokumente gegen das zweite Vergessen. [Concentration camp Flossenbürg in memory and presence: images and documents against the second forgetting].* Regensburg: Mittelbayerischer Verlag.

Herbert, S. (2000). For ethnography. *Progress in Human Geography, 24*(4), 550–568. doi:10.1191/030913200100189102

High, S. (2013). Embodied ways of listening: Oral history, genocide and the audio tour. *Anthropologica, 55*(1), 73–85.

Jacobeit, W., & Stegemann, W. (2004). *Fürstenberg/Havel - Ravensbrück. Beiträge zur Kulturgeschichte einer Region zwischen Brandenburg und Mecklenburg: Band 2: Wechselnde Machtverhältnisse im 20. Jahrhundert. [Fürstenberg/Havel - Ravensbrück. Contributions to the cultural history of a region between Brandenburg and Mecklenburg: Volume 2: Changing power relations in the 20th century].* Berlin: Hentrich und Hentrich Verlag .

Kawulich, B. B. (2005). Participant observation as a data collection method. *Forum Qualitative Sozialforschung/Forum: Qualitative Social Research* [online] *6*(2). Retrieved from http://www.qualitative-research.net/index.php/fqs/article/view/466

Keats, P. A. (2005). Vicarious witnessing in European Concentration Camps: Imagining the trauma of another. *Traumatology, 11*(3), 171–183. doi:10.1177/153476560501100303

Klüger, R. (2001). *Still alive: A Holocaust girlhood remembered.* New York: Feminist Press at the City University of New York.

Knigge, V. (2004). Museum oder Schädelstätte? Gedenkstätten als multiple Institutionen [Museums or places of skulls? Memorials as multiple institutions]. In *Stiftung Haus der Geschichte der Bundesrepublik Deutschland, ed. Museumsfragen. Gedenkstätten und Besucherforschung. [Questions about museums. Memorial sites and visitor research]* (pp. 17–33). Bonn: Stiftung Haus der Geschichte der Bundesrepublik Deutschland.

Knudsen, B. (2011). Thanatourism: Witnessing difficult pasts. *Tourist Studies, 11*(1), 55–72.

Köhler, R., & Plewe, J. T. (2001). *Baugeschichte Frauen-Konzentrationslager Ravensbrück. [The History of Construction of the Women's Concentration Camp Ravensbrück]. Schriftenreihe der Stiftung Brandenburgische Gedenkstätten.* Berlin: Edition Hentrich.

Küblböck, S. (2012). Sich selbst an dunklen Orten begegnen: Existentielle Authentizität als Potenzial des Dark Tourism. [To encounter oneself in dark places: Existential authenticity as the potential of dark tourism]. In H.-D. Quack and A. Steinecke (Eds.), *Dark tourism: Faszination des Schreckens. [Dark Tourism: Fascination with horror]* (pp.114–124). Paderborn: Selbstverl. des Faches Geographie, Fak. für Kulturwiss., Univ. Paderborn.

Lammert, M. (1965). *Will Lammert: Ravensbrück.* Berlin: Deutsche Akademie der Künste zu Berlin.

Lennon, J., & Foley, M. (2000). *Dark tourism: The attraction of death and disaster.* London; New York: Cengage Learning.

Light, D. (2017). Progress in dark tourism and thanatourism research: An uneasy relationship with heritage tourism. *Tourism Management, 61*, 275–301. doi:10.1016/j.tourman.2017.01.011

Malpass, J. (2011). Place and the problem of landscape. In J. Malpass (Ed.), *The place of landscape: Concepts, contexts, studies* (pp.3–26). Cambridge: MIT Press.

Manning, J. R. (2010). The palimpsest of memory: Auschwitz and Oświęcim. *Holocaust Studies, 16*(1–2), 229–256.

Marchetta, M. (2001). *Erinnerung und Demokratie. Holocaust Mahnmale und ihre Erinnerungspolitik: Das Beispiel Ravensbrück. [Memory and Democracy. Holocaust Memorials and their memory politics. The example of Ravensbrück]* Berlin: Metropol-Verlag.

Massey, D. (2005). *For space.* London: SAGE Publications Ltd.

McIntosh, A. J. (1999). Into the tourist's mind: Understanding the value of the heritage experience. *Journal of Travel & Tourism Marketing, 8*(1), 41–64. doi:10.1300/J073v08n01_03

Ministerium für Wissenschaft und Kultur Brandenburg. (2009). Geschichte vor Ort: Erinnerungskultur im Land Brandenburg für die Zeit von 1933 bis 1990 (Online) [History where it happened: The culture of remembrance in the Brandenburg region for the period 1933–1990]. Retrieved from https://mwfk.brandenburg.de/media_fast/4055/Konzept_GeschichtevorOrt.pdf

Nawijn, J., & Fricke, M.-C. (2015). Visitor emotions and behavioral intentions: The case of Concentration Camp Memorial Neuengamme. *International Journal of Tourism Research*, *17*(3), 221–228. doi:10.1002/jtr.1977

Nightingale, V. (2008). Why observation matters. In M. Pickering, (Ed.), *Research methods for cultural studies* (pp. 105–124). Edinburgh: Edinburgh University Press.

Nijhuis, S. (2019). Mapping the evolution of designed landscapes with GIS. In T. Coomans, B. Cattoor, & K. De Jongepp (Eds.), *Mapping landscapes in transformation multidisciplinary methods for historical analysis* (pp. 95–129). Leuven: Leuven University Press.

Oswalt, P., & Tischer, S. (1998). Ehemaliges Frauen-KZ Ravensbrück. [Former women's concentration camp Ravensbrück unpublished landscape architecture proposal submitted to Fürstenberg council]

Pereiro, X. (2010). Ethnographic research on cultural tourism: An anthropological view. In G. Richards & W. Munsters (Eds.), *Cultural tourism research methods* (pp.173–187). Wallingford: Cabi.

Pollock, G. (2003). Holocaust tourism: Being there, looking back and the ethics of spatial memory. In N. Lubbren & D. Crouch (Eds.), *Visual culture and tourism, English edition* (pp.175–190). Oxford: Berg.

Popescu, D. I. (2016). Post-witnessing the concentration camps: Paul Auster's and Angela Morgan Cutler's investigative and imaginative encounters with sites of mass murder. *Holocaust Studies*, *22*(2-3), 274–288. doi:10.1080/17504902.2016.1148880

Prosise, T. O. (2003). Prejudiced, historical witness, and responsible: Collective memory and liminality in the Beit Hashoah museum of tolerance. *Communication Quarterly*, *51*(3), 351–366. doi:10.1080/01463370309370161

Rapson, J. (2015). *Topographies of suffering: Buchenwald, Babi Yar, Lidice*. New York: Berghahn Books.

Reynolds, D. (2018). *Postcards from Auschwitz - Holocaust tourism and the meaning of remembrance*. New York: New York University Press.

Rickly-Boyd, J. M. (2013). Existential authenticity: Place matters. *Tourism Geographies*, *15*(4), 680–686. doi:10.1080/14616688.2012.762691

Schwarz, E., & Steppan, S. (1999). Die Entstehung der Nationalen Mahn-und Gedenkstätte Ravensbrück, 1945-1959 [The development of Ravensbrück memorial 1945-1959]. In I. Eschebach, S. Jacobeit, and S. Lanwerd (Eds.), *Die Sprache des Gedenkens. Zur Geschichte der Gedenkstätte Ravensbrück 1945-1995 [The language of commemoration. The history of Ravensbrück memorial site 1945-1995]*. Berlin: Hentrich Edition.

Shields, R. (1991). *Places on the margin: Alternative geographies of modernity*. London: Routledge.

Siegert, T. (1979). Das Konzentrationslager Flossenbürg. Ein Lager für Asoziale und Kriminelle [The concentration camp Flossenbürg. A camp for asocials and criminals]. In M. Broszat & E. Fröhlich (Eds.), *Bayern in der NS-Zeit [Bavaria during the NS regime]* (pp. 429–492.). Bd. 2. München: Oldenbourg Wissenschaftsverlag.

Skriebeleit, J. (2009). *Erinnerungsort Flossenbürg: Akteure, Zäsuren, Geschichtsbilder [Flossenbürg as a site of memory: Stakeholders, turning points and perceptions of history]*. Göttingen: Wallstein Verlag.

Skriebeleit, J. (2011). Nachwirkungen eines Konzentrationslagers [Aftermath of a concentration camp]. *Gedenkstättenforum - Rundbrief*, *159*, 21–27.

Skriebeleit, J. (2016). Relikte, Sinnstiftungen und memoriale Blueprints [Relics, meaning and memorial blueprints]. In E. Heitzer, G. Morsch, R. Traba, & K. Woniak, (Eds.), *Von Mahnstätten über zeithistorische Museen zu Orten des Massentourismus: Gedenkstätten an Orten von NS-Verbrechen in Polen und Deutschland [From memorials to contemporary museums to places of mass tourism: Memorials in places of Nazi crimes in Poland and Germany]* (pp.48–65). Berlin: Metropol-Verlag.

Stier, O. B. (2015). *Holocaust Icons: Symbolizing the Shoah in History and Memory*. New Brunswick, New Jersey: Rutgers University Press.

Stone, P. R. (2018). Dark tourism in an age of spectacular death. In R. Hartmann, R. Sharpley, T. Seaton, L. White, & P. R. Stone (Eds.), *The Palgrave handbook of dark tourism studies*. London: Palgrave Macmillan.

Sumartojo, S. (2019). Sensory impact: Memory, affect and sensory ethnography at official memory sites. In D. Drozdzewski & C. Birdsall (Eds.), *Doing memory research: New methods and approaches* (pp. 21–37). Singapore: Palgrave Macmillan.

Turner, V. W. (1969). *The ritual process: Structure and anti-structure*. Chicago: Aldine Pub. Co.

van Gennep, A. (1960). *The rites of passage*. London: Psychology Press.

Violi, P. (2012). Trauma site museums and politics of memory: Tuol Sleng, Villa Grimaldi and the Bologna Ustica Museum. *Theory, Culture & Society, 29*(1), 36–75. doi:10.1177/0263276411423035

Yair, G. (2014). Neutrality, objectivity, and dissociation: Cultural trauma and educational messages in German Holocaust Memorial Sites and Documentation Centers. *Holocaust and Genocide Studies, 28*(3), 482–509. doi:10.1093/hgs/dcu042

Zelizer, B. (1998). *Remembering to forget: Holocaust memory through the camera's eye*. Chicago: University of Chicago Press. doi:10.1086/ahr/106.4.1320

Dark tourism and moral disengagement in liminal spaces

Nitasha Sharma

ABSTRACT

Dark tourism, which deploys taboo subjects and commercially exploits the macabre, has always raised moral conflicts at a collective and individual level while providing new spaces in which morality is communicated, reconfigured and revitalized. Although earlier studies in dark tourism have focused upon the collective notions of morality with a considerable amount of discussion on the comprehension and the manner in which the history and information of dark tourist attractions are presented for tourist consumption, the individual differences of tourist morality and how tourists morally engage with death and its various forms of representation, has been neglected. In order to understand morally transgressive behavior displayed by tourists at emotionally sensitive or controversial sites and the various ways they justify their actions, the narratives of international tourists who are interested in death-related rituals at a cremation ground in India were collected and analyzed. Drawing upon a socio-cognitive theory, the moral mechanisms involved in tourist judgment towards photography of death-related rituals are discussed. It was observed that the cremation ground offers a liminal space for tourists to exercise their moral agency in an inhibitive form, as well as proactive form and that transgressive behavior among tourists is likely if they disengage from processes related to moral conduct using various moral disengagement mechanisms. This behavior arises due to an obscuring and fragmentation of human agency during moral disengagement thereby making it possible for tourists to not take ownership of the consequences of their actions.

摘要

黑暗旅游业利用禁忌主题和商业性的恐怖行为,总是在集体和个人层面引发道德冲突,同时为道德的交流、重构和振兴提供新的空间。虽然黑暗旅游早期的研究集中在道德的集体的观念,广泛讨论与阐释了针对旅游消费黑暗旅游吸引物历史与信息的展示方式,但是一直忽略了旅游者道德的个体差异以及游客道德层面接触死亡以及死亡的各种展示形式。为了了解游客在情感敏感或有争议的地点所表现出的道德越轨行为,以及他们为自己的行为辩护的各种方式,我们收集并分析了对印度火葬场与死亡有关的仪式感兴趣的国际游客的叙述。根据社会认知理论,讨论了游客对死亡相关仪式摄影的道德机制。研究发现,火葬场提供了一个阈

限空间, 让游客以抑制性和主动性的形式来发挥道德能动性, 如果
游客使用各种道德解脱机制来脱离与道德行为相关的过程, 就有
可能发生违反道德的行为。这种行为的产生是由于道德脱离过程
中人类行为主体的模糊和碎片化, 从而使游客有可能不对其行为
的后果承担责任。

Introduction

Morality is a socially constructed set of values that are agreed upon by individuals and societies (Pennycook, 1994). It differs within and between cultures and is embedded in relations of power and spatial contexts. According to Caton (2012), morality refers to the "human imaginative and discursive capacity for considering how things should be, as opposed to describing how things are-what is sometimes referred to as the "is" versus "ought" distinction" (p. 1906). Dark tourism is a social phenomenon where the notion of morality has been subjected to extensive interrogation, especially by the media. While the tourist motivations to visit sites of a sensitive nature may be diverse, dark tourism remains a morally relevant issue that involves a questioning of moral judgment (Rojek,1997; Stone, 2009). It has always raised issues of how morality is collectively conveyed and individually constructed. Dark tourism provides new spaces in which not only immorality is (re)presented for contemporary consumption, but also in which morality is communicated, reconfigured and revitalized (Stone, 2009). It deploys taboo subjects, commercially exploits the macabre and offers the tourist a liminal space for reassessment and reflexivity and may even allow a reconfiguration of moral reasoning and outlook (Stone, 2009).

Prior research in dark tourism has focused upon the collective notions of morality (e.g., moral issues related to collective memory, politics, commodification of tragedy and atrocity) and its institutional reconstruction through dark tourism but not much on the individual differences of tourist morality and moral consumption (Stone, 2009, 2011; Seaton & Lennon, 2004; Wight & Lennon, 2007). The discussions on morality in dark tourism have been about the comprehension and manner in which the history and information of dark tourist attractions are presented for tourist consumption but not much on how tourists morally engage with death and its various forms of representation. The process of individualization (in which traditional meaning systems and values diminish in importance in favor of personal considerations and decisions concerning values, norms and behaviors) has made "people more reliant upon themselves for moral instruction" (Stone & Sharpley, 2013, p. 62). Hence consumer behavior at an individual level is useful for understanding how individuals within contemporary society (and when placed in diverse situations) construct and reconstruct moral meanings and behave accordingly. Currently, there is a substantial amount of theoretical research available on dark tourism and morality or 'deviant leisure' (Stebbins, 1996; Stebbins, Rojek, & Sullivan, 2006). However, there are very few academic articles that explain the topic of morally transgressive behavior displayed by tourists at emotionally sensitive or controversial sites and the various ways the tourists justify their actions (Hodalska, 2017).

Dark tourism provides ample spaces to tourists who regularly find themselves in morally challenging situations, some of which they handle well, others, not (Fukui,

2015; Lawther, 2017). Consequently, the current study aims to understand the moral identity and mechanisms of moral judgement with respect to tourist consumption of death at a cremation ground. In doing so, the study demonstrates how tourist narratives at a cremation ground represent selective moral disengagement and why certain tourists act as conscientious moral agents when it comes to justifying transgressive behavior. Tourists can perform a place in different ways but transgressive behavior in dark tourism implies partaking in social, cultural and legal taboos which, in turn, are institutional prohibitions placed on determining what constitutes good or bad. There are numerous examples of tourist transgressive behavior reported in the media that have sparked moral outrage time and again. Examples include: tourists touching the dead bodies at Trunyan cemetery in Bali; tourists holding an inflatable sex doll at the 9/11 Memorial in New York; tourists taking selfies on the railway tracks at Auschwitz; tourists taking photographs with inappropriate poses at the Memorial to the Murdered Jews of Europe; tourists indulging in artwork or graffiti and defacing sacred monuments and buildings, and other acts of vandalism. In fact, an upsurge of photos on social media of tourists posing on the train tracks leading to the main gate of the Auschwitz Memorial forced the museum authorities to issue a statement on Twitter asking tourists to be more respectful while taking photos (Drury, 2019). While Sontag (1977) points out that photographs act as a screen or defense against anxiety in the face of horror, Hodalska (2017) states that tourists have been taking, stealing or buying souvenirs from sites of death, but today selfies have become the innovative way to demonstrate their presence in the places where others perished. In January 2017, an artist from Israel created a digital project called "Yolocaust" that involved photos taken from social media websites showing tourists posing or taking selfies at 'dark tourism' sites and superimposing these photos onto real archival footage of the Holocaust. This project was met with mixed reviews worldwide but it managed to highlight the moral issues associated with taking 'inappropriate' photos at sensitive dark tourism sites and the problem of tourist transgressive behavior.

The process by which individuals determine what is morally correct is an increasingly complex one (Treviño, Den Nieuwenboer, & Kish-Gephart, 2014). Nevertheless it is a topic worth exploring because dark tourism itself is somehow aberrant in both its production and consumption of taboo topics such as death and the (re)presentation of the dead. Using a socio-cognitive approach, the mechanism that enables otherwise considerate people to commit transgressive acts without experiencing moral distress and guilt, the objective of this research is to understand how tourists morally justify their transgressive behavior at emotionally sensitive sites such as a cremation ground. Transgressive behavior in this case implies taking photographs of the dead bodies and the mourners at a cremation ground despite a prohibitory warning and a local understanding that the dead should be respected. Scarles (2013), while explaining the ethics of the seemingly fleeting relationships between tourists and host communities that emerge during photographic encounters, states that photographing becomes a delicate balance— a series of compromises that often rely upon intuitive moral judgement, reasoning and reflective justification. It is this moral judgement, reasoning and the mechanisms behind it that this study focuses on. The tourist narratives explore the socio-psychological reasoning that underpin tourists' moral considerations on whether to click photographs or not. In doing so, the study focuses on the emergent tourist narratives which are an outcome of the interactions between tourists, death-ritual performers and locals who are photographed.

Literature review

Dark tourism has often been labelled as deviant and troubling and, in some cases, a source of moral panic by the media (Seaton & Lennon, 2004) suggesting that the commercialization of the macabre and tragedy is full of moral ambiguities. Clearly, dark tourism, despite its typological, interpretative, political and moral dilemmas, has (real and representative) death at its core and is often referred to as a postmodern phenomenon with an emphasis on spectacle (Foley & Lennon, 1996; Rojek, 1993). Stone (2009) suggests ethical ambiguities inherent within dark tourism are systematic of broader secular moral dilemmas in conveying narratives of death. In particular, he proposes dark tourism sites act as contemporary communicative spaces of morality. Further, he states that "dark tourism may not only act as a guardian of history in heritage terms, but also as moral guardian of a contemporary society which appears to be in a midst of resurgent effervescent moral vitality" and it can provide a new moral basis, because it has a variety of subtypes and can offer a range of morals and values. (Stone, 2009, p. 62). This means that dark tourism sites enable tourists to negotiate issues of moral concern and in the process, morality is revitalized in a society at a collective level.

The ethical dimensions of dark tourism have often been debated upon (Potts, 2012; Stone, 2009; Clark, 2014). Dark leisure experiences located within dark tourism, which are often perceived as morally suspect and deviant, might be viewed as legitimate and healthy when the broader cultural condition of secular society is taken into account (Stone & Sharpley, 2013). On the other hand, scholars (e.g., Dale & Robinson, 2011; Lennon, 2010; Lennon & Foley, 2000) have raised concern about the moral representation, acceptability and propriety of dark tourism sites. Most of the ethical discourse on morality within dark tourism has focused on how places associated with death and suffering are presented to their visitors. According to Robb (2009), the tourist has "long been derided in academic literature as a shallow thrill seeker, a consumer of inauthentic images of foreign lands, content to mistake simulacra for true knowledge of the cultural other" (p. 51). Light (2017) argues that claims of tourists being shallow thrill-seekers and behaving inappropriately at dark tourism sites, are founded on particular stereotypes of tourists that are rarely supported by empirical research with visitors. He points out that "while some instances of inappropriate behavior have attracted widespread media coverage, recent research indicates that many visitors are deeply engaged with the places of death and suffering that they visit" (p. 283).

During the mid-2000s, when the focus of research gradually moved to understanding visitor motivations to dark attractions and places, it was found that motivations of tourists could be diverse and there is little evidence that morbid curiosity and voyeurism is an important reason for visiting dark tourism sites (Dunkley, Morgan, & Westwood, 2007; Seaton & Lennon, 2004; Sharpley & Stone, 2009; Stone, 2005, 2006). Studies on tourist experience revealed that visiting dark tourism sites allows one to reflect on their own morality and behavior (Lisle, 2004; Stone, 2009). Despite the wide-ranging motivations and deeper connections that tourists develop with respect to dark tourism sites, transgressive acts and deviant behavior by tourists is a reality especially in this age of digital narcissism (e.g., provocative selfies at dark sites) and cannot be simply brushed aside as a form of "moral panic" created by the media. The outcome of this attitude and media blaming has mostly involved a vilification of the tourist without an actual attempt at understanding the psychological process that influences transgressive behavior and moral configuration among tourists. The following section describes moral disengagement and its relationship with human agency and liminality.

Moral disengagement and moral agency

Morality and moral behavior have been a widely discussed topic among scholars. There are several psychological theories on moral behavior such as the Theory of Moral Development (Kohlberg, 1971) and Moral Foundations Theory (Haidt & Grahm, 2007) as well as sociological theories on morality (Durkheim, 1965; Goffman, 1959; Weber, 1978; Collins, 2004). While sociologists have studied the larger societal frameworks and morality at a collective level, psychologists have focused on the individual as a unit and the source of moral action. Over the years, psychological studies have demonstrated the centrality of moral identity in determining moral action while investigating the relationship between moral judgments, moral behavior, and emotions. (Aquino, Freeman, Reed, Lim, & Felps, 2009; Frimer & Walker, 2009; Haidt, 2001; Hoffman, 2000). However, when it comes to understanding how individuals engage in cognitive strategies to change meanings in a particular situation or use psychosocial maneuvers to disengage from immoral behavior, it is the process of moral disengagement which seems to offer an explanation.

   A psychological mechanism that plays an important role in unethical decision making is moral disengagement that operates at both individual and collective levels (Bandura, 1999). Moral disengagement refers to the cognitive deactivation of moral self-regulatory processes in decision making. It mediates the relationship between the moral principles that individuals hold and their behavioral transgressions. Through this process, unethical decisions can be made without individuals feeling apparent guilt or self-censure (Bandura, 1999). In the context of tourism, these moral disengagement mechanisms are useful in explaining how tourists reconstruct their actions to appear less immoral resulting in shifting of ethical boundaries.

   According to Bandura (2002), individuals adopt standards of right and wrong that serve as guides and deterrents for conduct in developing moral agency. Moral disengagement is a self-regulatory process "where people monitor their conduct and the conditions under which it occurs, judge it in relation to their moral standards and perceived circumstances, and regulate their actions by the consequences they apply to themselves." He adds that "morality is rooted in a self-reactive selfhood, rather than in dispassionate abstract reasoning" and "moral actions are the product of the reciprocal interplay of cognitive, affective and social influences." (p.102). This implies that the ideological orientations of societies influence the form of moral justifications for an

---

Figure can be found in the original journal article

---

individual, but the individual also has the capacity to alter the social system through an exercise of his/her agency. This holds true for tourists who come from diverse cultural backgrounds, social realities and ideological systems that shape their moral perceptions and justifications. Therefore, the justification of moral judgements is relative rather than absolute (Bandura, 2002). Moral disengagement is believed to be a personal characteristic suggesting that people differ in their propensity to morally disengage (Moore, Detert, Klebe Treviño, Baker, & Mayer, 2012). These differences influence how individuals translate moral intentions into behavior (Martin, Kish-Gephart, & Detert, 2014; Moore et al., 2012). Analyzing how these psychological mechanisms of moral disengagement work in the dark tourism sector can help to understand implications for moral conduct of tourists and devise better management strategies at dark tourism sites to avoid conflicts, minimize tourist transgressive behavior and promote sober and respectful touristic engagement. Moral disengagement theory has already been used for empirical research across a number of disciplines and contexts such as child psychology (Obermann, 2013), organizational behavior (Martin et al., 2014; Cohen, Panter, Turan, Morse, & Kim, 2014), criminology (Cardwell et al., 2015), military behavior (McAlister, Bandura, & Owen, 2006), and sports psychology (Boardley & Kavussanu, 2008).

Moral disengagement is the process by which individuals rationalize engaging in transgressive behavior (Bandura, Barbaranelli, Caprara, & Pastorelli, 1996; Bandura, 1999, 2002) and through certain mechanisms that disengage self-sanctions from the behavior, they seek to validate or rationalize their decisions. These self-sanctions- guilt, shame, self-condemnation, etc. arise when personal moral standards are violated but once these self-sanctions are disengaged, individuals tend to indulge in transgressive acts (Bandura, 1999, 2002). According to Bandura (2002), individuals have moral standards but these do not function as fixed internal regulators of conduct. There are self-regulatory mechanisms which operate only when they are activated by surrounding activities or events. This selective activation and disengagement of self-sanctions may induce people to behave in diverse ways despite having similar moral standards. See Bandura (1986) for an illustration of moral control.

The process of moral disengagement unfolds through eight mechanisms grouped under four major sets of disengagement practices that individuals rely on to justify unethical behavior (Bandura, 1999). There are four loci of moral disengagement: behavioral, agency, effects and victim (Bandura, 2016). The first set of mechanisms involves cognitive construal and reconstruing the conduct so that it is not considered immoral (Bandura, 2002). . The second set of mechanisms involve minimizing personal involvement or obscuring personal agency. The third mechanism involves misrepresenting or discounting the resulting negative consequences while the fourth set involves blaming or devaluating the recipients of the unethical act. Through these disengagement mechanisms, individuals, who view themselves as ethical, deactivate the self-regulatory processes that would normally inhibit unethical behavior (Detert, Treviño, & Sweitzer, 2008; Tillman et al., 2018).

Further, human activities cannot be properly understood without taking into consideration the role of agency. Agency is the conscious and deliberate ability to act and implicitly no persons (at least those who are considering travelling) are without 'agency' (Lovelock, 2014).Moral agency is "an individual's ability to make moral judgments based on some notion of right and wrong and to be held accountable for these actions" (Taylor, 2003, p. 20). Within tourism, the notion of moral agency attributes to the tourist the capacity to process social information across different cultural milieus, engage in the construction of their own social context and experiences and devise different ways of justifying their actions, when confronted with moral dilemmas. Bandura's social cognitive theory is a robust and replicable model of moral agency where moral thought, self-evaluative reactions, moral conduct, and environmental influences operate together. Within this triadic model of reciprocal causation, moral agency is exercised through self-regulatory mechanisms (Bandura, 2016; Zsolnai, 2016). He also mentions that the regulation of moral conduct involves much more than moral reasoning because it is through the translation of moral reasoning into actions using self-regulatory mechanisms, that an individual's agency is exercised (Bandura, 1991). He asserts that personal moral agency determines if actors will engage in antisocial or pro-social behaviors (Bandura, 2004). According to Rachels and Rachels (2010), a responsible or conscientious moral agent is one who is concerned with the interests of everyone affected by what he/she does. The following paragraphs explain the role of liminality in moral configuration and its connection with moral agency.

Lovelock (2014) states that selective moral disengagement in tourism is easily possible due to the notion of liminality where moral agency also gets obscured by the neoliberal context that provide a structure in which immoral behavior is both expected and rewarded. This idea applies well to dark tourism which is considered as the correspondence of the neoliberal dispositive within the tourism sector (Korstanje & George, 2017). Biran, Poria, and Oren (2011) mentions that dark tourism may be perceived as a rite of social passage, given its transitional elements and its potential to influence the psychology and perception of individuals. Turner (1973) defined liminality as "any condition outside or on the peripheries of everyday life" (p. 47). Liminality has also been "frequently likened to death, to being in the womb, to invisibility, to darkness … " (Turner & Abrahams, 1969, p. 359). It is a transitional state, space or place and tourists become liminal people, "between places, times and conventions" (Pritchard & Morgan, 2006). Liminal times and spaces offer the possibilities for freedom, release and escape from quotidian constraints, routines and disciplines (Pritchard

& Morgan, 2006). In the context of tourism, liminal spaces offer the tourist a potential for adopting behaviors and identities that are outside the norm. Within the context of dark tourism, liminal spaces are those where tourist identity, moral perceptions and behavior are put to test. Moral decisions made within a liminal space are not conducive to 'staying within the rules'—where we are free to ignore any moral script that may be provided by wider society (Lovelock, 2014). Most importantly, they are also opportunities for transgression, subverting the social structure and an inversion of normal behavior.

A dark tourism site such as a cremation ground can be considered as a complex, culturally contested and ideologically laden liminal place. The cremation ground at Varanasi inclusive of all the death-related rituals is a threshold of transition and transgression - a place in between life and death, between the exotic and the familiar, the mundane and the extraordinary and between serenity and anxiety. It is a betwixt place, the crossing point of life's journey into the unknown. Although it is connected to experiences of death, dying and darkness but it is also connected to the possibility that it is just a temporary stop and the tourist will be back home safely and lead his daily life. Such a liminal, threshold place may offer freedom and peace for some, but are likely to cause anxiety, constraint or threat for others. As a liminal space, the cremation ground offers" the spatial presence and practice outside of the norms of the prevailing (enforced) social spatialization" (Shields, 1991, p. 210) and can become sites of 'resistant bodies' where normal rules and conventions can be temporarily suspended.

Bandura (2002) describes moral agency to be socially situated and exercised and moral actions being the products of the reciprocal interplay of personal and social influences. However, socio-structural theories and psychological theories represent different levels of causation with the explanation that human behavior cannot be understood fully in terms of social structural factors or psychological factors alone. Bandura (1986, 1997) advocates using a social cognitive theory that rejects a dualism between social structure and personal agency where socio-structural influences affect action via self-regulatory mechanisms within a unified causal structure. Therefore, using this socio-cognitive theoretical perspective in the context of dark tourism, it can be said that socio-structural practices at a site create liminal conditions (an in-between position) favorable for moral disengagement, where the tourist is in a flux and is torn between a set of (current and previously held) moral beliefs.

Methodology

The city of Varanasi in the state of Uttar Pradesh, India was chosen to be the study area. Varanasi, according to Hindu belief, is considered to be a holy city in India and attracts scores of both domestic and foreign tourists. Situated on the banks of the Ganga River, it is known as the "Great Cremation Ground" (Eck, 1983, p. 30) or the "Microcosm of the Universe" (Parry, 1994, p.11). Although formally labelled as a Hindu pilgrimage destination, the city has several spaces associated with death in the form of cremation grounds (Figure 2) and death hospices. With respect to the cremation ground, two death-related rituals within the domain of Hindu philosophy were

Figure 2. The cremation ground at Manikarnika ghat, Varanasi.
(Source: Author).

analyzed. The first type, the Hindu death ritual, broadly involves burning the deceased over a funeral pyre.

The second is a death-related ritual practiced by a group of ascetics, known as the Aghoris (Figure 3). This small sect of Hindu ascetics are rigid renouncers and worshippers of the Hindu deity, *Shiva*. Their rituals include performing austerities at the cremation ground, using skulls as food bowls, smearing one's body with ashes from the dead, coprophagy and necrophagy and meditating on top of corpses. In popular culture, Aghoris have also found mention in television media. Renowned documentaries on the Aghoris include 'Sadhus-India's Holy men', 'Varanasi, India: Beyond', 'The truth about Aghori', National Geographic's 'Aghoris' and CNN's documentary series 'Believer'. In 2017, journalist Reza Aslan ran into controversy for his alleged unethical portrayal of the Aghori sect as representing Hinduism and for consuming human brains during an Aghori ritual. Aslan followed up the episode's debut with a promotional post on Facebook, writing: "Want to know what a dead guy's brain tastes like? Charcoal. It was burnt to a crisp!" Several Indian and American Hindu groups claimed that the CNN series was "hinduphobic" and sensationalized aspects of the world's third largest religion (Safi, 2017).

For both the rituals mentioned above, the cremation ground (directly or indirectly) forms an integral part of the ritual space and involve a complex negotiation of sacred and profane. Moreover, both these rituals spark an interest among international tourists. The international tourist interest in the death-related rituals is supported by the fact that several privately-owned tour companies and operators offer "walking tours" that provide opportunities for tourists to witness the cremation grounds, popularly referred to as the 'Burning Ghats', and see the Aghoris and death-ritual performers.

Figure 3. An Aghori near the cremation ground in Varanasi.
(Source: Author).

A multi-method approach was adopted which predominantly involved collecting qualitative data and analyzing secondary sources of data, tourist narratives collected through semi-structured interviews, participant observation and a content analysis of tourist blogs, travel forums and travel websites (government and private). The fieldwork was carried out in May-August 2015 and December 2015– March 2016. The secondary sources of literature included background information about the Aghoris, information on Hindu society, death rituals and tourism inflow and outflow in Varanasi (Bakker, 1993; Barrett, 2008; Bloch & Parry, 1982; Doron, 2013; Eck, 1983; Parry, 1982, 1994). Participant observation was useful to ascertain the facial expressions and body language (Kawulich, 2005) of tourists and their behavior at the cremation ground as well as understand the nature of the death rituals. The sub-groups who were interviewed are the local people (performers) associated with death-related rituals and tourism (the Aghoris, the funerary workers and priests who perform death rituals at the cremation ground in Varanasi, local businessmen, tour operators and travel guides) and the international tourists who visit the cremation grounds to see these rituals. The semi-structured interviews were part of a larger study aimed at understanding tourist perceptions towards death. However, only the responses that involve taking photographs at the cremation ground and justification offered by the tourist have been considered for this analysis.

A convenience sampling technique was used, whereby the sampling population was present during field visits at the specific site. The target population consisted of those tourists who participated in tours taking them to the cremation ground. The respondents were international tourists predominantly from USA (16%), UK (19%),

Australia (15%), Canada (9%) and the rest from countries such as the Netherlands, Germany, Argentina, Italy, Russia, Spain, France, Switzerland, Colombia and Turkey. About 200 tourists were interviewed comprising 102 women and 98 men, out of which 120 tourist narratives were considered for the analysis as they admitted taking photographs at the cremation ground. The interview respondents were approached directly at the site and the purpose of the study was explained to them in detail. The respondents were given the choice to leave the interview at any point of time if they felt uncomfortable with the questions. The interview respondents were also given the assurance that their answers would be used solely for academic purpose and their personal information would be kept confidential. All the respondents that were approached agreed to participate in the interview except one. The tourists who admitted taking photographs were asked to describe the nature of the photographs they took and their reasons for doing so. Besides the tourists, the respondent sample also included two local death photographers. A deductive content analysis (Mayring, 2014) was carried out for the narratives obtained from the interviews, travel forums and private blogs. The content from websites of a few popular tour companies and agencies in Varanasi such as Varanasi Walks, Heritage Walks, Roobaroo Walks, Streetwise Varanasi Tours, Manglam Travels and Groovy Tours was also analyzed. The disengagement mechanisms were identified and sorted according to the categories mentioned by Bandura (1999, 2002).

Results

Contextualizing Bandura's (1986) model with respect to the cremation ground in Varanasi and for the sake of simplicity in analysis, the following have been categorized as reprehensible conduct, detrimental effect and victim:

Reprehensible conduct: Taking photographs of the deceased and their relatives without permission and ignoring the prohibitory warning, mockingly participating in the Aghori rituals and disrespecting them, etc.

Detrimental effects: Encroaching the personal space and privacy of mourners and the dead, purposeful or unintended construction of a negative public image of the ritual performers especially the Aghoris.

Victims: Family members of the deceased, dead bodies and the ritual performers.

Regarding the different moral mechanisms outlined by Bandura (1999), it was observed that in Varanasi, the most used were euphemistic labeling, moral justification, dehumanization and misrepresenting consequences while the rest of the mechanisms exhibited a lower percentage. The moral mechanism referred to as attribution of blame was found to be missing in the tourist narratives. The following sub-sections demonstrate how tourist behavior indicates an operation of the various mechanisms of moral disengagement at the cremation ground.

Euphemistic labelling

This is a means of reconstruing one's conduct by distorting language in such a manner that a seemingly unethical act appears respectable or ethical. This disengagement

Walk 6 Death & Rebirth in Banaras

Walk with us through the city of learning & burning and see Banaras when it is known as 'Mahashamstana', the great cremation ground of Shiva. It is here will you will traverse from the land of the living to the houses of the dying.

Perhaps an encounter with a black-clothed flesh-eating sadhu of the Aghor Ashram will give you will a taste of death and rebirth! If you chose the daytime version a small puja at the Sankata Devi Temple (the goddess of sorrows & a demon slayer) is participated in. If you chose to do this walk at night it ends with a visit for the 10:30 – 11:15pm Sankata Devi ritual worship service!

Figure 4. Death tour offered by the tour agency-Varanasi Walks.
Source: http://varanasiwalks.com/ ... , Accessed 3rd May 2014.

practice is significant in dark tourism marketing and plays an important role in pre-senting provocative narratives of a site to tourists in a manner that does not appear transgressive or unethical. Dark tourism markets in most cases, are quite well-developed especially those that involve a fun component such as ghost tours, dun-geon tours, etc. In contemporary society it is normal to deal with topics like death more in private than in public. In Varanasi, the public display of death at the crema-tion grounds and the necrophagous rituals of the Aghoris along with associated moral concerns poses a problem to the tour operators and agencies who want to effectively utilize the Western curiosity and fascination. Amidst the morality concerns associated with the commodification of death, the tourist websites advertising tours to the cre-mation ground, reveal a common feature, i.e., euphemistic labelling.

Bandura (1999) states that language shapes thought patterns on which actions are based and activities can take on different appearances depending on what they are called. Euphemistic language involves intricate rephrasing which makes an otherwise immoral or taboo activity acceptable and people feel that they are spared of being guilty. Gambino (1973) identified the different varieties of euphemisms, one of which relies on sanitizing language. Through the power of sanitized language, even killing a human being loses much of its repugnancy. For example, bombing missions are described as "servicing the target" (Bandura, 2002, p. 104). In the context of dark tour-ism, language is sanitized in a way by marketers to present death in an aesthetically pleasing manner thereby covering up the commodification of death for personal and monetary gain. The dark tourism market in Varanasi comprises death tours such as the 'Death and rebirth walk in Varanasi' which sanitizes the description of the cremation grounds by relying on its religious value (by making a reference to the Hindu deity *Shiva*), by creating an aura of mystery and referring to the cremation grounds as the 'burning ghats' and Varanasi as the 'city of learning and burning' (Figure 4). Death tours also tend to eulogize the process of death. Manikarnika Ghat is also famous by the name of *Mahasmasana* which means the 'great cremation ground'. It is considered that the one who is cremated at this place will attain salvation. Therefore, euphemistic labelling is particularly useful for influencing tourist behavior in dark tourism.

An important exonerative tool under euphemistic labelling is the agentless passive voice or transferring the tourist agency to a place, an inanimate object or a nameless force. It creates the appearance that reprehensible acts are the work of nameless forces, rather than people (Bolinger, 1982). This way unethical or transgressive actions of tourists are justified by transferring the agency to inanimate objects pointing towards a loss of human agency. In Varanasi, a few tourists at the cremation grounds justified taking photographs by a transfer of agency to the place, i.e., the cremation ground itself.

"The complexity of Varanasi and the cremation grounds attracted me."

"The eternal fire burning almost pulled me towards it."

By placing the tourist agency on the complexity of the cremation grounds and the funeral pyre, tourists exonerate themselves of their guilt despite a clear and written prohibition of photography at the site.

The marketing of death and its representational forms constitute a substantive moral debate within dark tourism. Dark tourism entrepreneurs, site managers and tour operators have a growing concern that tourists may find a site or a tour experience too negative to be entertaining, or too morally ambiguous to be assimilated. The early studies of dark tourism have frequently mentioned commodification (Foley & Lennon, 1996, 1997; Lennon & Foley, 1999, 2000; Dann & Potter, 2001; Gould, 2014; Murphy, 2015) and "kitchification" (Sharpley & Stone, 2009) with respect to dark heritage sites. This not only leads to distortion, sanitization and misrepresentation of tragic historical events but also creates a spectacle, simulation and replication of death in popular culture (Sharpley & Stone, 2009). The marketing of sensitive dark tourism sites and construction of place identity or image (or destination branding) has its own challenges and is a key determinant of consumer behavior in tourism studies. Euphemistic labelling is useful to understand how provocative narratives and site representations are sold to tourists in a way that does not violate their moral principles.

Moral justification

It is the disengagement practice that operates on the reconstruction of the behavior itself or when detrimental behavior is portrayed as personally and socially acceptable, serving worthy or a moral purpose. This way, individuals can act on a moral imperative and preserve their view of themselves as moral agents while indulging in the unethical act (Bandura, 2002). In case of the cremation grounds, moral justification is evident in the narratives of local professional death photographers as well as tourists who photograph the dead. For the death photographers of Varanasi, photographing the dead is just another means of earning their livelihood. Although it is not uncommon for relatives to pay these photographers to take one last photograph of the deceased, it still raises moral quandaries among the international tourists as well as for the photographers themselves. The moral justification that ensues is:

"I don't like my job but if a photo brings some solace to the grieving family, I feel satisfied. It is also a way to create one last memory of the dead and sometimes these photos are also used in the obituary column of the newspapers and insurance claims. I also try not to click photos of children, teenagers and pregnant women."

On the other hand, international tourists who indulge in death photography without permission from the mourners, justify the act as:

"I have captured some stunning and rare images that give a remarkable insight into the last hours of the Hindu body at Manikarnika Ghats". After all, it is the largest cremation site in Varanasi."

"Funeral practices are different all over the world but the Hindu death rituals are so transparent and raw that I couldn't stop taking photos. It's fascinating that they believe that if a person dies in Varanasi, his soul will escape the cycle of rebirth and attain moksha."

Another example of moral justification was observed in the monetary exchange between the tourists and the ritual performers (funerary workers) at the cremation ground. The funerary workers and the local touts, depending on their mood, sometimes allow tourists to take pictures from a discrete distance in exchange for money which is justified as "a donation to help buy wood for the poor". On the other hand, a tourist who was willing to pay money to a local tout for allowing him to take photos, remarked,

"I was offended by his hypocrisy and money-grabbing approach and wondered aloud… How much does it cost to pay for a destroyed soul?" (Cooper, 2011)

In this case, moral justification occurs both ways during a tourist-host encounter where the local tout tries to morally justify taking money and the tourist tries to morally justify taking photographs. The above examples illustrate the commodification of death rituals and a reconstruction of a prohibited act (photographing the dead) to making it personally and socially acceptable by serving a greater purpose like "creating memories" or "capturing Hindu funerary practices". The narratives subtly and discreetly point towards the Western tourist's fascination with death rituals in the East which is possibly rooted in notions of exotic "othering", colonial discourse, historical events and ideological movements.

Dehumanization

This moral disengagement practice operates on the recipients of the unethical act (Bandura, 2002). The strength of moral self-censure in tourist behavior depends on how the tourist perceives the destination and the hosts. Dehumanization is the process through which a person or group of people are denied subjectivity, individuality, agency, or distinctively human attributes (e.g., Sherwin, 1987). Tipler and Ruscher (2014) mention that three distinct components of agency may be denied or ascribed to others - affective agency (the ability of the other individual or group to experience emotion and possess desires), cognitive agency (the ability of the other to hold beliefs and think rationally) and behavioral agency (the ability of the other to produce a behavior and exhibit activity).

The other person or outgroup is no longer viewed as one with feelings, hopes and concerns, but objectified as a lesser sub-human or sub-group (Bandura, 2002). They are portrayed as mindless "savages", "gooks" and other despicable wretches (Ivie, 1980; Keen, 1986). For example, Greek torturers referred to their victims as "worms" (Gibson & Haritos-Fatouros, 1986) and Nazis regularly compared the Jews to "rats".

According to Kelman (1973), dehumanization involves denying a person "identity"—a perception of the person "as an individual, independent and distinguishable from others, capable of making choices" (p. 301). Haslam (2006) adds that when people are divested of an agentic aspect of humanness they are de-individuated, lose the capacity to evoke compassion and moral emotions. This is why dehumanization justifies treating others with less moral concern and empathy, and therefore validating transgressive behavior, moral exclusion and delegitimization of others.

This is similar to the idea of moral exclusion (Opotow, 1990) which is the process by which people are placed "outside the boundary in which moral values, rules, and considerations of fairness apply" (p.1) and includes a form of social conflict and feelings of disconnectedness. It occurs when groups or individuals are excluded from an ingroup's sphere of moral values, rules and beliefs. According to Haslam (2006), dehumanization is "just one of several extreme forms of moral exclusion, but Opotow (1990) described several milder processes like psychological distance (perceiving others as objects or as nonexistent), condescension (patronizing others as inferior, irrational and childlike), and technical orientation (a focus on means–end efficiency and mechanical routine)" (p. 254). Bandura's work on selective moral disengagement focuses at an individual level of the cognitive and affective mechanisms involved in exercise of moral agency.

The notion of dehumanization can be observed in the narratives of certain tourists and tourist websites where the Aghoris are usually described as the "eaters of the dead", "the legitimate cannibals of India", "the terrifying Aghori sadhus", "Aghori cannibals", "the living dead Aghori monks", "Aghori tantriks", "Murderer Aghori", "Necrophagous Aghori", etc. A few tourists despite their curiosity in the rituals of the Aghoris, considered them to be freaks and dangerous to others. A tourist when asked what he felt after meeting the Aghoris replied,

"Crazy people! I do not see that they are a nice role model for young people, what with all the cannibalism and smoking marihuana all day."

"Why is it necessary to have their presence in a (w)holy society?"

Another tourist said that he was scared of them and meeting them made him realize *"that it's possible to completely remove yourself from humanity"*.

The narratives indicate the denial of civility and refinement in the Aghoris reducing them to an outgroup that is dangerous to the society and humanity. The aspect of dehumanization was also observed at the cremation grounds where one of the tourists described the cremation ground as.

"The smell was overwhelming. I saw a charred foot coming out of the fire. How am I supposed to act here? Look? Don't look? What is the human body anyway? Humans are also meat at the end of the day. So what is the harm in taking photos?

In this case, the tourist denies the human nature attributes to the dead bodies and does not discriminate them from inanimate objects which helps him justify taking photographs.

People may be dehumanized not as representatives of a social group but as distinct individuals or members of a "generalized other" from which other individuals wish to distinguish themselves (Haslam, 2006). Hence, dehumanization is often mentioned in relation to ethnicity and race which also explains why the death of 'brown' bodies at the cremation ground in Varanasi is capable of evoking an interest among the 'white' tourists as well as challenging their emotions. Opotow (1990) also writes about the role of psychological distance as a form of moral exclusion linked to the objectification of others where people are seen as socially distant. In Varanasi, the tourists get an opportunity to compare their own culture, especially their religious and death-related rituals, with the culture of the host community. This has repeatedly been observed in the tourist narratives where the comparison between the death rituals in India and the West has been brought up. The 'Otherness' of dark tourism is universal, since every culture has its own way of handling the topic of death.

Disregarding or misrepresenting consequences

This method of disengagement disregards or misrepresents the consequences of action by generally minimizing the harm one causes or by avoiding the consequences. This involves selective inattention and subjectively cognitive distortion of effects of an action. This method of disengagement was also observed among tourists at the cremation ground where they justified taking photographs by saying:

> "I took photos of only the fire, not the bodies"

> "Only the animals wandering at the cremation ground"

> "I did not take photos near the fire or funeral pyre. I just took photos from the boat."

The first two narratives represent a cognitive distortion of the action and the third represents the acceptability of a prohibited action by distorting the physical distance of the subject from the site, i.e., the cremation ground.

Advantageous comparison

It is the type of disengagement practice involving an advantageous comparison in which one's unethical behavior is compared with an equally or greater unethical behavior for the sake of exoneration. This practice uses the contrast principle to make the transgressive act of a tourist look righteous because it is being compared against an action which is worse. Bandura (1990) provides the example of terrorists who often label their behavior as acts of selfless martyrdom by comparing them with widespread cruelties inflicted on the people with whom they identify.

In Varanasi, a tourist from Morocco admitted that he was extremely interested in the Aghoris and their rituals. He said,

> "I attended an Aghori ritual yesterday. I attended it but I did not participate in the proceedings because I do not like the idea of eating raw human flesh. I am fine with rituals or displays involving human skulls or bones but I don't like seeing stuff that involve the flesh and blood. I don't know how they do that."

The tourist here morally justifies his attendance at the ceremony by comparing his actions against the ritual performers. This restructuring of actions may at times, also lead to self-approval and self-valuation for the tourist.

Displacement of responsibility

This disengagement practice operates by obscuring or minimizing the agentive role of the tourist and by distorting the relationship between actions and the effects they cause. In this mechanism, the tourist agency is displaced to a legitimate authority in order to shrug off the responsibility of unethical actions and be spared of self-condemning reactions. People view their actions as legitimate because they are stemming from the dictates of authorities rather than personal judgement.

Despite the tourist exercising his/her agency in terms of choosing a destination representing death or meeting the Aghoris, the fact that dark tourism and the associated death tours legitimizes the public display and commodification of death, is a sufficient condition for tourists to feel less responsible or guilty by placing the moral agency on the tour guide, the tour company or the tourism niche market. For example, the responses of some tourists on being questioned why they took photographs at the cremation ground are:

"Because our tour guide said that we can do so."

"The tour company that I had contacted offers the cremation ground walk, so I thought I might as well make the most out of it."

These narratives demonstrate that the tourists view their act of clicking photographs as stemming from a legitimate authorization by the tour guide or the tourist agency. Another tourist who participated in the Aghori rituals said that:

"I tried to understand the complicated caste system in India and I tried to have empathy for the Aghoris who seemed to be in this life without choice. It's how the culture is where public display of death is acceptable."

In this case, the tourist justifies his act of engaging with the Aghoris and transfers his agency to the culture of the city which legitimizes the public display of death. He further blames an unknown authority (in this case, the caste system) that according to him, forces the Aghoris to practise these death-related rituals and considers his own behavior as an indirect act of obeying the social norms.

Diffusion of responsibility

In this mechanism, transgressive acts are attributed to group decisions instead of personal agency. This way personal agency is deliberately obscured and exercise of moral control is weakened exonerating the tourist from any form of personal responsibility or self-blame. According to Kelman (1973), personal agency may get obscured by social diffusion of responsibility which in turn, can be diffused by division of labour, group decision-making and collective action. This fragmentation of tourist agency and diffusion of responsibility is reminiscent of Turner's (1973) notion of communitas where tourists mingle with others beyond the normative bonds of home, classlessness ensues and relationships develop based on their common humanity and moral perceptions. It is liminality that leads to communitas, which is a firm 'social bond' occurring between those who share a liminal experience. A sense of communitas is demonstrated by different groups of tourists in multiple ways with respect to the death-related rituals in Varanasi. For example, it is often observed that in tour groups comprising a large number of tourists, if one tourist starts taking photographs of the dead bodies, there are many others in the group who follow the lead.

This is slightly similar to the concept of deindividuation in social psychology which refers to the diminishing of one's sense of individuality or loss of self-identity., when present in a group and the effect of a crowd or group on the behavior of an individual (Diener, 1980; Festinger, Pepitone, & Newcomb, 1952; Zimbardo, 1969). The authors claimed that an individual is "able to indulge in forms of behavior in which, when alone, they would not indulge" (p. 382). Consequently, this loss of self-identity is likely to encourage transgressive or deviant behavior (Diener, 1980; Zimbardo, 1969). Diener (1980) argued that deindividuation is facilitated by anonymous conditions within a group setting that cause individuals to lack awareness of who they are. It implies that anonymity provides an individual with protection from "the social disapproval or rejection likely to follow from non-adherence to the norm" (Mann, Newton, & Innes, 1982, p. 261). It has been found that anonymity influences negative social behavior (Zimbardo, 1969). The idea is that when everyone is responsible, no one really feels responsible and "any harm done by a group can always be attributed largely to the behavior of others". (Bandura et al., 1996, p. 365).

Discussion

The cremation ground in Varanasi offers the dark tourist a liminal space to perform activities that involve letting go of their moral and social restrictions. The moral dilemmas and uncertainty of tourists get compounded by the Aghori rituals, lifestyle, their philosophy of breaking social hierarchy, norms and taboos and engagement with the concept of death. It is an ethically and politically charged space providing the possibility of significant social and personal transformation amidst conflicts arising between moral self-sanctions and social sanctions. The tourists have the agency to decide what is right or wrong and act accordingly but sometimes, this agency tends to get obscured or fragmented, resulting in transgressive behavior. Bandura (1999) adds that the exercise of moral agency has dual aspects—inhibitive and proactive. While the inhibitive form, is manifested in the power to refrain from indulging in transgressive behavior, the proactive form of morality is expressed in the power to behave otherwise. This might explain why certain tourists exercise their moral agency and sometimes call out or reprimand fellow tourists if the latter are found violating moral standards and laws at a tourism site. Thus, liminal spaces in dark tourism allow tourists to exercise their moral agency in an inhibitive form as well as proactive form using various moral mechanisms.

Tourist transgressive behavior especially at emotionally sensitive sites is an important and controversial phenomenon. Until now, no study has attempted to analyze the psychological underpinnings or justifications that tourists have to offer in order to explain their acts of transgression. From describing dark tourists as craving for social media credibility to terming their behavior as downright disrespectful, previous studies and media articles on dark tourism have mostly vilified the dark tourist without an empirical investigation of their moral actions. Without defending the transgressive acts committed by the tourists, this article is the first attempt in dark tourism literature to classify collected tourist narratives and use those narratives to understand the psychological mechanisms that influence transgressive behavior at a sensitive site. Although reprehensible behavior cannot be easily caught and punished, analyzing how these psychological mechanisms of moral disengagement work in the dark tourism sector can help to understand implications for moral conduct of tourists and devise better management strategies and policies at dark tourism sites to avoid moral conflicts and minimize tourist transgressive behavior. For example, the moral mechanism displacement of responsibility reveals that tour operators and guides may sometimes, unconsciously play a role in encouraging tourists to break rules and hence, an important factor that needs to be incorporated in tour guide training and strategies to promote tourist awareness.

Finally, the study has its limitations in terms of using only Bandura's psychological theory to understand tourist transgressive behavior despite the theory being the only compelling one explaining moral disengagement from a psychological perspective and with a few moral mechanisms having similarities with other concepts in social psychology. The study is not all-encompassing and does not consider genetic conditions, more specifically psychiatric disorders, that could play a role in antisocial, or transgressive behavior. It also does not examine the differences in behavior among tourist subgroups based on gender, age, cultural background, etc. Further, due to different dark tourism site characteristics (such as history of the site; intensity and representation of death; prohibitions on tourist behavior; monitoring, compensations and regulatory fines associated with transgressive behavior, etc.), the moral mechanisms cannot necessarily be generalized.

Conclusion

Drawing on a robust and replicable social-cognitive theory of moral thought and action (Bandura, 1991, 1999), it was found that transgressive behavior among tourists at dark tourism sites which are also emotionally sensitive in nature, is more likely if they disengage from processes related to moral conduct. Bandura's theory is applicable across multiple domains (e.g., the entertainment, food or tobacco industry, gun control and climate change), and is useful to understand human behavior without subjecting the participants in experiments to questionable behavior or morally distressing questions on the part of experimenters. Sternberg (2016) while reviewing the theory, writes that although earlier studies mention that even good people can face moral dilemmas and be placed in situations that lead them to act in an inappropriate manner but "what has been missing before is an explanation of the mental mechanisms that lead people to do these things" (p. 2). This is a relevant point to consider in the context of dark tourism. Several of the moral mechanisms used to justify transgressive behavior has been supported by observations and other psychological concepts such as deindividuation and moral exclusion.

Dark tourism offers a liminal time and space and locates the activity within constructivist realms of meaning and meaning making (Sharpley & Stone, 2009). It is also within this liminal space that moral transgressions and transformations occur. Tourists morally justify their transgressive behavior at emotionally sensitive sites such as a cremation ground using various moral disengagement mechanisms. This behavior arises due to an obscuring and fragmentation of human agency during the moral disengagement process thereby making it possible for tourists to not take ownership of the consequences of their actions. The study also shows that the rhetoric of dark tourism sites, especially through euphemistic labelling, plays an important role in shaping tourist thought patterns which in turn, is likely to govern their actions and experiences.

While the study explains the various mechanisms of moral disengagement among tourists, it sets the stage for further psychological investigation to understand the underlying socio-cultural processes and factors at a dark tourism site that are likely to influence tourist behavior and moral perceptions. As Stone (2006) writes that not all dark tourism sites and its supplies have the same degree of darkness and ethics, it is clear that not all moral disengagement mechanisms will be operative at different dark tourism sites. Further, Johnson (2014) writes that while all people are susceptible to moral disengagement, some are more vulnerable than others due to such personal antecedents as lack of empathy, rigid and authoritarian beliefs, low self-esteem, and fear and anxiety. Hence, further studies can examine the interrelationships between socio-cultural factors influencing moral identity of tourists and personal factors such as fear of death and how this influence translates in cross-cultural encounters. It is possible that moral identities and the process of moral disengagement may operate differently when the tourists and the toured culture or object being represented at a dark tourism site, are culturally similar owing to a decreased possibility of "othering", psychological distance and moral exclusion. A possible hypothesis for future research could be higher the psychological distance between two cultures, the higher is the possibility for transgressive behavior among tourists.

Disclosure statement

No potential conflict of interest was reported by the author.

References

Aquino, K., Freeman, D., Reed, A., Lim, V. K. G., & Felps, W. (2009). Testing a social cognitive model of moral behavior: The interactive influence of situations and moral identity centrality. *Journal of Personality and Social Psychology, 97*(1), 123–141. doi:10.1037/a0015406

Bakker, H. T. (1993). Early mythology relating to Varanasi. In: R. P. B. Singh (Ed.). *Banaras, (Varanasi): Cosmic Order, Sacred City, Hindu Traditions* (pp. 21–28). Varanasi: Tara Book Agency.

Bandura, A. (1986). *Social foundation of thought and action: A social-cognitive view*. Englewood Cliffs. NJ: Prentice Hall.

Bandura, A. (1990). Mechanisms of moral disengagement. In W. Reich (Ed.), *Origins of terrorism: Psychologies, ideologies, theologies, states of mind* (pp. 161–191). Cambridge, Cambridge University Press.

Bandura, A. (1991). Social cognitive theory of moral thought and action. In W. M. Kurtines & J. L. Gewirtz (Eds.), *Handbook of moral behavior and development: Theory, research and applications* (Vol. 1, pp. 71–129).Hillsdale, NJ: Erlbaum.

Bandura, A. (1997). *Self-efficacy: The exercise of control*. New York, NY: Freeman.

Bandura, A. (1999). Moral disengagement in the perpetration of inhumanities. *Personality and Social Psychology Review*, 3(3), 193–209. doi:10.1207/s15327957pspr0303_3

Bandura, A. (2002). Selective moral disengagement in the exercise of moral agency. *Journal of Moral Education*, 31(2), 101–119. doi:10.1080/0305724022014322

Bandura, A. (2004). Selective exercise of moral agency. In Thorkildsen, T.A., & Walberg, H.J. (Eds.), *Nurturing morality* (pp. 37–57). Boston, MA: Springer.

Bandura, A. (2016). *Moral disengagement: How people do harm and live with themselves*. New York, NY: Worth Publishers.

Bandura, A., Barbaranelli, C., Caprara, G. V., & Pastorelli, C. (1996). Mechanisms of moral disengagement in the exercise of moral agency. *Journal of Personality and Social Psychology*, 71(2), 364–374. doi:10.1037/0022-3514.71.2.364

Barrett, R. L. (2008). *Aghor medicine: Pollution, death, and healing in northern India*. Berkeley, CA: University of California Press.

Biran, A., Poria, Y., & Oren, G. (2011). Sought experiences at (dark) heritage sites. *Annals of Tourism Research*, 38(3), 820–841. doi:10.1016/j.annals.2010.12.001

Bloch, M., & Parry, J. (1982). *Death and the regeneration of life*. New York, NY: Cambridge University Press.

Boardley, I. D., & Kavussanu, M. (2008). The moral disengagement in sport scale–short. *Journal of Sports Sciences*, 26(14), 1507–1517. doi:10.1080/02640410802315054

Bolinger, D. (1982). *Language-the loaded weapon: The use and abuse of language today*. London: Longman.

Cardwell, S. M., Piquero, A. R., Jennings, W. G., Copes, H., Schubert, C. A., & Mulvey, E. P. (2015). Variability in moral disengagement and its relation to offending in a sample of serious youthful offenders. *Criminal Justice and Behavior*, 42(8), 819–839. doi:10.1177/0093854814567472

Caton, K. (2012). Taking the moral turn in tourism studies. *Annals of Tourism Research*, 39(4), 1906–1928. doi:10.1016/j.annals.2012.05.021

Clark, L. B. (2014). Ethical spaces: Ethics and propriety in trauma tourism. In B. Sion (Ed.), *Death tourism: Disaster sites as recreational landscape* (pp. 9–35). London: Seagull.

Cohen, T. R., Panter, A. T., Turan, N., Morse, L., & Kim, Y. (2014). Moral character in the workplace. *Journal of Personality and Social Psychology*, 107(5), 943–963. doi:10.1037/a0037245

Collins, R. (2004). *Interaction ritual chains*. Princeton, NJ: Princeton University Press

Cooper, D. (2011, December 28). The Burning Ghats of Varanasi. [Blog post]. Retrieved from http://moissecooper.blogspot.com/2011/12/

Dale, C., & Robinson, N. (2011). Dark tourism. In P. S. Robinson Heitmann, & P. U. C. Dieke (Eds.), *Research themes for tourism* (pp. 205–217). Wallingford: CABI.

Dann, G. M. S., & Potter, R. B. (2001). Supplanting the planters: Hawking heritage in Barbados. *International Journal of Hospitality & Tourism Administration*, 2(3–4), 51–84. doi:10.1300/J149v02n03_03

Detert, J. R., Treviño, L. K., & Sweitzer, V. L. (2008). Moral disengagement in ethical decision making: A study of antecedents and outcomes. *Journal of Applied Psychology*, 93(2), 374–391. doi:10.1037/0021-9010.93.2.374

Diener, E. (1980). Deindividuation: The absence of self-awareness and self-regulation in group members. In P. B. Paulus (Ed.), *Psychology of group influence* (pp. 209–242). Hillsdale, NJ: Eribaum.

Doron, A. (2013). *Life on the Ganga: Boatmen and the ritual economy of Banaras.* New Delhi: Cambridge University Press India.

Drury, C. (2019, March 21). Auschwitz visitors told to stop posing for disrespectful photos at Nazi death camp. The Independent. Retrieved from https://www.independent.co.uk/news/world/europe/auschwitz-selfies-visitors-posing-railway-poland-a8833746.html

Dunkley, R. A., Morgan, N., & Westwood, S. (2007). A shot in the dark? Developing a new conceptual framework for thanatourism. *Asian Journal of Tourism and Hospitality, 1*(1), 54–63.

Durkheim, E. (1965). *The elementary forms of the religious life.* New York, NY: Free Press

Eck, D. L. (1983). *Banaras: city of light.* Princeton, NJ: Princeton University Press

Festinger, L., Pepitone, A., & Newcomb, T. (1952). Some consequences of deindividuation in a group. *Journal of Abnormal Psychology, 47*(2 Suppl.), 382–389. doi:10.1037/h0057906

Foley, M., & Lennon, J. J. (1996). JFK and dark tourism: A fascination with assassination. *International Journal of Heritage Studies, 2*(4), 198–211. doi:10.1080/13527259608722175

Foley, M., & Lennon, J. J. (1997). Dark tourism–an ethical dilemma. In *Hospitality, tourism and leisure management: Issues in strategy and culture* (pp. 153–164).

Frimer, J. A., & Walker, L. J. (2009). Reconciling the self and morality: An empirical model of moral centrality development. *Developmental Psychology, 45*(6), 1669–1681. doi:10.1037/a0017418

Fukui, M. (2015, April 22). What does the rise of 'dark tourism' mean? ABC RN. Retrieved from https://www.abc.net.au/radionational/programs/earshot/the-trouble-with-dark-tourism/6412726

Gambino, R. (1973). Watergate lingo: A language of non-responsibility. *Freedom at Issue, 22*(7–9), 15–17.

Gibson, J. T., & Haritos-Fatouros, M. (1986). The education of a torturer. Psychology Today, 50–58.

Goffman, E. (1959). *The presentation of self in everyday life.* Garden City, NY: Doubleday

Gould, M. R. (2014). Return to Alcatraz: Dark tourism and the representation of prison history. In B. Sion (Ed.), *Death tourism: Disaster sites as recreational landscape* (pp. 267–288). London: Seagull.

Haidt, J. (2001). The emotional dog and its rational tail: A social intuitionist approach to moral judgment. *Psychological Review, 108*(4), 814–834. doi:10.1037/0033-295X.108.4.814

Haidt, J., & Graham, J. (2007). When morality opposes justice: Conservatives have moral intuitions that liberals may not recognize. *Social Justice Research, 20*(1), 98–116. doi:10.1007/s11211-007-0034-z

Haslam, N. (2006). Dehumanization: An integrative review. *Personality and Social Psychology Review, 10*(3), 252–264. doi:10.1207/s15327957pspr1003_4

Hodalska, M. (2017). Selfies at horror sites: Dark tourism, ghoulish souvenirs and digital narcissism. *Zeszyty Prasoznawcze, 230*(2), 405–423.

Hoffman, M. L. (2000). *Empathy and moral development: Implications for caring and justice.* New York, NY: Cambridge University Press.

Ivie, R. L. (1980). Images of savagery in American justifications for war. *Communication Monographs, 47*(4), 279–294. doi:10.1080/03637758009376037

Johnson, C. E. (2014). Why "good" followers go "bad": The power of moral disengagement. *Journal of Leadership Education, 13*(4), 36–50. doi:10.12806/V13/I4/C6

Kawulich, B. B. (2005). Participant observation as a data collection method. *Forum Qualitative Sozialforschung/Forum: Qualitative Social Research, 6*(2). Retrieved from http://nbn-resolving.de/urn:Nbn.

Keen, S. (1986). *Faces of the enemy.* New York, NY: Harper & Row.

Kelman, H. G. (1973). Violence without moral restraint: Reflections on the dehumanization of victims and victimizers. *Journal of Social Issues, 29*(4), 25–61. doi:10.1111/j.1540-4560.1973.tb00102.x

Kohlberg, L. (1971). Stages of moral development as a basis for moral education. In C. M. Beck, B. S. Crittenden, & E. V. Sullivan (Eds.), *Moral education: Interdisciplinary approaches* (pp. 3-92). Toronto, Canada: Toronto University Press.

Korstanje, M., & George, B. (Eds.). (2017). *Virtual traumascapes and exploring the roots of dark tourism*. Hershey, PA: IGI Global.

Lawther, C. (2017, September 20). Dark tourism can be voyeuristic and exploitative – or if handled correctly, do a world of good. The Conversation. Retrieved from http://theconversa-tion.com/dark-tourism-can-be-voyeuristic-and-exploitative-or-if-handled-correctly-do-a-world-of-good-81504

Lennon, J. (2010). Dark tourism and sites of crime. In D. Botterill, & T. Jones (Eds.), *Tourism and crime: Key themes* (pp. 215–228). Oxford: Goodfellow Publishers

Lennon, J. J., & Foley, M. (1999). Interpretation of the unimaginable: The U.S. Holocaust Memorial Museum, Washington, D.C., and "dark tourism. *Journal of Travel Research, 38*(1), 46–50. doi:10.1177/004728759903800110

Lennon, J. J., & Foley, M. (2000). *Dark tourism: The attraction of death and disaster*. London: Continuum

Light, D. (2017). Progress in dark tourism and thanatourism research: An uneasy relationship with heritage tourism. *Tourism Management, 61*, 275–301. doi:10.1016/j.tourman.2017.01.011

Lisle, D. (2004). Gazing at ground Zero: Tourism, voyeurism and spectacle. *Journal for Cultural Research, 8*(1), 3–21. doi:10.1080/1479758042000797015

Lovelock, B. (2014). The moralization of flying: Cocktails in Seat 33G, famine and pestilence below. In M. Mostafanezhad & K. Hannam (Eds.), *Moral encounters in tourism* (pp. 153–168). New York, NY: Routledge.

Mann, L., Newton, J. W., & Innes, J. M. (1982). A test between deindividuation and emergent norm theories of crowd aggression. *Journal of Personality and Social Psychology, 42*(2), 260–272. doi:10.1037/0022-3514.42.2.260

Martin, S. R., Kish-Gephart, J. J., & Detert, J. R. (2014). Blind forces: Ethical infrastructures and moral disengagement in organizations. *Organizational Psychology Review, 4*(4), 295–325. doi: 10.1177/2041386613518576

Mayring, P. (2014). Qualitative content analysis: Theoretical foundation, basic procedures and software solution. Retrieved from http://nbn-resolving.de/urn:Nbn:de:0168-ssoar-395173

McAlister, A. L., Bandura, A., & Owen, S. V. (2006). Mechanisms of moral disengagement in sup-port of military force: The impact of Sept. 11. *Journal of Social and Clinical Psychology, 25*(2), 141–165. doi:10.1521/jscp.2006.25.2.141

Moore, C., Detert, J. R., Klebe Treviño, L., Baker, V. L., & Mayer, D. M. (2012). Why employees do bad things: Moral disengagement and unethical organizational behavior. *Personnel Psychology, 65*(1), 1–48. doi:10.1111/j.1744-6570.2011.01237.x

Murphy, B. (2015). Dark tourism and the Michelin World War 1 battlefield guides. *Journal of Franco-Irish Studies, 4*(1), 1–9.

Obermann, M. L. (2013). Temporal aspects of moral disengagement in school bullying: Crystallization or escalation? *Journal of School Violence, 12*(2), 193–210. doi:10.1080/15388220. 2013.766133

Opotow, S. (1990). Moral exclusion and injustice: An introduction. *Journal of Social Issues, 46*(1), 1–20. doi:10.1111/j.1540-4560.1990.tb00268.x

Parry, J. (1982). Sacrificial death and the necrophagous ascetic. In M. Bloch, & J. Parry (Eds.), *Death and the regeneration of life* (pp. 74–110). New York, NY: Cambridge University Press.

Parry, J. (1994). *Death in Banaras*. Cambridge, UK: Cambridge University Press.

Pennycook, A. (1994). *The cultural politics of English as an international language*. Harlow, Essex, UK: Longman Group Limited.

Potts, T. J. (2012). Dark tourism'and the 'kitschification'of 9/11. *Tourist Studies, 12*(3), 232–249. doi:10.1177/1468797612461083

Pritchard, A., & Morgan, N. (2006). Hotel Babylon? Exploring hotels as liminal sites of transition and transgression. *Tourism Management, 27*(5), 762–772. doi:10.1016/j.tourman.2005.05.015

Rachels, J., & Rachels, S. (2010). *The elements of modern philosophy*. New York, NY: McGraw-Hill.

Robb, E. (2009). Violence and recreation: Vacationing in the realm of dark tourism. *Anthropology and Humanism, 34*(1), 51–60. doi:10.1111/j.1548-1409.2009.01023.x

Rojek, C. (1993). *Ways of escape*. Basingstoke: MacMillan

Rojek, C. (1997). Indexing, dragging and the social construction of tourist sights. In C. Rojek, & J. Urry (Eds.), *Touring cultures: Transformations of travel and theory* (pp. 52–74). London: Routledge.

Safi, M. (2017, March 11). Reza Aslan outrages Hindus by eating human brains in CNN documentary. The Guardian. Retrieved from https://www.theguardian.com/world/2017/mar/10/reza-aslan-criticised-for-documentary-on-cannibalistic-hindus

Scarles, C. (2013). The ethics of tourist photography: Tourists' experiences of photographing locals in Peru. *Environment and Planning D: Society and Space, 31*(5), 897–917. doi:10.1068/d4511

Seaton, A., & Lennon, J. (2004). Moral panics, ulterior motives and alterior desires: Thanatourism in the early 21st century. In T. V. Singh (Ed.), *New horizons in tourism: Strange experiences and stranger practices* (pp. 63–82). Wallingford: CABI.

Sharpley, R., & Stone, P. R. (2009). (Re)presenting the macabre: Interpretation, kitschification and authenticity. In R. Sharpley & P. R. Stone (Eds.), *The darker side of travel: The theory and practice of dark tourism* (pp. 109–128).Bristol, UK: Channel View Publications.

Sherwin, S. (1987). Dehumanizing women: Treating persons as sex objects. *Canadian Journal of Philosophy, 17*(3), 671–681. doi:10.1080/00455091.1987.10716462

Shields, R. (1991). *Places on the margin: Alternative geographies of modernity.* London: Routledge.

Sontag, S. (1977). *On photography.* London: Anchor Books Doubleday

Stebbins, R. (1996). *Tolerable differences: Living with deviance* (2nd ed.). Toronto: McGraw-Hill Ryerson Limited.

Stebbins, R. A., Rojek, C., & Sullivan, A. M. (2006). Deviant leisure. *Leisure/Loisir, 30*(1), 3–231. doi: 10.1080/14927713.2006.9651338

Sternberg, R. J. (2016). When good, not so good, and downright evil people do bad things. *PsycCRITIQUES, 61*(8). doi:10.1037/a0040161

Stone, P. R. (2005). Dark tourism consumption e a call for research. *e-Review of Tourism Research, 3*(5), 109–117.

Stone, P. R. (2006). A dark tourism spectrum: Towards a typology of death and macabre related tourist sites, attractions and exhibitions. *Tourism, 54*(2), 145–160.

Stone, P. R. (2009). Dark tourism: Morality and new moral spaces. In R. Sharpley, & P. R. Stone (Eds.), *The darker side of travel: The theory and practice of dark tourism* (pp. 56–72). Bristol, UK: Channel View Publications

Stone, P. R. (2011). Dark tourism and the cadaveric carnival: Mediating life and death narratives at Gunther von Hagens' Body Worlds. *Current Issues in Tourism, 14*(7), 685–701. doi:10.1080/13683500.2011.563839

Stone, P. R., & Sharpley, R. (2013). Deviance, dark tourism and 'dark leisure. In S. Elkington & S. Gammon (Eds.), *Contemporary perspectives in leisure: Meanings, motives and lifelong learning: Meanings, motives and lifelong learning* (pp. 54–64).London, UK: Routledge.

Taylor, A. (2003). *Animals and ethics: An overview of the philosophical debate.* Peterborough, Ontario: Broadview Press.

Tillman, C., Gonzalez, K., Whitman, M. V., Crawford, W. S., & Hood, A. C. (2018). A multi-functional view of moral disengagement: Exploring the effects of learning the consequences. *Frontiers in Psychology. 8*(2286), 1–14. doi:10.3389/fpsyg.2017.02286

Tipler, C., & Ruscher, J. B. (2014). Agency's role in dehumanization: Non-human metaphors of out-groups. *Social and Personality Psychology Compass, 8*(5), 214–228. doi:10.1111/spc3.12100

Treviño, L. K., Den Nieuwenboer, N. A., & Kish-Gephart, J. J. (2014). (Un)ethical behavior in organizations. *Annual Review of Psychology, 65*, 635–660. doi:10.1146/annurev-psych-113011-143745

Turner, V. (1973). The center out there: Pilgrim's goal. *History of Religions, 12*(3), 191–230. doi:10.1086/462677

Turner, V., & Abrahams, R. D. (1969). Liminality and communitas. In V. Turner, R. D. Abrahams, & A. Harris (Eds.), *The ritual process: Structure and anti-structure* (pp. 94–113).Chicago, IL: Aldine Publishing.

Weber, M. (1978). Value-judgments in social science. In W. G. Runciman (Ed.), *Weber: Selections in translation* (pp. 69–98).New York, NY: Cambridge University Press.

Wight, A. C., & Lennon, J. J. (2007). Selective interpretation and eclectic human heritage in Lithuania. *Tourism Management*, *28*(2), 519–529.

Zimbardo, P. G. (1969). The human choice: Individuation, reason, and order versus deindividuation, impulse, and chaos. In W. D. Arnold & D. Levine (Eds.), *Nebraska symposium on motivation*, (pp. 237–307). Lincoln: University of Nebraska.

Zsolnai, L. (2016). Moral disengagement: How people do harm and live with themselves, by Albert Bandura. New York: Macmillan, 2016. 544 pp. ISBN: 978-1-4641-6005-9. *Business Ethics Quarterly*, *26*(3), 426–429. doi:10.1017/beq.2016.37

Liminality and difficult heritage in tourism

Velvet Nelson

ABSTRACT

Difficult heritage, rooted in difficult knowledge, is not simply difficult because of traumatic content but also because of the
responses it can provoke. These responses can include confusion,
anxiety, and empathy for the fear and suffering of others. As
such, difficult heritage sites can be problematic in tourism, which
is typically characterized by expectations of fun and relaxation.
Scholars recognize that the tourist experience is liminal in that
tourists occupy a state of limbo outside of their normal places
and lives. This article argues that difficult heritage can be a liminal
experience within tourism by critically analysing tourist reviews of
Bonaire's slave huts. The Caribbean island of Bonaire attracts
cruise tourists and tourists interested in water sports like snorkelling and diving. Yet, these tourists may visit the slave hut sites as
a secondary activity during their stay on the island. TripAdvisor
reviewers describe feelings of being both out of time and out of
place at the slave huts as they imagine the conditions the
enslaved would have experienced, and they describe emotional
responses ranging from sadness to revulsion. Additionally,
reviewers reflect on their visit to the slave huts after 'resuming'
their vacation, particularly focusing on the contrast between their
experiences. The approach of liminality has the potential to better
understand tourists' experiences of difficult heritage.

摘要

根植于艰困知识的艰困遗产, 不仅因为创伤性的内容, 而且因为它
可能引发的反应而变得困难。这些反应可能包括困惑、焦虑和对
他人的恐惧和痛苦的同情。因此, 困难的遗址在旅游业中可能是
值得商榷的, 旅游业的典型特征是对乐趣和放松的期望。学者们
认识到游客的体验是有阈限的, 游客在他们正常的地方和生活之
外处于一种不确定的状态。然而, 在旅游业中, 困难的遗产可能是
一种有阈限的体验, 例如, 可以通过批判性地分析加勒比博内尔岛
奴隶棚屋的游客评论看得出来。这些游客大多是游轮游客和对浮
潜和潜水等水上运动感兴趣的游客。然而, 他们在岛上逗留期间
可能会把参观奴隶棚屋作为次要活动。猫途鹰官网的评论者描述
了他们在想象被奴役者所经历的情况时, 在奴隶棚屋里感到时间
和地点都有不适的感觉, 他们描述了从悲伤到厌恶的情绪反应。
此外, 评论者还回顾了他们在"恢复"假期后参观奴隶小屋的经历,
尤其关注了他们前后经历的对比。阈限性的研究方法有助于对艰
困遗址的旅游体验有更深入的了解。

Introduction

Since the early 2000s, scholars have given increased attention to the relationship between liminality and tourism (e.g. Crang, 2004; Preston-Whyte, 2004; Pritchard & Morgan, 2006). The tourist experience may be understood as liminal in that tourists occupy a state of limbo outside of their normal places and lives. Studies have concentrated on particular tourist spaces, such as the beach (Preston-Whyte, 2004) and hotels (Pritchard & Morgan, 2006), or specific experiences, such as backpacking (Bui, Wilkins, & Lee, 2014) and festivals (Markwell & Waitt, 2009). However, these studies maintain the focus of such spaces/experiences as outside tourists' normal places and lives.

This study recognizes that tourist experiences are 'outside the norm' but also that tourism often has its own norms in terms of expectations of fun and relaxation. As such, experiences that do not meet these expectations may be seen as problematic. In particular, destinations around the world are increasingly acknowledging places associated with dark and difficult pasts. The framework of difficult heritage considers the challenges associated with both representing these pasts and experiencing them. Focusing on the latter, this project explores the idea of difficult heritage as a liminal experience within tourism. Sites associated with difficult heritage can present a stark contrast, physically and/or emotionally, to tourists' vacation experiences. Thus, they may find themselves once again 'betwixt-and-between' for the duration of their visit at the site, from just a few minutes to several hours.

This article specifically examines the liminality of difficult heritage through TripAdvisor reviews of slave huts on the Caribbean island of Bonaire. The first section introduces the concepts of difficult heritage and liminality as it pertains to tourism. The next section briefly reviews the research on slavery heritage tourism and provides some contextual information on tourism to Bonaire and the island's slave hut sites. The following section discusses TripAdvisor reviews as a source of data in tourism studies and considers the use of content and narrative analyses to examine these data. The last section examines key themes in review narratives. In particular, this section focuses on narrative descriptions of visitors' experiences at the slave huts, from crossing the (real or imagined) threshold that separates them, however briefly, from the physical and emotional contexts of their vacation in Bonaire, as well as their reflections on their experiences after their visit.

Difficult heritage and liminality

Scholars have noted the trend over the past two decades in which societies have given increased attention to 'dark' aspects of the past, such as violence, trauma, cruelty, or destruction (Arnold-de Siminie, 2013; Kidman, 2018; Logan & Reeves, 2009; Macdonald, 2016; Sather-Wagstaff, 2015; Simon, 2011a; Thomas, Seitsonen, & Herva, 2016). This trend has often been considered through the framework of black spot tourism, dark tourism, or thanatourism, in which people visit a range of sites and attractions associated with death and the macabre (Rojek, 1993; Stone, 2006). However, Thomas et al. (2016) argue that dark tourism is more complex and involves more varied motivations than simply a fascination with death. Kidron (2013) echoes this idea as she highlights tours that trace personal roots to 'dark' sites such as slave plantations, prisons, or concentration camps. Yankholmes and McKercher (2015) express concerns that placing dark heritage—in their case, slavery heritage—within the structure of dark tourism can oversimplify issues, including complicated emotional responses. To illustrate the point, Dunkley (2007) reflects on her own emotional response to the holocaust exhibition at London's Imperial War Museum. She writes, 'I began to cry, so upset about what I had just seen in the holocaust exhibition that I felt disillusioned with humanity, everything I knew to matter did not, along side this' (Dunkley, 2007, p. 372).

Efforts to further our understanding of, and the interest in, dark heritage have been couched in terms of dissonant, negative, undesirable, and increasingly difficult heritage. Sather-Wagstaff (2015) notes that dark heritage is grounded in difficult knowledge. The concept of difficult knowledge was developed in education but is increasingly applied in the context of museums and other places of memory (Zembylas, 2014). Difficult knowledge is not inherent in places, events, artifacts, images, or discourses (Samuels, 2015; Simon, 2011b; Zembylas, 2014). Thus, difficult knowledge is not simply difficult because of traumatic content; it is difficult because of the response it can provoke. Lehrer and Milton (2011, p. 7) note that what is 'more difficult [than content], perhaps, are questions of what such knowledge does to us—or what we do with it'.

Representations of trauma can be conceptually and emotionally unsettling (Zembylas, 2014, 2018). They can challenge an individual's expectations or beliefs and generate strong, complex, and possibly even conflicting emotions and responses including anger, anxiety, shame, or disappointment (Kidman, 2018; Macdonald, 2016; Simon, 2011a, 2011b). Such representations may even induce a sense of disorientation with a combination of confusion, anxiety, and empathy for the fear and suffering of others (Simon, 2011a). However, individuals will feel, understand, and interpret these representations differently based on their own experiences, perceptions, and frameworks (Zembylas, 2014) as well as their relationship to the event and those involved (Cohen, 2011). What is 'difficult' for one individual may not be so for another (Samuels, 2015).

Samuels (2015, p. 114) argues that the difficult heritage approach 'should draw attention to the process of dealing with problematic pasts most appropriately; the difficulty refers to the practice of heritage-making, not the site or event itself'. This requires us to recognize that there are challenges in both the representation of difficult histories and the experience of these representations (Zembylas, 2014). For example, Simon (2011a) considers the example of a museum exhibit displaying photographs of lynchings in the U.S. South. He discusses the controversial curatorial decision to minimize explanatory text. While some visitors complained about the lack of contextual information, the objective was to facilitate an intense visual and emotional experience of engaging with the photographs. Similarly, Forsdick (2014) describes an evolution from a passive 'sight-seeing' approach to a more active, participatory, and affective 'sight-involving' approach in the context of slavery heritage tourism. Such an approach can be both powerful and disruptive. As such, it may be instructive to consider difficult heritage from the perspective of liminality.

Preston-Whyte (2004, p. 349) describes liminality as 'an elusive concept'. The idea was first proposed by van Gennep in 1908 in the context of rites of passage. Such rites are marked by three phases: separation, transition, and incorporation (van Gennep, 1960). Turner (1974, 1977, 1979, 1982, 1986) adopted and extended van Gennep's use of liminal. The first phase refers to a separation from one's place in society, while the last phase refers to one's return. The middle phase is the liminal phase. Liminal comes from the Latin word *limen*, meaning threshold (Turner, 1974). Thus, 'this term, literally "being-on-a-threshold," means a state or process which is betwixt-and-between the normal, day-to-day cultural and social states and processes' (Turner, 1979, p. 465).

In this state, one may be out-of-place and/or out-of-time (Turner, 1982). Liminal spaces can be real places or literal thresholds, such as a doorway in a house (Thomassen, 2009), but they can also be imagined places (Thomassen, 2012) and the threshold to be crossed symbolic (Preston-Whyte, 2004). The liminal phase can last for an extended period of time or just a few moments (Thomassen, 2009). This state of 'limbo', that is unlike—or even the opposite of—the preceding state, is characterized by ambiguity. As such, it can create feelings of uncertainty and insecurity (Turner, 1982), and it can disrupt one's sense of self or place (Beech, 2011). Thus, experiences in such threshold states can be intense or difficult (Coleman (2019), and one would often return changed in some way (Turner, 1986).

For Turner (1974), liminality could refer to any condition outside, or on the periphery, of everyday life. Indeed, liminality has since been applied in various social and cultural contexts (Pritchard & Morgan, 2006). Turner (1977) initially proposed that leisure could be such an in-between state. Graburn (1989) also draws upon van Gennep when he likens tourism to a rite of passage in which one departs his or her ordinary life and returns home changed by the experience of the trip. Scholars in geography and tourism further explore the idea of tourism as liminal (e.g. Crang, 2004; Pritchard & Morgan, 2006). Tourists enter a period of limbo, where they are outside of their normal lives and places but are not fully a part of the places they visit either (Freidus & Romero-Daza, 2009). Tourist spaces are often viewed as places where social and cultural norms are suspended (Preston-Whyte, 2004; Pritchard & Morgan, 2006). In some contexts within tourism, this ambiguity may be seen as freeing (e.g. Bui et al., 2014; Freidus & Romero-Daza, 2009; Markwell & Waitt, 2009). However, Pritchard and Morgan (2006, p. 765) remind us that 'a liminal, threshold place may offer freedom for some, but unease, constraint or even threat for others'. In either case, we can consider individuals' reactions to such experiences, particularly upon their return (Thomassen, 2009).

This research seeks to consider sites of difficult heritage as liminal sites within tourism. While tourist spaces are 'outside the norm', tourism often has its own norms in that it is traditionally connected to pleasure, relaxation, fun, and escape. Scholars have recognized the inherent contradiction in tourism to sites associated with dark and difficult heritage where suffering and death are the opposite of these notions (Carter, 2016; Forsdick, 2014). This contradiction can be especially stark when tourists are not fully prepared for difficult experiences. For example, tourists may be motivated to travel to a place for leisure and recreation, but they choose to visit a heritage site to learn more about the place or simply as an activity to do there. Such a scenario has often played out in places like the U.S. South and the Caribbean, where heritage is very much tied up with issues of slavery.

Slavery heritage tourism research

Much of the academic literature on slavery heritage tourism has focused on the plantation museums that are an integral part of the heritage landscape in the U.S. South
(e.g. Alderman & Modlin, 2016; Butler, 2001; Butler, Carter, & Dwyer, 2008; Buzinde &
Santos, 2009; Carter, 2016; Carter, Butler, & Alderman, 2014; Dwyer, Butler, & Carter,
2013; Eichstedt & Small, 2002; Bright & Carter, 2016; Hanna, 2016; Modlin, 2008;
Modlin, Alderman, & Gentry, 2011; Potter, 2016; Small, 2013). Other studies have considered sites associated with the transatlantic slave trade, such as West African slave
'castles' (e.g. Boateng, Okoe, & Hinson, 2018; Bruner, 1996; Mowatt & Chancellor, 2011;
Yankholmes & McKercher, 2015), slavery museums (e.g. Alderman & Campbell, 2008;
Arnold-de Siminie, 2012; Cook, 2016), and slavery heritage trails (Best, 2017). In addition, scholars have called for greater recognition and representation of the role of
slavery and the contributions of the enslaved at other heritage sites (Gallas & DeWolf
Perry, 2014).

This literature has often focused on representations of slavery and the enslaved at
heritage sites. Early studies highlighted the lack of representations, namely the
absence of discussions of slavery and the enslaved in promotional materials and on
guided tours (Butler, 2001; Eichstedt & Small, 2002). While sites are increasingly recognizing slavery heritage, subsequent works have addressed ongoing representational
challenges, from the ways in which tour guides talk about the enslaved (Modlin, 2008;
Modlin et al., 2011) to the creation of spaces to talk about slavery (Hanna, 2016). In
addition, there has been considerable discussion about how representations of slavery
could be perceived by audiences. For example, Alderman (2010) frames his discussion
of the process of remembering slavery in the U.S. South in terms of commemorative
surrogation. Dwyer et al. (2013) note that such surrogates can provoke strong reactions if they are perceived as going too far in portraying slavery—or not far enough.

Studies also address visitor experiences and perspectives. Some use exit surveys at
plantation museums to identify visitors' sociodemographic characteristics, interest in
plantation narratives including slavery, and to a limited extent experiences at the
museum (Bright & Carter, 2016; Butler et al., 2008; Carter et al., 2014). Others use on-site
post-tour interviews to obtain greater insight into visitors' perceptions of and experience
at plantation museums (Alderman & Modlin, 2016; Buzinde & Santos, 2009). Mowatt and
Chancellor (2011) use a small sample of in-depth pre- and post-trip interviews with dia-
sporic visitors to examine not only their motivations for visiting a slavery heritage site
but also their emotions upon returning home. Finally, recent studies use TripAdvisor
reviews of sites associated with slavery heritage, including plantation museums in the
U.S. South (Carter, 2016) and slave castles in West Africa (Boateng et al., 2018). These
studies consider visitors' narratives of their experiences in their own words as well as
the ways in which they reflect on these experiences after their visit.

Bonaire's slave huts

Bonaire is a small island located north of the coast of Venezuela in the southern
Caribbean (Hofman & Haviser, 2015). The people who came to be known as the
Caquetío Indians had long inhabited the island prior to colonization (Antczak, 2018;

Figure 1. Worn informational site at the 'white slave' site (photograph by author).

West-Durán, 2003). The Spanish first arrived on the island at the end of the fifteenth century but generally considered it a 'useless' island (West-Durán, 2003). The first Dutch arrived in the early seventeenth century. They were particularly interested in salt from Bonaire, and in 1634, they invaded and took control of the island from the Spanish. Shortly thereafter, enslaved Africans were brought to the Dutch Caribbean and specifically to Bonaire to facilitate salt exploitation (Hofman & Haviser, 2015; West-Durán, 2003). More than two centuries later, in 1863, enslaved Africans in the Dutch possessions were emancipated (Klein, 1986). Since 2010, Bonaire has been classified as a special overseas municipality of the Netherlands; thus, the island is subject to Dutch regulations with some local authority over land use and preservation (Hofman & Haviser, 2015).

Tourism is a significant economic contributor for the island, accounting for 16.4% of gross domestic product as of 2012 (Statistics Netherlands, 2017). There has been some fluctuation in visitor numbers in recent years. In 2017, Bonaire received approximately 128,500 inbound visitors. This was down from 135,800 in 2016 due to problems with a regional airline. However, cruise passengers in 2017 reached 407,300. This represented an increase of 88% over 2016, which was partially attributed to a changes in cruise itineraries as a result of Hurricane Irma (Statistics Netherlands, 2018). The majority of inbound visitors are either Dutch citizens (including both those from the European part of the Netherlands and from the autonomous members of the Kingdom of the Netherlands such as Aruba, Curaçao, and Sint Maarten) or United States citizens. Scuba diving, snorkelling, and water sports like wind and kite surfing are among the most popular tourist activities (Statistics Netherlands, 2017).

In general, places in the Caribbean have been slow to recognize slavery heritage. On a tour of historical sites on an unidentified Caribbean island, Corkern (2004) was dismayed to find no discussion of slavery. Recent studies consider the legacies of the transatlantic slave trade as well as the ongoing efforts (and struggles) to develop slavery heritage sites in the region (Best, 2017; Catalani & Ackroyd, 2013; Forsdick, 2014). Among other challenges, Catalani and Ackroyd (2013) identify the 'spectacularization' of places in the Caribbean that brings attention to their natural beauty while neglecting their cultural and emotional value.

Antczak (2018) finds that Bonaire has largely been ignored in studies discussing the legacies of transatlantic slavery in the Caribbean and in heritage studies. Despite the presence of tangible and intangible heritage resources (Antczak, 2018; Hofman & Haviser, 2015), heritage tourism, and slavery heritage in particular, is a minor part of tourism for Bonaire. Today, there are several sites with 'slave huts' that are easily accessible from the main road on the southwestern part of the island. The huts date back to 1850 (Tourism Corporation Bonaire, 2018) and are thought to be the oldest buildings on the island (West-Durán, 2003). These very small structures located along the coast provided sleeping quarters for enslaved individuals working in the salt pans. They were used for this purpose only for a short time, as slavery was abolished in 1863. The huts are identified as a tourist attraction, although there is little in the way of tourist infrastructure at the sites. The 'white slave'[1] site has a faded and worn informational sign (Figure 1), while the 'red slave' site has sign dated 2007 that describes the salt pans and its 'workers'. The sites are considered a scenic attraction, with picturesque views of both the ocean with bright turquoise water and the distinctive landscape of the salt pans. In addition, the huts are used to mark popular dive sites (Figure 2).

Data and methodology

This study examines visitor narratives of experiences at Bonaire's slave huts in TripAdvisor reviews. Narratives play an important role in how we make sense of experiences and give them meaning (Caton & Santos, 2007). McCabe and Foster (2006) note the difficulties in obtaining visitor narratives of experiences as naturally occurring interaction data unaffected by the research process. Scholars have discussed the potential for user-generated content as a source of naturally occurring data. Such narratives are not reported for research purposes; thus, they are not influenced by researcher questions or perceptions about what is the expected or 'correct' answer (Volo, 2010). Other scholars have highlighted the potential for such data to yield insights into topics that might not be openly discussed (Thomas et al., 2016). While much of this discussion focused on the use of travel blogs (Bosangit, Dulnuan, & Mena, 2012; Nelson, 2015; Volo, 2010), Vásquez (2012) notes that scholars are giving more attention to 'small stories', particularly in light of trends in information and communication technologies. In the present digital environment, these small stories are told on a variety of social media platforms, including online review sites like TripAdvisor.

Figure 2. Scuba divers at the 'red slave' site (photograph by author).

TripAdvisor (2017) claims to be the world's largest travel site boasting approximately 760 million reviews of 8.3 million accommodations, airlines, experiences, and restaurants and the world's largest travel community with 490 million average monthly unique visitors as of July 2019. As the site has grown in significance, it has attracted the attention of tourism scholars (Law, 2006). Studies consider issues such as trust in and credibility of reviews (Ayeh, Au, & Law, 2013; Filieri, Alguezaui, & McLeay, 2015; Kusumasondjaja, Shanka, & Marchegiani, 2012), patterns in ratings (Banerjee & Chua, 2016; Miguéns, Baggio, & Costa, 2008), patterns among reviewers (Lee, Law, & Murphy, 2011), role of reviews in destination image formation (Garay Tamajón & Cànoves Valiente, 2017; Kladou & Mavragani, 2015), and reviews as narratives of experience (Crotts, Mason, & Davis, 2009; Vásquez, 2012). In addition, recent studies use TripAdvisor reviews to examine narratives of experiences at sites associated with dark heritage (Çakar, 2018) and slavery heritage more specifically, as identified above.

TripAdvisor reviewers describe their experiences at Bonaire's slave huts under the following categories: salt flats, slave huts, and witte (i.e. white) pan (ranked 20, 28, and 38, respectively, in 'things to do in Bonaire'). The original sample, collected in July 2018, consisted of 978 reviews. Data included rating value, textual description, date of posting, and reviewer country of origin if given. Upon initial inspection, posts that did not include textual description of the slave huts were eliminated (i.e. reviews discussing the white slave dive site as opposed to the slave huts). This yielded a sample of 653 reviews posted in eleven languages.

The author documented translations of reviews in all languages for preliminary analysis. 85.91% of these reviewers self-identify as coming from 36 countries as well as

Bonaire, Aruba, and Curaçao. This is consistent with Kladou and Mavragani's (2015) findings (i.e. 86.21% of reviewers self-identified country of origin). Reviewers from North America dominated the sample with 56.51% those who self-identified. This is also consistent with Kladou and Mavragani (2015). In this preliminary analysis, particular attention was given to Dutch language reviews, given the geopolitical relationship between Bonaire and the Netherlands. However, because English language reviews accounted for over 66.61% of the sample (435 reviews) and 63.89% of reviewers' countries of origin, as well as Bonaire and Curaçao, this language was selected for in-depth analysis. This corresponds with similar studies (see, e.g. Banerjee & Chua, 2016; Garay Tamajón & Cànoves Valiente, 2017). In particular, English serves as a lingua franca among tourists of diverse origins, and the use of the predominant language limits concerns about translation errors from multiple languages.

The number of reviews included in studies using TripAdvisor varies considerably based on the feature reviewed (e.g. hotels versus attractions) as well as study objectives and methodologies. For example, Banerjee and Chua (2016) used quantitative analysis to examine 37,652 hotel ratings, whereas Vásquez (2012) used qualitative analysis to examine just 100 hotel reviews. The final sample used in this research (435 reviews) is consistent with studies of similar study sites and methodologies (e.g. 436 reviews of Cape Coast Castle in Boateng et al., 2018; 330 reviews of Gallipoli war heritage memorials in Çakar, 2018; 200 reviews of Laura and Oak Alley plantation museums in Carter, 2016).

Qualitative approaches to TripAdvisor reviews primarily involve content analysis (Boateng et al., 2018; Çakar, 2018; Carter, 2016; Garay Tamajón & Cànoves Valiente, 2017; Kladou & Mavragani, 2015) and narrative analysis (Vásquez, 2012). This investigation used a thematic narrative analysis approach (Riessman, 2004) that combines the two methods. It is an inductive approach that allows the researcher to derive themes from detailed readings of the data as opposed to a priori expectations (Thomas, 2006). Thus, the preliminary analysis of all language reviews involved content analysis to gain familiarity with the data and to establish a set of descriptive codes from the data by tracking the frequency of key words and phrases. This was an iterative process to track frequencies and to establish reliability by ensuring consistency in tracking as well as to organize codes into categories. While this process was important for obtaining an overall understanding of the data, the imprecise wording of translations limits more comprehensive analysis. As such, the iterative process of content analysis was repeated again with the reviews posted in English. The author then identified key themes that emerged from the data.

This foundation provided the basis for more in-depth narrative analysis of the English language reviews. This method is frequently used to consider self-reflective accounts of tourist experiences (Rickly-Boyd, 2009). In addition, it allows the researcher to examine the narrative structure of these accounts to understand how tourists talk about experiences (McCabe & Foster, 2006). There is no single approach to narrative analysis (Laing & Crouch, 2009). In this research, narrative analysis was used to understand the context of the categories established through content analysis, to explore significant themes, and to consider the narrative structure of visitor descriptions of their experiences.

Findings

Reviews were posted between 2013 and 2018. Among reviewers who self-identified country of origin in the sample encompassing all languages, the United States comprised the single-largest demographic (i.e. 49.19%). The Netherlands comprised the second largest group (i.e. 18.34%). These two countries are the largest sources of visitors to Bonaire. The majority of reviewers (i.e. 73.35%) of reviewers gave the site a rating of good or excellent. However, there was a significant discrepancy in ratings between reviewers posting English and those posting in other languages (i.e. 77.01% reviewers rating good or excellent versus 66.06%). Of those English language reviewers who made a recommendation in their review, 77.62% encouraged readers to visit the site compared to 58.0% of reviewers posting in other languages.

To gain a better perspective on the relationship between Bonaire and the Netherlands, the author isolated the Dutch language reviews. 80.53% of reviewers who posted in this language and self-identified were from the Netherlands; an additional 7.08% came from Bonaire, Aruba, and Curaçao. It is worth noting that only 4.92% of Dutch language reviewers (all but one specifically identifying as from the Netherlands) connected the slave hut site to Dutch history or referred to it as 'our' history. Still, there was little discussion of what this meant for the reviewers. For example, a review titled 'This is too unfortunately our history', (Netherlands, 2017) did not discuss the history. Instead, the review was entirely descriptive in terms of location, size, construction material, etc. In addition, an equal percentage of these reviewers referred to the site as part of Bonaire's history.

Generally speaking, English language reviews were longer (i.e. on average 26% more words per review) and more reflective than Dutch language reviews. However, it is worth noting that reviewers from the Netherlands also comprised the fourth largest demographic among reviewers posting in English. Additionally, these reviewers came from all parts of the world including countries such as Guatemala, Croatia, South Africa, and China. For these reviewers, a tourist visit to Bonaire can be considered liminal. Suspended outside of their normal places and normal lives, they expect experiences of natural beauty as well as pleasure, recreation, and relaxation. Only a small minority of reviewers indicated a specific intention to visit the slave huts. One reviewer noted, 'We knew enough to read up on the history a bit before visiting' (Canada, 2018[2]), while two others stated that they had been to the site on a previous visit to the island. However, most indicated that their visit was one stop on a driving tour of the island or on a guided tour (e.g. a shore excursion from the cruise ship or in between dives) or something they simply stumbled upon. Since visitors were generally unaware of the site prior to the visit, there was little discussion of anticipation of or expectations for the experience in the reviews.

For many reviewers, the huts were something that could be seen if one were already driving that part of the island but not necessarily worth making a special trip. All of the reviewers who discussed duration of experience noted that the site did not require a long visit. Among these reviewers, 43.34% either specifically indicated that they spent less than 10 min at the site or noted that it could be seen in that amount of time. The longest stated visit was one hour. Reviewers presented the site as a part of Bonaire's history (the most frequent code). Moreover, 19.77% of all reviewers expressed the importance of learning about and, in particular, remembering the past.

Describing the place

Reviewers described the setting of the slave huts, particularly their location along the water's edge, in overwhelmingly positive terms. Beautiful, picturesque, and scenic were among some of the most frequent codes, while other terms included idyllic, tranquil, serene, and peaceful. For many, the natural beauty of the setting played an important role in creating a liminal experience because it made the difficult nature of the site all the more disconcerting. One reviewer noted, 'The ironic contrast between these huts and the surrounding beauty of the island will not be lost on you' (USA, 2018). Overall, reviewers considered the huts to be well preserved; however, a small minority expressed concern about the authenticity of the site. For example, considering the huts to be replicas, one reviewer felt they were not particularly interesting. Another felt that they were not necessarily reflective of the site's history: 'The huts were well restored and that maybe gives a bit too positive outlook of the situation at the days when these huts were in their original use' (Argentina, 2016).

One of the most significant themes in reviewers' descriptions was the size of the huts. Small and tiny were among the most frequent codes overall. Reviewers also focused on the feeling of the huts as tight, cramped, or stifling. One reviewer warned readers, 'Pictures do not do these huts justice. They are tinier than they appear' (USA, 2017). Some reviewers used their own height, or that of others they were with, to give readers perspective [e.g. 'My 5-foot wife could barely stand inside' (Canada, 2018)], while others compared the huts to the size of dog houses, doll houses, or small camping tents. The huts themselves were described as basic and minimal, little more than shelter and respite from environmental conditions. As with the beauty of the setting, this physical context of the huts played a role in creating a liminal experience, particularly as the visitors entered the huts (see 'Describing the experience' below).

The most common complaint about the site was the lack of contextual information about the huts themselves as well as the enslaved who used them. For example, a reviewer wrote, 'The slave huts are located on a beautiful part of the island and we found them to be quite interesting. I just wish there had been more information on them' (USA, 2016). Many cited the faded sign at the white slave site: 'It was very interesting but the sign is faded and washed out so I wasn't able to get more information on it until we go [sic] back to the resort and I could do a little online research (USA, 2017). The lack of information resulted in many different, and often conflicting, accounts of the site in reviews. For example, just over 10% of reviewers discussed the number of enslaved who would have occupied the space, and assertions ranged from two or three to 30. A small number of reviewers recommended that readers take a guided tour to get more information or to at least read up about the site prior to visiting. However, as expressed by a reviewer, the basic information on site allows people to 'feel' (USA, 2017). Indeed, many reviewers focused on experiential aspects of the visit, encouraging readers to see, touch, and pause, imagine, and reflect on life in that place in the past. This emphasis on 'sight-involving' is particularly important in creating a liminal experience. As discussed below, the reviewers who focused on the experiential aspects of their visit were the ones who expressed feelings of being out of time and place.

Describing the experience

Reviewers posting under the 'slave huts' category were most likely to elaborate on their experiences and share their emotional responses. For some, their arrival at the site was their threshold. Although, the environment appeared similar to what they had experienced elsewhere on the island, the 'feel' of the site was different. One reviewer wrote, 'What I will remember about this stop is the feeling I got when I was there. For me, there was a somberness about the place in spite of its beauty' (USA, 2016). Some generally cited an eerie feeling, while one described standing at the huts and feeling the souls of the people who once inhabited them (USA, 2017). Bell (1997) describes this as the ghosts of place and in fact argues that these ghosts play an important role in giving spaces meaning and creating places. Some experienced confusion and uncertainty as they processed what they were seeing. For example, several reviewers explained how they initially assumed the huts were used for keeping animals. 'Before I realized what these were for I thought they were for goats... Humbling and horrifying but important to see nonetheless' (USA, 2015). For many, however, their threshold was the physical entrance to the huts itself. 'It was one thing to see them but quite another when we crawled into one and tried to picture just what that would have been like hundreds of years ago' (USA, 2018).

These real places also became imagined ones as reviewers sought to envision what they would have been like when the huts were used. As such, they were liminal—out-of-time as well as out-of-place. They saw the physical conditions in a different light, from beautiful to threatening: 'You can only imagine the gruelling conditions that the slaves had to endure here, with the salt, sun and trade winds only adding to the discomfort and inhumane treatment they got in the first place' (UK, 2016). Indeed, many also tried to imagine the conditions of life and work in the salt pans at that time, described as harsh, brutal, cruel, and horrific. For example, one reviewer imagined up to 12 individuals in one hut, wearing 'salt-soaked clothing', unable to lie down to sleep (Canada, 2016).

Others further tried to conceive of how the enslaved would have felt: 'imagine the actual horror the slaves had to go through, cramming in such small places, in whatever weather, with creepy crawlies, hungry and tired, missing their loved ones' (Caribbean, 2017). Similarly, 'Imagine 8 people sharing one of these, facing out over the sea after months on a slave ship surrounded by suffering and death, trapped in a hell far from family or any known world' (USA, 2018). One reviewer wrote that s/he could almost feel the pain of the enslaved (Germany, 2017). This is similar to Kidron's (2013) description of how descendants of Holocaust victims sought to gain an 'empathetic feeling' of the experience. Yet, most reviewers still found their imagination to be inadequate. Nearly 20% of reviewers used terms such as hard to believe, difficult to comprehend, and can't imagine.

In this liminal state, reviewers were faced with some difficult emotions. Feelings of sadness were the most frequently expressed (12% of reviews). A reviewer wrote,

> We visited the slave huts on Bonaire as part of our land tour of the island. We felt deeply saddened by what they represented … These huts represent a desire to keep working to end oppression of any kind in human life (Canada, 2018).

Reviewers also commonly described the experience as sobering, humbling, moving, and heart-breaking. Others noted feelings of horror, revulsion, and shame. One reviewer noted her horror as she experienced the site, while her daughter was moved to tears (USA, 2018). Finally, a reviewer from the United States wrote that the site 'Brought back really bad memories to see how one human being could treat another human being like this' (USA, 2016).

Reflecting on the experience

Following the often-brief moments spent at the slave huts, visitors continued their vacation. Some reviewers indicated that the 'return' was not always easy. For example, one review was titled, 'make sure you have something upbeat to do afterward' (USA, 2018). Another reviewer on a dive vacation noted that s/he experienced mixed emotions in the time spent at the slave hut site 'contemplating the many lives torn apart by slavery'. After the visit, the reviewer noted that s/he needed to find 'a place of light and peace while diving afterward to spend a few moments accepting my own privilege to be able to be a visitor to this place and to be able to dive' (USA, 2016).

Similarly acknowledging their privilege as tourists, reviewers reflected on the sharp contrast between their experience at the slave huts and that of their vacation in general. For one reviewer, visiting the slave huts helped put his/her experiences in perspective. While this individual conceived his/her vacation on Bonaire as 'heaven', s/he drew upon the empathetic response to the experience of the slave huts and imagined that the enslaved would have conceived the same place as 'hell'. Focusing specifically on the physical context, a reviewer wrote,

> Visiting [the slave huts] is an important reminder of the different stages of the island's history and of how fortunate we tourists are to be able to enjoy all that nature has to offer on Bonaire, including our sleeping conditions that are certainly lavish, regardless of where one stays, in comparison to what these unfortunate slaves experienced (USA, 2018).

Another reviewer took the issue a step farther. After reflecting on the contrast between life for the enslaved and tourists, s/he asked readers to, 'imagine what it's like now with the sharp disparity between the rich who vacation or retire here and the indigenous people who barely scrape by on subsistence wages' (USA, 2018).

As stated by one reviewer, 'It doesn't take long to look at the slave huts, but the impression they left on me is lasting' (USA, 2017). While it is unlikely that the majority of reviewers experienced any significant personal changes as a result of their experience at this site, they nonetheless reflected on it later—at the very least to write their review. Some reviewers were still working through their emotions as they wrote their review. In particular, several struggled to frame their review and assign a rating. For example, one review was titled 'interestingly sad', as the reviewer explained that s/he struggled to find an appropriate title (Canada, 2018). Similarly, a reviewer wrote, 'It seemed wrong to give this attraction a very good review as it is a terrible reminder of the slave trade, but the huts have been well cared for' (UK, 2018).

Difficult heritage acknowledges that what is 'difficult' for some will not necessarily be difficult for others. Although many reviewers expressed their emotional response to the difficult topic of slavery, it was not a difficult or liminal experience for all. In a review titled 'fun and quick little detour!' the reviewer cheerfully wrote, 'It is worth a quick stop, read the sign and take a selfie from a hut. It's all part of taking in bonaire [sic] experience!' (USA, 2017). Similarly, another reviewer wrote, 'They are really cute little huts. We saw them in 2 locations not too far apart. Ones are in white and others are in beige. Go during sunset! They are awesome!' (USA, 2015). More than one reviewer commented that the place would make a good camping site, and several reviewers visited the slave hut sites simply to dive. One reviewer posting under the 'slave huts' category on TripAdvisor wrote, 'Theres [sic] not just the huts on the shore, even more interesting is the dive site' (USA, 2018).

The very different responses to the site created a source of tension. Reviewers commented on the lack of sensitivity displayed by other visitors. The presence of trucks, divers, and their equipment in particular was a point of contention. One reviewer noted that they were 'taken aback' by this (Germany, 2018), while another elaborated, 'I felt it was disrespectful and the divers that we encountered didn't seem to care or respect the grounds' (USA, 2018). Similarly, 'People were hanging around and washing their scuba gear. For this to be a part of history it is clearly not important to those who weren't affected by it' (USA, 2016). It is important to keep in mind, however, that this criticism is levied against a particularly visible group. In their own reviews, dive tourists also expressed a range of emotional responses. Other reviewers directed their criticism to visitors from the cruise ships.

> Wow. Honestly, if you visit these without taking the time to contemplate why they are here and what they are, you are TOTALLY missing the point and should get back on the cruise ship bubble you may have come from. It would be like visiting the Anne Frank house in Amsterdam and coming away with 'it was cozy' or Auschwitz near Kraków and thinking it was 'so spacious' (USA, 2015).

Reviewers also complained about the perceived insensitivity displayed in reviews themselves: 'Having just read a whole lot of earlier reviews, I was amazed at the absolute ignorance of the people submitting them: "…cute, amazing, great for a relax between dives, kept clean and tidy…" ???' (Canada, 2015). These responses, ranging from dismay to anger, offer further insight into the ways in which reviewers reflect on the liminal experience.

Discussion and conclusion

More places around the world are integrating sites associated with dark pasts into their tourism offer, yet these sites can be problematic in tourism. The perspective of difficult heritage recognizes that there are challenges associated with the processes of representing dark pasts as well as that of experiencing them. Yet, the literature particularly focuses on tourism to well-known sites, including UNESCO World Heritage

Sites, such as West African slave route sites or Nazi heritage sites (e.g. Macdonald, 2016; Sather-Wagstaff, 2015). While such sites face challenges with regards to tourist visits, tourists have expectations for and opportunities to prepare themselves for the experience, even if they ultimately find their expectations and/or preparation inadequate. Likewise, such sites often make provisions for visitor responses, such as spaces for visitors to try to make sense of (Dunkley, 2007) or to discuss their experiences (Simon, 2011a).

This research particularly seeks to consider engagements with difficult heritage that are simply one part of—and a contrast to—a larger tourist experience and thereby represent a liminal experience within tourism. Tourists to Bonaire are neither heritage tourists nor 'dark' tourists. One reviewer acknowledged 'It is easy to go to a place like Bonaire and ignore the history' (USA, 2017). Visitors came to the slave huts because tourist literature highlighted the site as a part of the island's history, because the site was a stop on an island tour, or because they simply saw it as they were driving by. As many were not even aware of the site, they were not expecting or prepared for a difficult experience. The stark contrast, physically and/or emotionally, to their vacation experiences can be especially disconcerting. Thus, while the vacation experience is liminal in that it displaces visitors from their normal places and lives, they may find themselves displaced once again at the slave hut site.

Entering the site, or even the huts themselves, many visitors crossed a threshold that separated the physical and emotional contexts of their vacations and their experiences at the site. In a brief period of limbo, the real place became an imagined one as they tried to envision life for the enslaved in nineteenth century Bonaire and to empathize with their experiences. The lack of detailed contextual information about the huts or the enslaved facilitates a more intense experience, in line with Forsdick's (2014) idea of an affective 'sight-involving' approach. Then, after a few moments or longer, visitors returned to their 'normal' vacations and eventually to their normal lives. Yet, many continued to reflect on the experience of the slave huts after their visit. In particular, a subset of reviewers focused on the contrast between their experiences in Bonaire in general and those at the slave huts.

The experience clearly was not difficult for all of the visitors who reviewed the site. Some visitors would not be deterred from their touristic purposes or motivations, as seen in the reviews complaining about the divers at the site. Indeed, some reviewers themselves reiterated this with statements such as, 'There is a [sic] interesting history panel to read. The real reason to get there is the dive site...' (Canada, 2017) and 'Remember, you are here to dive' (USA, 2017). However, purpose of the trip does not offer sufficient explanation for reviewers' responses to the experience. Other reviewers who indicated that they were on Bonaire to dive expressed varied emotional responses to the site (e.g. shocked, humbled, grateful, etc.).

Likewise, country of origin is an inadequate predictor of response. Although English language reviews were used for the in-depth analysis discussed here, reviewers nonetheless represented 26 different countries. Vastly varied responses are seen among reviewers from any of the countries included in the sample. For example, people in the United States continue to struggle with their own country's history of slavery. This is reflected in the different 'interpretive communities' identified among tourists to plantations in Louisiana's River Road region (Alderman & Modlin, 2016). The majority of tourists surveyed (over 85%) were from the United States (Forbes Bright & Carter, 2016). Among these tourists, some clearly expressed that they did not want slavery to be discussed on plantation tours, while others expressed a strong desire to hear more about the topic (Alderman & Modlin, 2016). Similar responses can be seen among the reviews in this study, from complete lack of interest [e.g. 'What's the point?' (USA, 2017)] to statements about the significance of the site [e.g. 'It is important that these huts are main-tained to remind us all that history should not repeat itself' (USA, 2015)].

One of the key limitations associated with the use of TripAdvisor reviews as a source of data is the lack of contextual information, ranging from demographic data like race/ethnicity or level of education to values and experiences. More nuanced information about reviewers could yield greater insight into responses, particularly why some visitors were affected by the experience and others were not. The literature on difficult knowledge reminds us that individuals interpret and feel representations differently based on their unique set of experiences, relationships, and conceptual frameworks (Zembylas, 2014). Thus, to fully unpack the personal perspectives and/or family histories that would yield a greater understanding of reviewer responses, such as the American reviewer who commented that Bonaire's slave huts 'brought back really bad memories' (USA, 2016), methods such as in-depth interviews might be necessary. Additionally, the fact that the researcher does not have the opportunity to follow up on and further explore key themes raised in the reviews is another limitation of the study.

On the other hand, TripAdvisor reviews give us access to visitors' narratives that describe their experiences and emotional responses—or lack thereof—in their own words. This is important in light of difficult heritage, where responses can vary widely and may be conflicting. Indeed, responses may not even be predicted, which could limit a researcher-designed survey. The anonymous and unprompted nature of reviews has the potential to provide more honest responses than an interview, especially for those individuals who expressed no interest or regard for the history of slavery in their reviews. Post-visit reviews submitted online also give visitors an opportunity to pro-cess their experiences, as opposed to on-site interviews. In this case study, some reviewers even discussed how they reflected on their experience after their visit to the slave hut site. The reflective reviews become personal narratives of experience that express internal conflicts and emotions. As Dunkley (2007) finds, these aspects are often lost in the structure of traditional research methods, in her case, a questionnaire.

To further explore the liminality of difficult heritage in tourism and to address these limitations, additional research will incorporate a post-trip interview component (see, for example, Mowatt & Chancellor, 2011). This will provide more in-depth narratives of experiences at the slave hut sites, reflections on these experiences, and reflections on these experiences with relation to the larger trip as well as greater opportunities to explore the factors that contribute to the responses to these experiences. Comparative research will also be undertaken at other slavery heritage sites in the region. In par-ticular, the researcher would like to examine sites with minimal infrastructure and/or interpretation similar to Bonaire's slave huts (e.g. sites along Guadeloupe's 'La route de l'esclave') along with those that are more developed (e.g. Martinique's 'La savane des esclaves') to consider the extent to which the nature of the site shapes the liminality of the experience.

Societies around the world are increasingly recognizing 'dark' aspects of the past and creating opportunities for visitors to learn about or commemorate such issues or events. As such, dark tourism experiences are becoming more diverse, and both motivations for visiting and emotional responses to them are becoming more complex. Scholars have proposed the frame of difficult heritage to particularly consider responses to traumatic content; yet, research continues to focus on high-profile sites for which visitors expect and prepare for potentially difficult experiences. Further research is needed to understand the experiences of visitors who neither expect nor are prepared to encounter difficult heritage. For this aim, this work employs the perspective of liminality. This perspective provides a lens to contextualize the feelings of being out of space and time expressed by visitors to Bonaire's slave huts.

Notes

1. The naming of the sites refers to the colour of the adjacent obelisks used as navigational shore markers to guide ships coming in to load salt.
2. Reviewer names/usernames have been omitted. For reference in this discussion, origin of reviewer and date of review are indicated.

Disclosure statement

No potential conflict of interest was reported by the author.

References

Alderman, D. H. (2010). Surrogation and the politics of remembering slavery in Savannah, Georgia (USA). *Journal of Historical Geography, 36*(1), 90–101. doi:10.1016/j.jhg.2009.08.001

Alderman, D. H., & Campbell, R. M. (2008). Symbolic excavation and the artefact politics of remembering slavery in the American South: Observations from Walterboro, South Carolina. *Southeastern Geographer, 48*, 338–355.

Alderman, D. H., & Modlin, E. A. (2016). On the political utterances of plantation tourists: Vocalizing the memory of slavery on River Road. *Journal of Heritage Tourism, 11*, 275–289. doi: 10.1080/1743873X.2015.1100623

Antczak, O. (2018). *Unpicking a feeling: Interrogating the role of heritage in indigenous collective identity formation on the Caribbean island of Bonaire* (Doctoral dissertation). University of Cambridge, Cambridge. Retrieved from https://www.repository.cam.ac.uk/bitstream/handle/1810/284389/Dissertation%20Oliver%20 Final.pdf?sequence=1&isAllowed=y

Arnold-de Siminie, S. (2012). The 'moving' image: Empathy and projection in the International Slavery Museum, Liverpool. *Journal of Educational Media, Memory, and Society, 4*, 23–40.

Arnold-de Siminie, S. (2013). *Mediating memory in the museum: Trauma, empathy, nostalgia*. Houndmills: Palgrave Macmillan.

Ayeh, J. K., Au, N., & Law, R. (2013). "Do we believe in TripAdvisor?" Examining credibility perceptions and online travelers' attitude toward using user-generated content. *Journal of Travel Research, 52*, 437–452. doi:10.1177/0047287512475217

Banerjee, S., & Chua, A.Y.K. (2016). In search of patterns among travelers' hotel ratings in TripAdvisor. *Tourism Management, 53*, 125–131.

Beech, N. (2011). Liminality and the practices of identity reconstruction. *Human Relations, 64*, 285–302. doi:10.1177/0018726710371235

Bell, M. M. (1997). The ghosts of place. *Theory and Society, 26*, 813–836.

Best, M. N. (2017). Freedom footprints: The Barbados story' – a slavery heritage trail. *Journal of Heritage Tourism, 12*, 474–488. doi:10.1080/1743873X.2016.1255220

Boateng, H., Okoe, A. F., & Hinson, R. E. (2018). Dark tourism: Exploring tourist's experience at the Cape Coast Castle, Ghana. *Tourism Management Perspectives, 27*, 104–110. doi:10.1016/j. tmp.2018.05.004

Bosangit, C., Dulnuan, J., & Mena, M. (2012). Using travel blogs to examine the postconsumption behaviour of tourists. *Journal of Vacation Marketing, 18*, 207–219. doi:10.1177/1356766712449367

Bright, C. F., & Carter, P. (2016). Who are they? Visitors to Louisiana's River Road plantations. *Journal of Heritage Tourism, 11*, 262–274. doi:10.1080/1743873X.2015.1100627

Bruner, E. M. (1996). Tourism in Ghana: The representation of slavery and the return of the black diaspora. *American Anthropologist, 98*, 290–304. doi:10.1525/aa.1996.98.2.02a00060

Bui, H. T., Wilkins, H., & Lee, Y. (2014). Liminal experience of East Asian backpackers. *Tourist Studies, 14*, 126–143. doi:10.1177/1468797614532179

Butler, D. L. (2001). Whitewashing plantations. *International Journal of Hospitality & Tourism Administration, 2*, 163–175. doi:10.1300/J149v02n03_07

Butler, D. L., Carter, P. L., & Dwyer, O. J. (2008). Imagining plantations: Slavery, dominant narratives, and the foreign born. *Southeastern Geographer, 48*, 288–302.

Buzinde, C. N., & Santos, C. S. (2009). Interpreting slavery tourism. *Annals of Tourism Research, 36*, 439–458. doi:10.1016/j.annals.2009.02.003

Çakar, K. (2018). Experiences of visitors to Gallipoli, a nostalgia-themed dark tourism destination: An insight from TripAdvisor. *International Journal of Tourism Cities, 4*(1), 98–109. doi:10.1108/IJTC-03-2017-0018

Carter, P., Butler, D. L., & Alderman, D. H. (2014). The house that story built: The place of slavery in plantation museum narratives. *The Professional Geographer, 66*, 547–557. doi:10.1080/00330124.2014.921016

Carter, P. L. (2016). Where are the enslaved?: TripAdvisor and the narrative landscapes of southern plantation museums. *Journal of Heritage Tourism, 11*, 235–249. doi:10.1080/1743873X.2015.1100625

Catalani, A., & Ackroyd, T. (2013). Inheriting slavery: Making sense of a difficult heritage. *Journal of Heritage Tourism, 8*, 337–346. doi:10.1080/1743873X.2013.766199

Caton, K., & Santos, C. A. (2007). Heritage tourism on Route 66: Deconstructing heritage. *Journal of Travel Research, 45*, 371–386. doi:10.1177/0047287507299572

Cohen, E. H. (2011). Educational dark tourism at an *in populo* site: The Holocaust museum in Jerusalem. *Annals of Tourism Research, 38*(1), 193–209. doi:10.1016/j.annals.2010.08.003

Coleman, S. (2019). From the liminal to the lateral: Urban religion in English cathedrals. *Tourism Geographies, 21*(3), 384–404. doi:10.1080/14616688.2018.1449236

Cook, M. R. (2016). Counter-narratives of slavery in the Deep South: The politics of empathy along and beyond River Road. *Journal of Heritage Tourism, 11*, 290–308. doi:10.1080/1743873X.2015.1100624

Corkern, W. (2004). Heritage tourism: Where public and history don't always meet. *American Studies International, 42*, 7–16.

Crang, M. (2004). Cultural geographies of tourism. In A. A. Lew, C. M. Hall, & A. M. Williams (Eds.), *A companion to tourism* (pp. 74–84). Malden: Blackwell Publishing.

Crotts, J. C., Mason, P. R., & Davis, B. (2009). Measuring guest satisfaction and competitive position in the hospitality and tourism industry: An application of stance-shift analysis to travel blog narratives. *Journal of Travel Research*, 48, 139–151. doi:10.1177/0047287508328795

Dunkley, R. A. (2007). Re-peopling tourism: A 'hot approach' to studying thanatourist experiences. In I. Ateljevic, A. Pritchard, & N. Morgan (Eds.), *The critical turn in tourism studies: Innovative research methodologies* (pp. 371–385). Amsterdam: Elsevier.

Dwyer, O., Butler, D., & Carter, P. (2013). Commemorative surrogation and the American South's changing heritage landscape. *Tourism Geographies*, 15, 424–443. doi:10.1080/14616688.2012.699091

Eichstedt, J., & Small, S. (2002). *Representations of slavery: Race and ideology in southern plantation museums*. Washington, DC: Smithsonian Institution Press.

Filieri, R., Alguezaui, S., & McLeay, F. (2015). Why do travelers trust TripAdivsor? Antecedents of trust towards consumer-generated media and its influence on recommendation adoption and word of mouth. *Tourism Management*, 51, 174–185. doi:10.1016/j.tourman.2015.05.007

Forsdick, C. (2014). Travel, slavery, memory: Thanatourism in the French Atlantic. *Postcolonial Studies*, 17, 251–265. doi:10.1080/13688790.2014.993427

Freidus, A., & Romero-Daza, N. (2009). The space between: Globalization, liminal spaces and personal relations in rural Costa Rica. *Gender, Place and Culture*, 16, 683–702. doi:10.1080/09663690903279146

Gallas, K. L., & DeWolf Perry, J. (2014). Comprehensive content and contested historical narratives. In K. L. Gallas & J. DeWolf Perry (Eds.), *Interpreting slavery at museums and historic sites* (pp. 1–20). Lanham: Rowman & Littlefield Publishers.

Garay Tamajón, L., & Cànoves Valiente, G. (2017). Barcelona seen through the eyes of TripAdvisor: Actors, typologies and components of destination image in social media platforms. *Current Issues in Tourism*, 20(1), 33–37. doi:10.1080/13683500.2015.1073229

Graburn, N. H. H. (1989). Tourism: The sacred journey. In V. L. Smith (Ed.), *Hosts and guests: The anthropology of tourism* (2nd ed., pp. 21–36). Philadelphia: University of Pennsylvania Press.

Hanna, S. P. (2016). Placing the enslaved at Oak Alley Plantation: Narratives, spatial contexts, and the limits of surrogation. *Journal of Heritage Tourism*, 11, 219–234. doi:10.1080/1743873X.2015.1100628

Hofman, C. L., & Haviser, J. B. (2015). Introduction. In C. L. Hofman & J. B. Haviser (Eds.), *Managing our past into the future: Archaeological heritage management in the Dutch Caribbean* (pp. 27–36). Leiden: Sidestone Press.

Kidman, J. (2018). Pedagogies of forgetting: Colonial encounters and nationhood at New Zealand's National Museum. In T. Epstein & C. L. Peck (Eds.), *Teaching and learning difficult histories in international contexts: A critical sociocultural approach* (pp. 95–108). New York, NY: Routledge.

Kidron, C. A. (2013). Being there together: Dark family tourism and the emotive experience of co-presence in the holocaust past. *Annals of Tourism Research*, 41, 175–194. doi:10.1016/j.annals.2012.12.009

Kladou, S., & Mavragani, E. (2015). Assessing destination image: An online marketing approach and the case of TripAdvisor. *Journal of Destination Marketing & Management*, 4, 187–193. doi:10.1016/j.jdmm.2015.04.003

Klein, H. S. (1986). *African slavery in Latin America and the Caribbean*. New York, NY: Oxford University Press.

Kusumasondjaja, S., Shanka, T., & Marchegiani, C. (2012). Credibility of online reviews and initial trust: The roles of reviewer's identity and review valence. *Journal of Vacation Marketing*, 18, 185–195. doi:10.1177/1356766712449365

Laing, J. H., & Crouch, G. I. (2009). Myth, adventure and fantasy at the frontier: Metaphors and imagery behind an extraordinary travel experience. *International Journal of Tourism Research*, 11, 127–141. doi:10.1002/jtr.716

Law, R. (2006). Internet and tourism—part XXI: TripAdvisor. *Journal of Travel & Tourism Marketing*, 20(1), 75–77. doi:10.1300/J073v20n01_06

Lee, H., Law, R., & Murphy, J. (2011). Helpful reviewers in TripAdvisor, an online travel community. *Journal of Travel & Tourism Marketing, 28*, 675–688. doi:10.1080/10548408.2011.611739

Lehrer, E., & Milton, C. E. (2011). Introduction: Witness to witnessing. In E. Lehrer, C. E. Milton, &
M. E. Patterson (Eds.), *Curating difficult knowledge: Violent pasts in public places* (pp. 1–22).
Houndmills: Palgrave Macmillan.

Logan, W., & Reeves, K. (2009). Introduction: Remembering places of pain and shame. In W.
Logan & K. Reeves (Eds.), *Places of pain and shame: Dealing with 'difficult heritage'* (pp. 1–22).
Houndmills: Palgrave Macmillan.

Macdonald, S. (2016). Is 'difficult heritage' still 'difficult'? Why public acknowledgement of past
perpetration may no longer be so unsettling to collective identities. *Museum International,
265–268*, 6–22.

Markwell, K., & Waitt, G. (2009). Festivals, space and sexuality: Gay pride in Australia. *Tourism
Geographies, 11*, 143–168.

McCabe, S., & Foster, C. (2006). The role and function of narrative in tourist interaction. *Journal
of Tourism and Cultural Change, 4*, 194–215.

Miguéns, J., Baggio, R., & Costa, C. (2008, May). Social media and tourism destinations:
TripAdvisor case study. Proceedings of IASK Advances in Tourism Research 2008 (pp. 1–6).
Aveiro, Portugal.

Modlin, J., E. A. (2008). Tales told on the tour: Mythic representations of slavery by docents at
North Carolina plantation museums. *Southeastern Geographer, 48*, 265–287.

Modlin, E. A, Jr., Alderman, D. H., & Gentry, G. W. (2011). Tour guides as creators of empathy:
The role of affective inequality in marginalizing the enslaved at plantation house museums.
Tourist Studies, 11(1), 3–19.

Mowatt, R. A., & Chancellor, C. H. (2011). Visiting death and life: Dark tourism and slave castles.
Annals of Tourism Research, 38, 1410–1434.

Nelson, V. (2015). Tourist identities in narratives of unexpected adventure in Madeira.
International Journal of Tourism Research, 17, 537–544.

Potter, A. E. (2016). 'She goes into character as the lady of the house': Tour guides, performance,
and the southern plantation. *Journal of Heritage Tourism, 11*, 250–261.

Preston-Whyte, R. (2004). The beach as a liminal space. In A. A. Lew, C. M. Hall, & A. M. Williams
(Eds.), *A companion to tourism* (pp. 349–359). Malden: Blackwell Publishing.

Pritchard, A., & Morgan, N. (2006). Hotel Babylon? Exploring hotels as liminal sites of transition
and transgression. *Tourism Management, 27*, 762–772.

Rickly-Boyd, J. M. (2009). The tourist narrative. *Tourist Studies, 9*, 259–280.

Riessman, C. K. (2004). Narrative analysis. In M. S. Lewis-Beck, A. Bryman, & T. F. Liao (Eds.), *The
SAGE encyclopedia of social science research methods* (Vol. 1, pp. 705–708). Thousand Oaks:
SAGE Publications.

Rojek, C. (1993). *Ways of escape: Modern transformations in leisure and travel.* Houndmills:
Macmillan Press.

Samuels, J. (2015). Difficult heritage: Coming 'to terms' with Sicily's Fascist past. In K. Lafrenz
Samuels & T. Rice (Eds.), *Heritage keywords: Rhetoric and redescription in cultural heritage* (pp.
111–128). Boulder: University of Colorado Press.

Sather-Wagstaff, J. (2015). Heritage and memory. In E. Waterton & S. Watson (Eds.), *The Palgrave
handbook of contemporary heritage research* (pp. 191–204). Houndmills: Palgrave Macmillan.

Simon, R. I. (2011a). A shock to thought: Curatorial judgment and the public exhibition of
'difficult knowledge. *Memory Studies, 4*, 432–449.

Simon, R. I. (2011b). Afterword: The turn to pedagogy: A needed conversation on the practice of
curating difficult knowledge. In E. Lehrer, C. E. Milton, & M. E. Patterson (Eds.), *Curating difficult knowledge: Violent pasts in public places* (pp. 193–209). Houndmills: Palgrave Macmillan.

Small, S. (2013). Still back of the Big House: Slave cabins and slavery in southern heritage tourism. *Tourism Geographies, 15*, 405–423.

Statistics Netherlands. (2017). Trends in the Caribbean Netherlands 2017. The Hague: Statistics
Netherlands. Retrieved from Statistics Netherlands website: https://www.cbs.nl/en-gb/publica-
tion/2017/50/trends-in-the-caribbean-netherlands-2017

Statistics Netherlands. (2018). *Tourism in the Caribbean Netherlands in 2017*. The Hague: Statistics Netherlands. Retrieved from Bonaire Official Tourism website: https://www.tourismbonaire.com.

Stone, P. R. (2006). A dark tourism spectrum: Towards a typology of death and macabre related tourist sites, attractions and exhibitions. *Tourism, 54*, 145–160.

Thomas, D. R. (2006). A general inductive approach for analysing qualitative evaluation data. *American Journal of Evaluation, 27*, 237–246.

Thomas, S., Seitsonen, O., & Herva, V. (2016). Nazi memorabilia, dark heritage and treasure hunting as 'alternative' tourism: Understanding the fascination with the material remains of World War II in Northern Finland. *Journal of Field Archaeology, 41*, 331–343.

Thomassen, B. (2009). The uses and meanings of liminality. *International Political Anthropology, 2*(1), 5–22.

Thomassen, B. (2012). Revisiting liminality: The danger of empty spaces. In H. Andrews & L. Roberts (Eds.), *Liminal landscapes: Travel, experience and spaces in-between* (pp. 21–35). London: Routledge.

Tourism Corporation Bonaire. (2018). Bonaire official tourism site. Retrieved from https://www.tourismbonaire.com

TripAdvisor. (2017). TripAdvisor media center. Retrieved from https://tripadvisor.mediaroom.com/us-about-us

Turner, V. (1974). *Dramas, fields, and metaphors: Symbolic action in human society*. Ithaca: Cornell University Press.

Turner, V. (1977). Variations on a theme of liminality. In S. F. Moore & B. G. Myerhoff (Eds.), *Secular ritual* (pp. 36–52). Amsterdam: Van Gorcum.

Turner, V. (1979). Frame, flow and reflection: Ritual and drama as public liminality. *Japanese Journal of Religious Studies, 6*, 465–499.

Turner, V. (1982). *From ritual to theatre: The human seriousness of play*. New York City: Performing Arts Journal Publications.

Turner, V. (1986). *The anthropology of performance*. New York City: PAJ Publications.

van Gennep, A. (1960). *The rites of passage* (M. B. Vizedom & G. L. Caffee, Trans.). Chicago: The University of Chicago Press.

Vásquez, C. (2012). Narrativity and involvement in online consumer reviews: The case of TripAdvisor. *Narrative Inquiry, 22*(1), 105–121.

Volo, S. (2010). Bloggers' reported tourist experiences: Their utility as a tourism data source and their effect on prospective tourists. *Journal of Vacation Marketing, 16*, 297–311.

West-Durán, A. (2003). The Netherlands Antilles (Curaçao, Bonaire, St. Eustatius, Saba), Aruba, and St. Maarten. In A. West-Durán (Ed.), *African Caribbeans: A reference guide* (pp. 141–156). Westport, CT: Greenwood Press.

Yankholmes, A., & McKercher, B. (2015). Rethinking slavery heritage tourism. *Journal of Heritage Tourism, 10*, 233–247.

Zembylas, M. (2014). Theorizing 'difficult knowledge' in the aftermath of the 'affective turn': Implications for curriculum and pedagogy in handling traumatic representations. *Curriculum Inquiry, 44*, 390–412.

Zembylas, M. (2018). Teacher resistance towards difficult histories: The centrality of affect in disrupting teacher learning. In T. Epstein & C. L. Peck (Eds.), *Teaching and learning difficult histories in international contexts: A critical sociocultural approach* (pp. 189–202). New York: Routledge.

Communitas in fright tourism

Robert S. Bristow

ABSTRACT

Liminality offers an explanation of the threshold one passes through as they enter a tourist destination. Beginning with the anticipation phase of the experience a tourist travels to a destination for an on-site experience. Multiple thresholds occur for the tourist, yet during the periods prior to the actual event, motivations will likely draw or repel the individual. For dark tourism research none have reviewed these liminal experiences in fright tourism, the more entertaining and lighter aspect of the dark elder. To better understand the anticipation stage of the liminal experience, the influence of fear while entering a haunted attraction is explored. Fear is expected to contribute to the fun of these haunted attractions. During this liminal phase, communitas evolve where the social bonding of the visitors develops during the encounter. Characteristics of these groups are examined in this exploratory study.

摘要

阈限为人们进入旅游目的地所经历的临界状态提供了一种解释。从体验的预期阶段开始, 游客前往目的地进行现场体验。游客会出现多个临界点, 但在实际活动之前, 动机可能会吸引或排斥游客。对于黑暗旅游的研究, 没有人评论过这些在恐惧旅游中的阈限体验, 黑暗旅游中老年游客更有趣和更轻松的方面。为了更好地理解阈限体验的预期阶段, 我们探讨了进入闹鬼景点时恐惧的影响。恐惧被认为是这些闹鬼景点的乐趣之一。在这一阈限阶段, 旅游者在这种旅游偶遇中发展出社会连接, 随之演化出旅游者共同体。本探索研究探讨了这些群体的特征。

Introduction

Macabre related tourism is nothing new. Travelers have visited famous tombs over the millennia and excursions to sites of human conflict has been popular for about as long (Boorstin, 1992/1961; Collins-Kreiner, 2016; Dale & Robinson, 2011; Hartmann, 2014; Lennon & Foley, 2000a; Seaton, 1996). Boorstin (1992/1961) notes for example, that tours to hangings in the United Kingdom were widely found in the early 19th century. These forms of macabre tourism exist under the general heading of heritage tourism. Collectively these travels are known as thanatourism (Seaton, 1996), dark tourism (Foley & Lennon, 1996) and others. From this origin, for the past two decades researchers have sought to understand the relationship between tourists and death around the globe (Bowman & Pezzullo, 2009; Light, 2017).

Research devoted to death related themes in tourism has explored the interest in sites of the holocaust (Lennon & Foley, 2000b; Miles, 2002), slavery (Mowatt & Chancellor, 2011; Rice, 2009), disasters (Robbie, 2008; Stone, 2013b; Yankovska & Hannam, 2014), genocide (Beech, 2000; Isaac & Çakmak, 2016), prisons (Goc, 2002; Strange & Kempa, 2003; Wilson, 2004), and dark fun factories (Stone, 2006; Stone, 2010). In view of this wide interest and the associated demand of death related tourism, it appears that dark tourism opportunities contribute to the "tourist gaze" (Seaton & Lennon, 2004; Stone, 2006; Stone & Sharpley, 2008; Urry & Larsen, 2011).

Multiple attempts to understand the motivation for dark tourism exist. If we explore the demand side of dark tourism, Seaton (1996) advocates a behavioral approach in thanatourism, driven by the motivations toward visiting sites found along a continuum. At one end is the fascination with death where the traveler has no personal connection with the deceased. At the opposite end, the traveler is familiar with the deceased and the visit is more important on a personal level. This end of Seaton's (1996) continuum includes religious ceremonies where we can find the reenactment of death. Sharpley (2005) builds on Seaton's thesis by suggesting a "paler" shared experience of dark tourism. The consumption of the dark experience is still driven by the interest in death, but brings people together in celebration, remembrance or mourning. It also creates of collective communal celebration similar to Turner's (1969) Communitas.

On the other hand Stone (2006) offers his dark tourism spectrum. His darkest to lightest framework is anchored by 'sites of death and suffering' and at the lighter end 'sites associated with death and suffering.' At the darkest end, authentic horror-related tourism opportunities seek to preserve the message the site exhibits. But he also recognized that not all sites of death or those associated with death are authentic. This opens the definition of dark tourism to include those non-authentic sites that provide a unique opportunity for entertainment tourism (Stone, 2006). Another study of dark tourism motivations was proposed by Raine (2013) where a dark tourist spectrum includes nine types of dark tourists. For the darker end, a more spiritual and deeply engaged experience is found. At her lightest end, the passive recreationists' visit is a more spontaneous and superficial visit. The motivation of dark attractions varies by the type of person as much as the type of destination. In sum, these authors suggest different motivations feed the interest in dark tourism.

Much of the interest in death is reinforced by popular media and the insatiable appetite for real frightful events around the world. For instance, the *Tragical History of the Life and Death of Doctor Faustus,* the late 16th century theatrical production, was an early dramatization of human horrors. And the early 20th century German silent horror films *Das Cabinet des Dr. Caligari* (1919) and *Nosferatu* (1921) brought terror to the masses and fed the demand for terror entertainment (Tamborini & Weaver, 1996). Engaging the spectator in cinematic horror entertainment rose to a pinnacle during the 1950s and 60s as ballyhoo-extraordinaire William Castle produced and directed *Macabre* (1958) and *House on Haunted Hill* (1959) to the delight and fright of the audiences (Clepper, 2016). This sustained fascination with fear has become part of our entertainment package. Likewise, recent research in Eastern Europe discovered that some dark destinations in Poland include elements of both fear and fun linking the two different motivations. "Death is inextricably connected with fear … but also entertainment" (Tanaś, 2014, p. 22). Consequently for entertainment, the feelings of fear may motivate the tourist.

Beyond media, ghoulish entertainment has grown from the travelling carnivals over the past centuries. Ripley's Believe It or Not, carnival freak shows and other displays of the unusual fed the appetite of tourists and peaked in the late 19th century (Bogdan, 1988). Today this interest continues even though we live in a world of terror, bombings and other human atrocities, fueling a voyeuristic appeal of the macabre (Christie & Lauro, 2011; Buda & McIntosh, 2013). Given the preponderance of popular media devoted to horror, this essay explores the relationship of these real life fears for a lighter and more entertaining form of dark tourism called fright tourism.

The rest of this paper follows this structure. A literature review highlights four main themes. First a brief discussion of liminality, liminoid and communitas' theories related to tourism is introduced. This is then linked to travel behavior representing a liminoid event. Fear related motivations felt during the liminoid phases in a fright tourism attraction is next explained. The research hypothesis linking liminoid, communitas, travel behavior and fear is then introduced within the summary of the literature. Next the methods for testing communitas in fright tourism are found including the survey instrument utilized in this paper. Results are discussed and the paper ends with some concluding remarks.

Literature

Liminality is anthropologically associated with the *Rites of Passage* (van Gennep, 1909/1960). Examples of the passages are the periods exhibited by the transition from adolescence to adulthood, getting married or having a child. One would expect this transition to be filled with fears, given the uncertainties that lie ahead. During the passage three unique and distinct phases are found. Beginning with separation, a pre-liminal phase, one is separated from a normal environment. Next the individual faces an ambiguous and unknown period called liminal. This second phase is temporary and fleeting. Finally, the rite of incorporation (post-liminal phase) evolves when the individual moves to a higher social status with greater responsibilities.

Turner (1969) built on this concept and noted the liminal period as one that is 'betwixt and between.' As an example, the individual is neither a boy nor a man. There is a loss of power and control (i.e., uncertainties) during the liminal phase and this is a common element as one moves through the stages. Noting that not all liminal events are rituals, Turner (1974) generalized the simple movement from one stage to another, and called it liminoid. This flexibility has opened the opportunity for the social sciences to explore human behavior in a more holistic manner.

Tourism scholars have explored liminality for over thirty years (Andrews & Roberts, 2012; Brooker & Joppe, 2014; Crouch, 2000; Lett, 1983; Light, 2009; Preston-Whyte, 2004; Pritchard & Morgan, 2006; Varley, 2011). The tourist is known to be a consumer of place, but also one who produces that space (Crouch, 2000). As an example,

Pritchard and Morgan (2006) explored the liminality of a hotel, where guests behave in a different manner than one would find at home. This suggests the on-site hotel experience could be encouraged by an unseen influence. The breadth and depth of understanding the transitional period of travel is an important one to understand since it can impact the overall encounter for the visitor.

Adding to this ambiguity, Preston-Whyte (2004, p. 249) states "(l)iminality is an elusive concept." Thomassen (2009, p. 5) adds that "(l)iminality is indeed not *any* concept. Liminality does not and cannot "explain". In Liminality there is no certainty concerning the outcome." Given that liminality has become as Downey, Kinane, and Parker (2016, p. 3) call the "catch-all expression for an ambiguous, transitional, or interstitial spatio-temporal dimensions" here we are challenged with defining it under those restraints in the tourist experience.

For dark heritage tourism there is a logical ambiguity since these spaces can be viewed as both sacred and dreadful (Osbaldiston & Petray, 2011). This double role of dark sites means the tourist may be attracted and repelled at the same time. One's fear may either attract the individual to a dark destination, but may also act as a barrier to travel. Morbid curiosity may attract visitation for some while others decide not to visit at all. Taking into consideration the dangerous uncertainty of liminality and an association with death (Andrews & Roberts, 2012), linking dark tourism encounters with liminality makes sense.

During this liminal period, Turner (1969) noted the formation of a community called communitas. This refers to the realization of a social bond between strangers who, regardless of their individual backgrounds, temporarily find that they have a shared interest during the liminal phase. In the historic ritualized experience, they are also beholden to the elders, so this bond develops among the individuals that break down the social norms and the differentiation between classes. All are now equal as they face the unknown of the future.

Communitas are also found in tourist groups where social inhibitions are loosened (Campo & Ryan, 2008; Lett, 1983; Yarnal & Kerstetter, 2005). Night-time entertainment in urban centers is a good example where social norms are relaxed (Campo & Ryan, 2008). Typically these districts attract a younger clientele who are fearless in their behavior. Equally, Lett (1983) found yacht tourism in the British Virgin Islands yields freedom to behave beyond the standards of normal accepted life. The communitas formed during this ludic experience is fun, freely created and liminal.

For many trips, tour packages are supported by staff to assist the travelers. These guides are credited for a significant contribution to the tourist experience (Cohen, 1985; Yankovska & Hannam, 2014). In addition to normal customer service roles, the tour staff steer the visitors to bond in the touristic communitas. This guidance is important since like the liminal elders, the staff in tourist settings choreograph the tourists' experience (Eco, 1986; Gentry, 2007; Weiler & Black, 2015).

Travel phases

Travel involves movement. The opportunity to break away from the norms of daily life is an important aspect of tourism. Yet liminality is a logical evolution for tourists since they are leaving the comfort of home to travel, crossing some threshold or boundary to some unknown experience (Goodnow & Ruddell, 2009). The authors suggest that in addition to physical preparation for an adventure tour, the process includes the evolution of some spiritual journey. One needs to be physically and emotionally prepared for the travel experience since there are unknowns to be encountered. These unknowns might represent the fears that must be overcome during the pre-liminal and liminal phases as described by van Gennep (1909/1960).

The traveler will think about the trip, travel to it, enjoy some onsite time, return home and later have memories. These five phases are what Clawson and Knetsch (1966) called the recreation experience and offers a fuller explanation of the entirety of the tourist event. Others propose similar descriptions of the tourist event (Hunter & Shaw, 2007; Lew, 2012; Light, 2009; Nelson, 2017; White & White, 2004). And just like the ritualized experience written by van Gennep (1909/1960) the traveler can anticipate several transitions. Anticipation of the unknown is found during several stages of the experience and may not be merely confined to the pre-travel phase. There may be no clear transition during the liminal experience resulting in multiple liminal encounters where individuals wait to move to the next phase. For example, Nelson (2017) suggests the blending of the on-site experience with anticipation. For this study, the anticipation and travel to phases provide a logical transformation from a pre-liminal to liminal experience as one leaves home and awaits the unknown and potential fearful future.

Fear and fright tourism

The study of fear has a long history. Hall (1897) was one of the earliest scholars to undertake this task and discovered fears of the supernatural are one of the most common experienced by people, driven by the unknown. Darkness, ghosts, dreams and solitude were feared by nearly fifty percent of his sample of 1701. Interestingly, "celestial phenomena" including weather was the most feared (Hall, 1897, p. 152). And coincidentally these are not unlike the typical fears that tourists may face during their travels today (Dolnicar, 2005).

Whether it is death, or dark or fright, fear is expected to contribute some emotions to the tourist (Stone, 2006). For the most part, fear studies in tourism have concentrated on the physical risk of adventure tourism (Carnicelli-Filho, Schwartz, & Tahara, 2010), psychological harm (Biran & Buda, 2018) consumer behaviour (Dolnicar, 2005), terrorism (Floyd, Gibson, Pennington-Gray, & Thapa, 2004), and even the paranormal (Holloway, 2010; Mathe-Soulek, Aguirre, & Dallinger, 2016; Rittichainuwat, 2011). In these cases, the fear of the unknown is the feeling one may have when the hairs of the back of the neck rise. That fear may not be seen, but it is certainly felt during the encounter (Heholt & Downing, 2016).

Like the spectrum of dark tourism, these examples illustrate the variety of fears a tourist may face, suggesting the tourists' sensation seeking behavior could even be immoral, unhealthy or dangerous (Williams, 2009). Following the long standing demand for fear related entertainment, this interest in the "bizarre, the morbid and the strange" changes the definition of dark tourism where the abandonment of historic references takes place to one based on the influence of modern day horrors (Ryan, 2005, p. 148). In these cases, death may be real or just hinted for the tourist.

Dark tourism research on the demand side has explored the motivation and characteristics of the tourist (Bigley, Lee, Chon, & Yoon, 2010; Blom, 2000; Fonseca, Seabra, & Silva, 2015), "ghoulish titillation" (Wilson, 2008, p. 169) and a fascination with evil (Lennon, 2010). But here we are specifically judging fear as a motivation and a pull factor to an attraction, (Ashworth & Isaac, 2015) especially for the lighter forms of dark tourism. The attraction to fear is atypical for most tourist opportunities, yet in this case is expected to not only contribute to the experience but may enhance it as well.

A fear of the macabre and tourism is one for debate and yields, if anything, acknowledgment of the breadth and depth of death enhanced tourist attractions. Light (2017) reviewed this history and found no clear consensus of how to approach death related tourism research. There continues to be some debate regarding the moral ramifications of studying death and tourism (Stone, 2013a). Since there are so many ways to explain dark tourism (e.g., Raine, 2013; Seaton, 1996; Sharpley, 2005; Stone, 2006; Stone & Sharpley, 2008), one unified theme is the lighter/paler/inauthentic aspect under investigation in this paper.

Commodification of dark tourism themes are found for ghosts in Scotland (Inglis & Holmes, 2003), and the horrific exhibition of the Salem Witch Trials in Massachusetts (Olbrys Gencarella, 2007; Weir, 2012). Business operators in Salem, for example, acknowledge the interest in providing both fear and fun experiences for the dark attractions in Witch City (Weidmann, 2016). Yet this commodification is not widely accepted. The additional responsibility and challenges facing some communities are being felt as they grasp with the demand of a dark attraction (Heidelberg, 2015). But since most dark tourism sites are intrinsically tied to specific resources, the advancement of lighter forms of dark tourism is possible in more destinations around the globe since they are not place dependent.

A recent review of dark tourist destinations in London found the most popular were the lighter forms that emphasize entertainment (Powell & Iankova, 2016; Powell, Kennell, & Barton, 2018). Haunted attractions include many facilities managed by the Merlin Entertainments Group who oversee Madame Tussauds and The Dungeons. Madame Tussauds Wax Museum is particularly interesting since Eco (1986) notes we know the figures are fake but we still are attracted to them. Sites for lighter dark tourism may exhibit "hyper reality" experiences desired by tourists (Eco, 1986; Seaton, 2009). Given the rise in popularity of lighter dark tourism, another term is needed.

Fright tourism occurs when a tourist seeks a scary opportunity for pleasure at a destination that may have a sinister history or may be promoted to have one (Bristow & Newman, 2004). Key in this experience is the demand for something viewed as 'fearful' and 'fun', while the supply is expected to exhibit some horrific heritage or the manifestation as such. The demand for fearful fun is viewed as a motivation of the visitor and death-related supply is set up to accommodate that demand.

Moreover, fright tourism seeks an inauthentic encounter via the liminal experience that is temporary and fleeting yielding some escapism. Tourists want the thrill of a good time, but also desire the shudder of the bad (Eco, 1986). Therefore, you cannot assess fright tourism in the same manner as the more traditional dark tourism model.

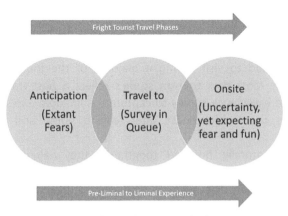

Figure 1. Model of fright tourist travel phases (Source: Author).

After all, entertainment is certainly absent from a pilgrimage or an educational opportunity that may drive the interest in the more traditional dark tourism.

This review has illustrated the literature on liminality, liminoid and communitas and blended these themes to a better understanding of the anticipation and travel to phases for tourists. Fear is an attraction in fright tourism since the participant also knows it will be fun. By asking fright tourists about their fears during the anticipation phase (Clawson & Knetsch, 1966) also known as pre-liminal phase (van Gennep, 1909/1960), we gain an understanding of how fears influence our motivation prior to entering a fun, yet scary liminal haunted attraction. This relationship is illustrated in Figure 1 and links the theories of travel phases to liminality as our fright tourist leaves the safety of home to enter a haunted attraction.

For this analysis, since visitors to a haunted attraction will travel with family and/or friends, it is expected that fear will vary across communitas. Family fears may be different than those exhibited by fright tourists who travel with friends. It is hypothesized that since fright tourists seek a fearful and fun experience by attending a haunted attraction, capturing their impressions of fears at the point of most vulnerability, that is, the pre-liminal phase while waiting in line, will yield a better understanding of fears for these tourists.

Methods

The bulk of research on dark tourism is based on qualitative and observational methods (Light, 2017). This makes sense since the place attachment attributed to these sites is often personal and moving, especially for pilgrimages. Sharpley (2009) also notes the preponderance of studies have surveyed the supply side of dark tourism without exploring elements of the demand. For this study a quantitative instrument explores fears in a liminal experience.

To understand the fears found in liminal communitas, participants visiting a haunted attraction were sought. A well-attended attraction called DementedFX, in Holyoke, Massachusetts was selected as the site for the survey. The site is an old factory building in a former industrial/commercial zoned district that adds to the mysterious ambiance of the experience. To assess the measures of fear of participants a survey instrument was prepared. The instrument was administered to the guests wait-ing in the queue, that is the pre-liminal phase, to enter the haunted house. The attrac-tion was open evenings on weekends during the month of October 2016. The dates were randomly selected to visit during a majority of the fourteen nights that the attraction was open. Most dark tourism studies reflect a post travel experience (see Bittner, 2011). A pre experience survey to capture the liminoid experience is used here and better reflects the liminal phase after leaving home and before the actual onsite experience.

Participants were naturally "huddled" together as they waited in line. Like the lim-inal ritual, the movement from one stage to the next is controlled by the "elders" or the haunted attraction staff. The queue is similar to the beach, neither land nor water (Preston-Whyte, 2004); you are not safe nor are you in hell, yet. The elders have strict control of you, symbolically moving into a higher status of being immersed in the hyper-reality of fright tourism. This immersion as Podoshen (2013) in his dark music entertainment research suggests, permits the tourist to fully experience death related emotions. Like dark music, this entertainment is based on a visit to a haunted attraction.

The haunted attraction staff is instrumental in the liminal experience, just like the elders in the ritual. Eco (1986, p. 48) explains the tourist/staff relationship akin to the management of Disneyland as "a place of total passivity. Its visitor must agree to behave like its robots." Controlling the liminal phase during a period of greatest vul-nerability enhances the liminal nature for the guests. This is a known point of anticipa-tion that heightens the experience (Light, 2009).

Fright tourists were grouped as they entered the attraction so the first step was to introduce the study to the guests and ask for a spokesperson to represent the group in the survey. Next the group identity was determined for the travelling companions as friends, family or both. Each spokesperson was asked "Ok, next I am going to ask your opinion about how frightful the following terms are to you. On a scale of 1-10 with 1 being not frightful and 10 being most frightful." Examples of the real fears explored are crime, natural disasters, personal phobias, future health and others. To test the fear characteristics of communitas, a Principal Component Analysis (PCA) is used to reduce the number of fears into a smaller set of factors to help define how similar fears may be viewed.

This tool creates a set of new variables that are exact mathematical (transforma-tions) of the original data (Nie, Hull, Jenkins, Steinbrenner, & Bent, 1975). Further each factor (component) are independent (uncorrelated) of one another and will result on a smaller set of groups of variables. Finally the first component represents the largest amount of variance in the data (Kim & Mueller, 1978). This identifies the set of most important fears for the group.

Tourism scholars have used PCA or the variant Factor Analysis to study motivations for the traveler (Chang, 2017; Chen & Tsai, 2019; Kozak, 2002; Meng, Tepanon, & Uysal, 2008). Chen and Tsai (2019) found several key motivations related to visitation to dark destinations including personal, spiritual, experience, physical and emotional. These factors are tied to history of the Kinmen Battlefield, Taiwan and illustrate examples of

Table 1. Descriptive statistics for the fear measures.

Fear	N	Mean	SD
Crime (Murder, rape, theft, fraud)	171	5.8012	2.8586
Government (Corruption, privacy, immigration, trust, control)	170	6.0706	3.2189
Human-caused Disasters (Climate change, terrorism, war, environmental disaster)	171	7.0058	2.5286
Natural Disasters (Earthquakes, droughts, floods, hurricanes)	169	5.8698	2.7026
Personal Phobias (Tight spaces, darkness, insects)	166	5.4217	3.1742
Personal Health (Death, illness, injury)	166	5.3253	3.0375
Financial Future (Running out of money, loss of jobs, housing)	167	6.7246	2.8950
Technology (Artificial intelligence, invasion of privacy, cyber terrorism, drones)	167	4.4970	2.9836

Note: Responses recorded on a 1-10 scale with 10 being most frightful.

motivations driving visitation. Chang (2017) discovered fears and other intense negative emotions, for tourists visiting dark destinations using this approach.

One hundred and seventy one surveys were administered to a spokesperson of each group representing a total of 570 visitors. Average group size was four and equally made up of women and men. The data represents an approximate sample of 5.7% of the 10,000 paying guests.

Results

In order to assess the fears of the visitors, the spokesperson was asked to rate how frightful eight different fears were to them on a scale of 1-10 with 1 being not frightful and 10 being most frightful. The survey was administered to the guests while in the queue. Nearly eighty percent of the sample had visited some haunted attraction in the past showing the popularity and continued commitment of guests to haunted attractions. Of that number, only nine had visited DementedFX before. Typically fright attractions will have similar scares e.g., tight spaces, strobe lights, loud sounds and so on, yet the draw to haunted attractions is the unexpected (Hoedt, 2009).

For the overall sample, the strongest fear is found for Human-Caused Disasters (mean = 7.00/10.00). Further this fear is fairly consistent among the sample with the smallest standard deviation (SD = 2.52) indicating a general consensus in the importance of that fear. Least fearful is technology (mean = 4.49, SD = 2.98). Table 1 provides the mean values and standard deviation of fears for the fright tourists.

The fundamental theme here is fear. Given this underlying construct it is hypothesized that additional analysis may group like fears to define the manner in which fear contributes to the motivations of the fright tourists. To explore the characteristics of the communitas a principle component analysis was performed. As a data reduction procedure, the statistics yield a smaller set of groups to help explain the common concerns of fear by those who visited the haunted attraction with friends, family or a combination of both. Groups of friends made up 56 percent of the sample (n = 94), family groups totaled 26.3 percent (45) and groups comprised of both total 16.4 percent (28). Cronbach's Alpha for the all the fear measures is 0.709, illustrative of a reliable and consistent survey instrument made up of Likert style questions (Vaske, 2008).

The principal component analysis with varimax rotation with Kaiser Normalization was performed on the measures of fear for the entire sample (Table 2). Correlations range from 0.04 to 0.29 suggesting a large amount of independence among the fears and communalities range from 0.358 to 0.656. The correlation matrix determinant of

Table 2. Principal component analysis for fear measures in fright tourism.

Fear	Loading	Eigenvalue	Variance Explained	Cumulative Variance Explained	Alpha
Factor 1 (Certain Fears)		2.703	33.787	33.787	0.678
Crime	0.652				
Human-caused disasters	0.646				
Natural disasters	0.706				
Personal Phobias	0.557				
Personal Health	0.659				
Factor 2 (Uncertain Fears)		1.138	14.224	48.011	0.539
Government	0.808				
Financial Future	0.618				
Technology	0.662				

Note: KMO = 0.771, Bartlett's Chi Square = 187.93, p = 0.000, Correlation Matrix Determinant = 0.303.

0.303 and is greater than 0.0001 indicating a low collinearity. Bartlett's Test of Sphericity was highly significant at p = 0.000 (Field, 2013). The Kaiser-Meyer-Olkin Measure of Sampling Adequacy was 0.771 which is above the acceptable limit of 0.50 (Kaiser & Rice, 1974). The eight fears were reduced to two factors exceeding an eigenvalue of 1.0 and after the varimax rotation, the two factors accounted for 48.01 percent of the variance. This result yields a modest explanation, but given the number of fears (8) compared to the sample size (171) while the intercorrelation of the fears is so weak, no reduction in the number of fears is recommended.

The first factor includes Crime, Human-Caused Disasters, Natural Disasters, Personal Phobias, and Personal Health. These account for 33.8 percent of the variance and have similar loadings. These fears may be thought as certain since they are well known. The second factor includes Government, Financial Future and Technology and yield a cumulative 48.01 percent variance explained. Collectively these fears may represent the uncertain fears, given the great variability. Though modest in explanation, as an initial exploration into the motivations of fright tourists, it does begin to explore contributions of fear as an attractive pull to fright attractions.

Similar factors are found for those who visited the haunted attraction with Friends (Table 3). The loadings are different, even though the factors are grouped in the same manner as the principal component analysis of entire sample. Those visiting the haunted attraction yield a similar cumulative variance (48.79%) and one possible explanation for the similar factors may be that the friends are the largest group in our sample with 94 groups of friends out of a total of 171 sampled and the sub group (friends) behaves like the entire sample. Further this internal consistency is adequate with Cronbach's alphas yielding 0.678 for the first component.

The results for families are found in Table 4. Interestingly just one factor is found for families. The communitas of family members seems to illustrate a common shared experience. Perhaps less uncertainty or variation of fears is experienced by families and that all fears, regardless of the impact on motivations, contribute to the visitation. For example, had the family experienced in some manner the devastation of a natural disaster like a hurricane it is likely the effect would have been felt by all, unlike those groups traveling with friends who may not have the same history. Also the family bond might already be strong through the anticipation phase of the fright tourism experience. However, since only one factor is found for families, the PCA does not

Table 3. Principal component analysis for fear measures for friends.

Fear Friends	Mean	Loading	Eigenvalue	Variance Explained	Cumulative Variance Explained	Alpha
Factor 1			2.325	29.067	29.067	0.678
Natural Disasters	5.677	0.776				
Crime	5.659	0.685				
Personal Health	5.355	0.616				
Personal Phobias	5.538	0.588				
Human-caused Disasters	7.042	0.554				
Factor 2			1.578	19.726	48.792	0.539
Government	6.074	0.793				
Technology	4.142	0.723				
Financial Future	6.527	0.62				

Note: KMO = 0.671, Bartlett's Chi Square = 99.635, p = 0.000, Correlation Matrix Determinant = 0.308.

Table 4. Principal component analysis for fear measures for family.

Fear Family	Mean	Loading	Eigenvalue	Variance Explained	Cumulative Variance Explained	Alpha
Human-caused Disasters	7.066	0.794	3.673	45.911	45.911	0.709
Natural Disasters	6.204	0.757				
Personal Health	5.659	0.733				
Technology	4.431	0.697				
Financial Future	3.386	0.645				
Personal Phobias	5.181	0.638				
Crime	6.133	0.590				
Government	6.288	0.524				

Note: KMO = 0.769, Bartlett's Chi Square = 104.944, p = 0.000, Correlation Matrix Determinant = 0.065.

Table 5. Principal component analysis for fear measures for both friends and family.

Fear Friends/Family	Mean	Loading	Eigen value	Variance explained	Cumulative variance explained	Alpha
Factor 1			2.377	29.718	29.718	0.596
Natural Disasters	5.71	0.819				
Financial Future	6.64	0.745				
Personal Phobias	5.70	0.741				
Technology	5.50	0.718				
Factor 2			1.754	21.922	51.641	0.456
Crime	6.03	0.786				
Government	5.70	0.747				
Human-caused Disasters	6.96	0.620				
Factor 3			1.065	13.313	64.954	na
Personal Health	4.71	0.881				

Note: KMO = 0.521, Bartlett's Chi Square = 42.276, p = 0.041, Correlation Matrix Determinant = 0.140.

provide an adequate explanation of the similarities of fears for family fright tourists. Additional exploration is warranted.

The final Principle Component Analysis is shown for groups travelling with both friends and family. Table 5 highlights the three factors discovered and yielded the highest Cumulative Variance Explained of 64.95 percent. While this group is the small-est of the sample (16.4%) it is interesting to note how the factors change. The third and solitary factor of Personal Health accounted for 13.3 percent of the variance. This may reflect the private nature of one's health, something that may be shared with a family member while not with a friend.

Cronbach Alpha reported is 0.596 for the first component and 0.456 for the second. Both are below the accepted threshold of 0.65 (Vaske, 2008). Give the small cohort here, the blending of companions with family and friends does not yield a strong enough description offered by the PCA. Likewise, the Bartlett's Test of Sphericity was just significant at $p = 0.041$ (Field, 2013). Communitas may not be strong when the companions are both friends and families. In order to identify common fears for communitas made up of friends and families, a larger sample is needed.

While the PCA groupings for friends and families are significant, the results are just modest. Increasing the ratio of fear variables based on sample size may improve the explanation (Field, 2013). For example, Meng et al. (2008) only included the destination attributes that had highest importance ratings. For the study here, the least important fear is technology (mean $= 4.49$, SD $= 2.98$). A repeat of PCA was performed without this variable and yielded similar results in terms of Cronbach's Alpha, correlation tables' determinant, KMO and Bartlett's Test of Sphericity significance. In these cases the change in statistical values was approximately five percent indicating only a modest change in importance. Also, in all cases, the significance of the statistics did not change so dropping the least important fear does not improve the explanation.

Likewise if we eliminate the fear that has the weakest overall loading (i.e., Phobia $= 0.556$ in Table 2) and rerun the analysis, an improvement may be found. A repeat of all the tests found the results to be relatively the same. The lack of differences may indicate the model for family and friends, while just acceptable and modest, is reliable for this exploratory study.

Discussion

In this study linking fears to the anticipation stage of the fright tourism experience, several unique findings are noted. The Principle Component Analysis provided some similarities and differences of the fears by those traveling with friends, family or a combination of both. The interviewer asked the spokesperson of the group to identify how fearful a set of fears are to them while the group was waiting in line for the haunted attraction. This period reflects the end of the travel to phase of the experience and the beginning of the on-site visit. It is a pre-liminal period since the individuals have left the safety of home and are preparing to enter the unknown haunted attraction (Figure 1).

Similar results are found between those traveling with friends and the analysis conducted for the entire sample. While sample sizes may offer one explanation, it might also be suggested that the results reflect the general feelings of a population just prior to the US Presidential election in November 2016. Government, financial future and technology were common concerns during the period. The other factor included fears that are more universally known. Typically, in travel decisions, groups of friends may count on one leader to make the plans (Decrop, 2006). The leader may consult with all members before taking the trip, but is still the organizer of the event. So it is possible the leader (survey spokesperson) may not reflect the general consensus of the communitas. The spokesperson's opinion however is respected.

Overall, given the statistical significance, groups composed of friends yield the most interesting results for the study. Since participants are friends, and the there is no knowing how long or deep the friendship may be, one can only speculate on how communitas' bond under this scenario. Further, the spokesperson may have asked the remainder of the group about fears, but in many cases, just answered the question under the circumstance of the survey design. In any case, a communita based on friend membership does provide an initial hint on the certain and uncertain fears facing the fright tourists.

Family ties in communitas are one possible reason for a unidimensional factor, even though not all families may share the same values and differences may still exist. It also represents the explanation that the fears are commonly linked as one factor in the statistics. However, Bilu (1988) found impediments in familial communitas. That is should the group be made up of siblings, the interfamily relationship can modify the experiences of a communita building pilgrimage. Sibling rivalry may dilute the bond in a communita. Yet family ties are generally longer than friendships and thereby support the scale of fears are found along a common agreement.

On the other hand families with children typically leave the decision making to the adult parents (Decrop, 2006). The unidimensional fears then may represent the collective and common fears. In either case, while it is known that the party was made up of family members, the composition of the family is not known.

Finally, groups made up of family and friends yielded three factors. One might have expected the factors to be the same as the entire sample, but that is not the case. Personal health stands out as a solitary dimension, uniquely absent from the other two factors. Since health concerns may be general (e.g., need to watch my diet) or severe, (e.g., need to watch my diet after that heart attack), the degree of importance can vary tremendously. And perhaps this is the reason for the third factor. Additionally since it is not known about the composition of the party, that is how many friends versus family comprise the group, the group interaction can vary tremendously. Given the small size of this cohort (16.4%) caution to the reader is needed due the relative size of the sample to the number of fears.

Gender differences were not considered for fear even though research has found that safety concerns varied between gender. Heimtun and Abelsen (2012) found this difference but also discovered men may still fear public spaces. If the men were fearless we did not test this. The reason for this decision is that since spokespersons for each group was self-selected. Some members of the group were not interested in the interview, while others tried to interject their opinion of the fears. We simply do not know the role of the spokesperson. They could have been the parent, the group guide or simply one that was interested in participating in the survey.

Conclusion

Fright tourism, despite the popularity in the UK and the US, has not been explored to the same extent as the darker parent. In part this may be due to the lack of respectability of this form of tourism. After all, fright tourism reminds us of "our collective and unacceptable past" (Lennon, 2017, p. 243). Yet a taste of a fright tourist experience may be enough for tourists since it provides the thrill without the risk (Boorstin (1992/1961). Boorstin (1992/1961, p. 79) even suggests the modern American tourist seeks "pseudo-events" and has come to expect "more strangeness and more familiarity" in that experience. Pseudo-events offer a nice description of leisure pursuits given the motivation to escape during a vacation and is certainly one found in fright tourism where fear and fun are sought.

Fright tourism management should pay attention to the assessment of fears by their guests. Catering to these fears can enhance the fear and fun of the visit. For example, Olsen (2002) recommends that the tourism industry create and construct destinations expecting tourist interaction to match an expected ritualized behavior. While in most cases, fear is a barrier to travel, nevertheless for the fright tourist it becomes actually an attraction, unlike most dark tourism sites. This movement is found in Figure one and links the travel phases with liminality, illustrating the importance of a fright attraction offering both fear and fun.

Shared experiences in communitas provide an opportunity for belonging in dark marginal spaces leaving liminoid experiences as a major importance (Varley, 2011). This danger is important in fright tourism. Still the communitas in fright tourism build on the liminal experience and "make events fun" (Chalip, 2006, p.124). Management is also aware that some individuals may be more sensitive to fear. A common tactic in haunted attractions is to have a "safe word" or even "help" where the staff will step outside of character to assist and escort the scared visitor safely out.

The recollection phase of the experience (Clawson & Knetsch, 1966) also explains the post liminal phase of the fright experience. This could be an area of future study since most dark tourism quantitative research has explored the post travel experience. For example, reviewing dark tourist travel blogs, Isaac and Çakmak (2016) found emotions ranging from shock to horror for the appraisals.

Is the interest in fright tourism waning? Perhaps not, since Wright (2017) suggests that many attractions in the future will have a "terror" theme building on the news and current events like September 11th, the Paris Terrorism Attack and natural disasters like the 2004 Indian Ocean tsunami. In this fear driven world, we can expect that individuals will continue to seek opportunities to be scared to death and return safely home.

Disclosure statement

No potential conflict of interest was reported by the authors.

ORCID

Robert S. Bristow (iD) http://orcid.org/0000-0001-7927-794X

References

Andrews, H., & Roberts, L. (Eds.). (2012). *Liminal landscapes: Travel, experience and spaces in-between*. New York: Routledge.

Ashworth, G. J., & Isaac, R. K. (2015). Have we illuminated the dark? Shifting perspectives on 'dark' tourism. *Tourism Recreation Research*, 40(3), 316–325. doi:10.1080/02508281.2015.1075726

Beech, J. (2000). The enigma of holocaust sites as tourist attractions – The case of Buchenwald. *Managing Leisure*, 5(1), 29–41. doi:10.1080/136067100375722

Bigley, J. D., Lee, C. K., Chon, J., & Yoon, Y. (2010). Motivations for war-related tourism: A case of DMZ visitors in Korea. *Tourism Geographies, 12*(3), 371–394. doi:10.1080/14616688.2010. 494687

Bilu, Y. (1988). The inner limits of communitas: A covert dimension of pilgrimage experience. Ethos, *16*(3), 302–325. doi:10.1525/eth.1988.16.3.02a00050

Biran, A., & Buda, D. M. (2018). Unravelling fear of death motives in dark tourism. In P. Stone (Ed.), *The Palgrave handbook of dark tourism studies* (pp. 515–532). London: Palgrave Macmillan.

Bittner, M. (2011). Dark tourism-evaluation of visitors experience after visiting thantological tourist attractions. Turizam, *15*(4), 148–158. doi:10.5937/Turizam1104148B

Blom, T. (2000). Morbid tourism-a postmodern market niche with an example from Althorp. *Norsk Geografisk Tidsskrift - Norwegian Journal of Geography, 54*(1), 29–36. doi:10.1080/ 002919500423564

Bogdan, R. (1988). *Freak show: Presenting human oddities for amusement and profit.* Chicago: University of Chicago Press.

Boorstin, D. J. (1992/1961). *The image: A guide to pseudo-events in America.* New York: Random House.

Bowman, M. S., & Pezzullo, P. C. (2009). What's so 'dark' about 'dark tourism'? Death, tours, and performance. *Tourist Studies, 9*(3), 187–202. doi:10.1177/1468797610382699

Bristow, R. S., & Newman, M. (2004). Myth vs. fact: An exploration of fright tourism. In K. Bricker, (comp., Ed.), *Proceedings of the 2004 northeastern recreation research symposium* (pp. 215–221). Gen. Tech. Rep. NE-326. Newtown Square, PA: U.S. Department of Agriculture, Forest Service, Northeastern Research Station.

Brooker, E., & Joppe, M. (2014). Developing a tourism innovation typology: Leveraging liminal insights. *Journal of Travel Research, 53*(4), 500–508. doi:10.1177/0047287513497839

Buda, D. M., & McIntosh, A. J. (2013). Dark tourism and voyeurism: Tourist arrested for "spying" in Iran. *International Journal of Culture, Tourism and Hospitality Research, 7*(3), 214–226. doi:10. 1108/IJCTHR-07-2012-0059

Campo, D., & Ryan, B. (2008). The entertainment zone: Unplanned nightlife and the revitalization of the American downtown. *Journal of Urban Design, 13*(3), 291–315. doi:10.1080/ 13574800802319543

Carnicelli-Filho, S., Schwartz, G. M., & Tahara, A. K. (2010). Fear and adventure tourism in Brazil. *Tourism Management, 31*(6), 953–956. doi:10.1016/j.tourman.2009.07.013

Chalip, L. (2006). Towards social leverage of sport events. *Journal of Sport & Tourism, 11*(2), 109–127. doi:10.1080/14775080601155126

Chang, L. (2017). Tourists' perception of dark tourism and its impact on their emotional experience and geopolitical knowledge: A comparative study of local and non-local tourist. *Journal of Tourism Research & Hospitality, 6*(3), 1–5. doi:10.4172/2324-8807.1000169

Chen, C. M., & Tsai, T. H. (2019). Tourist motivations in relation to a battlefield: A case study of Kinmen. *Tourism Geographies, 21*(1), 78–101. doi:10.1080/14616688.2017.1385094

Christie, D., & Lauro, S.J. (2011). *Better off dead: The evolution of the zombie as post-human.* New York: Fordham University Press, 1–296

Clawson, M., & Knetsch, J. L. (1966). *Economics of outdoor recreation.* Baltimore: Johns Hopkins Press.

Clepper, C. (2016). Death by fright": Risk, consent, and evidentiary objects in William Castle's rigged houses. *Film History, 28*(3), 54–84.

Cohen, E. (1985). The tourist guide: The origins, structure and dynamics of a role. *Annals of Tourism Research, 12*(1), 5–29. doi:10.1016/0160-7383(85)90037-4

Collins-Kreiner, N. (2016). The lifecycle of concepts: The case of 'Pilgrimage Tourism. *Tourism Geographies, 18*(3), 322–334. doi:10.1080/14616688.2016.1155077

Crouch, D. (2000). Places around us: Embodied geographies in leisure and tourism. *Leisure Studies, 19* (2), 63–76. doi:10.1080/026143600374752

Dale, S., & Robinson, N. (2011). Dark tourism. In P. Robinson, S. Heitman, & P. Dieke (Eds.), *Research themes for tourism.* Oxford: CABI.

Decrop, A. (2006). *Vacation decision making.* Oxford: CABI.

Dolnicar, S. (2005). Understanding barriers to leisure travel: Tourist fears as a marketing basis. *Journal of Vacation Marketing, 11*(3), 197–208. doi:10.1177/1356766705055706

Downey, D., Kinane, I., & Parker, E. (2016). *Landscapes of liminality: Between space and place.* London: Rowman & Littlefield International.

Eco, U. (1986). *Travels in hyper reality: Essays.* San Diego, CA: Houghton Mifflin Harcourt.

Field, A. (2013). *Discovering statistics using IBM SPSS statistics.* Beverly Hills, CA: Sage.

Floyd, M. F., Gibson, H., Pennington-Gray, L., & Thapa, B. (2004). The effect of risk perceptions on intentions to travel in the aftermath of September 11, 2001. *Journal of Travel & Tourism Marketing, 15*(2-3), 19–38. doi:10.1300/J073v15n02_02

Foley, M., & Lennon, J. J. (1996). JFK and dark tourism: A fascination with assassination. *International Journal of Heritage Studies, 2*(4), 198–211. doi:10.1080/13527259608722175

Fonseca, A. P., Seabra, C., & Silva, C. (2015). Dark tourism: Concepts, typologies and sites. *Journal of Tourism Research & Hospitality, 2*, 1–6.

Gentry, G. W. (2007). Walking with the dead: The place of ghost walk tourism in Savannah, Georgia. *Southeastern Geographer, 47*(2), 222–238. doi:10.1353/sgo.2007.0023

Goc, N. E. (2002). From convict prison to the Gothic ruins of tourist attraction. *Historic Environment, 16*(3), 22–26.

Goodnow, J. M., & Ruddell, E. (2009). An illustration of the quest genre as spiritual metaphor in adventure travel narratives. *Leisure/Loisir, 33*(1), 241–267. doi:10.1080/14927713.2009.9651438

Hall, G. S. (1897). A study of fears. *The American Journal of Psychology, 8*(2), 147–249. doi:10.2307/1410940

Hartmann, R. (2014). Dark tourism, thanatourism, and dissonance in heritage tourism management: New directions in contemporary tourism research. *Journal of Heritage Tourism, 9*(2), 166–182. doi:10.1080/1743873X.2013.807266

Heholt, R., & Downing, N. (Eds.). (2016). *Haunted landscapes: Super-nature and the environment.* London: Rowman & Littlefield International.

Heidelberg, B. A. W. (2015). Managing ghosts: Exploring local government involvement in dark tourism. *Journal of Heritage Tourism, 10*(1), 74–90. doi:10.1080/1743873X.2014.953538

Heimtun, B., & Abelsen, B. (2012). The tourist experience and bonding. *Current Issues in Tourism, 15*(5), 425–439. doi:10.1080/13683500.2011.609275

Hoedt, M. (2009). Keeping a distance: The joy of haunted attractions. *The Irish Journal of Gothic and Horror Studies, 7*, 34–46.

Holloway, J. (2010). Legend-tripping in spooky spaces: Ghost tourism and infrastructures of enchantment. *Environment and Planning D: Society and Space, 28*(4), 618–637. doi:10.1068/d9909

Hunter, C., & Shaw, J. (2007). The ecological footprint as a key indicator of sustainable tourism. *Tourism Management, 28*(1), 46–57. doi:10.1016/j.tourman.2005.07.016

Inglis, D., & Holmes, M. (2003). Highland and other haunts: Ghosts in Scottish tourism. *Annals of Tourism Research, 30*(1), 50–63. doi:10.1016/S0160-7383(02)00031-2

Isaac, R. K., & Çakmak, E. (2016). Understanding the motivations and emotions of visitors at Tuol Sleng genocide prison museum (S-21) in Phnom Penh, Cambodia. *International Journal of Tourism Cities, 2*(3), 232–247. doi:10.1108/IJTC-06-2016-0014

Kaiser, H. F., & Rice, J. (1974). Little jiffy, mark IV. *Educational and Psychological Measurement, 34*(1), 111–117. doi:10.1177/001316447403400115

Kim, J. O., & Mueller, C. W. (1978). *Introduction to factor analysis: What it is and how to do it* (Vol. 13, p. 193). Beverly Hills, CA: Sage.

Kozak, M. (2002). Comparative analysis of tourist motivations by nationality and destinations. *Tourism Management, 23*(3), 221–232. doi:10.1016/S0261-5177(01)00090-5

Lennon, J. (2010). Dark tourism and sites of crime. In D. Botterill & T. Jones (Eds.), *Tourism and crime: Key themes* (pp. 215–228). Oxford: Goodfellow.

Lennon, J. J. (2017). Conclusion: Dark tourism in a digital post-truth society. *Worldwide Hospitality and Tourism Themes, 9*(2), 240–244. doi:10.1108/WHATT-12-2016-0075

Lennon, J. J., & Foley, M. (2000a). *Dark tourism.* Andover, UK: Cengage Learning EMEA.

Lennon, J. J., & Foley, M. (2000b). Interpretation of the unimaginable: The US Holocaust Memorial Museum, Washington, DC, and "dark tourism. *Journal of Travel Research, 38*(1), 46–50. doi:10.1177/004728759903800110

Lett, J. W. Jr, (1983). Ludic and liminoid aspects of charter yacht tourism in the Caribbean. *Annals of Tourism Research, 10*(1), 35–56. doi:10.1016/0160-7383(83)90114-7

Lew, A. A. (2012). Tourism incognita: experiencing the liminal edge of destination places. *Études Caribéennes, 19* 1–12. doi:10.4000/etudescaribeennes.5232

Light, D. (2009). Performing Transylvania: Tourism, fantasy and play in a liminal place. *Tourist Studies, 9* (3), 240–258. doi:10.1177/1468797610382707

Light, D. (2017). Progress in dark tourism and thanatourism research: An uneasy relationship with heritage tourism. *Tourism Management, 61*, 275–301. doi:10.1016/j.tourman.2017.01.011

Mathe-Soulek, K., Aguirre, G. C., & Dallinger, I. (2016). You look like you've seen a ghost: A preliminary exploration in price and customer satisfaction differences at haunted hotel properties. *Journal of Tourism Insights, 7*(1), 1. doi:10.9707/2328-0824.1058

Meng, F., Tepanon, Y., & Uysal, M. (2008). Measuring tourist satisfaction by attribute and motivation: The case of a nature-based resort. *Journal of Vacation Marketing, 14*(1), 41–56. doi:10.1177/1356766707084218

Miles, W. (2002). Auschwitz: Museum interpretation and darker tourism. *Annals of Tourism Research, 29*(4), 1175–1178. doi:10.1016/S0160-7383(02)00054-3

Mowatt, R. A., & Chancellor, C. H. (2011). Visiting death and life: Dark tourism and slave castles. *Annals of Tourism Research, 38*(4), 1410–1434. doi:10.1016/j.annals.2011.03.012

Nelson, V. (2017). *An introduction to the geography of tourism*. Landham, MD: Rowman & Littlefield.

Nie, N. H., Hull, C. H., Jenkins, J. G., Steinbrenner, K., & Bent, D. H. (1975). *SPSS-statistical package for the social sciences*. 2nd ed. New York: McGraw-Hill.

Olbrys Gencarella, S. (2007). Touring history: Guidebooks and the commodification of the Salem Witch Trials. *The Journal of American Culture, 30*(3), 271–284. doi:10.1111/j.1542-734X.2007.00556.x

Olsen, K. (2002). Authenticity as a concept in tourism research: The social organization of the experience of authenticity. *Tourist Studies, 2*(2), 159–182. doi:10.1177/146879702761936644

Osbaldiston, N., & Petray, T. (2011). The role of horror and dread in the sacred experience. *Tourist Studies, 11*(2), 175–190. doi:10.1177/1468797611424955

Podoshen, J. S. (2013). Dark tourism motivations: Simulation, emotional contagion and topographic comparison. *Tourism Management, 35*, 263–271. doi:10.1016/j.tourman.2012.08.002

Powell, R., & Iankova, K. (2016). Dark London: Dimensions and characteristics of dark tourism supply in the UK capital. Anatolia, *27*(3), 339–351. doi:10.1080/13032917.2016.1191764

Powell, R., Kennell, J., & Barton, C. (2018). Dark cities: A dark tourism index for Europe's tourism cities, based on the analysis of DMO websites. *International Journal of Tourism Cities, 4*(1), 4–21. doi:10.1108/IJTC-09-2017-0046

Preston-Whyte, R. (2004). The beach as a liminal space. In A. Lew, C. M. Hall, & A. Williams (Eds.), *The Blackwell's tourism companion* (pp. 249–259). Oxford: Blackwell.

Pritchard, A., & Morgan, N. (2006). Hotel Babylon? Exploring hotels as liminal sites of transition and transgression. *Tourism Management, 27*(5), 762–772. doi:10.1016/j.tourman.2005.05.015

Raine, R. (2013). A dark tourist spectrum. *International Journal of Culture, Tourism and Hospitality Research, 7*(3), 242–256. doi:10.1108/IJCTHR-05-2012-0037

Rice, A. (2009). Museums, memorials and plantation houses in the Black Atlantic: Slavery and the development of dark tourism. In R. Sharpley, & P. R. Stone, (Eds.). *The darker side of travel: The theory and practice of dark tourism* (pp. 224–246). Bristol: Channel View Publications.

Rittichainuwat, B. (2011). Ghosts: A travel barrier to tourism recovery. *Annals of Tourism Research, 38*(2), 437–459. doi:10.1016/j.annals.2010.10.001

Robbie, D. (2008). Touring Katrina: Authentic identities and disaster tourism in New Orleans. *Journal of Heritage Tourism, 3*(4), 257–266. doi:10.1080/17438730802366557

Ryan, C. (2005). Dark tourism - An introduction. In C. Ryan, S. Page, & M. Aicken (Eds.), *Taking tourism to the limits* (pp. 187–190). London: Routledge.

Seaton, A. V. (1996). Guided by the dark: From thanatopsis to thanatourism. *International Journal of Heritage Studies, 2*(4), 234–244. doi:10.1080/13527259608722178

Seaton, T. (2009). Thanatourism and its discontents: An appraisal of a decade's work with some future issues and directions. In T. Tazim and M. Robinson (Eds.), *Sage Handbook of tourism studies* (Chapter 29, pp. 521–541). Los Angeles: Sage.

Seaton, A. V., & Lennon, J. J. (2004). Thanatourism in the early 21st century: Moral panics, ulterior motives and alterior desires. In T. V. Singh (Ed.), *New horizons in tourism: Strange experiences and stranger practices* (pp. 63–82). Wallingford, UK: CABI Publishing.

Sharpley, R. (2005). Travels to the edge of darkness: Towards a typology of dark tourism. In C. Ryan, S. Page and M. Aitken (Eds.), *Taking Tourism to the Limits: Issues, Concepts and Managerial Perspectives* (pp. 217–228). London: Routledge.

Sharpley, R. (2009). Shedding light on dark tourism: An introduction. In R. Sharpley & P. R. Stone (Eds.), *The darker side of travel: The theory and practice of dark tourism* (pp. 3–22). Bristol: Channel View Publications.

Stone, P. R. (2006). A dark tourism spectrum: Towards a typology of death and macabre related tourist sites, attractions and exhibitions. *Turizam: Znanstveno-Stručni Časopis, 54*(2), 145–160.

Stone, P. R. (2010). Death, dying and dark tourism in contemporary society: A theoretical and empirical analysis. PhD diss., University of Central Lancashire.

Stone, P. (2013a). Dark tourism scholarship: A critical review. *International Journal of Culture, Tourism and Hospitality Research, 7*(3), 307–318. doi:10.1108/IJCTHR-06-2013-0039

Stone, P. (2013b). Dark tourism, heterotopias and post-apocalyptic places: The case of Chernobyl. In L. White & E. Frew, *Dark tourism and place identity: Managing and interpreting dark places* (pp. 79–93). London: Routledge.

Stone, P., & Sharpley, R. (2008). Consuming dark tourism: A thanatological perspective. *Annals of Tourism Research, 35*(2), 574–595. doi:10.1016/j.annals.2008.02.003

Strange, C., & Kempa, M. (2003). Shades of dark tourism: Alcatraz and Robben Island. *Annals of Tourism Research, 30*(2), 386–405. doi:10.1016/S0160-7383(02)00102-0

Tamborini, R., & Weaver, J. (1996). Frightening entertainment: A historical perspective of fictional horror. In *Horror films: Current research on audience preferences and reactions* (pp. 1–13). New York: Routledge.

Tanaś, S. (2014). Tourism 'death space' and Thanatourism in Poland. *Current Issues of Tourism Research, 3*(1), 22–27.

Thomassen, B. (2009). The uses and meanings of liminality. *International Political Anthropology, 2*(1), 5–27.

Turner, V. (1969). Liminality and communitas. In *The ritual process: Structure and anti-structure* (pp. 94–113, 125–30). Chicago: Aldine

Turner, V. (1974). Liminal to liminoid, in play, flow, and ritual: An essay in comparative symbology. *Rice Institute Pamphlet-Rice University Studies, 60*(3), 53–92.

Urry, J., & Larsen, J. (2011). *The tourist gaze 3.0*. London: Sage Publications Limited.

van Gennep, A. (1909/1960). *The rites of passage*. Chicago: University of Chicago Press.

Varley, P. J. (2011). Sea kayakers at the margins: The liminoid character of contemporary adventures. *Leisure Studies, 30*(1), 85–98. doi:10.1080/02614361003749801

Vaske, J. J. (2008). *Survey research and analysis: Applications in parks, recreation and human dimensions*. State College, PA: Venture.

Weidmann, S. (2016). What screams are made of: Selling emotions with tourist promotional rack cards. In *6th Advances in Hospitality & Tourism Marketing & Management Conference*, Guangzhou, China. (p. 144–148

Weiler, B., & Black, R. (2015). The changing face of the tour guide: One-way communicator to choreographer to co-creator of the tourist experience. *Tourism Recreation Research, 40*(3), 364–378. doi:10.1080/02508281.2015.1083742)

Weir, R. E. (2012). Bewitched and bewildered: Salem witches, empty factories, and tourist dollars. *Historical Journal of Massachusetts, 40*, 178–211.

Williams, D. J. (2009). Deviant leisure: Rethinking "the good, the bad, and the ugly. *Leisure Sciences, 31*(2), 207–213. doi:10.1080/01490400802686110

Wilson, J. Z. (2004). Dark tourism and the celebrity prisoner: Front and back regions in representations of an Australian historical prison. *Journal of Australian Studies, 28*(82), 1–13. doi:10.
1080/14443050409387951

White, N. R., & White, P.B. (2004). Travel as transition: Identity and place. *Annals of Tourism
Research, 31* (1), 200–218. doi:10.1016/j.annals.2003.10.005

Wright, D. W. M. (2017). Terror park: A future theme park in 2100. *Futures*. doi:10.1016/j.futures.
2017.11.002

Yankovska, G., & Hannam, K. (2014). Dark and toxic tourism in the Chernobyl exclusion zone.
Current Issues in Tourism, 17(10), 929–939. doi:10.1080/13683500.2013.820260

Yarnal, C. M., & Kerstetter, D. (2005). Casting off: An exploration of cruise ship space, group tour
behavior, and social interaction. *Journal of Travel Research, 43*(4), 368–379. doi:10.1177/
0047287505274650

South African township residents describe the liminal potentialities of tourism

Meghan L. Muldoon

ABSTRACT

The townships of South Africa are peri-urban neighbourhoods defined by racial segregation, economic disparity, and geographic isolation. A product of the racist policies of apartheid, these spaces exist as exclusively black or 'coloured' neighbourhoods that present limited opportunities for mobility for residents. Since the end of apartheid, townships have increasingly come up under the tourists' gaze as sites/sights of resistance, difference, and, urban adventure. While much of tourism scholarship on liminality to date has focused on tourism landscapes creating liminal opportunities for tourists, this paper details how tourism encounters may also become liminal opportunities for tourism hosts under certain conditions. While the tourism encounters take place in the familiar landscape that is home, they become liminal occasions in which to come face-to-face with the previously inaccessible Other and transform one's relationship with them, with themselves, and with their home space. In conducting a critical discourse analysis with the texts of interviews with 16 township residents, a number of liminal moments were identified in participants' descriptions of tourism encounters. Themes identified in this research include: (1) *Pertaining to a change in social standing, economic state, relationships to/with the other;* (2) *Desire for engagement, transformation through encounter;* (3) *Transformation of one's understanding of the physical landscape,* and; (4) *Transformation of one's understanding of self.* These themes are elucidated through the use of creative analytic practice (CAP) and demonstrate that while tourism encounters in the spaces of home do not involve a physical relocation, they can have a transformative effect in people for whom such encounters with the Other were previously forbidden.

摘要

南非的城镇是由种族隔离、经济差异和地理隔离所界定的城市周边社区。作为种族隔离政策的产物, 这些空间完全以黑人或"有色人种"社区的形式存在, 为居民提供了有限的流动机会。自从种族隔离制度结束以来, 这些城镇越来越多地出现在游客的视线中, 成为抵抗、差异和城市探险的场所。虽然目前关于阈限的旅游研究大多集中在为游客创造阈限机会的旅游景观上, 但本文详细介绍了在一定条件下, 旅游地主客相遇如何也可能成为旅游东道主的阈限时刻。当旅游地主客相遇发生在熟悉的景观中, 比如发生在家附近, 旅游地的主客相遇就成为阈限时刻, 在此旅游东道主面对面地与以前不曾接触的他人相处, 这种相处改变了一个人的关系,与他们自己以及与他们家园空间的关系。在对16名乡镇居民的访谈文本进行批判性话语分析时，参与者在描述与旅游者相遇时发现了一些阈限时刻。本研究确定的主题包括:(1)有关社会地位、经济状况以及与他人的关系的变化; (2)对与旅游者接触的渴望以及通过接触发生的变化;(3)对自然景观的认识的转变; (4)对自我认识的转变。这些主题是通过创造性分析实践(CAP)进行了阐述，表明，虽然在家园空间中的旅游相遇不涉及物理空间的迁移，但它们可以对那些以前禁止与他人发生此类相遇的人产生转变效果。

Introduction

Conceptualized by van Gennep (1909) and further elucidated by Turner (1967, 1974), liminality was originally conceptualized to describe that period of 'betwixt and between' (Turner, 1974, p. 14) of human rites of passage, consisting of: a pre-liminary stage, where one distances themself from previous ways of life; a liminal stage consisting of the period of transition, and; a post-liminal stage where they begin to acquaint themself with their new way of life (Thomassen, 2012; Van Gennep, 1909). Since Turner revived the concept of liminality in his work with the Ndembu people (1967, 1969), liminality has been used to describe transitory states, landscapes, and experiences in the fields of sociology, geography, and anthropology, among others. Only comparatively recently has liminality come to be examined in the realm of tourism scholarship – surprising, given how much of the tourism experience – the absence of the comforts of home, the confrontation with new cultures, the physical movement from one place to another, and the lack of societal 'norms' – all connote the liminal.

To date, tourism scholarship has considered the liminal in the context of hotels (Pritchard & Morgan, 2006; Underthun & Jordhus-Lier, 2018), beaches (Andrews & Roberts, 2012; Preston-Whyte, 2004; Shields, 1991), dark tourism spaces (Lennon & Foley, 1999), Dracula (Light, 2009; Reijnders, 2011), barrier reefs (Povilanskas & Armaitiené, 2014), airports (Huang, Xiao, & Wang, 2018), backpacking (Bui, Wilkins, & Lee, 2014), stripping (Ryan & Martin, 2001), and Harry Potter (Lee, 2012). What all these studies have in common is their focus on the tourist experiencing liminality in the tourism space or place, or how the tourism landscape or site creates a liminal locale whereby tourists (or highly mobile tourism workers, in the case of Underthun & Jordhus-Lier, 2018) are encountering difference that has transformative potential.

The research described in this paper has found that familiar spaces – spaces of home – can also be transformative, given certain conditions. Tourism in the townships of South Africa can create this potential. Geographically bounded, racially segregated, and visibly impoverished, townships are physically and imaginatively constructed spaces of difference. A product of the racist policies of apartheid – the South African government's social and political policy meaning 'apart-hood,' townships were created as exclusively black or coloured spaces of oppression where economic and educational opportunities were curtailed, and they continue to be characterized by woefully inadequate infrastructure and impoverished housing today.

Tourism to the townships began in the late 1980s and early 1990s, as social justice activists strove to bring international attention to the racist atrocities of the apartheid government (Freire-Medeiros, 2013; Steinbrink, Frenzel & Koens, 2012). Since the end of apartheid in 1994, South Africa has become a world-class tourism destination, welcoming 10.29 million visitors in 2017 (IOL, 2017), up from an all-time low of 37,430 in 1979 (Trading Economics, 2018), and the frequency of tours to the townships has increased accordingly. Reconstructed as sites of historical significance and resistance to injustice, townships are spaces wherein tourists are assured of encountering the 'real' South Africa (Freire-Medeiros, 2013; Frenzel, 2016; Koens & Thomas, 2016; Rolfes, Steinbrink, & Uhl, 2009; Steinbrink et al., 2012).

In this paper, I define the concept of liminality and how it has been taken up in the tourism literature. I go on to describe my own research into the host's gaze with township residents living in the Cape Town area, and how their perceptions of the tourists in their home spaces differed from my own preconceived expectations of resentment and irritation at being the constant focus of the tourists' gaze. Instead, participants in this research described the liminal potentialities of encountering the tourists in the township space, where white (tourists) and black (hosts) are able to come together, share in one another's stories, and break down some of the racialized barriers once instituted by law, and still very much a reality of day-to-day life in much of South Africa. While tourists may or may not come away from those encounters feeling transformed, for the residents that I spoke with, hosting tourists meant sharing in an otherwise impossible meeting with the other. As one participant stated, 'Just being given a little bit of attention, you know, even if it's five minutes, it changes their lives. Like forever.'

Literature review

Liminality, from the Latin *limen* meaning 'threshold,' was first coined by van Gennep (1909) to describe those rites of passage present in every society that mark the transition between one state of being or identity to another, emergent state (Thomassen, 2009, 2012). Liminality refers to that sense of in-betweenness, when one is leaving behind a previous way of being but has not yet arrived at what comes next (Augé, 1995; Meethan, 2012; Thomassen, 2009, 2012). It has been described as 'the transitional period or phase of a rite of passage during which the participant lacks social status or rank, remains anonymous, shows obedience and humility, and follows prescribed forms of conduct, dress, etc.' (dictionary.com). The accustomed order of things becomes suspended, creating a state of chaos and uncertainty, but this fluidity and disorder is also productive of potentiality, leading to new identities, customs, or institutions (Andrews & Roberts, 2012; Thomassen, 2009, 2012; Turner, 1969; Underthun & Jordhus-Lier, 2018). As Turner (1974) explained, 'liminal individuals are neither here nor there; they are betwixt and between the positions assigned and arrayed by law, custom, convention, and ceremonial' (p. 95), a process by which 'the very structure of society [is] temporarily suspended' (Szakolczai, 2009, p. 142)

Since van Gennep's (1909) original conceptualization, which was rediscovered and revitalized by the work of Turner (1967, 1969, 1974, 1982), the term liminality has come to describe periods of social or political change as well (Pritchard & Morgan, 2006; Thomassen, 2009, 2012; Underthun & Jordhus-Lier, 2018). Thus, liminality may be intentionally brought about via proscribed rituals or may be accidental in the case of a loss or turbulent event that has thrown an individual's known world into turmoil (Andrews & Roberts, 2012). Liminality also implies a temporality, as it is an imperman-ent state of non-being in between (Andrews & Roberts, 2012; Preston-Whyte, 2004; Pritchard & Morgan, 2006; Thomassen, 2012). However, the temporal can refer to a moment, a given period, or even an epoch of many years (Thomassen, 2009). Likewise, liminal subjects may be individuals, groups, or entire societies as they transi-tion from one form of being to another (Thomassen, 2009). Finally, more recent research also suggests that liminality may be distinguished according to its scale, in terms of how mildly or powerfully the liminal moment is experienced (Thomassen, 2009, 2012; Underthun & Jordhus-Lier, 2018).

Of particular interest to tourism scholarship is the consideration of the ways in which *place* may also be liminal (Andrews & Roberts, 2012; Lew, 2012; Meethan, 2012; Preston-Whyte, 2004; Pritchard & Morgan, 2006; Shields, 1991; Underthun & Jordhus-Lier, 2018). The classic example is that of the beach, that place between the land and the sea, where so-called 'normal' modes of behaviour and dress may be eschewed (Andrews & Roberts, 2012; Meethan, 2012; Pritchard & Morgan, 2006; Shields, 1991; Thomassen, 2012). Referring to a 'threshold' immediately evokes the notion of place, the physical reality of a boundary that must be crossed or a doorway passed through (Andrews & Roberts, 2012; Lew, 2012; Thomassen, 2012). Taking the notion further, current conceptualizations of place recognize that it does not merely exist as a phys-ical reality but is also socially constructed and imbued with meaning and value (Jaimangal-Jones, Pritchard, & Morgan, 2010; Meethan, 2012). The meaning of a par-ticular place changes over time, and the ways in which people understand place nat-uralize and reinforce socio-cultural norms and hierarchies (Pritchard & Morgan, 2006). Liminal places, places of transition, movement, and uncertainty become attractive: they are invested with possibility, with breaking free of everyday ways of being and interacting (Preston-Whyte, 2004; Pritchard & Morgan, 2006; Shields, 1991; Thomassen, 2012; Urry, 2003). As such, these become 'spaces of performativity, places of intersec-tion and interaction where roles and identities can be negotiated and embodied' (Meethan, 2012, p. 69). According to Shields (1991), liminal spaces represent 'a liber-ation from the regimes of normative practices and performance codes of mundane life' (p. 47). These are also sites of disquiet and unease, requiring the traveller to move from the known to an unknown and unpredictable new reality (Lew, 2012; Nisbet, 1969; Preston-Whyte, 2004; Pritchard & Morgan, 2006; Thomassen, 2012; Turner, 1977; Underthun & Jordhus-Lier, 2018).

Tourism spaces are also sites of ludic inbetweenness, occupied temporarily by trav-ellers who are away from their familiar scenery and customs (Meethan, 2012, p. 70; Preston-Whyte, 2004; Urry, 2003). This period away from home represents a liminal space in which one has left the known realm of home and has entered a space in which 'disorder, antistructure, and experimental behaviour' are experienced (Brooker & Joppe, 2014, p. 501; Urry, 2003). Tourists themselves have been described as liminal, as they occupy the in-between of past and future realities, with little to do with scheduling, labour, and customariness (Burns, 1999; Pritchard & Morgan, 2006; Ryan & Hall, 2001). Urry (2003) describes how the tourist moves away from the 'familiar place to a far place' (p. 12) and engages in worshipful practices through which intense social bonds are formed and the tourist emerges with enhanced social standing. The implication is that when we travel we enter a liminal phase and space and return home changed by our experiences away.

Thomassen (2012) and Horvath, Thomassen, and Wydra (2009) propose that liminal moments disrupt or dissolve existing social hierarchies, making way for a possible cultural hybridity in which difference can be experienced without prevailing power relationships or binaries. Turner (1974) introduces the notion of *communitas*, in which coming together in spaces of liminality, through tourism or otherwise, becomes a unifying force, creating a shared sense of community amongst participants in that space (Simmel, 1994). The temporally disrupted social hierarchies thus allow for new ways of knowing and thinking about the Other, leading to more inclusive and embracive forms of social order (Simmel, 1994; Thomassen, 2012; Turner, 1969; Underthun & Jordhus-Lier, 2018). Tourism encounters in the townships of South Africa have exactly this transformative potential, however these encounters become liminal for those who reside in the townships; the experiencing of meeting and hosting tourists temporally transforming the familiar space into one of liminal potentiality.

Context of the townships

Townships are spaces of geographic, social, educational, and economic segregation (Freire-Medeiros, 2013; Frenzel, 2016; Koens & Thomas, 2016; Rolfes, 2010; Rolfes, Steinbrink, & Uhl, 2009). Created as residential neighbourhoods for black or coloured South Africans, these areas were occupied only by persons of a designated race, and when desirable urban areas were declared 'whites-only' by the apartheid government people already living there were forcibly removed to the townships without compensation. Characterized by inadequate housing, poor infrastructure, and limited access to services such as electricity and garbage collection, the townships today continue to be exclusively racially homogenous spaces. Designed with only one road leading in and out and typically separated from the rest of the urban environment by a highway or an industrial zone, townships were spaces that white South Africans did not enter, and black and coloured South Africans required a government-issued pass in order to leave. These geographically-constructed spaces of difference are immediately visible to anyone visiting the area of Cape Town.

Methods

In undertaking this discourse analysis, I analysed the 327 pages of transcripts collected over the course of interviews conducted by me with research participants. While liminality was not the original focus of my research, notions of liminality emerged strongly as I interviewed township residents about their experiences with and perceptions of tourists. Following Waitt (2005), I undertook a critical discourse analysis through a careful consideration of the interview texts, guided by the question; 'In what ways can tourism encounters be expressed as liminal in terms of personal identity, relationships to/with Others, and relationships to/with the physical environment?' The 16 participants (eight men and eight women) in this research were all residents of one of three townships and were all identified through a combination of tourism encounters, personal relationships, and snowball sampling. All but one of the participants were of black Xhosa descent; the one exception was a white Afrikaans man living in the township with his family.

A number of themes began to emerge from this analysis, which shall be discussed in greater detail below. I felt that my own understanding of the data, and my communication thereof, might be further elucidated through the use of creative analytic practice. Creative analytic practice, or CAP, gives academic writers the opportunity to explore scholarly creativity in writing that breaks free from traditional restrictions on form (Berbary, 2011; McKeown, 2015; Parry & Johnson, 2007; Richardson, 1997, 2000). It acknowledges that writing is in itself a scholarly practice and through writing researchers come to better understand the topics that they study (Richardson, 1997). Finally, CAP eschews the dull, staid writing of traditional academic research and places its value in being aesthetically appealing, in additional to academically rigorous (Berbary, 2011; Caulley, 2008; McKeown, 2015; Parry & Johnson, 2007; Richardson, 1997, 2000). This helps to make the work more accessible to lay audiences, potentially broadening the scope of the influence of the work (Berbary, 2011; McKeown, 2015; Parry & Johnson, 2007).

At the outset of this discourse analysis, I developed a number of themes that had emerged within my original analysis of the research texts that I felt pertained to the topic of liminality. These were: *Pertaining to a change in social standing, economic state, relationships to/with the Other; Change in the present, change for the future; Desire for engagement, transformation through encounter; Transformation of one's understanding of the physical landscape; Transformation of one's understanding of self*, and; *Also liminal for the tourists?*. My analysis involved a close reading of all of the interview texts and coding of participants' responses into one or more of these thematic areas. My analysis did not uncover any substantive texts related to the themes of *Change in the present, change for the future* or *Also liminal for the tourists?* and these themes were therefore eliminated from further analysis. An additional theme, *Opposite of liminal*, emerged over the course of this analysis. It was through this coding of the interview texts that the voices and mannerisms of the research participants were recalled to my mind and an imagined dialogue began to emerge. I began categorizing the participants' words into 'characters' within each of the themes, characters which broadly represented the people that I met during my research. The four initial themes that remained following my analysis are represented in the imagined dialogue and further discussed below. The fifth theme, *Opposite of liminal*, did not make its way into the dialogue and is briefly considered in the discussion section.

Out of this analysis, I created three composite characters that represent many of the characteristics of the participants that I spoke with over the course of this research. These are a tour guide, a Mama who hosts tourists, and a young man who does not have access to the tourists (and therefore, the profits to be gained from tourism). These characters are all drawn from the people that I met through my research, however constructed in such a way that they remain anonymous. Their words are drawn primarily verbatim from the transcripts – where I have added words for conversational flow I have presented them in italics. I also took some creative license in that the texts that I used in this fictionalized dialogue are not necessarily true to character, meaning for example that some of the words that Mama Luxande says in this dialogue may have originally been spoken by someone more closely identified with the role of a tour guide. My intention in creating this dialogue is not to convince the reader of an event that occurred, but rather to present, in their own words, some of the issues related to tourism raised by the participants which pertained to the liminal. Before moving on to the dialogue, it is important to acknowledge that this dialogue is written by me. The text is presented, as much as possible, in the exact words of the participants, however I was the person who chose what words to replicate here and how to arrange them.

Our cast of (composite) characters

Mama Luxande is a 56-year-old woman living in the largest township in the Cape Town area. She lives in a shack with her husband, his cousin from the Eastern Cape, her adult son, two teenaged daughters, and three grandchildren whom she is helping to raise. Her family lives on the incomes her husband and cousin-in-law bring in working in a local butcher shop, while her son continues to try and find work. Mama spends most days at the women's empowerment centre, running after-school programmes for local kids, serving hot lunches to people in need, and making handicrafts for the van-loads of tourists that visit the centre several times a day. Having had minimal access to formal education growing up under apartheid, Mama is happy to have found work at the new centre which allows her to get out of the house, work with the other women that she has come to love, and provide a steady source of income for her family.

Mpho is a tour guide working with a Cape Town-based company that offers tours in her home township. Still in her early 20s, her income – though unpredictable – helps support her mother and five siblings living in their one-bedroom apartment in one of the new hostel buildings. She enjoys getting to interact with the tourists and knows that she is fortunate to have an income given her age and gender, however her long term dream is to return to school to train for a job as a telemarketer.

Bongani is 30 years old and has lived in the township all his life. Despite having finished secondary school, he has been unable to find formal employment, although he is heavily involved in local arts and theatre initiatives. Bongani sees the tourists coming to the townships and resents the money that is being made by his friends and neighbours who are involved in the tourism industry. He feels that more should be done at the local level to ensure that tourism revenues are distributed more equally throughout the community. Despite his desire for greater involvement, he dislikes the affectations adopted by those who have contact with the tourists and has questions about the motivations of the tourists in coming to visit the townships.

Setting the scene

We enter on a dusty, unpaved street high up on the hill in the township. The street is narrow, with brightly painted corrugated tin shacks clustered closely at its edges. Illegal powerlines crisscross the skyline and provide dim lighting and some warmth to the densely packed housing. Many of these shacks have stood for decades, despite them once having been considered to be merely temporary until the family was able to build a more suitable home. Lines of laundry flap in the breeze; the air is chilly on this winter's July afternoon, although the threatening rain has not yet started to fall. As we approach the intersection of two roads, a rusty yellow dumpster comes into view, overflowing with garbage in the empty lot on the corner. A stray dog saunters lazily by, taking a casual sniff at the dumpster's erstwhile contents, now strewn about the lot. You catch a whiff of garbage – unpleasant to be sure, but probably nothing like what it must smell like in the high heat of January. On the other side of the intersection you see a two-story building with a sign: Legacy Childcare Centre. Faded plastic toys litter the yard beyond the chain-link fence, and the building's walls are adorned with hand-painted dancing lions and zebras and rainbow-coloured ABCs. From within, you are able to just catch the sound of small voices raised together in the singing of a Xhosa nursery rhyme. Two women stand together in the dust of the street, one young, the other approaching her old age, both waiting for the children in their families to finish their school day. The younger of the two has bright, laughing brown eyes, closely cropped hair, and wears blue jeans, a green wind breaker jacket, and broken-in sneakers. The elder woman wears a resplendent blue and orange shweshwe wrapped securely around her thickening waistline, a Co-Operators Team Building Event 2007! t-shirt, and plastic sandals. Her black synthetic curls peek through from beneath the iqhiya knotted about her head. The Mama has just finished congratulating the younger woman on her new position as a township tour guide.

Mama Luxande: We are lucky. The people who come from other places or another world they come to us and we are the friends of these people. They are not, no you are blacks, I am white. No, no, no, no they say hi how are you and then we make friends and that's why I like it.

Mpho: It's helping our country a lot. Because if there were not any international people coming, you know, even younger kids, like from that generation would still not know how to relate to white people. Because they don't see them, they only know that my mom works for the white person who is the boss. So that understanding or the mentality that you were given in the past that white people are superior, you know, you need to respect them, so it's kind of like fading out, now the society is seeing them like people, you know like they're like people like us, they can laugh at our jokes, they can sit down, they can eat what we eat, you know. But to most local people it's like they don't know that.

Mama Luxande: *Not long ago* I didn't have any job, now I'm there at [*the women's empowerment center*] because of the tourists. *If not for* the tourist that built *that* building *then* maybe I was not going to have a shelter to come to every day and do the beadwork and have this opportunity to have a job. So, I think the tourists can help us. When I look at the tourists I always think okay they can change our lives.

As the women are talking, the child care centre's double doors swing open, and a sea of small children, laughing and still singing, emerge and careen down the front steps. The pompoms on their pastel coloured knitted hats bounce up and down as they run towards the previously unnoticed playground equipment. A tall, thin man descends the steps more slowly behind them. His short hair and mustache are both neatly trimmed, and he wears a navy polo shirt and pressed brown trousers. Every Tuesday, you can find Bongani at the day care centre, volunteering his time to teach the children traditional Xhosa songs. He approaches and greets the women – Mama Luxande is a friend of his mother's - and joins their conversation.

Bongani: I grew up not knowing how to talk to a white person. You know, that these people are actually even making an effort to recognize that I even am alive, you know, is a huge thing. That, that now these kids that we have now know what a white person is because they can run to them.

Mpho: That's the central part, most definitely. The human to human interaction. That's the central part of our operation.

Mama Luxande: You know, what I like about it, it's we feel so, me I feel so happy when they ask me how do we live, how do we feel when they come here, so you know, I told them that you know what, we are all one. So, we are all human beings, so when I am seeing you, it's like I mean we all, we don't think the same. Some of them when they are seeing the tourists are coming around they are saying ah we are going to have money. It's not like that.

Bongani: I think that the idea that a person that I see as a superior person or a person that is better than me, the idea that a person like that can come and walk in the same street as I live makes me, even if there's no money it does something for my self-esteem. It means I'm a person too. It means … people, people don't look at me the way I look at myself, it means … some people realize that I exist in this world. So, it's a, it's that self-affirmation and confirmation of existence that comes with it as well.

Mpho: When I sum up my tour I say to them like even though you think this is about you, you know, but you don't even know about that kid, but you made that kid feel special at that time, you know, taking your time, playing with your expensive shoes, you know. Letting go and just, you know, being there. So, it means a lot to them.

Mama Luxande: But it's also learning that people are happy even if they don't have anything, and just being given a little bit of attention, you know, even if it's 5 minutes, it changes their lives. Like forever. They feel special in that particular time. 'Cause these kids they come from different tough households [*she gestures towards the children massing at the top of the playground's metal domed climbing structure*].

Mpho: *And* now the township is becoming safer and safer because more internationals are coming.

Mama Luxande: *I see that the* people come closer to the women, trying to know how they do this, how they do the beadwork. So, for me it *is* interesting to see a tourist doing this. It's where we can benefit and also they benefit from us by knowing how to do this. They see the womens who are very strong. The strong womens, yes.

Mpho: People they can keep on coming to the township, because we are getting a lot of the opportunities as the people they are staying here, they are opening our minds, they are helping the kindergartens people. Now no one is having the reason of just staying home telling us, or telling the people that no I don't have money to go to school, no, no people are telling people that now. Because they know that they are getting helped from elsewhere. Yes.

Mama Luxande: Tourism is trying to heal the wounds of coming from a divided society where we were separated, we had white people that were staying in white communities, we had black people that were staying in black communities, and social activities yet again were also separated. *When I was a younger woman* we went to different schools, we went to different hospitals and services, we went to different jobs, and amongst many things you will find that the policies during that specific time were harsher very, very harsh in actual fact on the native or the black people. *We were told to carry passbooks with us* all the time. Without that passbook you will be beaten, arrested, and in some circumstances deported to the homeland where you originated from, so it was a more of a difficult process, some of them were even chased and bitten by dogs just because they, they were told they came into a country that was never theirs which is quite, you know, very sad. So, we came from a dark process in our society. Now healing those wounds is about saying we are all human beings. The opportunities that you never had during that specific apartheid time that would include not going to school, not being employed in a particular working job and not developing your own livelihood or your life, so the opportunity now is to say is let's heal those wounds, let's help you enjoy life, let's help you engage with people that you were not, you were separated from, meaning different colours. Let's speak, let's talk about who we are and who you are and let's learn from each other.

Bongani: It's where you come from. This spot is where I come from. You know, when tourism transforms another community, if I may call places like Obs and stuff a community, when it can transform the minds of that community and make those people that have a hip life there want to come and be here, then obviously the ones from here that went away from here because they are all high and mighty and over there, they will be so ashamed of what they are doing that they will want to come with those guys and help them explain what it is. 'Cause my friend who is in Constantia or wherever, said to me no man you need to take me to *the township*. I can't say no because I'm too high and mighty. I'm forced now to tell them what is happening there. It places me in a position where I'm obligated to actually promote my own place.

Mpho: So, the question that raises for me *is*, does having all of the white people from Obs and all the tourists decide that *the township* is cool then make it cool for all the black people who have left?

Bongani: What they don't know is that unconsciously they are really learning how to love themselves and their own people. They are, they are doing it because they are forced, or they are doing it because they are being told that you should do this. They are carrying on the hipness, you know, but they are not aware of the fact that they are doing the right thing even for themselves, it becomes therapy for them, doing that. *It becomes* an opportunity for them to re-learn themselves. Now I have to tell *this white tourist* that we are from here, we come from this place, we grew up like this. By doing that I am re-learning, I am learning how to love myself again, I am learning to appreciate myself more. Now next week when *the white tourist* is not here to walk, to want to go to *the township* I drive myself alone to *the township* now, because I've seen that, it's not so bad, you know. So again, so it becomes a re-conscientization of the other as well.

The winter rain that has been threatening finally begins to fall. The children on the jungle gym scatter, still laughing and now shrieking at the coldness of the drops. Mama gathers her granddaughter, Mpho her youngest brother, and they bid farewell to Bongani and one another and proceed in their opposite directions towards home.

Discussion/conclusion

Notions of liminality emerge at several points during this fictionalized discussion. Through the course of this discourse analysis, I identified liminal moments in terms of changes in one's social status, economic state, and relationships with the Other. Mama and Mpho both talk about how the opportunity to have a job would not have been possible without the presence of the tourists, and Mpho contends that the tourists make it difficult for community members to sit at home and not work, since these opportunities now exist for everyone. Most significant here are the ways in which our three characters discuss the ways in which tourism encounters are transforming their relationships to/with the white Other. Framed within the context of South Africa's history of colonial violence, tourism is bringing white tourists into the formerly forbidden black spaces of the townships, and the tourism encounter facilitates a playful coming together of white and black people in that space. As Holst (2018) informs us, tourism encounters in the global South typically do not bring tourists and hosts together in egalitarian exchanges: hosts are usually maids, cooks, drivers, etc. Township tourism, as a specific form of slum tourism, is therefore an important area of study because of its central focus on bringing hosts and guests together on an equal footing to learn about one another's lives (Holst, 2018). The racial aspect in South Africa, in particular, makes this an exchange brimming with liminal potential. The characters in the dialogue feel visible in the tourism encounter, they recognize that tourism is changing the ways in which township residents, particularly children, are coming to know and interact with white people. Despite the fact that very few tourists to the townships are in fact white South Africans, these township residents feel that tourism is changing the nature of racialized relationships in their country.

Related to this, tourism in the townships is also understood to have liminal potential in terms of one's understanding of self. Bongani talks about how a person who is perceived as 'superior' coming to see where he lives and walk in the same streets as he does something for his self-esteem, that it means that he is a person as well. I personally found this perspective unsettling, and firmly rooted in Fanon (1967) and Mbembe's (2001) notions of internalized colonialism, however this understanding of the transformation of self was clearly deeply felt by Bongani. Both Mpho and Mama Luxande remark at how encounters in tourism are particularly transformative for the children growing up in the townships, that the tourists have no idea how impactful their taking the time to play with a child can be for them.

A third theme that emerged from Bongani's perspective is that tourism can also inspire liminal moments in terms of residents' understandings of their own physical environment. In the national consciousness, townships have historically been constructed as negative spaces, spaces of isolation and racialized oppression, places to escape from. The tourists perceive the townships as spaces of cultural value and interest, and these spaces then come to be re-framed in the eyes of their residents. Even though in some ways this viewpoint is still suggestive of black South Africans desiring what white people have determined to be desirable, township residents are coming to see their spaces as having value, they are re-learning to love their own space. In this way, according to Bongani, they are unconsciously learning to take pride in their space, and by extension, in themselves.

While the above dialogue presents a snapshot of how some township residents characterized their experiences with tourism as liminal, I would be remiss in not asserting that this is far from a complete picture of how tourism is understood in the townships. The generation of young people in South Africa born around independence in 1994 are known collectively as 'the born-frees.' Absent from my transcripts are any interviews with township residents of this generation, although in my personal conversations with some of them I came away with an understanding that they do not have the same feelings around the valuing of the white gaze that the older research participants spoke about. These younger South Africans did not grow up under a political system that reinforced their inferiority to whites in every aspect of society; instead, they were told that they were growing up in a society in which all races are equal. Some have hotly disputed Bongani's perspective that coming up under the white tourist's gaze affirmed his own identity and existence.

My other caveat is that in many instances research participants expressed concern about how township residents were perceived by the tourists. One questioned the preconceived biases that tourists may impose on the residents. Several made reference to notions of 'poverty porn.' While the majority of participants' reflections of their experiences with tourism spoke of positive potentialities, there was an ever-present undercurrent that was concerned with tourists' representations of themselves and their space as being one-dimensionally impoverished and disempowered.

Despite these hesitations, a powerful liminal thread ran throughout the narratives of tourism encounters that were shared with me by residents of the townships. This research moves beyond the confines of perceiving liminal tourism moments as existing purely from the tourist's perspective, and while the township residents represented in the above dialogue do not move beyond their home space and continue to be oppressed by systemic power imbalances in South Africa, liminal possibilities exist in the ways in which residents' relationships to the white Other are transformed. Participants in this research spoke about children growing up to not fear white people, to be able to run to them and play football with them, whereas in their own childhoods they were forbidden from speaking to white people. I would argue that South Africa has been occupying its own liminal moment since apartheid ended in 1994, as it slowly moves towards a more balanced and egalitarian society. South African society is in a period of active transition, moving intentionally away from what it was before through to what it is striving to become. While all societies evolve and change, it is rarer for nation-states to deliberately set aside what they had been – politically, economically, socially, and geographically – and become something new. These touristic encounters are operating within these transitory processes, as residents of the townships increasingly come to understand that they need no longer be second-class citizens in their own country.

There is no reconciliation without proximity (which certainly does not imply that proximity is the only condition for reconciliation), and through encounters with the Other in the spaces of the townships, residents and tourists are taking a moment to share in one another's humanity, to experience the *communitas* described by Turner (1974) and Urry (2003). Further, the photographs taken by the research participants connote the 'carnivalesque' (Shields, 1991), a ludic coming together that moves beyond a mere commercial transaction (see Figures 1–3).

Far from a purely materialistic exchange, tourism encounters in the townships are helping to break down three centuries of racial isolation and oppression. The desire to connect, to share in one another's experiences, and to resist the notions of difference between white and black that were instituted during apartheid were powerful

Figure 1. Tourists and township residents dancing at the Seniors' Centre (Source: Author).

Figure 2. A tourist and township residents singing at the Women's Empowerment Centre (Source: Author).

Figure 3. Ladies at the Women's Empowerment Centre (Source: Author).

common themes in this research. By presenting some of these ideas in the form of a creatively constructed dialogue between three township residents, I offer here a glimpse into how tourism encounters are productive of liminal possibilities in tourism to the townships.

Disclosure statement

No potential conflict of interest was reported by the author.

Funding

This research was generously funded through a Doctoral Award from the Government of Canada Social Science and Humanities Research Council (SSHRC).

References

Andrews, H., & Roberts, L. (2012). *Liminal landscapes: Travel, experience and spaces in-between*. New York, NY: Routledge.

Augé, M. (1995). *Non-places: Introduction to and anthropology of supermodernity. (J. Howe, trans.).* London: Verso.

Berbary, L. (2011). Poststructural *writerly* representation: Screenplay as creative analytic practice. *Qualitative Inquiry, 17*(2), 186–196. doi:10.1177/1077800410393887

Brooker, E., & Joppe, M. (2014). Developing a tourism innovation typology: Leveraging liminal insights. *Journal of Travel Research, 53*(4), 500–508. doi:10.1177/0047287513497839

Bui, H. T., Wilkins, H., & Lee, Y. S. (2014). Liminal experiences od East Asian backpackers. *Tourist Studies, 14*(2), 126–143. doi:10.1177/1468797614532179

Burns, P. (1999). *An introduction to tourism and anthropology.* New York, NY: Routledge.

Caulley, D. (2008). Making qualitative research reports less boring: The techniques of writing creative nonfiction. *Qualitative Inquiry, 14*(3), 424–449. doi:10.1177/1077800407311961

Dictionary.com (2018). *Liminality.* Retrieved October 2, 2018 from https://www.dictionary.com/browse/liminality?s=t

Fanon, F. (1967). *Black skin, white masks.* New York, NY: Grove Press.

Freire-Medeiros, B. (2013). *Touring poverty.* New York, NY: Routledge.

Frenzel, F. (2016). *Slumming it.* London: Zed Books.

Holst, T. (2018). *The affective negotiation of slum tourism: City walks in Delhi.* New York, NY: Routledge.

Horvath, A., Thomassen, B., & Wydra, H. (2009). Introduction: Liminality and cultures of change. *International Political Anthropology, 2*(1), 1.

Huang, W., Xiao, H., & Wang, S. (2018). Airports as liminal space. *Annals of Tourism Research, 70,* 1–13. doi:10.1016/j.annals.2018.02.003

IOL (2017). *South Africa's tourism stats for 2017.* Retrieved October 3, 2018 from https://www.iol.co.za/travel/travel-news/south-africas-tourism-stats-for-2017-13415216

Jaimangal-Jones, D., Pritchard, A., & Morgan, N. (2010). Going the distance: Locating journey, liminality and rites of passage in dance music experiences. *Leisure Studies, 29*(3), 253–268. doi:10.1080/02614361003749793

Koens, K., & Thomas, R. (2016). You know that's a rip-off": Policies and practices surrounding micro-enterprises and poverty alleviation in South African township tourism. *Journal of Sustainable Tourism, 24*(12), 1641–1654. doi:10.1080/09669582.2016.1145230

Lee, C. (2012). Have magic, will travel': Tourism and Harry Potter's United (magical) Kingdom. *Tourist Studies, 12*(1), 52–69. doi:10.1177/1468797612438438

Lennon, J. J., & Foley, M. (1999). Interpretation of the unimaginable: The U.S. Holocause Memorial Museum, Washington, D.C., and 'dark tourism. *Journal of Travel Research, 38*(1), 46–50. doi:10.1177/004728759903800110

Lew, A. (2012). Tourism incognita: Experiencing the liminal edge of destination places. *Études Caribéennes, 19.* doi:10.4000/etudescaribeennes.5232

Light, D. (2009). Performing Transylvania: Tourism, fantasy and play in a liminal place. *Tourist Studies, 9*(3), 240–258. doi:10.1177/1468797610382707

Mbembe, A. (2001). *On the postcolony.* Berkley, CA: University of California Press.

McKeown, J. (2015). *Single and ready to mingle? A feminist exploration of singlehood, dating, and leisure* (Doctoral dissertation). Retrieved from UWSpace https://uwspace-uwaterloo-ca.proxy.lib.uwaterloo.ca/handle/10012/9449

Meethan, K. (2012). Walking the edges: Towards a visual ethnography of beachscapes. In H. Andrews & L. Roberts (Eds.), *Liminal landscapes: Travel, experience and spaces in-between* (pp. 69–86). New York, NY: Routledge.

Nisbet, R. (1969). *Social change and history: Aspects of the western theory of development.* London: Oxford University Press.

Parry, D., & Johnson, C. (2007). Contextualizing leisure research to encompass complexity in lived leisure experience: The need for creative analytic practice. *Leisure Sciences, 29*(2), 119–130. doi:10.1080/01490400601160721

Povilanskas, R., & Armaitienė, A. (2014). Marketing of coastal barrier spits as liminal spaces of creativity. *Procedia - Social and Behavioral Sciences, 148,* 397–403. doi:10.1016/j.sbspro.2014.07.058

Preston-Whyte, R. (2004). The beach as a liminal space. In A.A. Lew, C.M. Hall, & A.M. Williams (Eds.), *A companion to tourism* (pp. 349–359). Oxford: Blackwell.

Pritchard, A., & Morgan, N. (2006). Hotel Babylon? Exploring hotels as liminal sites of transition and transgression. *Tourism Management, 27*(5), 762–772. doi:10.1016/j.tourman.2005.05.015

Reijnders, S. (2011). Stalking the count: Dracula, fandom, and tourism. *Annals of Tourism Research, 38*(1), 231–248. doi:10.1016/j.annals.2010.08.006

Richardson, L. (1997). *Fields of play: Constructing an academic life.* New Brunswick, NJ: Rutgers University Press.

Richardson, L. (2000). Writing: A method of inquiry. In N. Denzin & Y. Lincoln (Eds.), *The handbook of qualitative research* (2nd ed.) (pp. 923–948). Thousand Oaks, CA: Sage Publications Ltd.

Rolfes, M. (2010). Poverty tourism: Theoretical reflections and empirical findings regarding an extraordinary form of tourism. *GeoJournal, 75*(5), 421–442. doi:10.1007/s10708-009-9311-8

Rolfes, M., Steinbrink, M., & Uhl, C. (2009). *Township as attraction: An empirical study of township tourism in Cape Town.* Praxis Kultur-Und Sozialgeographie, 46, Potsdam, Germany: Universitätsverlag Potsdam.

Ryan, C., & Hall, C. M. (2001). *Sex tourism: Marginal people and liminalities.* London: Routledge.

Ryan, C., & Martin, A. (2001). Tourists and strippers: Liminal theatre. *Annals of Tourism Research, 28*(1), 140–163. doi:10.1016/S0160-7383(00)00015-3

Shields, R. (1991). *Places on the margin.* New York, NY: Routledge.

Simmel, G. (1994). Bridge and Door. *Theory, Culture, and Society, 11*(1), 5–10. doi:10.1177/026327694011001002

Steinbrink, M., Frenzel, F., & Koens, K. (2012). Development and globalization of a new trend in tourism. In F. Frenzel, K. Koens, & M. Steinbrink (Eds.), *Slum tourism: Poverty, power and ethics* (pp. 1–18). New York, NY: Routledge.

Szakolczai, A. (2009). Liminality and experience: Structuring transitory situations and transformative events. *International Political Anthropology, 2*(1), 141–172.

Trading Economics (2018). *South Africa tourist arrivals.* Retrieved October 3, 2018 from https://tradingeconomics.com/south-africa/tourist-arrivals

Thomassen, B. (2009). The uses and meanings of liminality. *International Political Anthropology, 2*(1), 5.

Thomassen, B. (2012). Revisiting liminality: The danger of empty spaces. In H. Andrews & L. Roberts (Eds.), *Liminal landscapes: Travel, experience and spaces in-between* (pp. 21–35). London: Routledge.

Turner, V. (1967). *The forest of symbols.* Ithaca, NY: Cornell University Press.

Turner, V. (1969). *The ritual process: Structure and anti-structure.* Ithaca, NY: Cornell University Press.

Turner, V. (1974). *Dramas, fields, and metaphors: Symbolic action in human society.* Ithaca, NY: Cornell University Press.

Turner, V. (1982). *From ritual to theatre: The human seriousness of play.* New York, NY: Performing Arts Journal Publications.

Underthun, A., & Jordhus-Lier, D. C. (2018). Liminality at work in Norwegian hotels. *Tourism Geographies, 20*(1), 11–28. doi:10.1080/14616688.2017.1314546

Urry, J. (2003). The sociology of tourism. In C. Cooper (Ed.). *Classic reviews in tourism* (p. 9–21). Clevedon: Channel View.

Van Gennep, A. (1960). *The rites of passage.* Chicago, IL: Chicago University Press, (Original Publication 1909).

Waitt, G. R. (2005). Doing discourse analysis. In I. Hay (Ed.), *Qualitative research methods in human geography* (pp. 163–191). Oxford, UK: Oxford University Press.

Between space and place in mountaineering: navigating risk, death, and power

Maggie C. Miller (ID) and Heather Mair

ABSTRACT

The liminal status of mountains makes them attractive destinations for adventure, and related tourism and recreation activities. Stemming from critiques of Nepal's growing adventure tourism industry, and recognising the centrality of Sherpas' roles within it, of interest are the ways Climbing Sherpas experience liminality in mountaineering. Liminality, an anthropological concept introduced by Arnold van Gennep (1960), becomes transformative as Sherpas use encounters with death and periods of uncertainty to take stock of the purpose of their lives. Moreover, analysis of narrative findings reveal that Sherpas assert individual freedom and collective agency in response to the dangers and demands of Nepal's commercial mountaineering industry, thereby shifting power relations on the mountainside. These findings challenge assumptions of immobile host populations that underlie some of the current understandings within tourism scholarship. Additionally, exploring the liminal landscapes of the mountainside draws attention to critical concerns regarding tourism (and its associated industries) as a mechanism for economic development.

摘要

登山的极限状态使山峰成为探险和相关旅游娱乐活动的有吸引力的目的地。源于对尼泊尔不断增长的探险旅游产业的评论,并认识到夏尔巴人在登山中所扮演的核心角色,有趣的是,登山的夏尔巴人在登山过程中体验阈限的方式。阈限是阿诺德·范·根内普(Arnold van Gennep, 1960)提出的一个人类学概念,随着夏尔巴人利用死亡的遭遇和不确定时期来评估他们生活的目的,阈限变得具有变革性。此外,对叙事结果的分析表明,夏尔巴人坚持个人自由和集体代理,以应对尼泊尔商业登山行业的危险和需求,从而改变了山峰上的权力关系。这些发现挑战了固有的接待国人口的假设,这些假设构成了旅游学术界目前一些认识的基础。此外,探索山峰的极限景观也引起了人们对旅游业(及其相关产业)作为经济发展机制的批判性的关切。

Introduction

Liminal places and spaces are tied to both physical environments, and the landscapes of our mind. Hereby place embodies a sense of human familiarity, while space represents geographical uncertainty and those coordinates of interaction which are not yet known (Downey, Kinane, & Parker, 2016; Seamon & Sowers, 2008). In many ways liminality connotes these spatial dimensions, whereby a threshold becomes 'a boundary, a border, a transitional landscape, or a doorway in Simmel's sense of a physical as well as a psychic space of potentiality' (Andrews & Robert, 2012, p. 1). The in-between nature of liminality represents freedom from traditional constrictions, but can also imply an unsettledness in which nothing really matters (Downey et al., 2016). For example, works by Preston-Whyte (2004) and Shields (1991) highlight how the ill-defined margin between land and sea contributes to the unterritorialised and liminal status of the beach, and thus marks it as a place for temporary escape.

Like the beach, mountains can be experienced as liminal landscapes. Situated at the borders – often between countries, mountains are spaces of uncertainty. They are wild and rugged places, often defined by their unpredictable weather patterns and objective dangers, making them inherently risky (Apollo, 2017; Attard, 2003; Beedie & Hudson, 2003). Thus mountains are particularly attractive destinations for adventure and related tourism and recreation activities. Beedie and Hudson (2003) contend that the locations themselves are steeped in 'actual and symbolic representations of adventure' (p. 626). For instance, the summit is a feature significant to mountaineering culture, and the perils and uncertainties of reaching this limit create a fascination for many to visit mountainous landscapes. Frohlick (2003) connects the Himalayas, specif- ically Mt. Everest, with Löfgren's (1999) notion of the 'global beach'; Everest captivates the public's imagination as a 'truly global iconography' (p. 215). Although there are countless beaches (mountains in the case of this research) a select few 'capture the mind's eye as *the* quintessential beach' (Frohlick, 2003, p. 529, emphasis in original). As the tallest mountain in the world, Mt. Everest was and continues to be, *the* moun- tain to climb, a final frontier and 'popular vacationscape for extreme adventure seekers' (Frohlick, 2003, p. 529).

The mountaineering and adventure tourism industries of Nepal have seen remark- able growth since the successful summit of Mt. Everest in 1953 by Tenzing Norgay Sherpa, a Nepali native, and Edmund Hillary, a visiting New Zealander (D'Aliesio, 2012; Rogers & Aitchison, 1998; Schaffer, 2013). Over 37,000 visitors endeavour the popular Mt. Everest Basecamp Trek annually, while there have been 8306 successful summits of its peak (Arnette, 2017; Mu & Nepal, 2016; Schaffer, 2013). However, critics argue that the boundaries between mountaineering and tourism are increasingly blurring, contributing to the popularity of mountains as well as the ways that mountaineering is understood and practiced (cf. Apollo, 2017; Beedie & Hudson, 2003; Pomfret, 2006). Indeed, 'Mountaineering expeditions are no longer the preserve of experienced moun- taineers' (Beedie & Hudson, 2003, p. 632). Today, a typical expedition up one of Nepal's mountains may include seasoned-mountaineers and tourists side by side: sim- ply those who are willing to spend significant amounts of money for the pursuit of adventure, regardless of prior experience (Beedie & Hudson, 2003; Swarbrooke, Beard, Leckie, & Pomfret, 2003; Williams & Soutar, 2009).

In the confines of commercial Himalayan expeditions, relationships on the moun- tainside are deeply rooted in financial power. For instance, foreign mountaineers pay tens of thousands of dollars for the privilege of climbing Mt. Everest, and Sherpas, an ethnic population of Tibetan descent (native to the highland regions of Nepal) are paid to help them reach its summit. Acting as high-altitude guides and porters, Climbing Sherpas commit themselves to securing and saving the lives of their clients by doing much of the dangerous labour like fixing ropes, setting up camps, and carrying supplies high into the mountains (Davis, 2014; National Public Radio [NPR], 2013; Payne & Shrestha, 2014; Peedom, 2015). Despite their efforts, it is impossible to completely eliminate the danger that is ever-present in these liminal landscapes. Every year deaths among climbers and guides continue to occur. To date, over 288 mountaineers have lost their lives attempting the Everest summit; approximately 40% of these deaths represent Sherpas and other Nepali natives (Brown, 2014; Himalayan Database, 2017 as seen in Arnette, 2017).

While mountains are playscapes to some, they remain a place of work for others. Thereby the continued growth of Nepal's mountaineering and adventure tourism industries calls attention to the ways in which these liminal spaces are experienced. Of interest is not only the experiences of foreigners who come to climb, but also the local communities whose difficult and often dangerous labour facilitates the development and operation of mountains as commercial spaces. Drawing on fieldwork observations and interviews from a larger research project (Miller, 2017), this paper explores the dimensions that exist *between* space and place in mountaineering. Specifically, the concept of liminality is used as an apparatus for exploring Climbing Sherpas' narratives to glean insights about the interplay of pride, risk, power, and death in experiences of freedom on the Nepali mountainside. To begin, the spatial dimensions of liminality are examined before an unpacking of Climbing Sherpas' experiences. Therein, key narrative findings are woven together with secondary sources in an attempt to explore, and problematise mountains as complex, contested, and power laden spaces.

Liminal dimensions of the mountainside

Liminality, an anthropological concept introduced by Arnold van Gennep (1960) and further conceptualised by Victor Turner (1969) may be regarded as a cultural apparatus characterised by heightened reflexivity, in which individuals are able to reflect on and critique normative social structures as well as explore new possibilities. The concept first appeared in van Gennep's *Rites de Passage*, what he understood as 'rites that accompany every change of place, state, social position, and age' (Turner, 1969, p. 94). These rites were often enacted within tribal initiation rituals, provoking 'transition' through three distinct phases: separation, margin, and aggregation (or reincorporation) (van Gennep, 1960). Turner (1969) further developed understandings of the second, margin phase, what he called a 'liminal period', recognising that the characteristics of the individual undergoing the ritual become ambiguous as she or he 'passes through a cultural realm that has few or none of the attributes of past or coming state' (1969, p. 351). In these moments it is as though individuals are reduced to a universal or uniform condition to be transformed, emerging from their symbolic ceremony with 'additional powers to enable them to cope with their new station in life' (Turner 1969, p. 351). Correspondingly, moments of liminality foster space for an individual to actively consider the possibilities for constructing new cultural resources and altering strategies of action (Howard-Grenville, Golden-Biddle, Irwin, & Mao, 2011).

The application of liminality has often privileged the abovementioned temporal dimensions, and though these ideas are referred to later it is relevant to first recognise the spatial dimensions of liminality (Thomassen, 2012). The term liminal derives from the Latin word *limen* meaning 'threshold' (Turner, 1969). According to Thomassen (2012), van Gennep himself saw thresholds as structurally equivalent to the margin phase of a ritual passage, indicating that the physical passage of a threshold is as integral as, and often precedes, the rite of a spiritual passage. A threshold can be concrete, such as a doorway or portal, as well as extended areas or zones like monasteries, airports, countries themselves, or even borders between nations (Thomassen, 2012). Landlocked between the Chinese region of Xizang (Tibet) and India, Nepal's borders help to define it politically. However, these nations share another kind of border – a threshold unmatched by any other place on earth: the Himalayan mountain range. Nepal houses 8 out of 14 of the world's highest peaks, each reaching elevations above 8,000 m – the tallest of these is Mt. Everest (8,848 m).

Mountains are sometimes wild yet civilised; they indicate passage but also assent, and thus expressions of liminality in such spaces are various (Attard, 2003). The unspoiled nature of mountains becomes a source of inspiration, revelation, and transformation – a reprieve from the stresses of daily life (Bernbaum, 1997; Godde, Price, & Zimmermann, 1996). In turn they evoke feelings of fear, reverence, and awe, perpetuating notions of romantic idealism amongst urban-dwelling populations (Cooper, 1997; Monz, 2000). Mountains are also perceived as a kind of limbo, a waiting place for the dead, and not dead (Attard, 2003). Thereby, they become a symbolic threshold – the *limen* – a transitional space. Moreover, many travellers and writers (see for example, Percy Shelley's *Mont Blanc*) have likened mountains, and more broadly wilderness terrains, to ruins of an ancient castles, residuum of forgotten cultures – a world that became before people (Attard, 2003). Sublime and beautiful in such Western contexts, mountains 'became a potential point of access to the new world and the old' (Attard, 2003, p. 9) and further contributed to narratives of lost or fabled civilisations (cf. Hilton, 1933).

In the case of the Himalayas, mountains often represent spiritual centres; places of power and worship; and houses of deities (Bernbaum, 1997). Historically, the native populations of these highlands understood them as the home of their gods. Thus, when they engaged these spaces they did so with utmost respect, trying to refrain from polluting or profaning the mountains in hopes of keeping the gods happy (Ortner, 1999). According to Sherry Ortner's (1999) ethnographic work on Sherpas' religious values, actions that constitute mountain pollutions included:

> Going high on the mountain or stepping on the summit; killing animals or otherwise shedding blood on the mountain; dropping human excretions on the mountain; burning garbage on the mountain or otherwise creating bad smells; and finally, having women on the mountain at all, having women menstruating on the mountain, or having people engage in sexual relations on the mountain. (127)

Behaviours like these are said to increase the potential for angry gods, followed by negative consequences (e.g., sickness, bad luck, accidents, death, etc.) (Ortner, 1999;

Pemba Sherpa, personal communication, April 14, 2015). As early as the turn of the twentieth century, *lamas*, trained and authorised Tibetan Buddhism specialists, warned against climbing the peaks of the Himalayas (Ortner, 1999).

Yet, these sacred landscapes, with their remote and majestic beauty, are increasingly sought after as tourist destinations as they can foster spaces for reflection, as well as provide opportunities for stimulation, excitement, and adventure (Apollo, 2017; Beedie & Hudson, 2003). Indeed, mountains exert a 'fatal power of attraction on the human mind' as places to explore the limits of the human body (MacFarlane, 2003, p. 16). Douglas (2007) contends it is the 'brilliant world of dazzling snow and ice and cobalt skies beyond' that appeals to individuals who aspire to climb mountains (p. 11). Within such limits exist the excitement of new experiences, physical challenges, and confrontation with 'otherness' (Beedie, 2008; Christiansen, 1990). In the 1950s the Himalayas became the place to go for the global climbing elite. In part this was due to the re-opening of the Nepali border in 1951, but also because many of these mountains had yet to be summited (Bhattarai, Conway, & Shrestha, 2005; Hansen, 1995). The summit can be understood as a final frontier, the last point between solid ground and the sky above, and as such a 'metaphor for the limits of our quotidian comfort zone' (Beedie, 2008, p. 175). Found at the fringes, Thomassen (2012) reminds us that liminal landscapes implicate the existence of a boundary, and such limit 'is not simply there: it is there to be confronted'. (p. 21). Correspondingly, the famous George Mallory quote still rings true for many mountaineers and adventure tourists as they assess their own motivations to conquer some of the world's highest peaks: 'Because it's there'. (Guggleberger, 2015; New York Times, 1923).

Spaces of self-making and risk-taking

Mountains and their summits are exemplars of in-between spaces, zones of liminality steeped with adventure. With adventure comes uncertainty, and undeniably it is this uncertainty, and risk of personal harm (or even death) that generates excitement for individuals who pursue activities set in challenging or adventurous contexts (Cater, 2006; Lepp & Gibson, 2008; Robinson, 2004). According to Ibrahim and Cordes (2002), simple involvement in 'adventurous' or 'extreme' activities is enough to present inherent aspects of risk. Risk, as it relates to adventure, is often linked to fear and contributes to narratives of hedonism, whereby participants of these activities '*play with* their fears' (Cater, 2006, p. 322, emphasis in original). Indeed individuals acceptance of risk is complex and underpinned by a myriad of socio-psychological factors (cf. Ryan, 2013), but the dangerous nature of mountaineering is admitted to be, by many mountaineers, part of the attraction of – and the fun in – climbing (Ebert & Robertson, 2013). Furthermore, Ortner (1997) explains that risk of a serious or fatal accident produces a high payoff in meaning. She describes the meaning Western mountaineers, whom she calls *sahibs*[1], gleaned from the sport:

> It's about the moral fiber of the inner self, about the nature of bonding and friendship, about the peace and calm of high cold places against the noise and bustle of modern society. All of this makes the risk of accident and death worthwhile. (p. 139)

Seemingly, adventurous individuals are 'searching for something within themselves' and it is through giving themselves up to the 'vagaries of nature' that they may confront realities that are not otherwise encountered (Palmer, 2004, p. 67). Thus, mountains as liminal landscapes can become spaces for 'suspensions of quotidian reality [...] privileged spaces where people are allowed to think about how they think, about the terms in which they conduct their thinking, or to feel about how they feel in daily life' (Turner, 1987, p. 102). Reflecting this sentiment, Kelly's (2000) research around alpine exploration in the Canadian Rockies (between 1885 and 1925) recognises that 'Mountains were not something looked at or even merely scrambled over, they were a place for self-expression and self-discovery' (Kelly, 2000, p. 272).

Mountaineering and the desire to stand on the top of the world were not always significant to Sherpas' lives (cf. Adams, 1992; Ortner, 1999). Rather, the thirteen Climbing Sherpas' stories collected in Nepal in 2015 (see Miller, 2017) contribute to a discourse of development. Indeed, the allure of Mt. Everest and the decision to attempt to stand on its summit are inextricably linked with the meanings attached to climbing and successfully reaching the top. Just as foreign mountaineers chase their Everest dreams, the motivations for Sherpas to climb are increasingly related to notions of pride, conquest, and self-expression. Mingma, a Climbing Sherpa and one of the research participants, suggested that Sherpas feel proud to stand on the world's tallest mountain. 'That's why it's good for me too', he confirmed. Many Climbing Sherpas confessed that they took on their first few pursuits as a personal challenge or goal. Ang Phurba, recalled, 'That [first] time I don't look the money, just the top. That time I'm thinking just one time, one day I climb the Everest'. Similarly, Rinchen reminisced, 'First time top is important for life. Important for life, record also, that time I'm very happy. And next many times climbing is my job'. These emergent storylines disrupt previous research understandings of money being the key driver for Sherpas' participation in mountaineering expeditions (Bott, 2009; Ortner, 1997, 1999). Instead, Sherpas' stories have begun to converge with those of their foreign clients in terms of cultural meaning and identity (cf. Beck, 1992; Neale, 2002), and are enmeshed with narratives of risk.

The Sherpa participants discussed the risky nature of climbing in the Himalayas, as they told stories of camps being swept away by avalanches, clients running out of oxygen, and friends slipping off cliffs or falling into crevasses. Many Climbing Sherpas engage these liminal spaces, and their associated bodily risks, because of perceived meaning and implications for identity and self-making. In these instances, climbing can be understood as an individualised 'project of self', which is connected to the reproduction of social identities through risk performance (Bott, 2009; Palmer, 2004; Rhinehart, 2003). As discussed in Elsrud's (2001) work on behaviours of backpackers, acts of risk-taking are used as tools for, and symbols of, distinction between *self* and the *self of others*. Within their experiences of risk on mountains like Mt. Everest, the Climbing Sherpas distinguished themselves through interconnecting stories of risk, pride, and conquest. This nexus is illuminated by a discussion had with Tashi about summiting Mt. Everest ten times. He explained:

> My dreams when I've done ten times then I stop, I'm thinking that. If I done it ten times, I also might be counted as the famous one ... My plan is that last year [2014], that if I've done [the summit ten times], then I'd stop, and after I have to go guiding, just basecamp and below.

At the time of his interview (March 24, 2015) Tashi had already successfully summited Mt. Everest nine times. As a result of the 2014 avalanche, he did not achieve his dream, and therefore planned to attempt the summit again during the spring 2015 climbing season. Unfortunately, this also proved to be another failed attempt due to the April 25th 2015 earthquake.

Tashi's mention of stopping and his vision of 'guiding below basecamp' once he achieved the ten summits illuminates understandings of the risks involved with his high-altitude mountaineering job, while the disastrous avalanche and earthquake that stopped him from reaching this goal further emphasise the risky and potentially fatal nature of his continued attempts. Conflicting with these risks however, were Tashi's desire to stand on the summit ten times to be recognised as famous, his subsequent decision to climb Mt. Everest again in the Spring of 2016 (which was successful), and his eventual travel to the USA in June 2016 to climb Mt. Denali. Emerging from Tashi's risk-taking were tales of meaning that illuminate a process of identity construction, to distinguish himself from other Sherpa mountaineers. This finding aligns with Elsrud's (2001) notion of participants' tales of risk and adventure, whereby novelty and difference were storylines told in their own efforts to narrate identity. This is further echoed in a recent interview conducted by *Independent* media with Kami Rita Sherpa as he prepared for a record-breaking summit attempt during the 2018 Everest season. Kami explained, 'I want to set a new record not just for myself but for my family, the Sherpa people and for my country, Nepal' (Gurubacharya, 2018). Kami Rita is now the world record holder for most successful ascents of Mt. Everest with twenty-four summits.

Understanding the conquest of mountains as sport rather than solely as work illuminates complexities of Sherpas' stories and how negotiations of their place within mountaineering challenge the relationship between 'us' and 'them' in these liminal spaces. Moreover, Climbing Sherpas' narratives of risk-taking for record-setting achievements advance adventure tourism discourses, which recognise danger as a new element of the 'tourist gaze' (Bott, 2009, p. 289). While such aspects of risk strengthen the appeal of mountain pursuits for Sherpas, it should be briefly emphasised that the effects of money continue to pervade these spaces, contributing to complex dynamics of risk, which according to Bott (2009) are affected by the 'economic power imbalance' implicit in the relationship between commercial expeditions and their hired support (e.g., Climbing Sherpas and porters) (p. 288). Undeniably, financial incentives still compel some Sherpas to assume greater responsibilities (e.g., carrying heavier loads), and consequently an increased level of risk.

Encounters with fear and death

The complex dynamics of risk within these landscapes draws attention to Climbing Sherpas' physiological and mental capacities. There is a widespread perception of Sherpas as 'superhuman' with regard to their physical capability at high altitudes (cf. Adams, 1992, 1996; Neale, 2002). While Sherpas do possess a tremendous level of strength and aptitude for the mountain environment, they are also invariably human, and as such are equally susceptible to human emotions, including feelings of fear and anxiety when faced with situations that pose extreme risk or danger (as any other mountaineer might be). This human side of Sherpas is seemingly one which the industry (e.g., mountaineering outfitters) as well as Climbing Sherpas themselves, strive to suppress from their public image and identity; perhaps in part because the perception of 'strength' plays a critical role in Sherpas' employability. In Carnicelli-Filho's (2013) work around 'emotion management' of adventure guides, he proposes 'a guide who loses the ability to manage emotions such as fear and anxiety can be seen as inadequate for real or perceived risk activities' (p. 193). This would, of course, have major implications for business prospects for Sherpas as professional guides and experts, whose industry relies on clients placing their trust and lives in Sherpas' hands. Therefore, the performance of emotional strength by Sherpas is often bolstered.

When risk is perceived as being higher than competence and skill, fear and anxiety ensue (Cater, 2006; Mu & Nepal, 2016). Fear feels dangerous (cf. Buda, 2015), and if not properly managed can itself add increased risk and danger to an already dangerous situation. Therefore, a large part of Sherpas' roles on the mountainside is, in a sense, to minimise risk through the mitigation of fear experienced by their clients and themselves (Carnicelli-Filho, 2013). Effective management of fear becomes a necessity in an industry situated in a hazardous environment where bodily risks can easily lead to fatalities. For instance, Da Gelje recalled the fear that accompanied one of his first expeditions on Mt. Everest:

> When I'm climbing to Camp III, first time. Very, very, very difficult. I am very afraid ... Before, I was never a climbing guide there. Very danger. 'How do I go down?' Very difficult for my body and my mind. So just I'm thinking after that, 'Okay not only me. I have many friends, many people here. What are they doing? I must also follow that.'[That's] my thinking.

As Da Gelje inwardly manages his emotions and thoughts, he watches fellow climbers perform the necessary skills, and mimics them to appear outwardly competent and capable. Similarly, Dorchi recalled a slow and dangerous climb he endured with limited vision, a result of snow blindness or *ultraviolet (UV) keratitis* (Boyd, 2015): 'My eyes were swollen from 6:00pm onward. I couldn't shout or cry. It's a shame to cry'. The deliberate acts of Da Gelje and Dorchi can be understood as 'emotional work', which is used to actively control the degree and quality of emotions or feelings to achieve a particular impression (Hochschild, 1979, p. 561). Drawing on Goffman's understandings, Elsrud (2001) explained, 'a strong character is not generated through facing the risk whining, shivering, and crying', rather, risk and fear are managed with courage, composure, and 'gameness' (p. 603).

Beneath the surface of some of these performances lie narratives of fear and anxiety. For instance, in answering a question about what his job was like, Phuri let out a gasp and proclaimed, 'It's a scary one, man! I'm scared, along with the foreign climbers'. As he continued to describe his push towards the Mt. Everest summit, Phuri depicted his experience of feeling fear. 'It's very dangerous. Look, we have to put the ladders [over the crevasses] to cross. Due to fear sometimes our body was a little bit shaky too'. Moreover, when discussing their own brushes with death, many of the Climbing Sherpas retreated to laughter. This laughter and humour replaced fear, sorrow, or disbelief – reactions that can appear to be rather incongruous. For instance,

Da Gelje recounted his rescue attempt of a dying Russian mountaineer. 'No move. No life. So I give ... CPR, breath to him ... Many times I do that [Laughs]'. While erupting in a bout of laughter, he continued and confirmed, 'No, no. Not coming back'. Within stories about death, laughter seemingly serves as a natural and nervous response to the uncomfortable-nonpareil and inevitable nature of death (Berger, 1967; Stone, 2009; Yalom, 1980) – a mere attempt to silence fear?

The fear (and subsequently the laughter, silence, or avoidance) expressed by Sherpas within their interviews can be understood as 'death anxiety', 'mortal terror', or 'fear of finitude', all of which speak to the awareness of the fragility of our material existence (Berger, 1967; Varley, 2006; Yalom, 1980). These confrontations with mortality are propelled by urgent experiences or what Berger (1967) identifies as 'marginal situations', which include but are not limited to one's own death or the collapse of some fundamental meaning-providing schema (see also Yalom, 1980). For instance, Lhakpa Dorji illustrated his own marginal situation, describing a time when clients left him stranded on the South Summit of Mt. Everest:

> ... they [the clients] leave me behind, and they run before, down. Then I am alone ... I'm so tired, and I get the ice in my goggle, the sweat. When I almost get to the last camp I couldn't see, then I fell down ... It's about 250 m, about nearly 300m I fell down, like rolling down. I don't know how long I was *dead*. I thought [it's] like a dream, like when I woke up I had no goggles. I had no ice axe ... Then after that I get to [camp at] South Col at 6:30pm. Then other members, about three members in the South Col, they don't care [for] me. They didn't know where I was ... When I was there I am so cold, I no can walk that time. I tried to make a cup of ice and tried to make the water. I couldn't eat anything, I didn't drink the water. The whole night I couldn't sleep.

Situations like these threaten what Giddens (1991) refers to as 'ontological security'. Individuals' rely on structure and security in order to make sense of their lives and daily experiences; however, while climbing, risk-taking, and more poignantly, when confronting death, Sherpas may be exposed to dread, fear, or heightened anxieties (Giddens, 1991; Stone, 2009). In Giddens' (1991) words, 'Death becomes point zero: it is nothing more or less than the moment at which human control over human existence finds an outer limit' (p. 162).

Consequently, from these liminal moments come contemplations of one's own existential position within the material-physical world (Berger, 1967). This is highlighted in Dawa's unexpected encounter with an avalanche while working for a commercial expedition team on Mt. Everest. He explained:

> I remember an avalanche. I tried to stop myself from being taken with an ice axe, trying
>
> to get it into snow, but it was fresh snow so it took all of us down. I was found at the head
>
> of avalanche with my body upside down. When I woke up, it was morning, and I was
>
> lying down with oxygen and glucose water on ... I was pretty homesick after that accident.
>
> I wanted to go home.

Scholars who take up notions of liminality suggest that those affected by disasters, death, and the like find themselves 'betwixt and between' their life prior to the event and an uncertain sense of the future (Cheung & McColl-Kennedy, 2015;

Turner, 1979, p. 465). According to Jencson (2001) these moments mark the transition of an individual from one status to another, which is often accompanied by considerable stress, doubts, and fear about an uncertain future. For instance, Dawa's near miss triggered what he articulated as 'homesickness,' a longing for what he had known before the expedition while he contemplated his current position on the mountain. This sense of fear and uncertainty was emphasised in other Sherpas' narratives as well. Mingma described, 'At the time when the avalanche was coming, I was thinking of where to run and how to save my life. Nothing else was in my mind'. The desperation in Mingma's actions was triggered by the disastrous potential of the avalanche; survival was the only thing that mattered in those heighted moments of uncertainty.

A glimpse of death or a taste of risk illuminates the mutability of human beings (Lewis, 2000). Moreover, the uncertainties that accompany Climbing Sherpas' encounters with death foster potential to radically challenge social constructions within mountaineering (Berger, 1967). In Yalom's words, 'though the physicality of death destroys an individual, the idea of death can save him' (1980, p. 159). These ideas are explored next.

Moments of agency and potentiality

As a moment of liminality, a close encounter with death encourages individuals to return to their fundamental priorities and thoughtfully deliberate what is truly important and meaningful (Cheung & McColl-Kennedy, 2015; Oliver-Smith & Hoffman, 1999). Death enacts a vast influence upon existence and our conduct, in which we can understand the way we live and grow (Yalom, 1980). Thereby, individuals emerge from their marginal situations – their run-ins with death or the idea of it – with 'additional powers to enable them to cope with their new station in life' (Turner, 1969, p. 351). From devastating and uncertain moments, the Climbing Sherpas expanded their sense of self and community, and mountaineering accidents became purpose-revealing experiences producing moments of transformation and survival. For instance, Dawa indicated a change in his own conduct after his brush with death. His homesickness led him to eventually walk away from his position on the mountain, forfeiting his income from that particular expedition. Dawa remembered:

> The next morning, I walked down to my home in Phortse through Pangboche, where I had a cousin. I got to my cousin's home and at the same moment they were talking about me being taken by the avalanche. One of my cousins was crying thinking I was gone forever. They were happy to see me back... After that I didn't return up.

According to Oliver-Smith and Hoffman (1999), 'Disasters take people back to fundamentals' (p. 1). In devastating moments 'victims' expand their sense of self, community, and purpose-revealing experiences of transformation and survival (Jencson, 2001). Undeniably, chaos, irrationality and death are most often evoked in what Varley (2011) calls 'Dionysiac experiences'; however, he argues that the sense of community, stillness and tranquillity that settles afterwards is of equal importance.

Encounters with death impel Sherpas to actively consider the possibilities of constructing a new life. It is from these liminal moments that some Sherpas began to understand the meaning of life differently, while others exercised their power more freely. For instance, Rinchen discussed a time when a paying client, against his recommendation, resumed climbing towards the Mt. Everest summit during a storm – a dream that could not be stopped by hazardous risks or a knowledgeable guide. In response to how he navigated this scenario, Rinchen declared, 'Not going I ... People not listening. Why I do this? 'No, go yourself.' Life is for life, I don't go, I don't go. Please, money is nothing'. Similarly, Lakpa confirmed that when clients 'don't listen' this becomes 'their own responsibility'. When faced with a sufficient level of risk (of death) on the mountain, despite the presence of various forms of power (e.g., money, client gaze, etc.), Sherpas take responsibility for their own lives. Hereby, the Climbing Sherpas' individual agency, their actions and words, disrupt the power and structures that have traditionally contributed to their actions and relationships on the mountainside.

In liminal moments on the mountainside, power is shifted and new freedoms and actions are enacted. Mälksoo (2012) recognises, 'the strength of liminality as the phase of pure possibility underscores the potential power of agency in the liminal process', in which existing realities are restructured to create new ones (p. 489). Narratives of agency emerge within the Climbing Sherpas' navigations of death. For example, Lhakpa Dorji, who was left by his clients and fell nearly 300 meters while descending Mt. Everest, explained his reactions during a subsequent mountaineering expedition. He exclaimed:

> I thought that time, no more ... I was in Camp II, and they pressured me [to join] another team for another summit. I said 'NO!' Then they bring me to Basecamp and they talk a lot of questions. 'Please go do another summit.' And I said, 'NO!'

The positive and transformative aspect of death and disaster is illuminated in the power and agency enacted by Lhakpa Dorji. As he navigated away from the undesirable trajectory of the mountaineering industry, despite the potential economic loss he might have incurred, Lhakpa Dorji created a new reality for himself. Death (or the idea of it) fostered a space to evaluate his continued involvement in the mountaineering industry: an industry that so often places Climbing Sherpas' lives at risk.

The prevailing agency and freedoms of the Sherpa participants of this research can also be seen on a larger, community scale. For instance, in 2014 the mountaineering industry was effectively blamed for the deaths of sixteen Sherpa and Nepali climbers. Mingma explained, 'Lots of Sherpas died on the same day, so everyone decided not to continue ... Since that route was not safe, we were not ready to risk our life'. In his interview, Kaji expounded upon why expeditions on Mt. Everest were halted in 2014: 'After that, Everest was closed. Not by the government, by the Climbing Sherpas. They all said 'let's not climb this time' ... in the mountain we have to respect for tourist, and tourist also have to respect Sherpa'. Therein, the climbing community (in particular the Sherpa and Nepali climbers) moved from the initial shock of the disaster through a liminal moment, which constituted a formative experience for the collective.

Cheung and McColl-Kennedy (2015) suggest that during periods of disaster and displacement, a strong collective bond is formed. Lakpa reflected on how the climbing community transitioned from this tragic accident, recognising some of the reasons why Climbing Sherpas collectively decided to stop climbing in 2014:

That year, you know it's so many accidents, so all the climbers they decide to close. It was black year, bad luck, so many friends lost ... You lose some business, but sixteen, seventeen people died, and after if you continue, you know people psychologically affected, not good feeling.

Those affected by a difficult event may be stripped of their familiar institutions, routines, and resources, a grim situation that entails individuals to come together to find new ways to deal with the challenges of the circumstances of their new emerging worlds (Cheung & McColl-Kennedy, 2015; Oliver-Smith & Hoffman, 1999). Collective agency was activated as the Sherpas disregarded the pressures of commercial climbing teams. Rinchen acknowledged that working on Mt. Everest is not the only employment opportunity in the Solukhumbu region. He proclaimed, 'Money is pay, okay, but safety is life ... Life is important. Money we will make next year. Next day. Another job, many jobs, not only mountaineering Everest'. Evoked by the very act of imagining new boundaries, liminality can help communities find a source of renewal, as they begin to acknowledge the power of their collective agency to create a new setting or 'structure'; one that can be regarded as better than the old (Mälksoo, 2012).

Concluding thoughts

Liminality, as taken up here, highlights and challenges the ways we engage with mountainous landscapes – the way they are developed and managed – recognising the allure they have, but also the power they hold. Mountaineers, and their desire to derive meaning from their adventures, paved the way for emerging niches of adventure tourism in the Nepali Himalaya. Moreover, Mt. Everest presents the ultimate boundary – the border between the earth and the heavens – and thousands of people, mountaineers, adventurers, and tourists alike, have been drawn to this liminal space to test their own limits. Within these spaces Climbing Sherpas are also proud risk-takers, and accomplished mountaineers in their own right. They admittedly take on some of their own Everest pursuits as sport, rather than solely as work. Such narratives of risk-taking and self-making contribute to the complexities of these liminal landscapes, challenging the oversimplified claims that Sherpas climb primarily for moneymaking efforts; thereby disrupting oppositional binaries of East/West and us/them and the problematic tendency in tourism studies to render tourism's 'hosts' as static and immobile.

Nevertheless, we are reminded 'spaces mean different things to different people at different times and represent, reinforce, idealise and naturalise socio-cultural power relations' (Pritchard & Morgan, 2006, p. 763). Sherpas are paid to help foreign mountaineers to the summit, and thereby mountains as liminal landscapes can be experienced quite differently. For Climbing Sherpas, there is a balance between providing the service expected while managing the responsibility of safety, and navigating the significant risks that accompany these extreme endeavours. As discussed earlier, the mediation of their emotions is instrumental to Sherpas' navigations of risks and danger; research findings that further support work put forward by Carnicelli-Filho (2013) and Hochschild (1979) around the performance of emotional labour. However, more salient to this work is the transformative potency of liminal moments, as they created space for Sherpas to reconsider power imbalances on the mountain, and thereby their continued involvement in an industry that so often places their lives at risk.

Though experienced as destabilising and life threatening in the moment, confrontations with death create *a pause* in the everyday, rupturing the status quo. Within this pause, individuals and communities may take stock of their lives, and often consider new trajectories and future possibilities. Therein, death, as the ultimate boundary, reveals insight into freedom, power and development. Rather than being static, vulnerable, and powerless, Sherpas assume active roles in mountaineering and adventure tourism. Power relations shift on the Nepali mountainside as Sherpas demonstrate agency to say 'no' to commercial industry interests. From moments of liminality presented by confrontations with mortality, come opportunities for reflection, consideration, and the questioning of development – challenging the way forward for the people and industries that thrive within the Himalayas.

Note

1. Sahib is a Hindi term meaning "boss" or "master" or (in address) "sir." Sherpas used this term to both refer to and address the international climbers, namely Western climbers, up until the 1970s. Thus, Ortner used this word throughout her work to identify the international climbers. She believed it signalled the lingering colonial influence, and the continuing inequality in the Sherpa-Climber relationship (Ortner, 1997, 1999).

Disclosure statement

No potential conflict of interest was reported by the authors.

ORCID

Maggie C. Miller ⓘ http://orcid.org/0000-0001-6848-5866

References

Adams, V. (1992). Tourism and Sherpas. *Annals of Tourism Research, 19*(3), 534–554. doi:10.1016/0160-7383(92)90135-C

Adams, V. (1996). *Tigers of the snow and other virtual Sherpas: An ethnography of Himalayan encounters*. Princeton, NJ: Princeton University Press.

Andrews, H., & Robert, L. (2012). Introduction: Re-mapping liminality. In H. Andrews, & L. Roberts (Eds.), *Liminal landscapes: Travel, experience and spaces in-between* (pp. 1–17). London: Routledge.

Apollo, M. (2017). The true accessibility of mountaineering: The case of the High Himalayas. *Journal of Outdoor Recreation & Tourism, 17*, 29–43. doi:10.1016/j.jort.2016.12.001

Arnette, A. (2017). Everest by the numbers: 2018 edition [Blog post]. Retrieved from http://www.alanarnette.com/blog/2016/12/30/everest-by-the-numbers-2017-edition/

Attard, K. P. (2003). *Lost and found: A literary cultural history of the Blue Mountains* (Unpublished doctoral dissertation). Western Sydney University, New South Wales, Australia.

Beck, U. (1992). *Risk society: Towards a new modernity*. London: Sage.

Beedie, P. (2008). Adventure tourism as a 'new frontier' in leisure. *World Leisure Journal, 3*, 173–183. doi:10.1080/04419057.2008.9674551

Beedie, P., & Hudson, S. (2003). Emergence of mountain-based adventure tourism. *Annals of Tourism Research, 30*(3), 625–643. doi:10.1016/S0160-7383(03)00043-4

Berger, P. L. (1967). *The sacred canopy: Elements of a sociological theory of religion*. New York: Doubleday.

Bernbaum, E. (1997). The spiritual and cultural significance of mountains. In B. Messerli and J. D. Ives (Eds.), *Mountains of the world: A global priority* (pp. 39–60). London: Parthenon Press.

Bhattarai, K., Conway, D., & Shrestha, N. (2005). Tourism, terrorism, and turmoil in Nepal. *Annals of Tourism Research, 32*(3), 669–688. doi:10.1016/j.annals.2004.08.007

Bott, E. (2009). Big mountain, big name: Globalised relations of risk in Himalayan mountaineering. *Journal of Tourism & Cultural Change, 7*(4), 287–301. doi:10.1080/14766820903521785

Boyd, K. (2015). What is photokeratitis, including snow blindness? *American Academy of Opthalmology*. Retrieved from https://www.aao.org/eye-health/diseases/photokeratitis-snow-blindness

Brown, C. (2014). Sherpas: The invisible men of Everest. *National Geographic*. Retrieved from http://news.nationalgeographic.com/news/special-features/2014/04/140426-sherpa-culture-everest-disaster.

Buda, D. M. (2015). The death drive in tourism studies. *Annals of Tourism Research, 50*, 39–51. doi:10.1016/j.annals.2014.10.008

Carnicelli-Filho, S. (2013). The emotional life of adventure guides. *Annals of Tourism Research, 43*, 192–209. doi:10.1016/j.annals.2013.05.003

Cater, C. I. (2006). Playing with risk? Participant perceptions of risk and management implications in adventure tourism. *Tourism Management, 27*(2), 317–325. doi:10.1016/j.tourman.2004.10.005

Cheung, L., & McColl-Kennedy, J. R. (2015). Resource integration in liminal periods: Transitioning to transformative service. *Journal of Services Marketing, 29*(6/7), 485–497. doi:10.1108/JSM-01-2015-0055

Christiansen, D. (1990). Adventure tourism. In J. Miles & S. Priest (Eds.), *Adventure education* (pp. 433–442). State College, PA: Venture Publishing.

Cooper, A. (1997). *Sacred mountains: Ancient wisdom and modern meanings*. Edinburgh, UK: Floris Books.

D'Aliesio, R. (2012). Grieving man rebukes guides for failing to halt wife's Everest trek. *The Globe and Mail*. Retrieved from http://www.theglobeandmail.com/news/national/grieving-man-rebukes-guides-for-failing-to-halt-wifes-everest-trek/article4544432/

Davis, W. (2014) As equals on the mountain, the Sherpas deserve better. *The Globe and Mail*. Retrieved from http://www.theglobeandmail.com/opinion/as-equals-on-the-mountain-the-sherpas-deserve-better/article18209186/

Douglas, E. (2007). The mother of all climbs. *The Guardian, The Observer*. Retrieved from https://www.theguardian.com/travel/2007/aug/26/switzerland.climbingholidays

Downey, D., Kinane, I., & Parker, E. (2016). *Landscapes of liminality: Between space and place*. London: Rowman & Littlefield.

Ebert, P. A., & Robertson, S. (2013). A plea for risk. *Royal Institute of Philosophy Supplement, 73*, 45–64. doi:10.1017/S1358246113000271

Elsrud, T. (2001). Risk creation in traveling: Backpacker adventure narration. *Annals of Tourism Research, 28*(3), 597–617. doi:10.1016/S0160-7383(00)00061-X

Frohlick, S. (2003). Negotiating the 'Global' within the global playscapes of Mount Everest. *Canadian Review of Sociology/Revue Canadienne de Sociologie, 3*(5), 525–542. doi:10.1111/j.1755-618X.2003.tb00003.x

Giddens, A. (1991). *Modernity and self-identity: Self and society in the late modern age*. Stanford, CA: Stanford University Press.

Godde, M. F., Price, M. F., & Zimmermann, F. M. (1996). *Tourism and development in mountain regions*. New York, NY: CABI Publishing.

Guggleberger, M. (2015). Climbing beyond the summits: Social and global aspects of women's expeditions in the Himalayas. *The International Journal of the History of Sport, 32*(4), 597–613.

Gurubacharya, B. (2018). Veteran Sherpa tries to reach top of Mount Everest for record-breaking 22nd time. *Independent*. Retrieved from https://www.independent.co.uk/news/world/asia/mount-everest-world-record-climbs-sherpa-kami-rita-latest-nepal-kathmandu-a8298926.html

Hansen, P. H. (1995). Albert Smith, the Alpine Club, and the invention of mountaineering in mid-Victorian Britain. *Journal of British Studies, 34*(3), 300–324. doi:10.1086/386080

Hilton, J. (1933). *Lost Horizon*. New York, NY: William Morrow & Company, Inc.

Hochschild, A. R. (1979). Emotion work, feeling rules, and social structure. *American Journal of Sociology, 85*(3), 551–575. doi:10.1086/227049

Howard-Grenville, J., Golden-Biddle, K., Irwin, J., & Mao, J. (2011). Liminality as cultural process for cultural change. *Organization Science, 22*(2), 522–539. doi:10.1287/orsc.1100.0554

Ibrahim, H., & Cordes, K. A. (2002). *Outdoor recreation: Enrichment for a lifetime* (2nd ed.). Champaign: Sagamore Publishing.

Jencson, L. (2001). Disastrous rites: Liminality and communitas in a flood crisis. *Anthropology & Humanism, 26*(1), 46–58. doi:10.1525/ahu.2001.26.1.46

Kelly, C. J. (2000). *"Thrilling and marvellous experiences": Place and subjectivity in Canadian climbing narratives, 1885–1925* (Unpublished doctoral dissertation). University of Waterloo, Waterloo, Ontario, Canada.

Lepp, A., & Gibson, H. (2008). Sensation seeking and tourism: Tourist role, perception of risk and destination choice. *Tourism Management, 29*(4), 740–750. doi:10.1016/j.tourman.2007.08.002

Lewis, N. (2000). The climbing body, nature, and the experience of modernity. *Body & Society, 6*(3–4), 58–80. doi:10.1177/1357034X00006003004

Löfgren, O. (1999). *On holiday: A history of vacationing*. Berkley: University of California Press.

MacFarlane, R. (2003). *Mountains of the mind*. London, UK: Granta Publications.

Mälksoo, M. (2012). The challenge of liminality for international relations theory. *Review of International Studies, 38*(2), 481–494. doi:10.1017/S0260210511000829

Miller, M. C. (2017). *An exploration of Sherpas' narratives of living and dying in Mountaineering* (Unpublished doctoral dissertation). University of Waterloo, Waterloo, Ontario, Canada.

Monz, C. (2000). Recreation resource assessment and monitoring techniques for mountain regions. In P. Godde, M. Price, & F. Zimmermann (Eds.), *Tourism and development in mountain regions* (pp. 47–68). New York, NY: CABI Publishing.

Mu, Y., & Nepal, S. (2016). High mountain adventure tourism: Trekkers' perceptions of risk and death in Mt. Everest region, Nepal. *Asia Pacific Journal of Tourism Research, 21*(5), 500–511. doi:10.1080/10941665.2015.1062787

National Public Radio. (2013). On Mount Everest, Sherpa guides bear the brunt of the danger. *NPR Fresh Air*. Retrieved from http://www.npr.org/2013/08/14/206704533/on-mounteverest-sherpa-guides-bear-the-brunt-of-the-danger.

Neale, J. (2002). *Tigers of the snow: How one fateful climb made the Sherpas mountaineering legends*. London: Abacus.

Nepal, S. K. (2016). Tourism and change in Nepal's Mt. Everest region. In H. Richins and J. S. Hull (Eds.), *Mountain tourism: Experiences, communities, environments, and sustainable futures* (pp. 285–294). Wallingford: CAB International. doi:10.1079/9781780644608.0000

New York Times. (1923). Climbing Mount Everest is work for supermen. *New York Times*. Retrieved from http://graphics8.nytimes.com/packages/pdf/arts/mallory1923.pdf

Oliver-Smith, A., & Hoffman, S. M. (1999). *The angry earth: Disaster in anthropological perspective*. New York, NY: Routledge.

Ortner, S. B. (1997). Thick resistance: Death and cultural construction of agency in Himalayan mountaineering. *Representations, 59*(Beyond), 135–162. doi:10.2307/2928818

Ortner, S. B. (1999). *Life and death on Mt. Everest: Sherpas and Himalayan mountaineering.* Princeton, NJ: Princeton University Press.

Palmer, C. (2004). Death, danger and the selling of risk in adventure sports. In B. Wheaton (Ed.), *Lifestyle sport: Consumption, identity and difference* (pp. 205–215). London: Routledge.

Payne, E., & Shrestha, M. (2014) Avalanche kills 12 in single deadliest accidents on Mount Everest. *CNN World.* Retrieved from http://www.cnn.com/2014/04/18/world/asia/nepal-everestavalanche/

Peedom, J. (Director). (2015). *Sherpa: Trouble on Everest* [Documentary]. Australia: Screen Australia.

Pomfret, G. (2006). Mountaineering adventure tourists: A conceptual framework for research. *Tourism Management, 27*(1), 113–123. doi:10.1016/j.tourman.2004.08.003

Pritchard, A., & Morgan, N. (2006). Hotel Babylon? Exploring hotels as liminal sites of transition and transgression. *Tourism Management, 27*, 762–772.

Preston-Whyte, R. (2004). The beach as a liminal space. In A. Lew, C. M. Hall, & A. Williams (Eds.), *The Blackwell's tourism companion* (pp. 249–259). Oxford: Blackwell.

Rhinehart, R. (2003). *To the extreme: Alternative sports inside and out.* New York: State University Press.

Robinson, V. (2004). Taking risks: Identity, masculinities and rock climbing. In B. Wheaton (Ed.), *Lifestyle sport: Consumption, identity and difference* (pp. 113–130). London: Routledge.

Ryan, C. (2013). Risk acceptance in adventure tourism—Paradox and context. In J. Wilks, J. Stephen, and F. Moore (Eds.), *Managing tourist health and safety in the new millennium* (pp. 75–86). London: Routledge.

Rogers, P., & Aitchison, J. (1998). *Towards sustainable tourism in the Everest region of Nepal.* Kathmandu: IUCN Nepal.

Schaffer, G. (2013). The disposable man: A western history of Sherpas on Everest. *Outside Magazine.* Retrieved from http://www.outsideonline.com/outdooradventure/climbing/mountaineering/Disposable-Man-History-of-the-Sherpa-on-Everest.html.

Seamon, D., & Sowers, J. (2008). Place and Placelessness. In P. Hubbard, R. Kitchen, and G. Vallentines (Eds.), *Key texts in human geography* (pp. 43–51). Los Angeles: Sage.

Shields, R. (1991). *Places on the margin: Alternative geographies of modernity.* London: Routledge.

Stone, P. R. (2009). Making absent death present: Consuming dark tourism in contemporary society. In R. Sharpley and P. R. Stone (Eds.), *The darker side of travel: The theory and practice of dark tourism.* Bristol, UK: Channel View Publications.

Swarbrooke, J., Beard, C., Leckie, S., & Pomfret, G. (2003). *Adventure tourism: The new frontier.* London: Butterworth-Heinemann.

Thomassen, B. (2012). Revisting liminality: The danger of empty spaces. In H. Andrews & L. Roberts (Eds.), *Liminal landscapes: Travel, experience and spaces in-between* (pp. 21–35). London: Routledge.

Turner, V. (1969). *The ritual process: Structure and anti-structure.* Chicago: Aldine Press.

Turner, V. (1979). Frame, flow and reflection: Ritual and drama as public liminality. *Japanese Journal of Religious Studies, 6*(4), 465–499. doi:10.18874/jjrs.6.4.1979.465-499

Turner, V. (1987). *The anthropology of performance.* New York: Performance Arts Journal Publications.

van Gennep, A. (1960). *The rites of passage.* Chicago: University of Chicago Press.

Varley, P. (2006). Confecting adventure and playing with meaning: The adventure commodification continuum. *Journal of Sport & Tourism, 11*(2), 173–194. doi:10.1080/14775080601155217

Varley, P. J. (2011). Sea kayakers at the margins: The liminoid character of contemporary adventures. *Leisure Studies, 30*(1), 85–98. doi:10.1080/02614361003749801

Williams, P., & Soutar, G. N. (2009). Value, satisfaction and behavioural intentions in an adventure tourism context. *Annals of Tourism Research, 36*(3), 413–438. doi:10.1016/j.annals.2009.02.002

Yalom, I. D. (1980). *Existential psychotherapy.* New York: Basic Books.

Change within the change: pregnancy, liminality and adventure tourism in Mexico

Isis Arlene Díaz-Carrión, Paola Vizcaino-Suárez and Hugo Gaggiotti

ABSTRACT

Despite the growing number of pregnant women engaging in outdoor adventure activities, very few studies have explored pregnancy or the specific needs and challenges of pregnant women in tourism research. To fill this gap in the literature, we examine the participation of pregnant women in adventure tourism through the theoretical lens of liminality. Conceptualising pregnancy as a liminal stage in which women are 'suspended' between two statuses, opens diverse possibilities to delve into women's experiences of embodiment, bodily image and control. In this sense, pregnancy is understood as an 'internal change', which adds specific challenges to women's practice of adventure tourism, including bodily changes and different perceptions of risk-taking. Similarly, the context of adventure tourism provides an ideal space to reflect on liminal transitions and the 'outside changes' that pregnant women go through in the predominantly masculinised spaces that characterise this tourism segment. Semi-structured interviews were conducted with 35 Mexican women who actively pursue adventure tourism and who had engaged in these activities during at least one pregnancy. The analysis indicates the importance of norms and social expectations experienced by pregnant women when doing adventure tourism. The concept of the 'rhizomatic body' proved to be a valuable tool when looking at the social taboos, prohibitions and rules that apply to pregnant women in specific sociocultural contexts (in this case, Mexico). By reframing and reconceptualising pregnant women and their practice of adventure activities, the social construction of pregnancy is elucidated. Finally, the study contributes to the understanding of alternative models and experiences of being a woman in gendered spaces, while shedding light on relevant behavioural patterns among pregnant tourists and the sociocultural impacts of these patterns.

摘要

尽管越来越多的孕妇参与户外探险活动, 但很少有研究探讨怀孕或者孕妇在旅游研究中的具体需求和挑战。为了填补这一文献的空白, 我们通过阈限的理论视角来考察孕妇参与冒险旅游的情况。本文将怀孕概念化为女性在两种状态之间"悬浮"的一个阈限阶段, 为深入研究女性的亲身化、身体形象和身体控制体验提供了

多种可能性。这个意义上, 怀孕被理解为一种"内在的变化", 这给
女性的冒险旅游实践增加了具体的挑战, 包括身体的变化和对冒
险的不同看法。类似地, 冒险旅游的语境提供了一个理想的空间
来反思孕妇在这个主要是男性化的空间中所经历的阈限过渡和"外
部变化"。本研究对35名墨西哥妇女进行了半结构式访谈, 这些妇
女积极追求冒险旅游, 并在至少一次怀孕期间参与了这些活动。
分析表明了孕妇在进行冒险旅游时所经历的规范和社会期望的重
要性。"根状体"的概念被证明是一种宝贵的工具, 有助于了解在特
定的社会文化背景下(在本例中为墨西哥)应用于孕妇的社会禁忌
、禁令和规则。通过对怀孕妇女及其冒险活动实践的重新构建和
概念化, 阐明了妊娠的社会建构过程。最后, 这项研究有助于理解
在性别空间中作为女性的其他模式和体验, 同时阐明怀孕游客的
相关行为模式以及这些模式的社会文化影响。

Introduction

Anthropologists have extensively theorised on the notion of liminality to explain the construction of meaning during critical social and life events and their associated rituals and ceremonies. A major life event that has been examined through the framework of liminality is pregnancy. Following Turner (1969) and Van Gennep (1960), during the liminal period of pregnancy, a woman is conceived as 'suspended' between two statuses (e.g. a working woman and a 'mother to be'), leading to the construction of multiple selves (Ladge, Clair, & Greenberg, 2012; Noble & Walker, 1997). The theoretical perspective of liminality has opened possibilities to examine women's experiences of embodiment, bodily image or control during pregnancy (Nash, 2012; Ogle, Tyner, & Schofield-Tomschin, 2013); as well as to understand normative (i.e. conforming to social norms) and non-normative pregnancy experiences (Côté-Arsenault, Brody, & Dombeck, 2009).

Adding to the literature on liminality and pregnancy, this paper seeks to examine the participation of pregnant women in adventure tourism, as a context in which women may craft or carefully produce a non-normative pregnancy. Tourism, and in particular, adventure tourism, serves as an ideal space to reflect on liminal transitions. It works as a place of freedom, role subversion and, as Graburn (1989) suggests, a place to experience separation from routinised lives, where it is possible to be temporarily free from secular obligations and imposed roles (Trauer & Ryan, 2005). The recent spatial turn within cultural geography, tourism and urban studies also offers creative ways of theorising the fluidity of social relations, paying particular attention to women's embodied practices (see Dallen, 2018; Hannam, Sheller, & Urry, 2006; Mahon-Daly & Andrews, 2002; Soja, 1989; Xu, 2018).

The liminal (and the liminoid) we explore here are not exclusively concerned with identity transformations. What intrigues us when studying the participation of pregnant women in adventure tourism is the kind of liminality that represents the transformation of social status and compliance with social norms (Van Gennep, 1960), while recreating antagonisms between settling and moving, between a pregnant body and a woman's body, a woman at risk and a child at risk. The point of such enquiry is to foreground transition, the inside change (pregnancy) within the outside change (participation in adventure tourism).

In the Mexican context, where we conducted our research, normative expectations of pregnancy sustain that risky activities should be avoided. Thus, pregnant women who participate in adventure tourism are seen as having a defiant attitude and are heavily questioned by different groups of people, including family members, friends, service providers and other tourists. The social relevance of this study lies precisely in highlighting how women struggle with the physical, psychological and sociocultural impacts of a major inside change (pregnancy), while exploring a context of external change (adventure tourism) in which women can resist some of the gendered ideologies associated with pregnancy.

The article is organised as follows. First, we present the liminal as a theoretical perspective and its application to explain pregnancy (internal change). We follow with an explanation of how liminality, pregnancy and adventure tourism (external change) interact. The research context (Mexico) and methodological choices are then explained, followed by the analysis and discussion of the findings. Finally, we present the study conclusions and recommendations for future research.

Liminality and pregnancy

The notion of liminality has been extensively theorised to make sense of change, mobility, transition, transit, in-between-ness and any state of hybridity or transformation
(Borg & Söderlund, 2013; Ibarra & Obodaru, 2016; Turner, 1974, 1987; Underthun & Jordhus-Lier, 2017; Van Gennep, 1960). Turner (1969, 1974, 1987) and Van Gennep (1960) focused on the in-between spaces and transitional moments when apparent distraction and ambiguity are experienced during rites of passage and transformations. Bridges ([1974] 1980) referred to the liminal as a 'neutral zone', a space of reconstruction or an empty space where a new sense of the self could gestate. A more sophisticated elaboration suggests the need to acknowledge the essentiality of the liminal and the need to consider mobile and nomadic transitions as existential conditions of the social to regenerate, even without a conscious intention (Braidotti, 1994). Social researchers have found inspiration in the concept of liminality to explain changes in everyday life and recent approaches highlight how liminality is embedded in daily practices with dual outcomes (Borg & Söderlund, 2013; Daniel & Ellis-Chadwick, 2016; Mahon-Daly & Andrews, 2002).

The theoretical perspective of liminality, in particular the contributions of Van Gennep (1960) and Turner (1969), are useful to view pregnancy as a transformational space between social structures, where women experience, navigate and enact an in-between identity. Ladge, Clair, and Greenberg (2012) describe how the individual and the social construction of pregnancy as a liminal state operate in working women. The authors emphasise the identity transition along the process and suggest that cross-domain identity transitions (i.e. those occurring when an individual's work identity must be adapted to integrate a non-work identity like motherhood), appear to differ in complexity from sequential identity transitions (e.g. the change from one job to another).

The literature on liminality and pregnancy has also examined the positive and negative effects of pregnancy on women's transformational stages (Aiken & Trussell, 2017; Hebl, King, Glick, Singletary, & Kazama, 2007; Jackson, 2009; Kawash, 2011). Particular attention has been given to norms and expectations, as they play a substantial role in women's identity and personal change (Aiken & Trussell, 2017; Davis-Floyd,

2003; Jordan, [1978] 1993; Mercer, 2004; Sánchez Bringas, Espinosa Islas, Ezcurdia, & Torres, 2004). Another relevant area of study is how pregnancy affects a woman's physical, psychological and social self (Côté-Arsenault et al., 2009). On a physical level, the changing body and the clothes women need to use epitomise the in-between status women experience during pregnancy and even after giving birth (Ogle et al., 2013). On a psychological and social level, the negotiations women undertake to move in and out of public spaces while breastfeeding can be constructed as a liminal act where different feelings, including shame, arise (Mahon-Daly & Andrews, 2002).

Cultural interpretations of liminality and pregnancy

The liminal is subject to cultural relativist interpretations. Comparative studies across societies have shown that the construction of the liminal state of pregnancy differs depending on the cultural context (Davis-Floyd, 2001; Jordan, [1978] 1993). In Western cultures, pregnancy is often viewed through a medical but not a sociocultural lens (Davis-Floyd, 1992; Davis-Floyd & Sargent, 1997). Western medicine tends to associate pregnancy with risk and the pregnant woman has been construed as a sick patient at risk of death (Lupton, 1994). Authors who adopt a sociocultural lens criticise the medical rhetoric that promotes the objectification of both patients and their bodies (Leder, 1992); while noting that societal and institutional advice interact with gender stereotypes and may be opposed to women's preferences (Mahon-Daly & Andrews, 2002).

The dominant medical view focuses on multiple phases of assistance, care and protection, but underscores how pregnancy contributes to a multiplicity of representations for women. The literature suggests that considering a pregnant woman only as a pregnant body in need of medical care limits the multifaceted and complex social nature of the woman and her individual status during gestation (Clarke, Shim, Mamo, Fosket, & Fishman, 2003; Colman & Colman, 1973/1974; Mahon-Daly & Andrews, 2002). Being aware of the liminal nature of pregnancy helps us to consider the rigidity of the ritualization that is usually embedded as an indissoluble part of the pregnancy, as well as the taboos associated with the uses of the female body during pregnancy and the fantasies constructed around the risk to the foetus.

Finally, research has signposted that context and culture mediate the liminal period of pregnancy and have an impact on women's experiences. Negative impacts emerge from the non-compliance with sociocultural norms or expectations. For example, in her examination of cultural models and pregnancy in the state of Jalisco, Mexico, Jackson (2009) concluded that pregnant women who did not comply with culturally appropriate behaviour, as a consequence of others' reactions, experienced higher rates of psychological and social stress. Likewise, in the United States, Hebl et al. (2007) found that pregnant women evoked hostile or benevolent reactions depending on whether they conformed to or strayed from the traditional feminine gender roles.

Liminality, pregnancy and adventure tourism

The previous section highlighted how normative experiences emerge from the interactions of cultural interpretations and traditions of pregnancy (e.g. the Western medical tradition), and the sociocultural constructions of gender and femininity, which impose restrictions on the 'pregnant body' (Lupton, 1994), including limitations to physical activity or sports. Even though moderate physical exercise is usually recommended during pregnancy in industrialized and emerging countries, women receive mixed messages about the type, frequency, intensity and duration of physical activity (for a systematic review see Sánchez García et al., 2016). This section expands the inquiry of liminality and pregnancy, by examining women's participation in adventure tourism as a context that opens possibilities for 'non-normative' pregnancy experiences.

Pregnancy has rarely been examined in tourism studies, except within the category of health and medical tourism (e.g. Hall, 2011). However, a few scholars have shown interest on the social implications of pregnancy for female travellers (Voigt & Laing, 2010); the restrictions imposed by this liminal state (Small, 2005); and its importance in crafting role identities (Klann, 2017). The studies on gender and adventure tourism have focused more broadly on analysing the different levels of female and male par- ticipation, showing an underrepresentation of women in outdoor activities (Clinch & Filimonau, 2016; Doran, 2016; Kay & Laberge, 2004; Roggenbuck & Lucas, 1987). Among the reasons suggested are the social actors' needs to avoid risk due to the instability and inconsistencies produced during the social construction of multiple selves (Mitchell, 1983).

In our view, adventure tourism constitutes a relevant activity to explore pregnant women's experiences of liminality. The river, the mountain, the sea, the gullies or the dunes are common scenarios of adventure tourism, but are not usually associated with pregnancy. In fact, adventure tourism has reinforced the masculinisation of these spaces through the links with physical strength, the challenge to nature and the assertive management of risk, characteristics traditionally ascribed to men (Clinch & Filimonau, 2016) as opposed to women or pregnant women. Furthermore, the gender and tourism scholarship has examined the devaluation of women's presence in adven- ture activities through promoting images of women's emotionality in the face of chal- lenges (Doran, 2016; Kay & Laberge, 2004), focusing on the caregiving aspects of these activities (Pomfret & Doran, 2015), or minimising women's technical capacity (Stoddart, 2010). These images contribute to the construction and naturalisation of gender roles and to the hyper masculinisation of adventure spaces that impose restric- tions to women, particularly to pregnant women.

The masculinisation of adventure spaces produces barriers that hinder women's participation and exclude them during pregnancy, but also during other stages of their life. For example, Díaz-Carrión (2012) reported the restrictions experienced by young local women interested in rafting in the state of Veracruz, Mexico; Kay and Laberge (2004) explained how motherhood has been constructed as a limitation to pursuing adventure race activities; while Doran (2016) pointed out the restraints expe- rienced by women mountaineers during their active life.

The rhizomatic body

Scholars have drawn from the literature on liminality, pregnancy and adventure tourism to examine the conditioning of women's expressions of corporality and the perceived barriers to women's access and use of adventure spaces (Comley, 2016). A relevant example of women's resistance to these barriers is the dynamic construction of women's bodily identity depicted by Knijnik, Horton, and Cruz (2010) in their work about the 'rhizomatic body' of Brazilian professional women surfers, who contest the normative female body and open new interpretations for multiple representations of femininity. The authors build on Markula's (2006) reading of Foucault, highlighting how the discourses around femininity and the feminine body may be used to dominate women. Recognising that no sport or recreation activity on its own facilitates liberating practices, Markula (2006) applies the Deleuzian 'rhizomatic' model of thinking to imagine feminine bodies in a positive light beyond the binary opposition between femininity and masculinity, allowing for a more fluid and changeable conceptualisation. Similarly, Mahon-Daly and Andrews (2002) explore how women who breastfeed in public spaces are in a liminal state of time and space, and experience this 'rhizomatic' or fluid body during the transition between biological and sociocultural roles.

Adventure tourism is a fruitful field of study for contesting the normative woman's body and understanding the representation of the 'rhizomatic body'. Kay and Laberge (2004) analysed further examples of how strong women with athletic bodies were criticised because of the normative constructions of the female soft and docile body. Similarly, Comley (2016) described how women surfers often experience conflict while receiving unwanted male attention and patronising. In this case, the 'rhizomatic body' had to navigate between traditionally feminine/masculine identities in a space where their presence was marginal. Pomfret and Doran (2015) highlighted women's abandonment or change in mountaineering habits because of pregnancy. In order to craft a different identity, some women climbers had to differentiate themselves from traditional femininity to be recognised by their commitment rather than their gender, just like the 'rhizomatic' Brazilian surfers. Alternatively, in Chisholm's (2008) study, climber Lynn Hill utilises her 'sexed body' to develop her own style and gain recognition in a male-dominated world where the feminine is often undervalued. Thus, Hill's experience exemplifies the potential for transformation through a process that is consistent with the 'rhizomatic body'.

In our opinion, the concept of the 'rhizomatic body' is useful when addressing liminality as a space for pregnant women to challenge and address taboos, prohibitions and rules. This notion can be applied to normative pregnancy when crafting non-normative pregnancy identities through the participation in adventure tourism. In consistency with the concept of liminality (Ibarra & Obodaru, 2016; Turner, 1969, 1974, 1987; Van Gennep, 1960), the 'rhizomatic body' embodies the construction of meaning through experiences of transitional moments characterised by ambiguity and transformation, emerging as a catalyst for alternative, non-normative pregnancy.

The experience of the 'rhizomatic body' is essentially liminoid. The liminoid implies the symbolic construction of the liminal passage and the transition according to how it is represented by the individual imaginary. When concrete and visible liminal phases are diluted, the liminoid (individual, ambiguous, not socially constrained transfigurations in space and time) occurs. It is a phase in which the transition has not taken place as a concrete ritual stage, but it is imagined in function of how it is individually constructed. In this case, the woman imagines herself through a state she's leaving, a *mujer* (a woman, unitary, a person) and a state she is acquiring, a *mamá* (a mother, plural, two people - she and her child). In the process of representing herself, the subject self-imposes what is symbolically acceptable and unacceptable. According to Turner (1974), the liminoid phase between leaving one state and taking up another is evidenced in the subject (dreams, fantasies, favourite reading and entertainment) and in those with whom she is leaving and joining (their myths about her, treatment of her, and so on).

Based on the literature review, we have constructed a model to guide the investigation of liminality, pregnancy and adventure tourism (see Figure 1). The theoretical perspective of liminality will allow us to explore pregnancy (inside change) as a liminal-liminoid state, constructed in the context of the particular Mexican cultural taboos, prohibitions and rules. We expect these normative interpretations to follow societal and institutional advice, while promoting gender stereotypes that influence women's behaviours (as per Mahon-Daly & Andrews, 2002). Given that play and performance are fundamental to understanding how the liminal and the liminoid states work, the pregnant woman must lend herself to playing the role of future mother and to become 'responsible' for taking care of her and the future baby. This role is symbolically constructed as opposed to a woman who participates in adventure tourism (external change), where risk, freedom or lack of control, among other characteristics can generate spaces for transgression and for the development of non-normative pregnancy experiences. In this sense, our study will investigate the relationship between liminality and pregnancy (inside change), within the unique context of adventure tourism (outside change), where women can resist some of the gender ideologies associated with pregnancy.

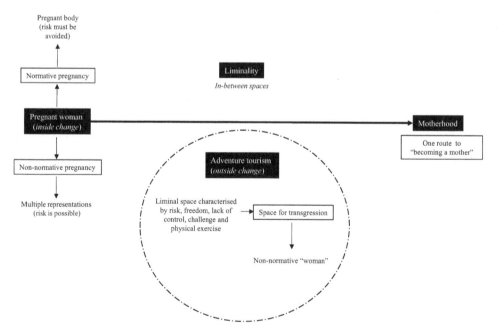

Figure 1. Liminality in pregnant women performing adventure tourism.
Source: Authors.

Method

The study's main purpose is to examine Mexican women's participation in adventure tourism during the liminal period of pregnancy, and to explore the possibilities for non-normative pregnancies. A qualitative design was adopted to facilitate the analysis of the gender dimensions in tourism (Nunkoo, Hall, & Ladsawut, 2017), as well as to understand the participants' context and pregnancy experiences (Martinez-Pascual, Abuin, Perez de Heredia, & Palacios-Ceña, 2016; Osuchowski-Sanchez, Tigges, Mendelson, Lobo & Clark, 2012).

Semi-structured interviews were chosen as the main data collection instrument in order to listen to participants' voices directly and to understand their 'interpretations, experiences and spatialities of social life' (Dowling, Lloyd, & Suchet-Pearson, 2016, p. 680). Tourism and geography scholars have found interviews a particularly useful method to examine bodily and gendered experiences (Bondi, 2003; Díaz-Carrión, 2012; McDowell, 1999; Seow & Brown, 2018), which make them an appropriate technique for this study. The interview guide was informed by the literature review on liminality, pregnancy and adventure tourism and covered questions on the adventure tourism experience, changes during pregnancy and gender roles and expectations, to apprehend the interpretations of normative and non-normative pregnancy in Mexican women.

During the first stage of research, key contacts were made in adventure tourism clubs and other formal associations, as well as through specialised adventure tourism agencies. A total of 35 semi-structured interviews were conducted through purposeful snowball sampling (Palinkas et al., 2015; Tajeddini, Ratten, & Denisa, 2017). Inclusion criteria were to be a Mexican woman and to have pursued adventure tourism activities during part of their pregnancy. Nearly half of the interviews were conducted face-to-face ($n = 15$). The rest were conducted using information and communication technologies (ICTs) and software applications (Skype, Google Hangouts, Facebook or WhatsApp). All of the interviews (face-to-face and non-face-to-face) were conducted in Spanish, audio recorded and then transcribed into text for analysis. Interviews lasted an average of 80 minutes and the transcriptions generated about 1,000 pages in Spanish. Pseudonyms were employed in lieu of participants' names and some demographic details were excluded from the results in order to ensure anonymity and confidentiality.

The demographics of the sample are presented in Table 1. The average age of women participants was 36.8 years, with an average number of 1.6 children aged 12.2 on average. Only one woman was retired, the remaining 34 worked in a diverse range of fields. 17 women work in the private sector, 13 in the public sector and the remaining 4 in the third sector (e.g. NGOs). The majority of the participants held a university degree (32). This is particularly relevant in a country where access to higher education is limited (Organisation for Economic Co-operation and Development (OECD), 2018).

Qualitative content analysis was employed to systematically examine the textual data with the purpose of elucidating themes (Bengtsson, 2016; Thomas, 1994). This technique has proved effective in previous gender and tourism studies to examine participants' lived experiences (Camprubí & Coromina, 2016; Hsieh & Shannon, 2005; Neuendorf, 2011). The systematic process entailed coding, examination of meaning

Table 1. Participants' demographics.

Name	Age	Occupation	State of Residence	Years practicing Adventure tourism	Activity performed	Age of children
Alicia	41	Entrepreneur & professor	Mexico City	13	mountaineering	15 & 12
Andrea	34	Travel agent	San Luis Potosí	12	climbing	8
Antonia	63	Consultant	Puebla	39	mountaineering	40 & 37
Ariana	32	Professor	Veracruz	15	caving	5 & 3
Aurora	50	Manager	Veracruz	28	scuba diving	24 & 21
Berenice	28	Professor	Mexico City	14	mountaineering	4
Carla	41	Entrepreneur	Veracruz	25	mountaineering	17
Cristina	53	Accountant	Puebla	26	mountaineering	28 & 24
Daniela	27	Dentist	Oaxaca	13	kayaking	2
Diana	40	Doctor	Baja California Sur	23	scuba diving	10 (twins)
Elena	29	Professor	Mexico City	13	abseiling	2
Elisa	35	PhD Student & Professor	Mexico City	21	caving	8 & 5
Ericka	26	Entrepreneur	Veracruz	12	kayaking	3
Evelyn	48	Dentist	Nuevo León	23	mountaineering	25, 21 & 18
Giselle	25	Accountant	Veracruz	9	kayaking	2
Gloria	65	Retired	Puebla	40	mountaineering	42, 39 & 37
Imelda	41	Consultant	Mexico City	22	paragliding	13 & 10
Irene	26	Entrepreneur	Baja California	8	abseiling	1
Karina	35	Lawyer & Consultant	Oaxaca	9	kayaking	7 & 4
Laura	29	Architect	Mexico City	12	abseiling	4 & 2
Liliana	41	Psychologist	Veracruz	12	rafting	15 & 11
Lina	33	Veterinarian	Baja California	11	surfing	5
Maritza	32	Entrepreneur	Baja California Sur	10	kayaking	2
Mireya	24	Dentist	Mexico City	4	abseiling	1
Nadia	26	Consultant	Veracruz	8	paragliding	4 & 2
Olga	33	Entrepreneur & Professor	Edo. de México	8	mountaineering	5
Patricia	49	Lawyer & Professor	Querétaro	25	mountaineering	23, 21 & 17
Raquel	50	Professor	Oaxaca	26	scuba diving	21
Rosario	27	Veterinarian	Oaxaca	13	rafting	5 & 3
Sara	39	Consultant	Mexico City	12	paragliding	9 & 6
Susana	26	Accountant	Baja California	11	surfing	4
Teresa	32	Professor	Sonora	15	abseiling	10 & 7
Verónica	41	Psychologist	Quintana Roo	15	scuba diving	9 & 6
Yuliana	38	Architect	Mexico City	16	surfing	10 & 7
Yulissa	31	Consultant	Mexico City	11	scuba diving	4

and provision of a description through both manifest and latent content analysis (Graneheim, Lindgren, & Lundman, 2017).

During the manifest content stage, we reviewed the surface structure of the discourse analysis in order to get a preliminary interpretation about the meanings of pregnancy. This first stage was useful to identify the informants' perception into the way pregnancy was experienced as a liminal state and the restrictions it imposed in the use of adventure tourism spaces. Reflective notes were generated to describe the

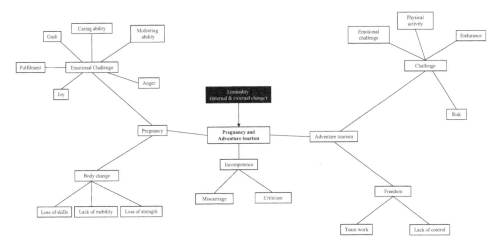

Figure 2. Concept map.
Source: Authors.

trends of participants' perspectives and to organise the initial codes (Hsieh & Shannon, 2005; Neuendorf, 2011). During the second phase of latent analysis, we focused on the underlying meaning through the construction of a concept map (see Figure 2). Following the strategies recommended by Hsieh and Shannon (2005), Bengtsson (2016) and Neuendorf (2011), the concept map summarized the recurrent unifying ideas that characterised the experiences of participants (i.e. emotional challenge, body change and freedom). The relevance of these themes was assessed in terms of capturing an important relation to the overall research question. This process was useful in understanding context as well as circumstances regarding pregnancy, liminality and adventure tourism.

Particular attention was devoted to identifying researcher biases or *a priori* assumptions. Some strategies employed to minimise bias over the course of analysis included: referring back to the theoretical framework, triangulating data (i.e. contrasting the interview data with the researcher observations and notes taken during the fieldwork), showing field notes to colleagues, and keeping the overall research question firmly in mind (Miles & Huberman, 1994). Initial impressions and interpretations of the data were revised through the hermeneutic spiral approach. Different interpretations were then examined and contextualised and agreements were reached on the meanings of the text within its context (Lindseth & Norberg, 2004). Member checking of the transcribed interviews and translated versions was also required (Lietz & Zayas, 2013).

Findings

According to the participants' age and life cycle stage, the following categories can be used to characterise women who engage in adventure tourism in Mexico. In order to explore pregnancy, the women from our sample fall under categories 3, 4 and 5:

1. children and adolescents,
2. women with no children,

3.   women with babies, 34.2%
4.   women with young children, 37.1% and
5.   women with older children, 28.5%.

As shown in Table 1, participants practised the following adventure tourism activities: abseiling, climbing, mountaineering, paragliding, caving, kayaking, rafting, surf and scuba diving. Sometimes they alternated between different adventure sports, but one activity prevailed. The choice of adventure activity was closely related to the place of residence. For instance, women who lived in Southern Mexico (e.g. Oaxaca, Veracruz, Quintana Roo) had more opportunities to engage in fresh water sports like kayaking or rafting in nearby rivers (10 out of 12), whereas those living in Central and Northern Mexico (e.g. Mexico City, Puebla, San Luis Potosí, Nuevo León) found abseiling, climbing, mountaineering or paragliding more accessible (16 out of 18). Women who lived in the Baja Peninsula preferred salt water activities like surfing or scuba diving (4 out of 5).

The average of years practising the activity was 16.4 and most women became involved in adventure tourism before having children. Only five of the interviewees got involved with adventure activities after having their first child, but experienced a second pregnancy while pursuing adventure activities. All women reported a break (of months, but in some cases of years) due to pregnancy and childbirth. All of the participants resided in cities and travelled to adventure tourism destinations to practise their preferred sport at least once a month. Those who did abseiling reported the possibility of training in sport facilities in their own cities, while those who engaged in water activities and lived near the sea also tried to train regularly. Even if some of these activities did not formally account as adventure tourism, they were seen as an extension of it because they were related to the tourists' training.

Every woman's story was unique, but two broad categories could be identified when exploring participants' introduction to adventure activities. For women over 55 years old, it was the relatives or someone who they were in a close relationship with (mainly a male member of the family such as the father, the brother, the husband or boyfriend) who invited them to try the activity. Women under 55 reported diverse forms of engagement with adventure tourism. Even if there may have been a male influencer, the presence of female friends or relatives who did adventure sports, or emerging connections through specialized clubs, became incentives to pursue adventure tourism. It was evident that the growing popularity of adventure tourism in Mexico has opened new gateways for women to engage in adventure activities.

All interviewees considered themselves as part of the expert sector (Giddy & Webb, 2018), even though a few of them had initially engaged with adventure tourism through a more commercial experience. This was more evident in the younger cohort from our sample. Women's main motivation to pursue adventure activities after trying them for the first time was to feel stronger and to experience risk after the successful engagement with challenging activities, as illustrated in the following account:

> I enjoy the way I feel after doing a difficult path or crowning, you know it is like 'resist you can do it' and then you get to the top and it is wow! Priceless.... you can apply that philosophy to your daily life too (Olga).

Similar to Olga, the majority of participants considered they experienced a liminal state of challenge and freedom and overcoming risks as motivation to practise adventure tourism. Even though their initial engagement in adventure tourism activities did not take place during pregnancy, we found that the motivation of overcoming risks in adventure tourism remained an important element during the liminal period of pregnancy. To be motivated to pursue adventure activities suggested to us how our participants tried to subvert the normative impositions of what pregnancy means in the Mexican context.

Freedom, risk and the pregnant woman

Freedom and risk are among the intrinsic characteristics of adventure tourism (Mu & Nepal, 2015) and they appeared as the main challenges for women, especially during pregnancy. Some of the participants practised adventure tourism before having children, but others already had offspring when they began to engage in adventure activities. Despite their initial condition, women in general struggled with the reconstruction of themselves while doing adventure tourism during their pregnancy. As stated previously, normative and non-normative pregnancy refers to specific cultural constructions (Jordan, [1978] 1993), thus the construction of women's own cultural scripts demands a certain amount of creativity (Ibarra & Obodaru, 2016) as Daniela recalled in her account:

> You know [adopting risk] is contrary to the idea of being a woman. This doesn't apply to men … it is understood that if men undertake risk this is normal … but if it is a woman [who undertakes risky activities] then it's madness, even if you do not want to have children.

As Mu and Nepal (2015) highlighted, adventure tourists have different perceptions of risk and according to their individual experiences, different strategies aimed to reduce the risk can be chosen. However, as Daniela stated above, this is not available to all and in the case of pregnant women risk could be amplified.

Normative expectations of pregnancy maintain that risky activities should be avoided. Pregnant women who participate in adventure tourism in Mexico are seen as having a defiant attitude. This was the case explained by Aurora:

> Some people didn't understand why I liked to practise adventure activities, they took me for a fool … well, it was worse when I became pregnant, even my mother didn't approve it.

Even though moderate physical activity is usually recommended during pregnancy, there is a lack of consensus if adventurous physical activities should be also prescribed to pregnant women (Mata et al., 2010). Most women interviewed were aware of the risks involving the practise of adventurous physical activities during pregnancy, but in their opinion a pregnant woman is able to do outdoor activities during the first months and eventually, introducing some changes in their routine, to continue with the activities:

> I stopped doing II or III class rafting, but I kept kayaking in flat waters, or if I was used to a solo kayak I changed to a tandem kayak, but my doctor told me I could keep practising

during the first months of pregnancy and until I considered and it wasn't strenuous activity and I think it was good because it helped me to relax (Rosario, 27 years-old).

Pregnancy could be an experience considered with several restrictions under the normative lens and the participation in adventure activities can be one of them. As Mata et al. (2010) stated some obstetricians and gynaecologists do not recommend the pursuit of physical activity during pregnancy. However, when some of our participants first learned about their pregnancy, they decided to continue engaging in adventure activities. An important number of participants recalled getting negative feedback from their gynaecologists and being disappointed. This situation is illustrated by Andrea:

> I was healthy but physicians considered climbing as a high risk activity for a pregnant woman even during the first months. I got scared especially when one told me that my insurance wouldn't cover any accident during the pregnancy, travel agencies didn't want to do it. I joined my friends sometimes .... I felt a lot of anger ... It was unfair. I quit during 3 or 4 years. Now I think I could have kept climbing but at that time I followed everything others told me about avoiding risk.

Andrea's testimony is an example of a normative ideal of pregnancy not only due to the importance given to medical opinion (including the advice by the insurance company or the travel agencies) where the absence of risk is regarded as the natural thing to do. Andrea's opinion also exposes the rupture from a normative experience characterised by self-fulfilment and maternal response. In her case, pregnancy was experienced as a process full of contradictory emotions, and having to quit climbing was felt as a big loss.

For Susana and Laura, medical support was considered as critical as family support in their search for constructing their own status as pregnant women.

> It isn't easy, for some people you are like crazy, others consider you are nuts or even stupid ... but if your body responds to you I think you should keep practising adventure activities (Susana).

Even if our participants struggled trying to balance the risk factor in their preferred activities, they ended up managing risk and pregnancy in a way that allowed them to perform a non-normative representation of themselves as pregnant women. They become more aware of the physiological challenges of their pregnant bodies rather than responding to the prevalent sociocultural norms and the social pressure. Laura considered that physiological changes and the characteristics of the outdoor activity were the main reasons to stop doing abseiling during her pregnancy:

> ... you know, your body changes and even if you are in a good shape as your weight increases you are less agile too ... your belly and hips fatten too .... it wasn't that I felt ridiculous .... it was more that it takes you twice as much energy .... but you know, when I was pregnant I wished there could be some indoor abseiling facilities for pregnant women .... it seemed like a good idea to me ... if there are yoga class for pregnant woman, why not?.

Laura thought abseiling was a safe activity, not exempt of risk but safe, and she did not recall receiving any medical recommendation to abandon the activity as long as she continued being healthy:

I think that some doctors are more traditional and others are less, in my case my gynaecologist was a woman who also, eventually, practised adventure activities … so she gave me some advice but it didn't feel like a warning or something.

Maritza, who kept doing kayak up until the last two months of her two pregnancies, reported a similar experience:

I lived abroad during my first pregnancy and doctors weren't as traditional as in Mexico and people are more used to outdoor activities … so I think it was important. So during my second pregnancy when a doctor told me about being careful I just didn't consider stop kayaking …. nothing had happened to me before, so it was safe. I had very good friends who encouraged me and took care of me so I didn't feel like an expat … although at one point I did feel that way (Maritza).

Alternatively, some of the participants considered their pregnancy to be more a normative experience. As Andrea stated, the pregnant woman who avoids risk is heavily enforced even when the woman has a record of either health or intensive physical activity. In the participant's opinion there is a relevant social representation of the pregnancy as a transitional stage where the pregnant woman will inevitably strengthen her maternal instinct in accordance with the normative experience:

Since you enjoy risk and freedom in adventure activities and you have faced some gendered questioning …. you think …. hey! It's over, but to be pregnant and to keep doing rafting is still a challenge … you even ponder if you really will be a bad mother because you put your baby at risk before birth (Maritza).

Participants confirmed that they stopped doing adventure activities once their pregnancy advanced (Alicia, Evelyn, Laura and Maritza). Even for those who continued to engage with other outdoor activities regarded as safer (e.g. hiking), their pregnancy eventually drove them away from all adventure activities. According to their testimonies, the decision to stop pursuing these activities mostly related to the changes they experienced in their bodies during pregnancy, rather than because of the need to avoid risk *per se*; as Aurora stated:

There's a time, during the last two months [of the pregnancy] that your body is heavy and it feels like you move in slow motion and it becomes uncomfortable …. you know, the adventure is not near your house so you have to travel and it is less enjoyable.

As is suggested by participants' testimonies, their embodied experience is full of negotiations to avoid being excluded from adventure spaces, where risk was considered a fundamental aspect of their narrative. Women also faced the external and internal questioning of their ability to care for their future child. As Andrea suggested in her account, in order to circumvent further criticism, some women opted to perform in concordance to the normative identity, but this decision was not necessarily free of emotional charge.

Embodying the pregnancy

In their research about body and surfers Knijnik et al. (2010) draw insights from the 'rhizomatic body' to explore the multiple and dynamic interactions over it, the way it is constructed and the way women try to liberate it. By using the concept of 'rhizomatic body' to analyse the case of pregnant woman who participate in adventure tourism, it is possible to examine the interconnections between the experiences of embodiment during pregnancy with the negative connotations of body transformations, which are clearly liminal, as illustrated in the following account:

> The way your body changes, you probably do not feel comfortable for a while .... well in fact I never felt comfortable at all! [laugh] (Maritza).

As well as positive connotations of body transformations:

> I became more confident ... I do not know I felt that way, to give birth can be messy but it is powerful at the same time. I was strong so to experience pregnancy with all that questioning and continue kayaking ... it was good (Maritza).

Participants built the narratives of their non-normative pregnancy with references to physiological changes as well as social pressure. A relevant factor for women to continue doing adventure activities during their pregnancy was having a supportive environment, as illustrated in Evelyn's account:

> Well, you get bigger and slower, eventually you know you can practise the activity but you feel sorry for slowing down the others ... but you know? I just had fantastic mates they not only took care of me but also encouraged me all the time (Evelyn).

Despite the bodily changes, some participants were also able to experience their pregnancy as a non-normative 'rhizomatic' state without major restrictions, as Alicia explained:

> You can't pretend nothing will happen, even if you dislike [the fact that] your body will change, your mind you know? in adventure activities both are inseparable, well both will change ... but change is ok ... so you just have to face it, not fight against, this isn't a fight, if you feel bad, stop doing it, or if you have to rest, you have to rest .... but do not allow others to decide [on your behalf].

The majority of participants expressed strong opinions about being able to have the final say regarding their participation in adventure tourism during pregnancy. As Susana pointed out:

> Decades ago pregnant women had to rest in their homes, physical exercise was banned, decades later it was ok to do some sports, but things keep changing and as long as your body responds you aren't risking anything, so just welcome your new temporal body and go for it [laughs].

Some of the negative consequences of bodily changes from the liminal period of pregnancy while engaging in adventure activities were related to specialised outfits:

> Nothing fits you, you have to use bigger footwear and clothing and it can be very expensive (Alicia).

Or equipment:

> Harnesses aren't designed for pregnant women ... there are some but it isn't easy to get them. I could get one because I bought it second hand from a woman who bought it in Canada, and when I didn't need it I sold it to another pregnant climber. But I was lucky it isn't easy to get one of them (Laura).

Outfit and equipment were considered important constraints that were not easily resolved for some activities. However, changes in outfit size or the need for special equipment during pregnancy may not be as recurrent in other activities:

I don't think that this will be relevant for rafting .... it depends on the body too ... some women don't experience the same symptoms [during pregnancy] nor in the same degree ... I just disliked my body when my life saver didn't close (Susana).

In order to embrace movement, freedom and risk beyond the normative experience, pregnant women had to deal with bodily changes and had to manage physically and emotionally challenging phases. This process of embodiment is full of liminal changes and has the potential to generate outcomes that can be employed to trigger richer non-normative experiences of pregnancy. The pursuit of adventure activities can be adjusted to create new identities for women in a sociocultural context where adventure, risk-taking and challenging physical activities are not legitimised for women in general, nor for pregnant women in particular. For instance, in Laura's personal process, challenge became the core element to construct a new representation of herself, through play and performance:

To me ... risk is something vital, I always liked outdoor activities and engaged in them since I was a child. I felt good while doing something different from the rest ... it was nice to be different I was able to create who I am. To think were you are going, to plan the trip, to do [adventure activities], it shapes you, it changes you, it makes you strong and you project it (Laura).

Instead of considering risk as something negative to avoid, Laura's account shows risk can be converted into a positive element in general and during pregnancy. In this sense, Laura was able to reinforce her non-normative experience:

When someone intended to convince me to stop I considered I was healthy ... I was in a good shape ... I felt good .... I enjoyed the experience ... my baby was fine too ... Why stop then?

For pregnant women this process of embodiment requires support and social guidance. Precisely, one of the main challenges for women who participated in adventure activities during pregnancy was obtaining the guidance necessary to craft their new role. Some women could get social support from medical professionals and other networks (family, friends, adventure clubs) and recognized the value of such networks (like Alicia, Evelyn or Susana); but at the end, the most relevant role was performed by the women themselves.

In their experience of this liminal process, women identified past experiences as a relevant resource to craft their new status as pregnant women. For instance, Alicia, described her achievement of constructing a more confident sense of self through her past involvement with play and performance:

It was more difficult the first time ... because ... you know everything is more difficult the first time ... I stopped climbing after the 5th month ... a lot of people ... my family and friends both questioned me ... first I tried to make fun of their questioning but at the end I was tired .... even my husband questioned me. When I became pregnant of my second child it was ... not easy because I also faced some questioning but I was more prepared and had more experience so it was less difficult.

Similar to Alicia, Susana also took advantage of past experiences, specifically based on references from her childhood: 'My mother isn't ... like the typical Mexican mother, so it was like hey! My brothers and I survived ... I was confident and it was very helpful'.

In order to pursue non-normative experiences in this liminal process, pregnant women who engaged in adventure tourism introduced risk as a crucial element, bringing together various personal resources, including past liminal experiences, in order to perform a positive embodied experience.

Discussion

Moderate exercise or physical activity is frequently recommended during pregnancy, but some hesitation still prevails. As a result, sports or strenuous activities are discouraged based on ethical issues rather than the risk itself (Mata et al., 2010; Sánchez García et al., 2016). In the Mexican context, since there does not seem to be a medical consensus on the level and type of physical activity during a healthy pregnancy, the challenge for pregnant tourists is to decide whether to continue or abandon adventure activities mainly based on social pressure and a combination of taboos, prohibitions and rules that discourage risk. We recognize that adventure activities are not exempt from risk for pregnant tourists, but we want to highlight how social restrictions seem to be the norm even in the cases where women are healthy and the physiological changes linked to pregnancy do not seem to endanger the woman or the foetus.

By conceptualising pregnancy as a liminal stage, we were able to explore the role of normative pregnancy and how some women are able to create alternative representations of pregnant women and generate non-normative experiences supported by their participation in adventure tourism. For these women, the crafting of a non-normative experience has to challenge cultural taboos, prohibitions and rules. Through the management of challenge, freedom and risk, adventure tourism spaces can become spaces for transgression where pregnant woman have the potential to construct alternative experiences during the liminal stage of pregnancy. Sánchez Bringas et al. (2004) remind us that new experiences can be interpreted from traditional models (i.e. normative pregnancy). However, this should not be considered as a limitation, because it is precisely during liminal stages that individuals can take advantage of the conflict and tensions generated through non-normative processes. For example, female adventure tourists have used the spaces of adventure to trigger non-normative processes (Kay & Laberge, 2004; Myers, 2010; Pomfret & Doran, 2015) just as Knijnik et al. (2010) considered, some pregnant women craft 'rhizomatic bodies' as a relevant process towards developing capacities that will help them during their pregnancy and ulterior motherhood.

The liminal state and the possibility to escape from everyday life lie at the core of any tourist activity. In adventure tourism spaces, female tourists can perform non-normative processes where challenge, freedom, lack of control and risk allow them to generate alternative representations of womanhood that differ from traditional or normative representations. Adventure spaces are then constructed as spaces for play and performance but also as spaces of transgression, where a pregnant woman can contest normative processes.

Traditions, cultural practices and symbolic constructions shape the way in which pregnant women create their identity. In the Mexican context, such restrictions become even more challenging for pregnant women who participate in adventure activities, especially when these activities are regarded as dangerous or physically demanding (e.g. rafting, abseiling, mountain biking or rock climbing, among others).

In this sense, the social construction of normative pregnancy as a liminal stage where risk is avoided has played a restrictive role that forces some women to abandon all adventure tourism activities during pregnancy.

Conclusions

Among our findings, we want to highlight the use of adventure activities as important in the crafting of non-normative pregnancy for those women who actively engaged in these activities before becoming pregnant. Further research on this topic could shed light on the construction and meanings of non-normative identities for female adventure tourists in different cultural contexts.

Due to the key components of physical challenge, risk and expertise, adventure tourism often appears as a liminal space not open to pregnant women due to normative expectations that dictate avoiding risk or strenuous physical exercise. In Mexico, pregnancy is a phase with strong symbolism attached to it, despite the social changes in reproductive behaviour experienced during the past few decades. As we stated before, pregnancy as a liminal phase tends to be strongly related to a normative experience that requires continuous medical surveillance. As exemplified in the accounts of the study participants, pregnant women who continued doing adventure activities engaged in processes of resistance, but also contributed to generating broader representations of what it is to be a woman. These women experienced non-normative liminality (centred on risk-taking), while contesting cultural taboos associated with the female body during pregnancy. Indeed, women potentially use the liminal spaces of adventure tourism for transformation, or even transgression, where they can break apart from the normative experience of 'being pregnant'.

Understanding the meaning of the liminality of pregnancy in women who participate in adventure tourism provides deeper insights into women's expectations and the way those expectations intertwine with social constructions of pregnancy and ulterior motherhood in Mexico. Such an understanding might be helpful in the crafting of more diverse models and experiences of being a woman in gendered spaces and for tourism and geography research to fully grasp behavioural patterns of pregnant tourists and their sociocultural impacts. Tourist enterprises could also benefit by redesigning their offers with a more diversified set of products depending on the phase of pregnancy (1, 2 or 3+ months of pregnancy), and the perceptions of what is 'adventurous' and what is not. Indeed, further research on the topic could be extended to other activities that women perform during pregnancy and that are not considered as 'adventurous' or risky, such as cleaning, washing, cooking or carrying babies and heavy shopping bags. Future research can also look at the role that private and public networks, such as family, friends, associations, and clubs play in supporting the construction of non-normative experiences for women in adventure tourism at different stages of their life cycle.

Acknowledgements

We thank the three anonymous reviewers for their valuable comments which helped to enhance the quality of the manuscript. We also thank Dr. Diana Marre (Autonomous University of Barcelona, Spain) for the detailed reading and comments that helped to improve the manuscript.

Disclosure statement

No potential conflict of interest was reported by the authors.

References

Aiken, A., & Trussell, J. (2017). Anticipated emotions about unintended pregnancy in relationship context: Are Latinas really happier? *Journal of Marriage and Family, 79*(2), 356–371. doi:10.1111/jomf.12338

Bengtsson, M. (2016). How to plan and perform a qualitative study using content analysis. *Nursingplus Open, 2*, 8–14. doi:10.1016/j.npls.2016.01.001

Bondi, L. (2003). Empathy and identification: Conceptual resources for feminist fieldwork. *ACME an International E-Journal for Critical Geographies, 2*(1), 64–76.

Borg, E., & Söderlund, J. (2013). Moving in, moving on: Liminality practices in project-based work. *Employee Relations, 36*(2), 182–197. doi:10.1108/ER-11-2012-0081

Braidotti, R. (1994). *Nomadic subjects: Embodiment and sexual difference in contemporary feminist theory*. New York, NY: Columbia University Press.

Bridges, W. ([1974] 1980). *Transitions*. Reading, MA: Addison-Wesley.

Camprubí, R., & Coromina, L. (2016). Content analysis in tourism research. *Tourism Management Perspectives, 18*, 134–140. doi:10.1016/j.tmp.2016.03.002

Chisholm, D. (2008). Climbing like a girl: An exemplary adventure in feminist phenomenology. *Hypatia, 23*(1), 9–40. doi:10.1111/j.1527-2001.2008.tb01164.x

Clarke, A. E., Shim, J. K., Mamo, L., Fosket, J. R., & Fishman, J. R. (2003). Biomedicalization: Technoscientific transformations of health, illness, and U.S. biomedicine. *American Sociological Review, 68*(2), 161–194. doi:10.2307/1519765

Clinch, H., & Filimonau, V. (2016). Instructors' perspectives on risk management within adventure tourism. *Tourism Planning & Development, 14*(2), 220–239. doi:10.1080/21568316.2016.1204360

Colman, S. D., & Colman, L. L. (1973/1974). Pregnancy as an altered state of consciousness. *Birth and Birth, 1*(1), 7–11. doi:10.1111/j.1523-536X.1973.tb00654.x

Comley, C. (2016). "We have to establish our territory": How women surfers 'carve out' gendered spaces within surfing. *Sport in Society, 19*(8-9), 1289–1298. doi:10.1080/17430437.2015.1133603

Côté-Arsenault, D., Brody, D., & Dombeck, M. T. (2009). Pregnancy as a rite of passage: Liminality, rituals & communitas. *Journal of Prenatal & Perinatal Psychology & Health, 24*(2), 69–78.

Dallen, J. T. (2018). Geography: The substance of tourism. *Tourism Geographies, 20*(1), 166–169.

Daniel, E., & Ellis-Chadwick, F. (2016). Entrepreneurship and liminality: The case of self-storage based businesses. *International Journal of Entrepreneurial Behavior & Research*, *22*(3), 436–457. doi:10.1108/IJEBR-01-2015-0015

Davis-Floyd, R. E. (1992). *Birth as an American rite of passage*. Los Angeles, CA: University of California Press.

Davis-Floyd, R. E. (2001). La Partera Profesional: Articulating identity and cultural space for a new kind of midwife in Mexico. *Medical Anthropology*, *20*(2-3), 185–244. doi:10.1080/01459740.2001.9966194

Davis-Floyd, R. E. (2003). *Birth as an American Rite of passage*. Berkeley, CA: University of California Press.

Davis-Floyd, R. E., & Sargent, C. F. (1997). Introduction. In R. E. Davis-Floyd & C. F. Sargent (Eds). *Childbirth and authoritative knowledge: Cross-cultural perspectives* (pp. 1–51). Berkeley, CA: University of California Press.

Díaz-Carrión, I. (2012). Turismo de aventura y participación de las mujeres en Jalcomulco (México) [Adventure tourism and women's participation in Jalcomulco (Mexico)]. *PASOS*, *10*(5), 531–542.

Doran, A. (2016). Empowerment and women in adventure tourism: A negotiated journey. *Journal of Sport & Tourism*, *20*(1), 57–80. doi:10.1080/14775085.2016.1176594

Dowling, R., Lloyd, K., & Suchet-Pearson, S. (2016). Qualitative methods 1: Enriching the interview. *Progress in Human Geography*, *40*(5), 679–686. doi:10.1177/0309132515596880

Giddy, J. K., & Webb, N. L. (2018). Environmental attitudes and adventure tourism motivations. *GeoJournal*, *83*(2), 275–287. doi:10.1007/s10708-017-9768-9

Graburn, N. H. H. (1989). Tourism: The sacred journey. In V. Smith (Ed.), *Hosts and guests: The anthropology of tourism* (pp. 21–52). Philadelphia, PA: University of Pennsylvania Press.

Graneheim, U. H., Lindgren, B.-M., & Lundman, B. (2017). Methodological challenges in qualitative content analysis: A discussion paper. *Nurse Education Today*, *56*, 29–34. doi:10.1016/j.nedt.2017.06.002

Hall, C. M. (2011). Health and medical tourism: A kill or cure for global public health? *Tourism Review*, *66*(1/2), 4–15.

Hannam, K., Sheller, M., & Urry, J. (2006). Editorial: Mobilities, immobilities and moorings. *Mobilities*, *1*(1), 1–22. doi:10.1080/17450100500489189

Hebl, M. R., King, E. B., Glick, P., Singletary, S. L., & Kazama, S. (2007). Hostile and benevolent reactions toward pregnant women: Complementary interpersonal punishments and rewards that maintain traditional roles. *Journal of Applied Psychology*, *92*(6), 1499–1511. doi:10.1037/0021-9010.92.6.1499

Hsieh, H. F., & Shannon, S. E. (2005). Three approaches to qualitative content analysis. *Qualitative Health Research*, *15*(9), 1277–1288.

Ibarra, H., & Obodaru, O. (2016). Betwixt and between identities: Liminal experiences in contemporary careers. *Research in Organizational Behavior*, *36*, 47–64. doi:10.1016/j.riob.2016.11.003

Jackson, M. A. (2009). *Cultural models, pregnancy, and stress: Examining intracultural variation in Jalisco, Mexico* (Unpublished doctoral dissertation). The University of Alabama, Tuscaloosa, AL. Retrieved from https://ir.ua.edu/handle/123456789/674

Jordan, B. ([1978] 1993). *Birth in four cultures, a cross-cultural investigation of childbirth in Yucatán, Holland, Sweden and the United States*. Long Grove, IL: Waveland Press.

Kawash, S. (2011). New directions in motherhood studies. *Signs: Journal of Women in Culture and Society*, *36*(4), 969–1003. doi:10.1086/658637

Kay, J., & Laberge, S. (2004). "Mandatory equipment": Women in adventure racing. In B. Wheaton (Ed). *Understanding lifestyle sports: Consumption, identity and difference* (pp. 154–174). New York, NY: Routledge.

Knijnik, J., Horton, P., & Cruz, L. (2010). Rhizomatic bodies, gendered waves: Transitional femininities in Brazilian Surf. *Sport in Society*, *13*(7-8), 1170–1185. doi:10.1080/17430431003780138

Klann, M. (2017). Babies in baskets: Motherhood, tourism, and American identity in Indian baby shows, 1916-1949. *Journal of Women's History*, *29*(2), 38–61. doi:10.1353/jowh.2017.0020

Ladge, J. J., Clair, J. A., & Greenberg, D. (2012). Cross-domain identity transition during liminal periods: Constructing multiple selves as professional and mother during pregnancy. *Academy of Management Journal, 55*(6), 1449–1471. doi:10.5465/amj.2010.0538

Leder, D. (1992). A tale of two bodies: The Cartesian corpse and the lived body. In D. Leder (Ed.). *The body in medical thought and practice* (pp. 17–35). Amsterdam: Kluwer Academic Publishers.

Lietz, C. A., & Zayas, L. E. (2013). Evaluating qualitative studies. In R. M. Grinnell, Jr. & Y. A. Unrau (Eds.). *Social work research and evaluation: Foundations of evidence-based practice* (pp. 595–605). Oxford: Oxford University Press.

Lindseth, A., & Norberg, A. (2004). A phenomenological hermeneutical method for researching lived experience. *Scandinavian Journal of Caring Sciences, 18*(2), 145–153. doi:10.1111/j.1471-6712.2004.00258.x

Lupton, D. (1994). *Medicine as culture: Illness, disease and the body in Western societies.* Thousand Oaks, CA: Sage.

Mahon-Daly, P., & Andrews, G. (2002). Liminality and breastfeeding: Women negotiating space and two bodies. *Health & Place, 8,* 61–76. doi:10.1016/S1353-8292(01)00026-0

Markula, P. (2006). Deleuze and the body without organs: Disreading the fit feminine identity. *Journal of Sport and Social Issues, 30*(1), 29–44. doi:10.1177/0193723505282469

Martinez-Pascual, B., Abuin, V., Perez de Heredia, M., & Palacios-Ceña, D. (2016). Experiencing the body during pregnancy: A qualitative research study among Spanish sportswomen. *Women & Health, 56*(3), 345–359. doi:10.1080/03630242.2015.1088118

Mata, F., Chulvi, I., Roig, J., Heredia, J., Isidro, F., Benítez Sillero, J. D. & Guillén del Castillo, M. (2010). Prescripción del ejercicio físico durante el embarazo [Prescription of physical exercise during pregnancy]. *Revista Andaluza de Medicina del Deporte, 3*(2), 68–79.

McDowell, L. (1999). *Gender, identity and place: Understanding feminist geographies.* Cambridge: Polity Press.

Mercer, R. T. (2004). Becoming a mother versus maternal role attainment. *Journal of Nursing Scholarship, 36*(3), 226–232. doi:10.1111/j.1547-5069.2004.04042.x

Miles, M. B., & Huberman, A. M. (1994). *Qualitative data analysis: An expanded sourcebook.* Thousand Oaks, CA: Sage.

Mitchell, G. (1983). *Mountain experience: The psychology and sociology of adventure.* Chicago, IL: Chicago University Press.

Mu, Y., & Nepal, S. (2015). High mountain adventure tourism: Trekkers' perceptions of risk and death in Mt. Everest Region, Nepal. *Asia Pacific Journal of Tourism Research. 21*(5). doi:10.1080/10941665.2015.1062787

Myers, L. (2010). Women travellers' adventure tourism experiences in New Zealand. *Annals of Leisure Research, 13*(1-2), 116–142. doi:10.1080/11745398.2010.9686841

Nash, M. (2012). Weighty matters: Negotiating 'fatness' and 'in-betweenness' in early pregnancy. *Feminism & Psychology, 22*(3), 307–323. doi:10.1177/0959353512445361

Neuendorf, K. A. (2011). Content analysis—A methodological primer for gender research. *Sex Roles, 64*(3-4), 276–289. doi:10.1007/s11199-010-9893-0

Noble, C. H., & Walker, B. A. (1997). Exploring the relationships among liminal transitions, symbolic consumption, and the extended self. *Psychology and Marketing, 14*(1), 29–47. doi:10.1002/(SICI)1520-6793(199701)14:1<29::AID-MAR3>3.0.CO;2-Q

Nunkoo, R., Hall, C. M., & Ladsawut, J. (2017). Gender and choice of methodology in tourism social science research. *Annals of Tourism, 63,* 203–222.

Ogle, J. P., Tyner, K. E., & Schofield-Tomschin, S. (2013). The role of maternity dress consumption in shaping the self and identity during the liminal transition of pregnancy. *Journal of Consumer Culture, 13*(2), 119–139. doi:10.1177/1469540513480161

Organisation for Economic Co-operation and Development (OECD). (2018). *Education at a glance 2018. OECD indicators. Mexico.* Retrieved from https://www.oecd-ilibrary.org/docserver/eag-2018-58-en.pdf?expires=1564343878&id=id&accname=guest&checksum=6C20BA8CE0901550314B704F33757064

Osuchowski-Sanchez, M. A., Tigges, B., Mendelson, C., Lobo, M., & Clark, L. (2012). Teen preg-nancy and parenting: A qualitative study into attitudes and behaviours of teenaged long-term Hispanics in New Mexico. *Journal of Research in Nursing*, *18*(3), 218–232. doi:10.1177/1744987112455422

Palinkas, L. A., Horwitz, S. M., Green, C. A., Wisdom, J. P., Duan, N., & Hoagwood, K. (2015). Purposeful sampling for qualitative data collection and analysis in mixed method implemen-tation research. *Administration and Policy in Mental Health and Mental Health Services Research*. *42*(5), 533–544. doi:10.1007/s10488-013-0528-y

Pomfret, G., & Doran, A. (2015). Gender and mountaineering tourism. In M. Ghazali, J. Higham, & A. Thompson-Carr (Eds.), *Mountaineering tourism* (pp. 138–155). Oxon: Routledge.

Roggenbuck, J. W., & Lucas, R. C. (1987). Wilderness use and user characteristics: A state-of-knowledge review. In R. C. Lucas (Ed.). *Proceedings of the National Wilderness Research Conference: Issues, state-of-knowledge, future directions* (pp. 245–264). Fort Collins, CO: USDA Forest Service.

Sánchez Bringas, Á., Espinosa Islas, S., Ezcurdia, C., & Torres, E. (2004). Nuevas maternidades o la desconstrucción de la maternidad en México [New motherhood or deconstruction of mother-hood in Mexico]. *Debate Feminista*, *30*, 55–86.

Sánchez García, J. C., Rodríguez Blanque, R., Sánchez López, A., Baena García, L., Suárez Manzano, S., & Aguilar Cordero, M. (2016). Efectos de la actividad física durante el embarazo y en la recuperación posparto: Protocolo de estudio. *Nutrición Hospitalaria*, *33*(5), 29–32. doi:10.20960/nh.756

Seow, D., & Brown, L. (2018). The solo female Asian tourist. *Current Issues in Tourism*, *21*(10), 1187–1206. doi:10.1080/13683500.2017.1423283

Small, J. (2005). Women's holidays: Disruption of the motherhood myth. *Tourism Review International*, *9*(2), 139–154. doi:10.3727/154427205774791645

Soja, E. W. (1989). *Postmodern geographies: The reassertion of space in critical social theory*. London: Verso.

Stoddart, M. (2010). Constructing masculinized sportscapes: Skiing, gender and nature in British Columbia, Canada. *International Review for the Sociology of Sport*, *46*(1), 108–124. doi:10.1177/1012690210373541

Tajeddini, K., Ratten, V., & Denisa, M. (2017). Female tourism entrepreneurs in Bali, Indonesia. *Journal of Hospitality and Tourism Management*, *31*, 52–58. doi:10.1016/j.jhtm.2016.10.004

Thomas, S. (1994). Artifactual study in the analysis of culture: A defense of content analysis in a postmodern age. *Communication Research*, *21*(6), 683–697. doi:10.1177/009365094021006002

Trauer, B., & Ryan, C. (2005). Destination image, romance and place experience—An application of intimacy theory in tourism. *Tourism Management*, *26*(4), 481–491. doi:10.1016/j.tourman.2004.02.014

Turner, V. (1969). *The ritual process*. Chicago, IL: Aldine.

Turner, V. (1974). Liminal to liminoid, in play, flow, and ritual: An essay in comparative symbol-ogy. *Rice Institute Pamphlet - Rice University Studies*, *60*(3), 53–92. http://hdl.handle.net/1911/63159.

Turner, V. (1987). Betwixt and between: The liminal period in rites of passage. In I. C. Mahdi, S. Foster, & M. Little (Eds.), *Betwixt and between: Patterns of and feminine initiation* (pp. 3–19). La Salle, IL: Open Court.

Underthun, A., & Jordhus-Lier, D.C. (2017). Liminality at work in Norwegian hotels. *Tourism Geographies*, *20*(1), 11–28. doi:10.1080/14616688.2017.1314546

Van Gennep, A. (1960). *The rites of passage*. Chicago, IL: The University of Chicago Press.

Voigt, C., & Laing, J. H. (2010). Journey into parenthood: Commodification of reproduction as a new tourism niche market. *Journal of Travel & Tourism Marketing*, *27*(3), 252–268. doi:10.1080/10548401003744685

Xu, H. (2018). Moving toward gender and tourism geographies studies. *Tourism Geographies*, *20*(4), 721–727. doi:10.1080/14616688.2018.1486878

Liminality at-sea: cruises to nowhere and their metaworlds

Bradley Rink (iD)

ABSTRACT

The concept of liminality informs the experience of tourism, yet little is known about how liminality is performed in the context of 'cruises to nowhere' that sacrifice terrestrial destinations for endless 'seascapes' of liminality. Fuelled by alcohol, round-the-clock parties and endless buffets, cruises to nowhere are an increasingly popular addition to the Southern African cruising season. Understood through a sample of South African based multi-day ocean-going cruises without a destination, results take literally the notion that tourist liminality involves boundary crossing into the unknown on the limitless horizon of the high seas. Using netnographic methods, boundary crossings are traced through the intended and practiced activities on-board cruise-to-nowhere experiences. Involving a mix of sun, sea, sex and especially alcohol, cruises to nowhere engineer the destination-free seascape as a liminoid playground. Reflecting on South African-based cruises to nowhere offered during the southern hemisphere summer cruising season, the findings of this research call for a more deliberate focus on the liminal aspects of ship-based tourism. At the same time, conclusions chart a course for what may be termed debauchery tourism. Building from work in cruise tourism geographies, alcotourism and party tourism, findings do not intend to moralise debaucherous shipboard tourism, but rather to explore the liminal setting of the cruise ship and the sea where cruises to nowhere offer round-the-clock drinking and partying as a liminal destination in and of itself.

摘要

阈限的概念是旅游体验的重要议题, 但人们对阈限如何在"无目的地巡航"的背景下表现却知之甚少, 无目的地巡航为大陆目的地贡献了阈限的无尽的海景。在不分昼夜的饮酒、派对与自助餐的刺激下, 无目的地巡航越来越成为南部非洲巡航季的新宠。通过一个以南非为基地的、没有目的地的多天海上巡航的样本, 研究结果从字面上理解了这样一个概念:游客的阈限涉及到穿越边界进入公海无限地平线上的未知领域。使用网络图的方法, 我们可以通过在无目的地巡游体验中船上预期和常规的活动来跟踪边界越界行为。无目的地航行将阳光、大海、性, 尤其是酒精混合在一起, 把这片没有确定航行目的的海洋景观设计成一个有限的游乐场。考虑到南半球夏季巡航季节提供的以南非为基地的无目的地巡航, 这项研究的结果呼吁更慎重地关注游轮旅游的限制因素。与此同时, 结论为所谓的纵情旅游制定了一个进程。基于邮轮旅游地理、美酒旅以及派对旅游的研究工作,本研究结果不打算为纵情邮轮旅游进行道德说教, 而是探索邮轮旅游以及这种无目的地海上巡游的限制因素。

Introduction

Debauchery, from the French *debaucher* [to lead astray], refers to a 'vicious indulgence in sensual pleasures' (OED Online, 2018). Such over-indulgence is, according to Butcher (2006), symbolic of mass tourism's excess and lack of self-restraint. Debauchery is evident in mass tourism's focus on 'sun, sea, sand and sex' in the holiday-making experience (Butcher, 2006, p. 71). While moral arguments may arise when discussing debauchery in combination with tourism (Caton, 2012), tourism scholars have long contended that the pursuit of pleasure, escape, relaxation and the satisfaction of the senses are at the heart of the tourist experience. Straying from the norms of everyday life is also at the heart of the concept of liminality which Selänniemi (2003) argues plays a central role in the escapist and out-of-the-ordinary experiences practiced by tourists on holiday. Whether liminal or not, tourism experiences typically take place in destinations—a region, city/town or specific site—where the tourist focuses the activities of their holiday. While some destinations may be spatially fixed, that does not imply that they are static. A destination might refer to a particular location, or might refer to the site of tourism activities that is mobile such as a cruise ship. In cruise tourism, the destination consists of both the ports of call that typically comprise the cruise itinerary (Rodrigue & Notteboom, 2013), as well as the ship itself (Dickinson & Vladimir, 1997; Wood, 2004; Weaver, 2005a). The port calls of seaborne cruises thus constitute a string of destinations where tourism activities take place, and where much of the economic and social impact from cruise tourism is focused (Satta, Parola, Penco, & Persico, 2015). With the increasing size, complexity and variety of pleasure-oriented offerings of contemporary cruise vessels, the cruise ship itself has become a destination. This process of 'destinization' of the cruise ship (Weaver, 2005a, p. 166) is clearly evident in the case of multi-day ocean-going cruises without port calls—referred to as 'cruises to nowhere'. On-board such cruises, the destination is the ship, and the ship is the destination. Weaver's (2005a) argument, like that which underpins this study, is a metaphorical one where the cruise ship serves as a self-contained site of leisure and holiday experiences. Much like a resort, they are self-contained, and in the case of cruises to nowhere limit the (liminal) holiday experience to the hull of the ship.

While liminality has informed the experience of tourism more broadly (Andrews & Roberts, 2012; Brooker & Joppe, 2014; Preston-Whyte, 2004; Pritchard & Morgan, 2006; Selänniemi, 2003), it has received little attention in the context of ship-based tourism. With the exception of Yarnal and Kerstetter (2005), few tourism scholars have explored liminality on the high seas. None have done so in the case of cruises without port calls. Understood through a sample of cruises to nowhere, this study takes literally the notion that tourist liminality involves boundary crossing into the unknown on the limitless horizon of the high seas. With a focus on cruises to nowhere, this study makes three primary contributions to the literature on tourism geographies. Firstly, the findings respond to Yarnal and Kerstetter's (2005) call for further investigation into the role that vacation spaces such as cruise ships play in individuals' lives. This study explores liminality at-sea from spatial, discursive and practice-based perspectives where boundary crossings are exemplified through the intended and practiced activities on-board cruise-to-nowhere experiences. Involving a mix of sun, sea, sex and especially alcohol, cruises to nowhere frame the destination-free seascape as a 'liminoid playground' (Selänniemi, 2003) where an individual may test the limits of their inhibitions with regard to alcohol, partying and sex. Second, this study seeks to extend the use of netnography as a methodological tool to embrace travel narratives that are produced for and shared with on-line communities. Based on a sample of netnographic accounts of cruise to nowhere experiences in the Southern African context, the study intends to further demonstrate the utility of online travel accounts in exploring the tourist experience. Finally, the results extend the concept of liminality in order to trace a preliminary understanding and call for more research into relatively unexplored waters to establish an agenda for what may be called 'debauchery tourism'. Through a discussion of netnographic data from cruises to nowhere, this study seeks to triangulate debauchery tourism at the intersection of cruise geographies, alcotourism, party tourism and metaspatiality. Findings do not intend to debate the moral aspects of tourism (Caton, 2012), but rather to explore the metaspatial, enclavic setting of cruises to nowhere that enable vicious indulgence in sensual pleasures as a liminal destination itself. With these objectives in mind, the remainder of this paper is divided into four sections. The first section moors the exploration of liminal seascapes through a review of literatures of tourism geographies of cruising, liminality, a combination of alcotourism and party tourism, as well as metaspatiality. The second section briefly describes the netnographic method used to gather data on cruises to nowhere, followed by the third section which presents findings derived from the data. Finally, I conclude with a discussion of the implications of these findings that together chart a course for the further study of debauchery tourism.

Literature review

Tourism geographies of cruising

Exploring the geographies of cruising includes a journey into a range of tourism places involved in cruise tourism encompassing: ports of call (Satta et al., 2015; Wilkinson, 1999); itineraries (Rodrigue & Notteboom, 2013); and ships themselves (Wood, 2004; Weaver, 2005a, 2018; Yarnal & Kerstetter, 2005). In spite of the original utilitarian purpose of sea-going ships in transporting passengers to a destination, the super-sized ships of today are themselves destinations that may overshadow the importance of ports of call (Weaver, 2005a, p. 166). Adding to that, Rodrigue and Notteboom (2013) suggest that contemporary cruise tourism is functionally focused on managerially driven itineraries rather than on destinations. Therefore, the geographies of contemporary cruising are a complex mix of fixed and mobile destinations including port cities and cruise ships. Most cruises are spatially and culturally distinguished by the ports of call they visit. Yet, some cruise companies include seaborne voyages without any ports of call—described by cruise companies and on-line traveller review forums as 'cruises to nowhere' (Cruise Critic, 2018a, 2018b). These voyages trade terrestrial destinations for on-board experiences of pleasure and liminality as the destination itself. The online cruise community Cruise Critic notes that

'A decade or so ago, a cruise to nowhere was best described as a party cruise. You sailed out of port on Friday afternoon and returned to shore 72 h later, after action-packed days and nights filled with eating, drinking and dancing' (Cruise Critic, 2018b, np).

Where such cruises are offered, they are typically themed 'around topics like food and wine, comedy and lifestyle' (Cruise Critic, 2018b, np). Temporally and spatially, cruises to nowhere are brief, and organised around a single port with an important element being that they sail into international waters.

'Typically they depart from and return to the same port and spend three days cruising up and down the coastline, far enough out to sea to legally operate the casino and duty-free shops. Some are less than 24 hours long' (Cruise Critic, 2018b, np).

While the space of the cruise ship, as argued by Weaver (2005a), may be seen as a space of containment, and a destination unto itself (Dickinson & Vladimir, 1997; Weaver, 2005a; Wood, 2004), the ship may also serve as a space of abandonment from the norms of everyday life. Thus, the space of the cruise ship has the potential to serve as a 'liminoid playground' (Selänniemi, 2003) where inhibitions toward sensual pleasures of alcohol, partying and sex fall away like the distant shore over the horizon. Absent from the literature of cruise tourism, however, is any discussion of cruises without ports of call such as those described above. In spite of this silence within the academy, so-called 'cruises to nowhere' offer the possibility to productively explore the concept of liminality and how it positions the tourist and their experiences at the edge of everyday life (Turner, 1974). Cruises to nowhere thus offer productive capacity to explore the spatial and social setting of the cruise ship and the sea where cruises to nowhere posit drinking and partying as a liminal destination in and of itself.

Liminality

The concept of liminality is understood through rites of passage (van Gennep, 1960) and is situated on the margins of everyday life (Turner, 1974). Liminality plays a critical role in the escapist and out-of-the-ordinary experiences practiced by tourists on holiday (Selänniemi, 2003). Turner describes the social and geographical elements of liminality as

'The passage from one social status to another is often accompanied by a parallel passage in space, a geographical movement from one place to another … or the literal crossing of a threshold which separates two distinct areas, one associated with the subject's pre-ritual or preliminal status, and the other with his post-ritual or postliminal status' (Turner, 1974, p. 58)

Turner's exploration of liminality hinges on the concept of *communitas*. In Turner's use, *communitas* refers to the 'modality of human interrelatedness' (1974, p. 76) where humans are conditioned to play certain roles. Turner expands on this when noting that

'...[C]ommunitas preserves individual distinctiveness...In people's social structural relationships they are by various abstract processes generalized and segmentalized into roles, statuses, classes, cultural sexes, conventional age divisions, ethnic affiliations, and so on (Turner, 1974, p. 77).

It is under such social conditions that humans are conditioned to play certain roles which are obedient to social norms. Liminality, in that case, is the crossing of the coded boundaries of societal expectation. Turner's concept of *communitas* includes spontaneous, ideological, and normative forms that each have relationships with liminoid phenomena (1974, p. 79). Of these three forms, it is the spontaneous that is most likely to be prevalent in the context of tourism. Spontaneous *communitas* finds individuals in the micro-community (of the ship, resort, etc.) becoming, in Turner's argument 'totally absorbed into a single, synchronized, fluid event' (1974, p. 79). It is in this temporal, event-based limitation where liminality in the context of tourism is understood as a 'time-limited escape from "normal life"' (Bell, 2008, p. 293). This temporal and spatial distinction of the liminality in tourism stems from Turner's juxtaposition of work and leisure. The liminal setting of tourism as a *leisure* pursuit—the opposite of *work* according to Turner (1974), provides

'...freedom to enter, even to generate new symbolic worlds of entertainment, sports, games, diversions of all kinds. It is, furthermore...freedom to transcend social structural limitations, freedom to play—with ideas, with fantasies, with words' (Turner, 1974, p. 68).

The concept of liminality thus helps to inform a range of tourist performances during the time away from work, and distant from societal expectations. This temporal and spatial break from normality is meant to be restorative, allowing the tourist to let go of work, 'let their hair down' (Yarnal & Kerstetter, 2005, p. 374), and practice new ways of being. Turner's contribution to our understanding of the extraordinary aspects of the tourism experience is evident both in the extreme example of 'the party animal' whose unbridled hedonism makes them an exceptional tourist subject (Diken & Laustsen, 2004), and in the everyday aspects of tourism as noted by Edensor (2007) who reminds us to recognise the mundane aspects of tourism experiences that are replete with their own 'rigid conventions, habits and routines' (Edensor, 2007, p. 200). Such a focus on liminality in the context of cruise ships has received little attention from tourism scholars, with the exception of Yarnal and Kerstetter (2005) who explore the social space and interactions amongst passengers on a 9-day, 8-night Caribbean cruise with four ports of call. Their research revealed the many ways that liminality is performed in the context of the cruise. As they reflect in their study,

'For some, "letting your hair down," meant drinking two glasses of wine at dinner instead of one. For others, it spanned a spectrum from drinking alcohol before noon, gambling beyond self-imposed limits, joking with crewmembers, and ordering three different desserts at a meal. From simple overindulgence in food or alcohol to lying out in the sun too long to overspending in the casino to having the opportunity to gossip for extended periods, many individuals took delight in the ship as a space for pleasure and indulgence' (Yarnal & Kerstetter, 2005, p. 374).

Like the example above, liminality in tourism is often associated with alcohol. The role of alcohol and partying thus informs the capacity of a holiday to provide an escape from normal life and the literal intoxication of a holiday sojourn. Next, I turn to exploring how alcohol and partying help to inform liminal experiences of cruises to nowhere on the high seas.

Alcotourism and party tourism

The influence of alcohol in the liminal tourist experience has received surprisingly little attention by scholars as noted by Bell (2008). In a tourist's quest to escape from norms and routine, the consumption of alcohol and partying late into the night form a critical part of the tourism experience. Such practices may be in stark contrast to attitudes toward and use of alcohol in domestic space (Holloway, Jayne, & Valentine, 2008). The concept of alcotourism, conceived by Bell (2008) and inspired by Moore (1995), provides an important precursor to this study. At the same time, the present research charts new territory for the application of alcotourism research to the context of the cruise ship. The nexus of alcohol and tourism, as explored by Thomas, Mura, and Romy (2018) influences both local and tourist cultures, while it also calls for a greater focus on the role of alcohol in tourism itself. In spite of the paucity of literature on the relationship between alcohol and tourism, Moore (1995) and Bell (2008) underscore the long-standing relationship between alcohol consumption and tourism. While the only seaborne example raised by Bell (2008, p. 30) are so-called 'booze cruises' that are economically-motivated shopping-trips for British tourists in search of cheaper French alcohol, drinking, and thus intoxication, forms an import pathway to pleasure and escape for much of cruise tourism. When it comes to cruise tourism in particular, alcohol plays an integral role in the experience both from the perspective of revenue generation for cruise companies (Weaver, 2005a) as well as the liminal pursuits of passengers. It is in the latter role where alcohol itself assumes its own agency as its consumption helps to frame both passenger motivations and their behaviours while at-sea. On-board a cruise ship—particularly in the case of cruises to nowhere—there are opportunities for drinking alcohol and partying at every turn, and few or limited consequences for drunkenness or debauchery. The availability of alcohol in a tourism setting is noted by Moore (1995, p. 301) as a contributing factor in increased consumption. As Moore notes, 'The alcohol availability literature provides support for the idea that increasing ease of physical and social access will be reflected in higher consumption rates' (Moore, 1995, p. 301). Without a destination, there is limited possibility for negative socio-cultural impacts of such tourism activities.

Similar to alcotourism, the literature of party tourism and hedonism in tourism, grounded in the work of such authors as Thurnell-Read (2012), may serve as a pre-cursor to understanding ship-based party tourism and its practices. However, unlike party tourism as situated by Thurnell-Read (2012) and Diken and Laustsen (2004), partying on the high seas without a destination does not result in contact with host culture(s) aside from the 'host' culture of the ship's crew. Without a destination, cruises to nowhere have limited possibilities for negative socio-cultural impacts as a result of behaviours that may otherwise contravene local norms. While a ship of passengers may comprise a degree of cultural diversity, there is nonetheless a limit to the exposure to cultural others. At the same time, this lack of contact with a host culture also limits the regulatory concerns that often come with the association between tourism and alcohol (Bell, 2008, p. 293), and the impacts that come with 'unsuitable behavior ... [and] the inappropriate use of public space that often results from party tourism (Thurnell-Read, 2012, p. 802). The shipboard environment provides a safe cocoon for liminoid exploits, far from land. Partying on-board a cruise to nowhere can thus offer maximum opportunities for alcohol-based revenue generation, and minimal concern for regulation of debaucherous activities. The party atmosphere of shipboard life makes way for multiple ways of satisfying pleasure. As Inglis (2000) highlights, seeking pleasure through the body is part of the liminal experience of tourism. The combination of alcohol and partying in tourist experiences serve as a pathway toward liminality. Both constitute a large part of the 'fun' element of cruising (Swarbrooke & Horner, 2007, p. 285) and thus contribute to the sense that alcohol and partying combine in a 'hedonistic cocktail of sea, sun and sex' (Diken & Laustsen, 2004, p. 100). In the case of cruises to nowhere with their round-the-clock parties and judgement-free environment, that debaucherous cocktails flow as endless as the limitless horizon at sea.

Containment and metaworlds

Before the super-sized cruise ships of today, the role of ocean-going vessels was to move people and goods between places (Weaver, 2005a, p. 166). Such ships carried migrants, business people and tourists. Whatever the motivation of passengers aboard ocean liners during this golden age of ship travel, they would have experienced the spaces of the ship as utilitarian as the purpose of their travel. Contemporary cruisers, however, experience super-sized ships as 'containers' for their holiday experience (Weaver, 2005a). Weaver explores how these modern mega-ships act as containers of the tourist experience. At the same time, the environmental bubble of the cruise ship, and in many cases private island enclaves visited by them, 'capture both tourists and their money' (Weaver, 2005a, 180). This sense of containment and enclosure in an environment that is spatially and/or culturally apart from the 'real' world is clearly articulated by Hottola's (2004, 2005, 2010) discussion of 'metaworlds'. A metaworld is a spatially and culturally distinct enclave where tourists seek to regain control over the cultural confusion that is experienced when coming in contact with a host culture (Hottola, 2005). Thus, the concept of metaspatiality and metaspatial enclaves serve as means to explore the contained spaces of the cruise ship. Using Hottola's (2010) argument, the metaspatial enclave of the cruise ship is a space where

... people may adopt and play with holiday identities and experiment with behavioural excesses, being temporally free of a number of norms prevalent both at home and abroad. (2010, np)

Hottola's argument, however, is based on the presumption of differences between host- and guest cultures, within the context of a culturally differentiated destination. While a cruise passenger on a typical voyage may encounter ports of call that expose them to cultural difference, cruises to nowhere provide an even more sequestered tourist experience that is contained within the hull of the ship itself. Cruise passengers and the crew that serve them are further segregated into distinct cultural worlds on the ship through which they move, eat, sleep, and socialise (Weaver, 2005a). Whereas

the behaviour and 'performance' of tourists in a typical tourist enclave may be moni-
tored and surveilled (Edensor, 2000), in the metaspatial enclave of a cruise ship, tourist
practices of liminality may be limited only by fellow tourists on the ship and the rules
of conduct governing shipboard safety. Moored by these literatures of tourism geographies of cruising, alcotourism, party tourism, and metaspatiality, I next turn to discussion of the method used in the exploration of liminal seascapes.

Method: exploring liminality at-sea

This study uses a qualitative approach to gather data from a variety of sources in
order to understand seaborne liminality. This approach intends to explore the ways in
which boundary crossings are anticipated, performed and reflected upon by passengers on-board cruises to nowhere. The principal sources of data were online, including
cruise community websites, travel reviews, social media posts, and websites dedicated
to cruises to nowhere. These sources are used following the netnographic method.
The online ethnographic method known as netnography is a form of internet-based
ethnography inspired by the growth of user-generated on-line content, referred to as
web 2.0. Netnography was coined by Kozinets (1997) and used initially for consumer
research (Kozinets, 1998, 2002, 2006, 2010). More recently, netnography has gained a
foothold within tourism and hospitality research where the tourist experience is concerned (Fitchett & Hoogendoorn, 2019; Jeacle & Carter, 2011; Mkono, 2012, 2013;
Mkono & Markwell, 2014; Rink, 2017). Engaging with online content in tourism
research thus reflects the ways in which individuals shape and understand their
worlds, and more specifically how they anticipate, perform and reflect on the time-limited period of the holiday. Much of this anticipation, performance and reflection happens on social media platforms, where the sharing of text, photo and short videos
amounts to the 'new postcard' (Munar & Jacobsen, 2014, p. 47) for the internet generation. As Zeng and Gerritsen (2014) discuss in their comprehensive review of social
media in tourism,

'Social media includes social networking sites, consumer review sites, content community sites, wikis, Internet forums and location-based social media. Social media has
emerged as the new way in which people connect socially, by integrating information
and communication technology (such as mobile and web-based technologies), social
interaction, and the construction of words, pictures, videos and audio. It is actually
more than a new way to communicate; it is an entire online environment built on participants' contributions and interactions' (Zeng & Gerritsen, 2014, p. 28).

Social media thus provides new terrain in which to explore tourism narratives, and
netnography serves as a systematic approach to gathering and making sense of such
data (Mkono & Markwell, 2014). Netnography allows researchers to value both the
mundane and the extraordinary (Rink, 2017) aspects of the tourist experience, and
thus the narratives gathered provide unique insights into a range of tourism phenomena. Given the increasing use of social media and user-generated online travel content, the netnographic method assists in capturing travel narratives as both relics of
the information age (Bissell, 2012) as well as data for better understanding the experiences that tourists have before, during and after their holiday. Being user-generated,

netnographic accounts of travel experience also have the additional benefit of being candid, and therefore a reflection of the extraordinary experiences of shipboard life. Even in cases where such accounts are potentially overstated and tinged with revelous bravado, these travel narratives signify the expectations of drunken, debaucherous behaviour that reinforce passengers' sense of 'spontaneous communitas' (Turner, 1974). For purposes of my study, I have sampled netnographic data related to 'cruises to nowhere' based on two inclusion criteria: (1) cruises that sail from South Africa into international waters and return to the original port of departure without any inter-mediate port calls; and (2) cruises that sail from South Africa into international waters and onward to a private, 'contained' destination (Weaver, 2005a) without border for-malities, returning to the original port of departure.

My netnographic approach was both active and passive. From the active perspec-tive, I became a member of the online cruise community Cruise Critic (www.cruise-critic.com). I created a user name that was my actual name (against the suggestion of the Cruise Critic community) so that I could be identified by potential respondents, and could be directly contacted with any queries. No user identities from this active netnographic method have been revealed in the course of this study, and all responses are treated as anonymous. Interacting with other members, I posed ques-tions on the Cruise Critic message board under the message thread 'South African Cruises to Nowhere'. I began the thread by revealing my interest in researching cruises to nowhere, and asked members of the community for their impressions on cruises to nowhere from those who have done such cruises from South Africa or elsewhere. I asked the online respondents to reflect on the motivations for embarking on such cruises; and to relate the pros and cons of such cruises. I finally posed the question of what it is like to be on a cruise to nowhere. Responses to the thread were limited, par-tially due to the fact that a large part of the Cruise Critic community is comprised of cruising enthusiasts from North America. In spite of this, respondents to the thread were nonetheless revealing with regard to the structure, motivations and activities on cruises to nowhere.

The opposite of this active approach is that of the 'passive lurker' (Mkono & Markwell, 2014, p. 290). Such an approach is characterised by the lack of direct inter-action between the researcher and on-line communities. The passive lurker gathers data anonymously from publicly accessible websites, while those who post on such sites are not aware of the role of the researcher in the study. This 'passive lurker' approach is one where the researcher does not interact with the on-line community such as I did with Cruise Critic, but one where texts in the form of written discussions and comments, and visual texts in the form of photographs and videos were viewed through a public forum. Given ethical and legal considerations governing the use of data from many travel websites and social media platforms (Rink, 2017), data from this passive lurker stance are neither used directly nor with attribution to those tourists who posted the content. The only exception is in the descriptions of cruises as taken from their respective cruise organiser or company. From this passive perspective, I reviewed and analysed content on websites and social media dedicated to two themed cruises to nowhere that sail from South African ports. Both cruises take place aboard the same cruise company's ships, yet each is distinct as described below. Two websites and several social media platforms were reviewed. They included: A public website developed for promoting the themed cruise to nowhere known as *Oh Ship* (http://www.ohship.co.za); a public Facebook group (https://en-gb.facebook.com/Smile904FM/videos/the-smile-all-80s-cruise-is-underway/1292955724106723/) and website for the themed cruise to nowhere known as the *Smile all 80 s Cruise* (http://www.smile904.fm/gallery/smile-all-80s-cruise/; and Twitter posts from @OhShipSA and posts with the hashtags #ohship2016, #ohship2017, and #ohship2018. While all of the above sites/platforms are publicly accessible, terms of use guide the ways in which information can be used. Using data from both active and the passive approaches, I performed a thematic content analysis of visual and written texts provided through the sources above. Such analysis focuses on examining 'story grammars' (Franzosi, 2004, p. 187) including the

' ... who, what, where, when, and why (and how); someone doing something, for or against someone else, in time and space; or subject-actionobject or, better, agent-action patient/beneficiary and their modifiers' (p. 187).

Table 1 illustrates an example of the framework of analysis that establishes the relationship between observed story grammars and debaucherous shipboard activities. Table 1 provides an example of thematic content analysis by illustrating some of the key elements and 'story grammars' from one data source (*Oh SHIP* 2016), using a coding schema based upon the literature from alcotourism (Bell, 2008) and party tourism (Diken & Laustsen, 2004; Thurnell-Read, 2012). The stories that tourists write about their holiday thus characterise the shipboard environment and the activities that comprise the cruise to nowhere experience with respect to temporal and spatial elements of alcohol use, reference to sex and sexuality, and partying. Supplementing the netnographic sources, I also include cruise company descriptions of cruises to nowhere from industry websites, and my own reflections as a passenger aboard a ship that over the past several years has been used for cruises to nowhere in the South African cruising season. While my voyage was not a cruise to nowhere, discussions with crew and reflections on the ship environment assist in making sense of other sources of data.

Liminality on the high seas

With the aim to explore how liminal boundary crossings are performed in the context of 'cruises to nowhere' from spatial, discursive and practice-based perspectives, I turn now to analysis of data from the netnographic method. Cruises to nowhere are a unique cruise tourism experience that sacrifice terrestrial destinations for the metaspatial enclave of the ship and endless 'seascapes' of liminality. Liminality in the case of cruises to nowhere is situated in the intersection of tensions between space and time; embodiment; and alcohol. Fuelled as they are by alcohol, round-the-clock parties and endless buffets, cruises to nowhere are an increasingly popular addition to the Southern African cruising season. As the on-line community Cruise Critic describes them,

'On these brief getaways, usually lasting just one or two nights (but sometimes three), ships sail out to international waters—usually just far enough so that they can open the casino and duty-free shopping—and then turn around and come back to

Table 1. Example of framework of analysis: from story grammars to debauchery (*Oh Ship 2016 After movie*).

Story grammar elements (Franzosi, 2004) who, what, where, when, and why (and how)	Coding schema: alcohol		Coding schema: sex and sexuality		Coding schema: partying		Notes
	Spatial (where)	Temporal (when)	Spatial (where)	Temporal (when)	Spatial (where)	Temporal (when)	
Opening scene: Man dancing in crowd with drinks in-hand	1	1			1		On the deck of the ship, in a crowd with drinks spilling as he turns around
Wide shot of deck filled with dancing passengers	1	1					Reinforcing the idea of spontaneous communitas
DJ calls out to the crowd, asking which men are single				1			He replies in disbelief, suggesting that not all of those present are single
DJ warns female passengers that if you call his room it's because he is in someone else's room			1	1			Flexible relationship status while on-board
DJ reminds passengers of the group call: Oh..SHIP					1		Reminds passengers of the group nature of the cruise and the alliteration between ship and shi*
Images of twerking in front of DJ and other dancers			1		1		The dancing has started early in the voyage, and scenes cut between day and night
Wet t-shirt contest on the pool deck		1	1	1	1		Sex and sexuality are openly displayed, celebrated and consumed by the crowd
Comment from passenger: 'the food is great, the music is pumping, that's all I wanna do'					1		Suggestion that the party does not stop
Crowds of passengers holding drinks have their photos taken in fancy dress		1			1		
Crowds of passengers dance in synchronized steps, drinks in hand	1	1			1		Reinforcing the idea of spontaneous communitas
Female passenger gets a lap-dance from a male passenger			1	1			Crowd gathers around as they dance
Entertainer sings a song suggesting 'chocolate love on the side'			1	1			Crowd roars with approval

the same port a day or two later. Passengers don't have the opportunity to set foot on land' (Cruise Critic, 2018a, np).

These quick cruises are designed to immerse—and thus contain—passengers within the ship's offerings. Cruises to nowhere are often operated on super-size ships (Weaver, 2005a) that have a range of revenue-capturing offerings. Cruise experts suggest that cruise companies offer cruises to nowhere for a variety of reasons including to attract new customers who, after trying a short cruise, will return to purchase another in future (Cruise Critic, 2018b). Cruises to nowhere are described by members of Cruise Critic, an online community of cruisers, as follows:

'The companies sometimes schedule cruises to nowhere ... to fill gaps. It's a perfect way for the line to make a few dollars while a cruise ship is lingering between shifts of its regular itineraries or preparing to reposition for the season' (Cruise Critic, 2018a, n.p.).

While the purpose of cruises to nowhere may be functional and managerial for cruise companies to fill gaps in a seasonal sailing schedule, for cruise passengers '... cruise-to-nowhere escapes pack in plenty of fun, allowing cruisers to leave it all behind on land and get lost at sea for a carefree day or two ... ' (Cruise Critic, 2018a, np), or a 'giant 3-day floating party' (Cruise Critic, 2018c, np). The cruises to nowhere sampled for this research differ in their ports of origin and thematic mix of music, entertainment and passenger profile. However, they share in common the key elements of cruises to nowhere, namely that they depart from port, sail into international waters, and return days later after a debaucherous sojourn on the high seas.

South African-based cruises to nowhere are offered by MSC Cruises, a privately owned Italian shipping company. They describe their two-night cruises to nowhere on their website as the 'perfect weekend getaway experience for those who are short on time, but in need of a break!' (MSC, 2018, np). They further add that such experiences are

'Ideal for first time cruisers, for couples or families wanting a quick escape, or for those wanting to celebrate their own personal occasions on board like bachelor parties or milestone birthdays' (MSC Cruises, 2018, np).

In spite of the fact that MSC includes 'families' amongst the potential clients of its cruises to nowhere, such short escapes are dominated by those who are crossing more substantial liminal boundaries, such as on the 2015 sailing of *Oh Ship* that included a wedding, as seen in a video posted on the voyage's website. Weddings, bachelor parties and milestone birthdays are all symbolic of liminal border crossings. Thurnell-Read (2012) makes the connection between bachelor parties and scripted drunkenness and other activities that must take place within them. Such parties represent 'a ritualised premarital event typically preceding the wedding by several weeks, in which the impending changing status of the soon-to-be-married man, the stag, is celebrated and signified' (Thurnell-Read, 2012, p. 801). Similarly, milestone birthdays celebrate the passage from one age-based social status to another. Cruises to nowhere thus become the ideal setting for enacting such border crossing. On their cruises to nowhere, MSC further promises that

'... a 2 night cruise to nowhere allows for a fabulous away from home experience. Hit the open waves, and experience the ship as the destination ... Value for money guaranteed, a 2 night cruise is a perfect fun filled break' (MSC Cruises, 2018, np).

One of the cruises to nowhere from Cape Town is the musically themed *Smile All 80s Cruise*. The cruise offers lovers of 80s music with a floating party on the high seas, sponsored by Smile FM, a regional radio station broadcasting from Cape Town that specialises in music from the 80s and 90s. In addition to a continuous party vibe, music, dancing and comedy acts, the *Smile All 80s Cruise* featured a Pac-Man themed evening with plenty of neon colours. The radio station's listenership also influences the profile of passengers aboard its cruise to nowhere. As the station describes in its profile (http://www.smile904.fm), nearly 75% of their listeners are white, with smaller fractions from other race groups.

Oh Ship is a Durban-based cruise that like the Cape Town cruises, takes place aboard an MSC vessel and is also sponsored by a radio station. Like *Smile All 80s Cruise*, *Oh Ship* is driven by corporate sponsorship from media and brands of alcoholic drinks. Initially sponsored primarily by popular radio station 5FM, the current headline sponsor of *Oh Ship* is now Metro FM. Metro FM broadcasts from Johannesburg to a nationwide audience that appeals to a young, urban, black listenership. As they note on their website, Metro FM is a 'progressive lifestyle brand [that] epitomizes black success and leadership, with attitude. Its listeners are high achievers with a lot of style, confidence, potential and the enviable ability to feel at home in modern South Africa' (http://beta.sabc.co.za/metrofm/about-us). The profile of the *Oh Ship* cruise to nowhere follows suit with a young, urban, black passenger profile. *Oh Ship* passengers take part in the cruise to nowhere seemingly to 'let their hair down'. Evidence of this comes in the form of social media posts and comments anticipating non-stop partying and 'living loud'. *Oh Ship* makes an intermediate (day-long) call at Portuguese Island, a small uninhabited private island off the coast of Mozambique. Portuguese Island is a contained enclave (Weaver, 2005a) that only serves the passengers of the ships that make anchor off its shore. The island provides visitors with opportunities to purchase locally-inspired drinks and food from the cruise company's kiosks. Thus, the metaspatial enclave is an extension of the enclavic bubble of the ship. *Oh Ship* is a cruise to nowhere by every definition.

Liminality in tension between space and time

Both the *Smile All 80s Cruise* and *Oh Ship* offer opportunities for tourist to test the waters of liminality. In a retrospective video of the 2017 *Oh Ship* experience, one video featured commentary from two smartly dressed black male passengers. Smiling and laughing as they spoke, one echoed the famous tagline for the 'sin city' of Las Vegas, adding 'They say whatever happens on *Oh Ship* stays on *Oh Ship*'. His interlocutor agrees, replying with a simple but poignant 'Crazy, crazy, crazy'. These comments set the tone for liminal experiences aboard cruises to nowhere. In contrast to terrestrial destinations that have some degree of spatial and temporal limits, the confines of a cruise to nowhere sit in tension between notions of space and time. Terrestrial destinations have limits imposed by a range of temporal and spatial elements including: operating hours of clubs and bars; regulation in serving alcohol such as liquor licenses and the temporal or spatial limits imposed by them; more conventional temporalities of day/night; cultural, safety or other restrictions that such temporalities may bring;

and broader socio-cultural norms that regulate behaviour. While cruise ships are governed by both maritime law and the conditions of carriage imposed by cruise company policies, the destination which is the cruise ship has very few if any of these restrictions. Aboard cruises to nowhere, parties continue throughout the day and night on account of the fact that the ship operates within its own space and time. As one passenger aboard Oh Ship 2015 notes 'It's a glorious day in the middle of nowhere'.

The space of the cruise to nowhere ship at once contains the passengers spatially within the hull while it also captures them as sources of revenue. At the same time that environmental bubble sequesters them from the outside world, the temporalities of day and night, and the restrictions that come with it. One reveller aboard the 2016 *Oh Ship* cruise reminisced about late-night partying noting that he only woke-up at 03:00am to catch a set of his favourite old school hip-hop DJ. Even at that hour, the environment was described by him and his fellow passengers as 'lit'. In other words, it was intoxicating in both literal and figurative terms. In the enclavic setting of the cruise to nowhere, the environmental bubble does not function to 'shield tourists from potentially unpleasant experiences' (Weaver, 2005b, p. 169), but rather to enable the extraordinary. In this case, the extraordinary is characterised by vicious indulgence in sensual pleasures that, while acutely focused and limited spatially to the constraints of the ship, are facilitated by the flexibility and openness of time. Vicious indulgence is also exhibited in bodies: how they move; how they are costumed often in more-than-human flights of fancy; and how they are desired, sexualised and consumed.

Bodies

The body plays a central role in tourist performances on cruises to nowhere: moving bodies, costumed bodies, more-than-human bodies, and sexualised bodies. As Crouch (2000, p. 63) concludes, the sensuous, social and poetic dimensions of embodiment play a critical role in understanding tourism. The body becomes a site of over-indulgence of alcohol and place in which identity can be celebrated. Passengers aboard *Oh Ship* celebrate black success, achievement, style and confidence through the adornment of their bodies in glamorous—and often revealing—clothing, while they dance in unison on the deck of the ship. Similarly, photos from *Smile All 80s Cruise* are replete with costumed and adorned bodies. The passenger bodies are in a variety of themed costumes, celebrating the out of the ordinary nature of the cruise experience. A tweet in advance of the 2016 *Oh Ship* voyage featured an animated .GIF revealing a packed dancefloor illuminated in neon colours. In the centre of the scene was a dancing costumed 'horse' (with two revellers inside) surrounded by a range of dancers in animal print clothing, urging the horse onto the dancefloor. The image suggests a wild animal-like party, a fantasy of liminal abandon within an environment of spontaneous communitas. Smile All 80s Cruise video posted on their public Facebook site (https://www.facebook.com/Smile904FM/videos/1298369483565347) highlights 'the party animals' and the party animals and friends as integral elements of the cruise experience. It also refers to 'Die Skandaal' [the scandal] of the voyage, where a host of cross-dressing men are seen parading across the pool deck, cheered and jeered-on by fellow passengers. Dressed in high-heels, bikini tops, and adorned with jewellery and make-up, these gender-bending performances are likely to be out of the ordinary for their actors. In this case, the cruise environment placed bodies in performances that they may have never enacted before. This segment of the video ends with an incomplete but familiar phrase: 'what happens on the ship...' All of this echoes Turner's (1974) reference to liminality's capacity to thrust individuals into new symbolic worlds free from structural limitations, and replete with fantasy and play (Turner, 1974, p. 68).

Sailing during the southern hemisphere's summer season, these cruises invite passengers to wear little clothing for much of the time on-deck. Women—and less-so men—are seen frequently in their bathing suits, dancing, catching sun, and posing for the camera. Wet t-shirt contests for women, and line-ups of topless men showing their abs are part of the *Oh Ship* experience. Sexualising the body is a central theme of videos from past voyages of *Oh Ship* as seen on their public website (http://www.ohship. co.za). Reflecting on *Oh Ship* in the video entitled '*Oh Ship* 2—What went down', a woman interviewed notes her interest in 'hot guys... some single, some not-so single'. Here she refers to the fact that relationship status is a flexible characteristic on-board the ship, and that in keeping with an earlier comment above, what happens on the ship stays on the ship. Flexible relationships are also an element of *Oh Ship* 5 in 2016. In that video, a DJ warns interested female passengers 'If you call my room and I don't answer, it's because I'm in somebody else's room, so don't call again'. Cabin-hopping seems the order of the voyage. If that is the case, then cruise sponsors have you covered. The retrospective movie from *Oh Ship* 3 opens with an interview of a passenger as he settles into his cabin. With a pumping house music track in the background, the passenger sits on the bed in his cabin and opens a welcome gift given to passengers by one of the sponsors, 'Lovers Plus', a brand of South African condoms. 'Lovers Plus have given us a party pack. We've got condoms, on condoms, on condoms, on condoms' he says as he tosses the assorted packs of foil-wrapped condoms at the camera. He concludes by saying 'let's all play safe, guys'. Bodies are seen in various states of undress in photos and videos posted both on social media and public sites dedicated to the sampled cruises to nowhere. What is most prevalent in all visual texts, however, is the presence of alcohol—in the sponsorships and in the hands of passengers—that underscores the importance of drinking on a cruise to nowhere.

Booze

Both frequent cruisers as well as those who are anticipating a cruise to nowhere experience express the limitless qualities of the ship environment. In describing cruises to nowhere, one on-line respondent noted that

... [cruises] to nowhere used to be popular [in the USA]... they were booze cruises. Cheap... the ship went out beyond the coast into international waters, opened up the duty free shops and you could buy all you wanted without paying duty back into the US. But our gov't stopped that, felt it was violating our cabotage laws.[1]

Another, from Durban, South Africa noted that

'...Cruises to nowhere are designed for those who wish to have a big, fat party. They have no destination where you can disembark and explore etc. You don't even need a passport. The crew lay on all sorts of entertainment and fun throughout the day and well into the night. If you want to relax and take things slow you might be annoyed by the party animals busting loose on these cruises. By South African standards, they are relatively inexpensive. The durations are short. No real time to be leisurely. If you want a peaceful cruise, rather save and book for longer trips ... '

The comments above are typical of how cruises to nowhere are understood in an on-line community of cruise enthusiasts. Both comments refer to the importance of alcohol in the cruise to nowhere experience. One respondent on a Durban-based cruise to nowhere agreed with the assessment that cruises to nowhere are 'booze cruises', and further backed this up by referring to a conversation with an entertainer they befriended on-board.

'... You cannot purchase an all-inclusive drinks package on South African based MSC cruises. Apparently, the ship ran out of alcohol when they did offer them. One of the entertainers that we befriended ... is a regular on the SA-based ships. She described the "party atmosphere" onboard and said that it's almost impossible to move for the bottles and glasses littered about the ship at night'.

This passenger's comments suggest that the liminal environment of a cruise to nowhere is not experienced the same for crew members who have to contend with the behaviour of passengers and the results of their debaucherous pursuits. For crew members that may already be working under difficult conditions, a cruise to nowhere may add to their misery.

Shaping metaspace

As limitless as it may seem for passengers, debauchery aboard a cruise to nowhere may be circumscribed by the invigilating eyes of crew members and the legal provisions from cruise company policy. The metaspatiality of the cruise ship is thus shaped as much by motivation and expectation as it is by service standards and policy. MSC's conditions of carriage (https://www.msccruises.co.za/en-za/Conditions-Of-Carriage.aspx) sets out such policies with regard to both passenger conduct generally, and alcohol use more specifically:

11.2 Passengers must at all times conduct themselves in a manner which respects the safety and privacy of other persons onboard.

11.3 Passengers must comply with any reasonable request made by any member of staff, the Master or his/her officers.

13.3 The Carrier and/or its servants and/or agents may refuse to serve a Passenger alcohol or further alcohol where in their reasonable opinion the Passenger is likely to be a danger and/or nuisance to himself/herself, other passengers and/or the Vessel.

Relationships between passengers (the guests) and crew (the hosts) are complex. While each is segregated within their own stratified metaworlds of the ship, that segregation is not absolute. While crew must interact with passengers in their various roles, the relationships are unequal and complicated by cruise company regulations and expectations of service standards. As a participant myself in a 'below decks' tour of the MSC Sinfonia during a 2018 cruise, the contrast between the domestic and social worlds of crew below desks was in stark contrast to that above.

In spite of the tension between passenger motivations and cruise company policies, cruises to nowhere exemplify a unique liminal destination where 'debaucherous' tourism can be explored within an enclavic seaborne bubble (Weaver, 2018) with a spontaneous sense of communitas, together with their fellow revellers. Such shipboard experiences mark the ship as a terra incognita (Lew, 2011) that is both destination and periphery. As is the case with stag tourism in Europe (Thurnell-Read, 2012), debaucherous tourists 'work collaboratively to define a destination according to expectations' (2012, p. 802). The combination of intention, encounter, and meaning-making result in a unique seaborne destination.

Conclusions: weighing anchor on debauchery tourism

Cruises to nowhere are unique in the cruise industry, offering passengers a contained holiday experience that is brief, cost-effective and limited to the space of the cruise vessel. Cruises to nowhere also offer an opportunity for young (or even not-so-young), first-time cruise passengers to sample the cruise experience. For a young demographic, interested in partying, the cruise to nowhere offers the possibility to combine party culture with an adventure on the high seas. Cruises to nowhere thus provide an entry point to a new cruise market at the same time they highlight a void in academic interest related to this rare cruise genre. An absence of literature focusing on cruises to nowhere leaves a gap in our understanding of the experience of such cruises. As a result, this study aimed to respond to Yarnal and Kerstetter's (2005) call for further investigation into the role that vacation spaces such as cruise ships play in individuals' lives. This exploration of liminality at-sea has taken spatial, discursive and practice-based perspectives where boundary crossings are traced through the intended and practiced activities on-board cruise-to-nowhere experiences. Relying on data from written and visual texts, the vacation space of the cruise ship emerges through a hedonistic mix of sun, sea, sex and especially alcohol. The uncommon ways in which cruises to nowhere contain space while they also liberating time situate the liminal setting of the cruise to nowhere in a unique environmental bubble. Whereas Weaver (2005) discusses containment on the cruise ship in terms of destinization, he also argues that the enclavic detachment of the ship is used to capture consumers and thus revenue. With cruises to nowhere, containment has additional meaning. On cruises to nowhere, consumers and the revenue that they generate are contained by the ship. However, that containment also enables an extraordinarily liminal experience that insulates passengers from contact with cultural others as it intensifies the group-based debaucherous behaviours that happen on the dance floor, in the bars and throughout the ship. In this way, cruises to nowhere frame the destination-free seascape as an exceptional liminoid playground.

My second aim was to further the use of netnography as a methodological tool to embrace travel narratives that are produced for and shared with on-line communities. Based on a sample of netnographic accounts of cruise to nowhere experiences in the Southern African context, I have demonstrated the role of on-line travel accounts in framing tourist practices both in terms of the experience being had in the present, and in anticipation of future voyages for those who consume such media. The netno-graphic data demonstrate, following Zeng and Gerritsen (2014) that social media is not simply about communication, but rather calls attention to the ways in which social media signifies a complete environment through which tourism practices are under-stood. Using this method also helps to spotlight the value of user-generated accounts of travel behaviour in understanding the tourism experience. Given the prevalent use of social media and user-generated content both in travel and everyday life, the net-nographic method may help tourism researchers to better understanding the experi-ences that tourists have before, during and after their holiday. Such accounts have the additional benefit of being candid—and thus an unvarnished reflection of the extraor-dinary experiences of shipboard life.

Finally, through my exploration of cruises to nowhere, I sought to extend the con-cept of liminality into a relatively unexplored tourism typology in order to trace a pre-liminary understanding and call for more research on what may be called 'debauchery tourism'. Why debauchery tourism? Understanding the ways in which passengers sat-isfy their vicious indulgence in sensual pleasures, the setting of a cruise to nowhere unlocks the productive potential of debauchery—not through a moral perspective, but through the ways that tourist intention, encounter, and meaning-making coalesce amidst the containment of the vessel. Cruises to nowhere have a metaspatiality that limits intercultural contact and strengthens the enclavic nature of the cruise ship as a destination and an environmental bubble. The experience of drinking alcohol and par-tying aboard the contained enclave of cruises to nowhere has much in common with alcotourism and its close relative party tourism (Bell, 2008). Both focus on boundary-crossing escapes from the ordinary in the context of tourism. However, the shipboard experience of cruises to nowhere are unique with respect to the degree that such lim-inal activities are contained in the metaspatial enclave of the ship. The metaspatial enclave of the cruise to nowhere does not require the same policing of boundaries that might otherwise characterise such tourist enclaves. As Edensor notes:

' ... enclavic space requires a continual policing of its boundaries, its inhabitants, its appearance, and the activities which occur within it, there is a sense in which touristic enclaves may be mobile entities, captured by the common phrase "environmental bubble"' (2000, p. 330).

The seaborne bubble of the cruise ship may be sold to potential cruise tourists for its pleasure potential, and for attracting first-time passengers (Weaver, 2018). This is especially so in the case of cruises to nowhere that serve as an entry point for first-time cruisers, as well as an enclavic metaspace for debaucherous tourism activities. The findings of this study reveal, following Hottola (2010), that the metaspatial zone of the cruise to nowhere provides a place for rest and liminal activities with a debau-cherous cruise tourist's primary reference group: other debauchery-seeking cruise tou-rists. The enclavic bubble of cruises to nowhere is fortified by the absence of port calls, and thus the ship alone remains the site of tourist performances that are shared with others through social media. While the lack of port calls on cruises to nowhere may have a managerial function in terms of providing opportunities for maximum use of resources (Cruise Critic, 2018a) and opportunities to expand cruise markets beyond middle- to upper-class tourists, such cruises also provide scope to understand a functional metaspace that exemplifies the liminal dimensions of tourism on the high seas. Such liminal experiences of tourists are shared through and re-inforced by social media (Bissell, 2012; Zeng & Gerritsen, 2014), and thus the debaucherous tourists perform collaborative work in defining the shipboard destination according to their expectations. The combination of intention, encounter, and meaning-making result in a unique seaborne destination. Within the enclave of the ship, passengers aboard cruises to nowhere have little chance of contravening local norms. With little possibility of causing negative socio-cultural impacts as a result of their behaviour, the horizon of liminal possibility is nearly endless. A passenger on-board Oh Ship 2017 sums up the meaning of such cruises for passengers, and provides a fitting way to conclude: 'I'm in the middle of nowhere, having the time of my life'.

Note

1. *Cabotage* is the transport of goods or passengers between two places in the same country by a transport operator from another country.

Disclosure statement

No potential conflict of interest was reported by the author.

ORCID

Bradley Rink (iD) http://orcid.org/0000-0002-2903-9561

References

Andrews, H., & L. Roberts (Eds.), (2012). *Minal landscapes: Travel, experience and spaces in-between*. London: Routledge.

Bell, D. (2008). Destination drinking: Toward a research agenda on alcotourism. *Drugs: Education, Prevention and Policy, 15*(3), 291–304. doi:10.1080/09687630801934089

Bissell, D. (2012). Mobile testimony in the information age: The powers of travel reviews. *International Journal of Cultural Studies, 15*(2), 149–164. doi:10.1177/1367877911416885

Brooker, E., & Joppe, M. (2014). Developing a tourism innovation typology: Leveraging liminal insights. *Journal of Travel Research, 53*(4), 500–508. doi:10.1177/0047287513497839

Butcher, J. (2006). *The moralisation of tourism: Sun, sand... and saving the world?* London. Routledge.

Caton, K. (2012). Taking the moral turn in tourism studies. *Annals of Tourism Research, 39*(4), 1906–1928. doi:10.1016/j.annals.2012.05.021

Crouch, D. (2000). Places around us: Embodied geographies in leisure and tourism. *Leisure Studies, 19*(1), 63–76. doi:10.1080/026143600374752

Cruise critic. (2018a). Cruises to Nowhere Basics. Retrieved from https://www.cruisecritic.com/articles.cfm?ID=1683

Cruise critic. (2018b). Australia Cruises to Nowhere. Retrieved from https://www.cruisecritic.com/articles.cfm?ID=1658

Cruise critic. (2018c). Member reviews, cruise to nowhere. Retrieved from https://www.cruise-critic.com/memberreviews/regions/cruise-to-nowhere/

Dickinson, R., & Vladimir, A. (1997). Selling the sea: An inside look at the cruise industry. New York: John Wiley & Sons.

Diken, B., & Laustsen, C. (2004). Sea, sun, sex and the discontents of pleasure. *Tourist Studies*, *4*(2), 99–114. doi:10.1177/1468797604054376

Edensor, T. (2000). Staging tourism: Tourists as performers. *Annals of Tourism Research*, *27*(2), 322–344. doi:10.1016/S0160-7383(99)00082-1

Edensor, T. (2007). Mundane mobilities, performances and spaces of tourism. *Social & Cultural Geography*, *8*, 199–215. doi:10.1080/14649360701360089

Fitchett, J. M., & Hoogendoorn, G. (2019). Exploring the climate sensitivity of tourists to South Africa through TripAdvisor reviews. *South African Geographical Journal*, *101*(1), 91–109. doi:10.1080/03736245.2018.1541022

Franzosi, R. (2004). Content analysis. In M.S. Lewis-Beck, A. Bryman, & T. Futing Liao (Eds.), *The SAGE Encyclopedia of social science research methods*. Thousand Oaks, CA. Sage.

Holloway, S. L., Jayne, M., & Valentine, G. (2008). 'Sainsbury's is my local': English alcohol policy, domestic drinking practices and the meaning of home. *Transactions of the Institute of British Geographers*, *33*(4), 532–547. doi:10.1111/j.1475-5661.2008.00322.x

Hottola, P. (2004). Culture confusion: Intercultural adaptation in tourism. *Annals of Tourism Research*, *31*(2), 447–466. doi:10.1016/j.annals.2004.01.003

Hottola, P. (2005). The metaspatialities of control management in tourism: Backpacking in India. *Tourism Geographies*, *7*(1), 1–22. doi:10.1080/1461668042000324030

Hottola, P. (2010). Tourism spaces, behaviours and cultures: The metaspatialities of tourism. J. Wilson (Eds.), *The Routledge handbook of tourism geographies* (1st ed.) Abingdon: Routledge.

Inglis, F. (2000). *The delicious history of the holiday*. London: Routledge.

Jeacle, I., & Carter, C. (2011). In TripAdvisor we trust: Rankings, calculative regimes and abstract systems. *Accounting, Organizations and Society*, *36*(4-5), 293–309. doi:10.1016/j.aos.2011.04.002

Lew, A. A. (2011). Tourism incognita: Experiencing the liminal edge of destination places. *Études Caribéennes*, *19*, 1–12. doi:10.4000/etudescaribeennes.5232

Mkono, M. (2012). Netnographic tourist research: The Internet as a virtual fieldwork site. *Tourism Analysis*, *17*(4), 553–555. doi:10.3727/108354212X13473157390966

Mkono, M. (2013). Netnography in qualitative tourism research. In J. Fountain & K. Moore (Eds.), *Tourism and global change: On the edge of big* [CAUTHE 2013 conference proceedings] (pp. 501–551). Lincoln: Cauthe.

Mkono, M., & Markwell, K. (2014). The application of netnography in tourism studies. *Annals of Tourism Research*, *48*, 289–291. doi:10.1016/j.annals.2014.07.005

Moore, R. (1995). Gender and alcohol use in a Greek tourist town. *Annals of Tourism Research*, *22*(2), 300–313. doi:10.1016/0160-7383(94)00078-6

MSC Cruises (2018). 2 night party cruises by MSC Cruises. Retrieved from https://www.msccruises.co.za/en-za/Cruise-Destinations/Cruise-To-Nowhere.aspx

Munar, A., & Jacobsen, J. (2014). Motivations for sharing tourism experiences through social media. *Tourism Management*, *43*, 46–54. doi:10.1016/j.tourman.2014.01.012

OED Online (2018). 'debauchery', Oxford University Press. Retrieved from http://www.oed.com/view/Entry/47861?redirectedFrom=debauchery&

Preston-Whyte, R. (2004). The beach as a liminal space. In A. Lew, C. M. Hall & A. Williams (Eds.), (Eds.), *The Blackwell's tourism companion* (pp. 249–259). Oxford. Blackwell.

Pritchard, A., & Morgan, N. (2006). Hotel Babylon? Exploring hotels as liminal sites of transition and transgression. *Tourism Management*, *27*(5), 762–772. doi:10.1016/j.tourman.2005.05.015

Rink, B. (2017). The aeromobile tourist gaze: Understanding tourism 'from above'. *Tourism Geographies*, *19*(5), 878–896. doi:10.1080/14616688.2017.1354391

Rodrigue, J. P., & Notteboom, T. (2013). The geography of cruises: Itineraries, not destinations. *Applied Geography*, *38*, 31–42. doi:10.1016/j.apgeog.2012.11.011

Satta, G., Parola, F., Penco, L., & Persico, L. (2015). Word of mouth and satisfaction in cruise port destinations. *Tourism Geographies*, *17*(1), 54–75. doi:10.1080/14616688.2014.938689

Selänniemi, T. (2003). On holiday in the liminoid playground: Place, time and self in tourism. In T. G. Bauer & B. McKercher (Eds.), *Sex and tourism: Journeys of romance, love, and lust* (pp. 19–31). New York. Haworth Hospitality Press.

Swarbrooke, J., & Horner, S. (2007). *Consumer behaviour in tourism*, 2nd ed. Amsterdam. Elsevier.

Thomas, T., Mura, P., & Romy, A. (2018). Tourism and the "dry law" in Kerala – exploring the nexus between tourism and alcohol. *Journal of Tourism and Cultural Change*, 1–14. doi:10.1080/14766825.2018.1471085

Thurnell-Read, T. (2012). Tourism place and space: British stag tourism in Poland. *Annals of Tourism Research*, *39*(2), 801–819. doi:10.1016/j.annals.2011.09.009

Turner, V. (1974). Liminal to liminoid, in play, flow, and ritual: An essay in comparative symbology. *Rice Institute Pamphlet-Rice University Studies*, *60*(3), 53–92.

van Gennep, A. (1960). *The rites of passage*. Chicago: University of Chicago Press.

Weaver, A. (2005a). Spaces of Containment and Revenue Capture: "Super-Sized" Cruise Ships as Mobile Tourism Enclaves. *Tourism Geographies*, *7*(2), 165–184. doi:10.1080/14616680500072398

Weaver, A. (2005b). The McDonaldization thesis and cruise tourism. *Annals of Tourism Research*, *32*(2), 346–366. doi:10.1016/j.annals.2004.07.005

Weaver, A. (2018). Selling bubbles at sea: Pleasurable enclosure or unwanted confinement?. *Tourism Geographies*, 1–16. doi:10.1080/14616688.2018.1437766

Wilkinson, P. (1999). Caribbean cruise tourism: Delusion? Illusion?. *Tourism Geographies*, *1*(3), 261–282. doi:10.1080/14616689908721321

Wood, R. (2004). Cruise ships: Deterritorialized destinations. In L. Lumdon & S. J. Page (Eds.), *Tourism and transport: Issues and agenda for the new millenium* (pp. 133–145). Amsterdam: Elsevier.

Yarnal, C. M., & Kerstetter, D. (2005). Casting off: An exploration of cruise ship space, group tour behavior, and social interaction. *Journal of Travel Research*, *43*(4), 368–379. doi:10.1177/0047287505274650

Zeng, B., & Gerritsen, R. (2014). What do we know about social media in tourism? A review. *Tourism Management Perspectives*, *10*, 27–36. doi:10.1016/j.tmp.2014.01.001

Liminality in nature-based tourism experiences as mediated through social media

Eugenio Conti ⓘ and Susanna Heldt Cassel ⓘ

ABSTRACT

The intersection between social media, liminality and nature-based tourism experiences hasn't been the focus of previous tourism research. Such intersection, on the other hand, is illustrative of how social media relate to the constitution and performance of tourism spatialities, tourist identities, storytelling and place-making, and can lead to relevant theoretical contributes. We aim to investigate how liminality is expressed in relation to nature-based experiences by tourists on social media, and what role social media plays in mediating liminality during nature-based tourism experiences. The analysis is based on a participatory net-nography of images and text posts, as well as online interviews with users of the popular social media Instagram. Findings show that the expression of tourism experiences in nature is closely related to specific notions of liminal otherness as opposed to the urban life and the everyday, where nature and wilderness are expressed as related to the genuine, the authentic and a true inner self. Creative combinations of pictures, captions and hashtags make it easier for tourists to express the contrast between the natural landscape and the everyday landscape once they returned home. These combinations also relate closely to performances of resistant and alternative selves and communities. At the same time, such performances are mediated and contested between freedom of self-expression, surveillance and social norms, an aspect that makes their liminal nature ambiguous.

摘要

社交媒体、阈限性与自然旅游体验之间的交叉领域, 尚未成为旅游研究的焦点。另一方面, 这个交叉领域说明了社交媒体与旅游空间的构成和展示、游客身份、叙事和地方营造之间的关系, 并可以产生相关的理论贡献。我们的目的是研究游客在社交媒体上如何表达自然体验方面的阈限, 以及社交媒体在自然旅游体验中对阈限的调节作用。这一分析基于对图片和文本帖子的参与式网络民族志研究, 以及对流行社交媒体Instagram (即时照片墙) 用户的在线访谈。研究结果表明, 旅游体验在自然中的表达与特定的、迥异于城市生活和日常体验的阈限差异性概念密切相关, 自

然和荒野被表达为与真实的、真正的和纯粹的内在自我相关。图
片、字幕和标签的创造性组合，让游客回到家后更容易表达自然
景观和日常景观之间的差异。这些组合也与抵抗的、另类的自我
社群的表演密切相关。与此同时，这些表演在自我表达自由、监
督和社会规范之间进行了调节和竞争，这使得它们的阈限性质变
得模糊不清。

Introduction

Several studies have found that tourism in nature provides sensations of amazement, peacefulness and awe. Nature is also perceived as a space in which identities are re-negotiated through spiritual growth, introspection and psychological regeneration (Heintzman, 2009). A growing number of tourists are willing to engage in inspiring and transformational experiences in nature in an attempt to achieve different senses of self and connections to the environment; Newsome, Moore, and Dowling (2012) argued that these aspects are at the very essence of tourism in natural areas.

The constant flux of exchanging information online and formation of online communities in which such information finds hubs, particularly through social media, has contributed to the development of new spatial 'cultures and practices' in tourism (Munar, Gyimóthy, & Cai, 2013, p. 2). This has dramatically affected not only how tourists experience places, but also how they actively construct them through personal stories, meanings and values (Ibid; Jaimangal-Jones, Pritchard, & Morgan, 2010; Pritchard & Morgan, 2006; Gyimóthy, 2013). On the other hand, if new virtual spaces of tourism (and the way such spaces relate with the physical ones) receive increasing attention in the tourism literature, it is also true that they have been investigated mostly to understand how they can be exploited by the tourism industry (Tribe & Mkono, 2017). Although recent trends in nature-based tourism have suggested an increasing demand for the use of technology and mobile-based applications (Elmahdy, Haukeland, & Fredman, 2017), studies by Dickinson et al. (2014), Dickinson, Hibbert, and Filimonau (2016), and Silas, Løvlie, and Ling (2016) have detected a perceived need to 'disconnect' from devices that dominate everyday life; this confirms dilemmas regarding the value of connectivity against a willingness to 'get away'.

However, a general advocacy and a post-positivist paradigm are still dominant, as are specific ontologies of technology (Munar et al., 2013; Lalicic & Weismayer, 2016). Gyimóthy (2013) notes how, despite the multifaceted content conveyed by social media and Web 2.0-based technologies, much of the current research still tends to consider Web 2.0 as a space where human communication, decision-making and usage are driven by generalized and rational processes of information exchange. If it is true that Web 2.0 is enabling users to communicate 'the real experience revealed by real people' (Leung, Law, Van Hoof, & Buhalis, 2013, p. 8), current and future research should adopt a more 'techspressive' view (Munar et al., 2013) and investigate the complex interactions between Web 2.0, tourism, place-making and identity, as expressed by complex user-generated narratives. By adopting critical and interpretive stances, as well as through innovative methodological approaches, the research in this field may be advanced (Ibid; Pink, 2013).

This study departs from such premises in order to explore the intersection among social media, liminality and nature-based tourism experiences. This intersection can be potentially illustrative of how the digital spatiality of social media relates to the themes of tourist identity building, self-realization, storytelling and place-making. Starting from the studies of Van Gennep (1960) over rites of passage, liminal spaces have been conceptualized as spaces in which a transition from a condition to another, and from the known to the unknown, is experienced. Consequently, tourism journeys have been represented as rites of passage that enable tourists to experience liminality, by introducing them into a space 'other' than the tourist's daily lifeworld, which often carries transformational aspects related with disconnecting/detoxifying from the daily struggles and re-connecting with one's spirituality, health and well-being in a genuine environment, as well as performing different identities and building new communities of value (Jaimangal-Jones et al., 2010; Pritchard & Morgan, 2006). Although studies have been produced about the intersection between tourism and liminality, no studies have been produced over a similar intersection between liminality, tourism and social media. Consequently, the paper's purpose is to explore expressions of liminality by tourists on social media, in relation to nature-based experiences, and how social media mediate liminality during nature-based tourism experiences. The analysis is based on a netnography of Instagram posts as well as online interviews with Instagram posters.

Theoretical background

Liminality

Liminality became a popular concept in the literature thanks to the studies of Arnold Van Gennep (1960) and the essays of Victor and Edith Turner (1974). Van Gennep used the term 'rites of passage' to label rituals accompanying a change in the individual or social status of a person, or even seasonal changes of entire societies. Such rites were distinguished in three phases: separation, transition and re-aggregation. The transition phase, which Van Gennep called the 'limen', was a phase characterized by a social ambiguity, in which the individual or the society was separated from a past social condition and yet not integrated into the new one. It was a sort of social and symbolic limbo in which, while transitioning from one condition to the other, most of the cultural and social rules, such as economical or legal ties, were modified or nullified (Van Gennep, 1960). Turner (1974, 1982) noted how this transition could be behavioral, symbolic, temporal and/or geographical, and underlined that it was characterized by a liberation from structural obligations proper of the social order, manifested through subversive and ludic events where people 'played' with the elements of the familiar and 'defamiliarized' them. *'Novelty emerges from unprecedented combinations of familiar elements'* (Turner, 1974, p. 59), and an anti-structure born out of a liminal and free creativity comes to balance and transform the pre-existing structure of top-down norms and statuses (Bigger, 2009).

One of Turner's recognized merits was to draw several parallels between the indigenous societies studied during his fieldwork and post-industrial Western societies: such contextual expansion critically contributed, later, in making the concept of liminality popular across a variety of disciplines (Andrews & Roberts, 2012; Wels, Van der

Waal, Spiegel, & Kamsteeg, 2011; Bigger, 2009; Thomassen, 2009, 2012). In the tourism literature, liminality has been used since Graburn (1978), often to define journeys, experiences, events, places and the tourists themselves. The concept has shown to be quite compatible with the tourism themes of escapism, transition and the carnival-esque: Tourists have been defined as liminal people who occupy an in-between state between spaces, times and social norms and who engage in journeys that bring them to distance from the old and within reach of the new (Burns, 1999; Jaimangal-Jones et al., 2010; White & White, 2004; Urry, 2002). White and White (2004) underlined the desire of long-term travellers in the Australian Outback to escape routine, social pres-sure and responsibilities, as well as the quest for exploring different paths of personal growth. Studying participants of dance music events, Jaimangal-Jones et al. (2010) reached to similar conclusions, also adding the search for spiritual fulfilment, the need to see unfamiliar places, and the enjoyment of transitory encounters.

The spatial contexts of these studies have also been defined as liminal: transitional spaces, neutral limbos, whose strange characteristics provide an environment in which aspects of the tourists' identities can be reflected back in a different light, and in which normal conventions do not apply (Ibid; White & White, 2004). Pritchard and Morgan (2006) explored the hotel as a liminal space, a ludic and unconventional site in which unusual rituals of romance and sexuality take place, old identities can be left aside, and new identities can be played with, constituted and performed. Similarly to the event stage and the Outback, hotels become spaces in which 'resistant bodies' (Shields, 1991) play and perform according to how they imagine themselves at the moment, suspending – even for a limited time – ranks, hierarchies and norms that would normally deny or limit these performances. Other studies associated similar qualities with the beach and seaside resorts (Shields, 1991). Generally, identities per-formed in these touristic liminal spaces can lead to bonding with new *communitas*, new and temporary communities characterized by the absence of rank, status and other normalized social structures that are present in everyday life (Ibid; Turner, 1974, 1982; White & White, 2004). Jaimangal-Jones et al. (2010) noted how even in isolated areas travellers seek a kind of sociability that marks a nostalgic reference to a sense of lost or desired community. Again, being "in-between" social connections of the norm and the creation of new ones remarks the liminal qualities of the spaces, situations and experiences in which the tourist is situated.

Nature-based tourism and liminality

Natural areas such as forests or deserts have been explicitly associated with liminality by Jaimangal-Jones et al. (2010) and White and White (2004), who quoted Bridges (1996) in arguing that since pre-industrial times a person in transition would leave the village and go out into an unfamiliar stretch of forest to remain for some time, deprived of his or her own everyday identity and cultural landscape, a landscape 'other' and pristine in which 'a new sense of self could gestate' (2004, p. 12; see also Newsome et al., 2012).

Attempts have been made to produce broad definitions of nature-based tourism, depending on the kind of activity that is organized or sought in natural areas

(Margaryan, 2017). These definition attempts also differ in terms of whether nature is the object or simply the setting of tourism consumption. This aspect led some authors to be cautious about including some forms of tourism within nature-based tourism, as in some instances they are closer to mass tourism (Newsome et al., 2012; Lindberg & Lindberg, 1991). Yet, authors such as Buckley (2011), Mayer, Müller, Woltering, Arnegger, and Job (2010) and Goodwin (1996) include a vast array of tourism activities and motivations within the nature-based tourism spectrum. Although associations of nature with liminality are not always explicit in the literature about nature-based tourism, implicit similarities are commonly present across a variety of activities, motivations and orientations that tourists might have with regard to experiencing nature. This may be reflected in the dimension of 'being outside of the ordinary' that is present in one of the broadest definition attempts, that of Fredman, Wall-Reinius, and Grundén (2012, p. 3), who depict nature-based tourism as *'human activities occurring when visiting nature areas outside the person's ordinary neighbourhood'*.

Vespestad and Lindberg (2011) extensive review of studies produced over nature-based tourism experiences confirmed that themes such as experiencing the extraordinary as a way of reaching new states of being, the seek for holiness and authenticity through the act of 'going back' to a landscape other and pristine, as well as the search to establish new communities of common values, are frequently emerging in the literature. Heintzman (2003, 2009) reviewed an extensive body of empirical studies on tourism and recreation in the wilderness and how they relate with spiritual growth and well-being. Introspection and spiritual growth were mostly present and associated with different activities across the majority of the studies presented. Spiritual experiences of this kind were mostly associated with being alone in the wilderness, but also with community-based adventurous activities such as canoe rafting. Of particular interest were the findings of Stringer and McAvoy (1992, in Heintzman, 2009), who made a clear connection between spiritual growth and the lack of constraints and responsibilities that one experiences in the wilderness, as well as the opposition of natural areas with the urban areas from which the tourists were coming.

Critical perspectives on liminality, tourism and social media

The concept of liminality has been subjected to criticism recently, particularly when it comes to the division between liminality and social constraint. As spaces get constructed by human beings, even liminal spaces are inevitably subjected to a degree of surveillance and scrutiny (Pritchard & Morgan, 2006). Surveillance and scrutiny are noteworthy to mention especially in relation to the dramatic role that the new digital spaces have on human life. Kozinets (2015, p. 75) noted that, while online, people are both subjects and agents of a degree of surveillance and exhibitionism which is difficult to experience in the real world, a state that the author calls 'multi-panopticon'. This becomes a theme of interest when coupled with the increased ubiquity that mobile-based technologies grant to digital spaces, which introduce users to several creative activities and, at the same time, force them into constant connectivity with their everyday network (Dickinson et al., 2014). Wilhoit (2017) noted how social pressures to keep constant connectivity could jeopardize liminal spatialities normally associated with freedom, creativity and imagination.

Similar aspects should be further investigated in tourism as well. Smartphones allow tourists to engage in the pre- and post-phases during the core of the experience by a variety of means (Dickinson et al., 2014; Fotis, Buhalis, & Rossides, 2011; Wang, Xiang, & Fesenmaier, 2014). For instance, by using social media apps, tourists can keep their connection with peers at home while away (Munar et al., 2013). If social media and mobile applications increasingly blur the borders between the before and the after with the actual experience, one could question how this is reflected on the way tourists experience liminality, given that a 'connection' with the separation and the re-aggregation is potentially never lost. Gretzel (2010) as well as Tribe and Mkono (2017), argued that this can affect the tourism experience by causing disengagement, disembodied experiences and a loss of sense of place, among other things. White and White (2007) and Silas et al. (2016) echoed this negative affection by underlining a conflicting tension between the act of going away, and breaking the routine, and the desire or need to maintain social interaction with the home environment. In agreement with these studies, Voase (2018) argued that smartphones force tourists to meet invasive expectations that can ultimately jeopardize any liminal separation phase that might relate to the tourism experience.

On the other hand, Wang et al. (2014) highlighted how mobile devices can provide tourists with a means to enhance creativity and spontaneity and to facilitate new interactions (see also Lamsfus, Wang, Alzua-Sorzabal, & Xiang, 2015). Although Voase pointed at how geographical locations 'become irrelevant' (2018, p. 386), Hinton and Hjorth (2013) contended that mobile devices generate spaces that are not entirely online, as they can have a geographical baseline (through GPS-assisted applications, for example), placing them somewhere in-between online and offline, spaces that could indeed be argued to be liminal in nature, that are always accessible by users. Madge and O'Connor (2005) and Cappellini and Yen (2016) argued these to be liminal and empowering spaces, in which users can explore and perform contrasting and liberating identities, echoing, therefore, the considerations made by Pritchard and Morgan (2006) and Shields (1991).

Instagram in tourism research

According to Verkasalo, López-Nicolás, Molina-Castillo, and Bouwman (2010), it would currently be an oversimplification to draw clear distinctions between users and non-users of smartphones; instead, it is important to distinguish between users and non-users of specific smartphone-enabled services. One of the factors that users find to be most important in making use of a definite Web 2.0-based platform is the degree of control and customization that can be exercised over it, given a specific aim. This is arguably one of the reasons for the skyrocketing popularity of the social media Instagram, which currently has more daily users than Twitter (Abbott, Donaghey, Hare, & Hopkins, 2013; Hu, Manikonda, & Kambhampati, 2014). While being based on the apparently simple function of sharing pictures online, Instagram enables users to manipulate them through post-processing, visual filters and by including text captions and geotags. According to Abbott et al. (2013), this enables users to express emotions, reflections and contexts that may not be otherwise evident in the pictures. The connectivity opportunities offered by Instagram are wider than those available with Facebook. To begin with, one does not need to be followed back in order to follow another user and interact, which can be done by liking and commenting posts, as well as by instant-messaging through the 'Direct' feature (which is a tool for getting in personal contact with those posting images on Instagram). Moreover, in addition to sharing their content with their followers, users are able to share their posts to users outside their circle, by turning single words typed in a post into hashtags, tagging pages and other users, as well as sharing the post on other social media (Cuomo, Tortora, Festa, Giordano, & Metallo, 2016; Fatanti & Suyadnya, 2015). By connecting online photography with a more personalized expression of being in a specific place in a specific way, Instagram is capable of conveying personalized definitions of space, time, experiences and the way these connect with the user's identity, interpretation and imagination (Lo & McKercher, 2015; Pink, 2006; Pearce & Moscardo, 2015). For these reasons, in particular, Instagram was chosen to address the issue at stake.

Instagram is mentioned in tourism research in relation to issues such as sustainability and digital marketing (e.g. Gössling, 2017; Kaur, 2017; Királová & Pavlíčeka, 2015). Yet few studies that focus on Instagram and/or online photography can be identified. Such studies depart largely from the dominant perspectives on technology described earlier, and explore exploitation potentials for tourism organizations, as well as the correlations between tourists' posts, destination image and consumption patterns (e.g. Stepchenkova & Zhan, 2013; Rossi, Boscaro, & Torsello, 2018; Latorre-Martínez, Iñiguez-Berrozpe, & Plumed-Lasarte, 2014; Shuqair & Cragg, 2017; Tenkanen et al., 2017). To the best of the author's knowledge, no study has so far been published on social media in relation to nature-based tourism besides Tenkanen et al. (2017). Most of the existing studies implement covert and/or quantitative data collection. Examples of notable exceptions are Fatanti and Suyadnya (2015), Baksi (2016) and Lo and McKercher (2015), who adopted photo-elicited interviews to deepen the understanding of posters' relationships with their posts.

Research methodology

Netnography is emerging as one of the most implemented methodologies for studies that relate with 'obtaining cultural understandings of human experience from online social interaction and content, and representing them as a form of research' (Kozinets, 2015, p. 17). Netnography has been praised for its immediacy, parsimony, and for its capacity to undertake unobtrusive data collection, as the researcher may access data without revealing his/her presence (Bartl, Kannan, & Stockinger, 2016). However, removing disclosure from netnography also means eliminating the capacity to fully understand cultural meanings and contexts attached to content, and the possibility to authenticate, dispute or extend the researcher's interpretations (Kozinets, 2015; Mkono & Markwell, 2014). As both these aspects were of primary importance in this study, participation was embraced in several data sources, which included online interviews, online observations and online document analysis, referred by Kozinets (2015) as elicited and archive data. Participation took place mainly through following pages and users, and by contacting users on Instagram Direct in the form of text-based chat interviews (Ibid; Salmons, 2014).

Most of the online observations were aimed to be external, meaning that they were not interfering with online communications of the users (Salmons, 2014). Following Kozinets (2015), disclosure was reinforced by making the researcher's identity clear and transparent at several levels: some information was added on the researcher's profile, and the research rationale was brought up several times during the online interviews. Emerging online interactions, even when not elicited, were coded though observational and reflective field notes (Kozinets, 2015) and were included in the findings when their content and/or the interaction with the researchers was judged to be appropriate given the research questions.

The data collection covered a period of approximately three months. An explorative approach was adopted (Salmons, 2014), which led to the final selection of a purposeful sample of 14 participants, with whom the researchers conducted a number of semi-structured online text-based interviews in English. Users were initially reached by using geotags of known national parks in Sweden. Participants encompassed different nationalities, including Swedish. The language of their posts was mostly English but included Swedish, German and Italian as well. Geotag-based data is considered as valuable when studying tourism spatialities and the way physical and digital spatialities relate with one another (Rossi et al., 2018). Geotags helped in assuring that relevant data was collected, given the research intent, as the researchers faced a lack of proper keywords (e.g. hashtags) which could help in distinguishing posts related with nature-based tourism experiences 'outside' the user's neighbourhood (Fredman et al., 2012). By typing the geotag of a given park on the Instagram search engine, the researchers were presented with all the posts created by Instagram's users with that geotag attached on his/her home feed. From there, a wide range of posts and user profiles could be assessed. The sample had a theoretical purpose, meaning that it was intentionally selected in order to obtain detailed data in relation to a given theoretical framework (Salmons, 2014). Consequently, the focus was on the appropriateness of the data rather than data generalization, and the sample was both emergent and critical, meaning that users were chosen as opportunities arose during the fieldwork, and selected based on how their characteristics could lead to rich data related to the advancing, understanding or explanation of the theoretical framework delineated above (Ibid; Patton, 2002). This meant that the final sample included users not selected according to the initial geotag input, and whose experience was located outside the initial National parks of reference. Further clarification was sometimes needed, during the interviews, regarding whether the post(s) examined were related to a tourism experience or not, as this aspect was a fundamental criterion in terms of inclusion/exclusion as the data collection proceeded.

General criteria established were: being an Instagram user and having post(s) whose visual and/or textual clues could suggest a degree of relevance with any aspect of liminality explained above. Therefore, the researchers' judgment over users' relevance started from the interpretation of visual and textual material that could be gathered from his/her posts (Willig, 2014). Nevertheless, the selection of participants tried to encompass users with different profile activities, (particularly in terms of number of posts, number of followers, number of likes/comments in a given post), as it was forecast that relevant data might have arisen from such differences. This was confirmed as the data collection proceeded. The final sample includes participants with more than 20k followers as well as less than 100, 'private' as well as 'public' profiles (meaning whether or not posts are accessible to users that do not follow the poster). Such aspects were not pre-determined systematic criteria, as it was judged that this would have threatened flexibility, potentially jeopardizing the discovery of information-rich data (Bryman & Bell, 2011). Other criteria which might be drawn from the participants' profile (e.g. frequency of posts in a given timeline) were not considered as excluding criteria for similar reasons. A degree of subjective judgement was inevitably involved in such sampling design, as it normally is in qualitative research (Marshall, 1996).

Findings and discussion

These sections present and discuss the findings from the analysis. The first part contains examples of different ways in which liminality is expressed through Instagram and how posters explain and relate to their posts, as found in on-line interviews. The final part of the section discusses the conceptual and general aspects of the findings and draws conclusions based on the findings of the study.

Opposing nature and the everyday: #survival, dirtiness, poetry and zen

The desire to escape routine and to transit into different or opposite zones, in which normal conventions associated with the daily life do not apply, has been linked to liminality in tourism by most of the reviewed studies (e.g., White & White, 2004; Jaimangal-Jones et al., 2010; Pritchard & Morgan, 2006). This aspect was noted in relation to several posts, in which a remarked opposition emerged between a lived or (imagined) daily space, connected with noise, stress, and commodities, and conversely a space connected with adventure, calm and survival. Instagram emerges as a digital spatiality that makes this opposition more visible, mainly through a relationship established between the picture and compelling text. This opposition was underlined by users. A caption in a post (a landscape photographed during a rainy sunrise) was explained as follows:

> With the caption I want to point out that in order to have great experiences, it is an advantage to get out of the comfort zone. [...] I think that there is no bad weather, just the wrong clothing. I also think it is important to go outside and to reconnect with nature without all the noise, stress and distraction city life includes. That's what I try to show. (Greg, Sept. 3, 2018)

Another tourist, who posted a picture taken during a winter hiking event in Skuleskogen National Park, with the caption *'Of all the paths you take in life, make sure a few of them are dirt'*, explained the rationale behind the post in the online interview as follows:

> It's good to occasionally tread off the beaten path, paved by 'modern-day expectations,' and go back to exploring. [The caption] sounds heavy, but basically just look up from all

the screens and experience life around you, not to just live digitally and secluded. [...] people often say 'live life' but they don't. That's a shame. (San, Sept. 6, 2018)

Similarly, the desire to reach new states of being and seek holiness and authenticity through the act of moving into a landscape 'other' and pristine (Vespestad & Lindberg, 2011; Heintzman, 2003, 2009) could also be noted, where these themes emerged by placing the 'otherness' of nature at the opposite of a stressful daily life. One poster included a poem by Emily Dickinson next to a set of pictures depicting a forest, which, for her before her audience, represent *'calm, silence, solitude. The Other from me, the non-human. Another language'*. Thus, the poem:

> sums up my sensations and what those pictures represent for me. That is, the affinity that one can feel when there is very little humanity around. Everything is in the beginning and in the end of the poem: I live fevered days, among lot of people. To take a day and to take yourself for a day elsewhere, without goals, without objectives to meet, to look, to listen and to feel ... at times it seems everything. (Clara, Aug. 21, 2018)

Similar feelings can sometimes be described just by one word, as exemplified by a poster whose one-word text caption – 'zen' – also expresses a space in which to disconnect, re-charge, meditate, where the poster is portrayed meditating while looking at a waterfall, immersed in the forest:

> I find it important to disconnect and admire the moment, to cherish the beauty around us, because we are kind of caught in a stressing environment, everyone is in a hurry, agitated, running from one place to another and we forget to be happy. [...]I am a spiritual person, I practise yoga, love the nature. [...] (Dina, Aug. 9, 2018)

The aforementioned themes can be related with a specific post that captures an emotion lived at the moment, but the relationship between intricate themes of personal growth, adventure and nature-based tourism experiences, and posts of reference, can be more complex and relate previously experienced spaces with new ones. Instagram leaves users free to reflect that in the way new posts relate to old posts. For example, one post portrayed a fountain in Tyresta National Park and included a critical reflection about technology, water and nature:

> If technology is really about extending our abilities, well, then today this has more technology than my phone or the satellite it uses for locating my position. Never forget the importance of water in one's life. Close your tap earlier than you use to tonight. (text caption from an Instagram post by Alex).

During the interview, the user specified how his experience at Tyresta in relation to such reflection echoed a previous tourist experience he had in the desert, in which water was highly rationed. These feelings were evident in previous posts about that experience: *'the experience in the desert changed me somehow. Therefore, the post'* (Alex, Sept. 2, 2018).

Resistant bodies: liberation, animals and mythological creatures

Performances of 'resistant bodies' take place in liminality when tourists feel free to imagine and play with new identities that challenge restrictions and norms proper of the daily life, even for a limited time (Pritchard & Morgan, 2006; White & White, 2004;

Jaimangal-Jones et al., 2010). These performances can also lead to an alternate social-ization, regardless of the restrictions that would be normally experienced. Through the same combination of captions and pictures mentioned above, Instagram facilitates the expression to those 'resistant bodies' that perform alternative ways of being in nature and being wild, given how they imagine themselves at the moment. Sometimes, the relationship with the theme of freedom from social constrains experienced in the daily life is evident, as explained in relation to some posts in which a poster poses without clothes, facing the wilderness:

> It's a great sense of becoming more free! Men have sexualized my breasts all my life and I have felt used too many times! So I'm taking the right to show them without being used by men back! [...] It can be shown not as a cry for validation, but more of an assertion! Like, here I am! It's MY body, I am free! (Amy, Sept. 3, 2018)

These correlations of themes are made clearer by hashtags such as #wilderness, and the included caption: 'To be fully human is to be wild [...] Wild is the soul where passion and creativity reside, and the quickening of your heart. Wild is what is real, and wild is your home'.

These performances can acquire an inedited and more complex strength thanks to Instagram's formatting options for posts and profiles. For instance, social norms and distinctions between animals and humans can be reversed: dogs can have Instagram profiles and speak about their experience in nature in first person, through text cap-tions and comments. By talking through their dog's voice, dog owners are, as one on-line interviewee expressed, able to:

> ... express the bond between the human and the dog; that is a strong bond between us and getting even stronger through experiencing things together. [...] Taking moments of serenity in nature with them. [...] Our connection is strengthened by this.

> [...] I also make it seem like he does this and that by himself, that he is more independent and can reason more human-like. (Lex, Sept. 4, 2018)

Tourists can move further by portraying themselves as magical beings, and the landscape they experienced can acquire magical features, through post-processing, descriptive texts, hashtags and even geotags. Thus, a mountain landscape can become 'Middle Earth' through typing it as a geotag that, despite not always being a clear expression of 'where am I', is certainly one of 'where I feel I am' or 'where I imagine to be' (Lo & McKercher, 2015). Hashtags such as #trollskog, #oldgods, #huldrefolk help to fixate qualities of a natural landscape as a gateway to another world. The relationship can acquire further expressive strength by bounding several posts or even entire pro-files to the same thematization. This was particularly clear in posts associated with paganism, or with profiles associated with fantasy impersonators. Users can label themselves as elves, fairies and witches to further express a distinct connection with places that they find suitable to be able to perform and play with such identities.

Although it might be interpreted as such by an external observer, these are not alternative identities performed in nature for the sake of Instagram itself, or for visibil-ity, and nor is Instagram the only space in which such identities exist. For instance, one poster described herself as an 'elven warrior', a 'proud ravenclaw' and a 'part-time knight', and uploaded pictures in which she performs as a medieval warrior, an elf or a druid. And yet, throughout the interview, she specified that *'my Instagram is about 'this is who I am', and not 'this is who I am aspiring to be"* (Eve, Sept. 5, 2018). Although she made it clear that she does not need social media for her self-expression, the interviewee sees Instagram as a space through which she can allow people to see parts of her life that she chooses to display (Eve, Sept. 5 2018). Many posts in her profile express closeness to nature as something mystical and spiritual, as exemplified by this caption: *'for when you walk amongst trees you may as well find questions you didn't know existed.'*

Another poster, Uva depicts herself, through post-processing modifications and a caption, as a tailed 'skogsrå' (a mythological creature of the Nordic folklore). She explained:

> My profile is a product of what I love and how I experience nature and see it. [...]It is who I am and what I love and how I love to express myself the best; otherwise I think I would have run out of ideas by now if that was not who I am [...] I feel very close to the tales of huldrefolk and many times I wondered if me myself is under a huldre spell because of my extreme love for roaming the woods. (Uva, Sept. 5, 2018)

Uva depicted several natural areas located between Norway and Sweden according to the themes mentioned above, and connected with the sacral, paganism and mythological creatures through text captions, post-processing and hashtags.

> I am myself very inspired by my old folklore of trolls, giants, fairies, etc. And the magical aspects of nature that goes hand in hand with me being a heathen, so for hashtags I think it is very connected. [...] my captions are what I feel and think and how I experience the woods with a hint of magic. (Uva, Sept. 5, 2018)

In all the above examples, Instagram does not emerge as a realm in which separate identities can exist, but rather as a space in which these identities can be performed, played with, re-imagined and expressed in a peculiar way. In this sense, Instagram provides an additional means to express the poster's creativity (Wang et al., 2014). It could be, as in the case of Lex, that the performance is close to what Madge and O'Connor (2005) defined as 'new selves', because the performance implies identifying oneself with a different being and, as will be shown further below, to new communities that transcend normally experienced bounds and roles. However, it is also true that, as Eve stated, what is performed on Instagram and what is performed in real life can exist more as a hybrid, without clear borders (Ibid), or as a performance that amplifies and/or reflects a liminality experienced in real life (Cappellini & Yen, 2016).

Transitioning

Transition lies at the very core of the concept of liminality (Thomassen, 2012). The act of 'transitioning' can be identified in at least two different dimensions. The first is a transition in the real world between an urban and daily-life landscape and nature, in which a new dimension is embraced and the daily life is left aside, demarcated by a sharp opposition, as shown above. The very nature of many Instagram posts is openly 'in-between' the urban and the natural, in which often the first is criticized, or separated from, and the second one celebrated. Several participants underlined how this opposition existed, even when it was not as immediately clear from the post as others, and was a meaningful part of their experience in the nature that they wanted to communicate. Here, Instagram is a space of free expressivity.

At the same time, another spatiality introduced by Instagram itself (and the mobile device that grants access to Instagram) is present when a visitor 'transits' from their real-life experience of a place into his/her user experience in the digital world. This transition was found to be uneasy, although it is 'technically' made easy by the device, because the digital realm of Instagram comes to be melted with the real-life experience in the nature, an aspect that the users considered with caution. All of the users interviewed chose their posts once they were back at home, or at least far from the nature experience that they were living in their real life, as they did not want their experience of a landscape 'other' and rich of meanings (later expressed through their Instagram posts) to interfere with their digital space. This also makes the expressions and the mediation of experiences and emotions staged, not only in terms of editing of photos but also in the context of post-reflection and post-experience narrations, allowed through Instagram (Abbott et al., 2013).

Generally, users did not mention significant issues or difficulties experienced in coping with transitioning from Instagram to the real world. However, one user accompanied the following caption to one of her posts:

> It's very important for me to find moments and things that bring me some peace. I've found that simple, productive household activities, reading, and being offline actually are quite helpful for me. […]. I feel like I'm moving past that [Instagram], making room for other things in life that are more important to me right now, such as mental peace and rest, schooling, a healthy and happy life and relationships with the people around me. (text caption from an Instagram post by Lae)

Lae, whose profile counts around 8500 followers, further explained the caption during the interview by stressing the sensation of addiction that she experienced when posting on Instagram: *'the more I distance myself from It, the more it tires me'* (Lae, Sept. 4, 2018).

Communitas: pages, comments, followers

Instagram provides users with many tools to connect with pages and other users, and to interact through comments and messages. Pages with a specific theme – like 'forest' ('let's get lost in the trees') 'divine_forest' ('let's get lost in the divine forest'), or 'norsewarriors' (a 'Viking community' from Asgard) – can be followed or tagged in order for a post to be included in their profile page, which in turn can generate comments or new followers. Some of the tourists interviewed appeared as followers of some of the aforementioned pages.

Even hashtags play an important role because they are not only keywords that help make a meaning clear, but also a link, that makes the image searchable through the Instagram engine. Users can even follow specific hashtags, as well as other users and pages, in order to make them visible in their feed. The existence of a specific 'audience' of reference is remarked by the participants, to whom the question of whether or not to use hashtags means being free to define specific audience and interactions, but also being free to connect with a specific selection of likeminded people, pages, or even specialized journals. On the contrary, Dina considered showing what is important for her, and specifically for the post showed above: *'the idea was disconnecting, and by using hashtags I would connect again. [...] I would alter the picture by adding a couple of hashtags'* (Dina, Aug. 9, 2018).

Across these disparate cases, it is important to note that users can choose freely the audience that they refer to, and that such choice is related with a particular way of being in a place that they transmit through the picture, whether this is well-being, silence, dirtiness, survival, mythological creatures or other 'dogs on Instagram'.

The communities generated by these mechanisms are liminal in the sense that they are joined, tagged or connected with one another by dynamics that can be different from the ones experienced in the daily life (White & White, 2004; Bigger, 2009). Even when users do not claim to follow specific groups or pages that relate with the themes of their profile, the idea of sharing and commenting their experience with others is important, just as it is important to interact through comments and to follow people who share similar interests.

Surveillance and commercialization

Many examples have been provided of Instagram's usability to play with one's idealized identity and experience of a place, as well as to perform oppositions with the user's daily life. These echo the characteristics of what Turner labelled the 'anti-structure' proper of liminality (Turner, 1974). Yet, caution should be taken in seeing a sharp binomial dichotomy between structure (out of Instagram) and anti-structure (Instagram). Specifically, the nature of Instagram as an area in which one can observe a 'dissolution of normative social structure' (Ibid, p. 70) is ambivalent. This aspect was elaborated by participants in different ways and particularly highlighted by the researchers' netnographic notes.

Posters are aware of the double nature of social media and the different roles they take on in real life versus on social media. At the same time, they reflect on the sometimes superficial quest for popularity. Popularity is a complex and vast topic that could only be touched here, yet still deserves a mention in the context of how the liminal aspects of creativity, freedom, and the forging of new communities relate with the perceived conformism, commoditization, and loss of authenticity. #instalike, #instafollow #instagood are some of the most popular hashtags that users apply to posts of a vast array of nature, although they have been criticized by many Instagram marketing practitioners for their excessive conformism: hashtags 'empty' of content, placed by users on posts due to a mainstream opinion that doing so makes the post more popular and visible. Nevertheless, such hashtags are used, and it is important to investigate the elements of standardization and conformism to a 'structure' that they trigger in otherwise creative and personal posts. Most of the users (particularly Dina and Clara, less than 400 followers) placed being popular and visible for the sake of it at the opposite of the way they express themselves, even by using hashtags. Lae (around 8500 followers) found it important to state: *'I've grown super, super-tired of the community and all these people being self-obsessed and playing popularity games. It's really all a big lie, I think'* (Lae, Sept. 4, 2018).

Yet, an important aspect elaborated from the researcher's netnographic notes was that when a user posted a picture with the hashtags mentioned above, it could lead to websites of companies that sell items related to camping, tour operators, professional photographers, or influencers, starting to follow the user. Accessing these pages/followers instantly brings promotional messages, which are either visually noticeable in the profile thanks to the profile branding or by the text included in the description.

Businesses that have an Instagram page can connect with users of interest as easily as was the case for the researchers, by following them and interacting with them through tags, comments, and messages. What is important to notice here is that, although a minimal degree of control is available for the user by deciding whether or not to 'follow back', an initial contact – however desirable – is possible. Such initial contact, even in the case of not following back, can lead to deeper interactions through messages, comments (which can range from a simple like to comments under posts such as 'follow my page', or even be more explicitly promotional) over which the user has little control.

Moreover, as is the case for social media such as Facebook, Instagram is run by ads, and the algorithm behind each user's timeline selects specific typologies of ads that might be interesting for the user, and position these ads in between the user's timeline. The researchers themselves could observe this particular aspect when, once related pages (regarding topics such as outdoorism, paganism, and forest therapy) were followed, ads with branding related to these pages (hiking equipment, clothes, craftsmanship, etc.) were repeatedly shown while scrolling the timeline. The resemblance of the posts in the ads to those spontaneously generated by the users was remarkable. Finally, market-based logics interfered in one case in which the very user, as well as posting in relation to her travels and experiences with nature, started using his/her profile for business reasons. As mentioned by Uva, whose profile counts more than 24,000 followers: *'How I express myself is just how I've always expressed myself, but I think I tweak it a bit. [...] I think more about what I write since I want to sell'* (Uva, Sept. 5 2018).

Two key aspects are here revealed. First, a theme of surveillance, both algorithm and popularity-based (Pritchard & Morgan, 2006; Kozinets, 2015). Second, a commercialization of a space whose capacity to foster the users' creativity and freedom to perform an alternative self was explained above. In other words, an intrusion of norms proper of the 'structure' (Turner, 1974), identified in the everyday neo-liberal economy, marketing and consumption, into what ideally should be an 'anti-structure' in which users are free to 'play with' idealized identities and enhanced expressions of otherness, made of #survival, #detox, #mothernature, #norrfolk, etc.

Conclusions

Findings have shown that the way in which liminality is expressed through the use of Instagram in relation to nature-based tourism experiences is about defining and expressing personal and social identity, but also about the transcending of borders between the self and the persona on Instagram in relation to nature. It is also about the staging of experiences through the post-processing of images and the adding of hashtags and geotags, which make the posts stand out and enhance their expression. The expression of tourism experiences in nature is closely related to specific notions of difference and otherness, as opposed to the urban life and the everyday, where nature and wilderness are expressed as related, for example, to the genuine, the authentic and the true inner self. The combinations of pictures, captions and hashtags were able to express more easily the opposition between the natural landscape and the everyday landscape.

Thus, Instagram offers a space in which the tourist can 'play' with symbolic tools in order to reflect on his/her own experience and deliver a message, whether this is a message of opposition among survival, adventure and comfort, or among stress, crowds and other social pressures as opposed to freedom, silence and meditation. Moreover, 'resistant bodies' are able to use Instagram's expressive tools and socialization platforms to perform parts of themselves alternative to the social norm and engage in a kind of sociality (through comments, followers and pages) that reflects such performance. In this way, Instagram enhances tourists' creativity in expressing a way of living the nature that contrast with standardized social pressures.

On the other hand, it is worth mentioning the co-presence of standardized logics proper of popularity-seeking, business and marketing, as well as the sometimes problematic nature of transitioning between Instagram and the real-life experience, which question the liminal qualities of Instagram. It could be noted that the posting on Instagram is closely related to popularity and the commercial and marketing purposes of businesses, which become intertwined with the communities and connect commercial messages with the posters and their emotions in sophisticated ways. This could be seen as a form of liminal space between the personal/emotional and the commercial.

It is true that some of the findings can somewhat blur the distinction between creative expressions of liminality and the intrusion of social and cultural pressures and norms, making the liminal nature of Instagram's performances ambiguous. Going back to 'classical' photography, Bourdieu and Whiteside (1996) had already noted how images taken by a specific individual inevitably carry a dramatic heritage of social norms and pressures about where the camera should aim. Pink (2006) argued that although these norms play certainly a role, it is important to caution against the reduction of individual creativity to collective norms and account for the individual creativity and innovation, specifically when related to individuals' unique biographies and skills. The present study provides important evidence in this sense, as both users' creativity and biographies can be seen in what they convey through their posts, whose purpose, according to their statements, does not relate with social pressures of visibility, but with the perceived need to express parts of their biography, even though the former pressure can sometimes be tangible. Nevertheless, it is still possible to be introduced to non-liminal elements of commoditization, marketing and consumption through targeted ads, posts, and users' activity.

As this is an exploratory study that was conducted with a somewhat limited sample, it is important to acknowledge certain limitations. Further research is needed on the issues raised by the findings and corroborated by several participants. For instance, a more detailed segmentation of the users of reference could be applied in order to identify important differences and similarities across different genders, generations or backgrounds. This study is widely based on data related to the post-phase of the tourism experience (both posts and reflections on the posts), and further research could add value by focusing on the relationship between nature-based tourism, liminality and social media by engaging in field-based methods. Other popular social media platforms, such as Twitter and Facebook, should be investigated with similar intents. The way these platforms relate with one another could also lead to new understanding of how new digital spatialities intersect with tourists' experience of places, identity building and place-making – aspects that have only started to be uncovered here.

ORCID

Eugenio Conti (iD) http://orcid.org/0000-0003-1763-140X
Susanna Heldt Cassel (iD) http://orcid.org/0000-0002-4919-4462

References

Abbott, W., Donaghey, J., Hare, J., & Hopkins, P. (2013). An Instagram is worth a thousand words: An industry panel and audience Q&A. *Library Hi Tech News, 30*(7), 1–6.
Andrews, H., & Roberts, L. (Eds.). (2012). *Liminal landscapes: Travel, experience and spaces in-between*. London: Routledge.
Baksi, A. (2016). Destination bonding: Hybrid cognition using Instagram. *Management Science Letters, 6*(1), 31–46. doi:10.5267/j.msl.2015.12.001
Bartl, M., Kannan, V. K., & Stockinger, H. (2016). A review and analysis of literature on netnography research. *International Journal of Technology Marketing, 11*(2), 165–196. doi:10.1504/IJTMKT.2016.075687
Bigger, S. (2009). Victor Turner, liminality, and cultural performance. *Journal of Beliefs & Values, 30*(2), 209–212. doi:10.1080/13617670903175238
Bridges, W. (1996). *Making Sense of Life's Changes*. London: Nicholas Brealey Publishing.
Bryman, A., & Bell, E. (2011). *Business research methods*. Oxford: Oxford University Press.
Buckley, R. (2011). Tourism and environment. *Annual Review of Environment and Resources, 36*(1), 397–416. doi:10.1146/annurev-environ-041210-132637
Bourdieu, P., & Whiteside, S. (1996). *Photography: A middle-brow art*. Stanford: Stanford University Press.
Burns, P. M. (1999). *An introduction to tourism & anthropology*. London: Routledge.

Cappellini, B., & Yen, D. A. W. (2016). A space of one's own: Spatial and identity liminality in an online community of mothers. *Journal of Marketing Management, 32*(13-14), 1260–1283. doi: 10.1080/0267257X.2016.1156725

Cuomo, M. T., Tortora, D., Festa, G., Giordano, A., & Metallo, G. (2016). Exploring consumer insights in wine marketing: An ethnographic research on# Winelovers. *Psychology & Marketing, 33*(12), 1082–1090. doi:10.1002/mar.20942

Dickinson, J. E., Ghali, K., Cherrett, T., Speed, C., Davies, N., & Norgate, S. (2014). Tourism and the smartphone app: Capabilities, emerging practice and scope in the travel domain. *Current Issues in Tourism, 17*(1), 84–101. doi:10.1080/13683500.2012.718323

Dickinson, J. E., Hibbert, J. F., & Filimonau, V. (2016). Mobile technology and the tourist experience: (Dis)connection at the campsite. *Tourism Management, 57*, 193–201. doi:10.1016/j.tourman.2016.06.005

Elmahdy, Y. M., Haukeland, J. V., & Fredman, P. (2017). Tourism megatrends, a literature review focused on nature-based tourism. MINA fagrapport 32, Norwegian University of Life Sciences.

Fatanti, M. N., & Suyadnya, I. W. (2015). Beyond user gaze: How Instagram creates tourism destination brand?. *Procedia - Social and Behavioral Sciences, 211*, 1089–1095. doi:10.1016/j.sbspro.2015.11.145

Fotis, J., Buhalis, D., & Rossides, N. (2011). Social media impact on holiday travel planning: The case. *International Journal of Online Marketing, 1*(4), 1–19. doi:10.4018/ijom.2011100101

Fredman, P., Wall-Reinius, S., & Grundén, A. (2012). The nature of nature in nature-based tourism. *Scandinavian Journal of Hospitality and Tourism, 12*(4), 289–309. doi:10.1080/15022250.2012.752893

Goodwin, H. (1996). In pursuit of ecotourism. *Biodiversity & Conservation, 5*(3), 277–291.

Gyimóthy, S. (2013). Symbolic convergence and tourism social media. In A. M. Munar, S. Gyimóthy, & L. Cai (Eds.), *Tourism social media: Transformations in identity, community and culture* (pp. 55–71). Bingley, UK: Emerald Group Publishing Limited.

Graburn, N. (1978). Tourism: The sacred journey. In V. L. Smith (Ed.), *Hosts and guests: The anthropology of tourism* (pp. 21–36). Oxford: Blackwell.

Gretzel, U. (2010). Travel in the network: Redirected gazes, ubiquitous connections and new frontiers. In *Post-global network and everyday life* (pp. 41–58). New York: Peter Lang.

Gössling, S. (2017). Tourism, information technologies and sustainability: An exploratory review. *Journal of Sustainable Tourism, 25*(7), 1024–1041. doi:10.1080/09669582.2015.1122017

Heintzman, P. (2003). The wilderness experience and spirituality what recent research tells us. *Journal of Physical Education, Recreation & Dance, 74*(6), 27–32. doi:10.1080/07303084.2003.10609216

Heintzman, P. (2009). Nature-based recreation and spirituality: A complex relationship. *Leisure Sciences, 32*(1), 72–89. doi:10.1080/01490400903430897

Hinton, S., & Hjorth, L. (2013). *Understanding social media*. London: Sage Publications Ltd.

Hu, Y., Manikonda, L., & Kambhampati, S. (2014). What we Instagram: A first analysis of instagram photo content and user types. In *Proceedings of the 8th International Conference on Weblogs and Social Media, ICWSM 2014* (pp. 595–598). Menlo Park, CA: The AAAI Press.

Kaur, G. (2017). The importance of digital marketing in the tourism industry. *International Journal of Research - Granthaalayah, 5*(6).

Királová, A., & Pavlíčeka, A. (2015). Development of social media strategies in tourism destination. *Procedia - Social and Behavioral Sciences, 175*, 358–366. doi:10.1016/j.sbspro.2015.01.1211

Kozinets, R. V. (2015). *Netnography: Redefined*. London: Sage Publications Ltd.

Jaimangal-Jones, D., Pritchard, A., & Morgan, N. (2010). Going the distance: Locating journey, liminality and rites of passage in dance music experiences. *Leisure Studies, 29*(3), 253–268. doi:10.1080/02614361003749793

Lamsfus, C., Wang, D., Alzua-Sorzabal, A., & Xiang, Z. (2015). Going mobile: Defining context for on-the-go travelers. *Journal of Travel Research, 54*(6), 691–701. doi:10.1177/0047287514538839

Lalicic, L., & Weismayer, C. (2016). The passionate use of mobiles phones among tourists. *Information Technology & Tourism, 16*(2), 153–173. doi:10.1007/s40558-015-0042-z

Latorre-Martínez, M. P., Iñíguez-Berrozpe, T., & Plumed-Lasarte, M. (2014). Image-focused social media for a market analysis of tourism consumption. *International Journal of Technology Management, 64*(1), 17–30. doi:10.1504/IJTM.2014.059234

Leung, D., Law, R., Van Hoof, H., & Buhalis, D. (2013). Social media in tourism and hospitality: A literature review. *Journal of Travel & Tourism Marketing, 30*(1–2), 3–22. doi:10.1080/10548408.2013.750919

Lindberg, K., & Lindberg, K. (1991). *Policies for maximizing nature tourism's ecological and economic benefits* (pp. 20–21). Washington, DC: World Resources Institute.

Lo, I. S., & McKercher, B. (2015). Ideal image in process: Online tourist photography and impression management. *Annals of Tourism Research, 52*, 104–116. doi:10.1016/j.annals.2015.02.019

Madge, C., & O'Connor, H. (2005). Mothers in the making? Exploring liminality in cyber/space. *Transactions of the Institute of British Geographers, 30*(1), 83–97. doi:10.1111/j.1475-5661.2005.00153.x

Margaryan, L. (2017). *Commercialization of nature through tourism* (Doctoral Dissertation, Mid Sweden University).

Marshall, M. N. (1996). Sampling for qualitative research. *Family Practice, 13*(6), 522–526. doi:10.1093/fampra/13.6.522

Mayer, M., Müller, M., Woltering, M., Arnegger, J., & Job, H. (2010). The economic impact of tourism in six German national parks. *Landscape and Urban Planning, 97*(2), 73–82. doi:10.1016/j.landurbplan.2010.04.013

Mkono, M., & Markwell, K. (2014). The application of netnography in tourism studies. *Annals of Tourism Research, 48*, 289–291. doi:10.1016/j.annals.2014.07.005

Munar, A. M., Gyimóthy, S., & Cai, L. (Eds.) (2013). *Tourism social media: Transformations in identity, community and culture*. Bingley, UK: Emerald Group Publishing.

Newsome, D., Moore, S. A., & Dowling, R. K. (2012). *Natural area tourism: Ecology, impacts and management* (Vol. 58). Bristol: Channel View Publications.

Patton, M. Q. (2002). *Qualitative research and evaluation methods*. California EU: Sage Publications Inc.

Pearce, J., & Moscardo, G. (2015). Social representations of tourist selfies: New challenges for sustainable tourism. In: *Conference Proceedings of BEST EN Think Tank XV* (pp. 9–73). Skukuza, Mpumalanga, South Africa.

Pink, S. (2006). *The future of visual anthropology: Engaging the senses*. London: Routledge.

Pink, S. (2013). *Doing visual ethnography*. London: Sage Publications Ltd

Pritchard, A., & Morgan, N. (2006). Hotel Babylon? Exploring hotels as liminal sites of transition and transgression. *Tourism Management, 27*(5), 762–772. doi:10.1016/j.tourman.2005.05.015

Rossi, L., Boscaro, E., & Torsello, A. (2018). Venice through the Lens of Instagram: A Visual Narrative of Tourism in Venice. In *Companion of the Web Conference 2018 on the Web Conference 2018* (pp. 1190–1197). International World Wide Web Conferences Steering Committee.

Salmons, J. (2014). *Qualitative online interviews: Strategies, design, and skills*. London: Sage Publications Ltd.

Silas, E., Løvlie, A. S., & Ling, R. (2016). The smartphone's role in the contemporary backpacking experience. *Networking Knowledge: Journal of the MeCCSA Postgraduate Network, 9*(6), 40–55.

Shields, R. (1991). *Places on the Margins*. London: Routledge.

Shuqair, S., & Cragg, P. (2017). The immediate impact of Instagram posts on changing the viewers'perceptions towards travel destinations. In *1st International Conference on Advanced Research (ICAR-2017)*, Manama, Bahrain.

Stepchenkova, S., & Zhan, F. (2013). Visual destination images of Peru: Comparative content analysis of DMO and user-generated photography. *Tourism Management, 36*, 590–601. doi:10.1016/j.tourman.2012.08.006

Tenkanen, H., Di Minin, E., Heikinheimo, V., Hausmann, A., Herbst, M., Kajala, L., & Toivonen, T. (2017). Instagram, Flickr, or Twitter: Assessing the usability of social media data for visitor monitoring in protected areas. *Scientific Reports, 7*(1), 17615. doi:10.1038/s41598-017-18007-4

Thomassen, B. (2009). The uses and meanings of liminality. *International Political Anthropology*, *2*(1), 5–27.

Thomassen, B. (2012). Revisiting liminality: The danger of empty spaces. In H. Andrews, & L. Roberts (Eds.) *Liminal landscapes* (pp. 37–51). London: Routledge.

Tribe, J., & Mkono, M. (2017). Not such smart tourism? The concept of e-lienation. *Annals of Tourism Research*, *66*, 105–115. doi:10.1016/j.annals.2017.07.001

Turner, V. (1974). Liminal to liminoid, in play, flow, and ritual: An essay in comparative symbology. *Rice Institute Pamphlet – Rice University Studies*, *60*(3).

Turner, V. W. (1982). *From ritual to theatre: The human seriousness of play*. New York: Paj Publications.

Urry, J. (2002). *The tourist gaze* (2nd ed.). London: Sage.

Van Gennep, A. (1960)[1908]. *The rites of passage*. Chicago: University of Chicago Press.

Verkasalo, H., López-Nicolás, C., Molina-Castillo, F. J., & Bouwman, H. (2010). Analysis of users and non-users of smartphone applications. *Telematics and Informatics*, *27*(3), 242–255. doi:10.1016/j.tele.2009.11.001

Vespestad, M. K., & Lindberg, F. (2011). Understanding nature-based tourist experiences: An ontological analysis. *Current Issues in Tourism*, *14*(6), 563–580. doi:10.1080/13683500.2010.513730

Voase, R. (2018). Holidays under the hegemony of hyper-connectivity: Getting away, but unable to escape?. *Leisure Studies*, *37*, 384–395 doi:10.1080/02614367.2018.1475503

Wang, D., Xiang, Z., & Fesenmaier, D. R. (2014). Adapting to the mobile world: A model of smartphone use. *Annals of Tourism Research*, *48*, 11–26. doi:10.1016/j.annals.2014.04.008

Wels, H., Van der Waal, K., Spiegel, A., & Kamsteeg, F. (2011). Victor Turner and liminality: An introduction. *Anthropology Southern Africa*, *34*(1-2), 1–4. doi:10.1080/23323256.2011.11500002

White, N. R., & White, P. B. (2004). Travel as transition: Identity and place. *Annals of Tourism Research*, *31*(1), 200–218. doi:10.1016/j.annals.2003.10.005

White, N. R., & White, P. B. (2007). Home and away: Tourists in. *Annals of Tourism Research*, *34*(1), 88–104. doi:10.1016/j.annals.2006.07.001

Wilhoit, E. D. (2017). My drive is my sacred time': commuting as routine liminality. *Culture and Organization*, *23*(4), 263–276.

Willig, C. (2014). Interpretation and analysis. In The SAGE *handbook of qualitative data analysis* (pp. 136–149). London: Sage.

Liminality Wanted. Liminal landscapes and literary spaces: The Way of St. James

Rubén C. Lois González and Lucrezia Lopez

ABSTRACT

The term limen was introduced to anthropological studies following Van Gennep's theories (1960) about liminality. Among them, Victor and Edith Turner (1978) defined pilgrimage as a *liminal experience,* as it implies being between two existential levels that, through rituality, favours reflection. In this sense, the case of The Way of St. James (Spain) is an interesting field or research as it is loaded with contemporary meanings. Its landscapes assume the nature of spiritual and therapeutic ones; here, the physical and built environment, social conditions and human perceptions produce an atmosphere favourable to spiritual healing. On the basis of these emotions, liminality is the essence of this pilgrimage experience, not only during the same, but especially afterwards. As a matter of fact, this spiritual journey involves the search for one's self once back home, thus acting in the process of formation of the individual. Drawing on the need for improving researches on landscape perception approach in tourism studies, we pretend to singularise the pilgrimage landscape from a liminal perspective in order to point out the need for liminality before, during and after the pilgrimage. This is achieved by exploring perceptions and emotions expressed in a corpus of travel literary production. These narrative works are not limited to describe the pilgrimage experiences; rather they make liminality a literary theme to magnify their experiences. As a result, the concept of *liminal literary landscape* is used to refer to pilgrims' desire to revive liminality through the pages of travel narratives, in order to continue enjoying these emotions and feelings. These travel narratives are producing new literary modes based on the geographical exploration of the landscapes of The Way in relation to human feelings.

摘要

根据范热内谱1960年提出的阀限理论, 阀限这个术语引入到人类学研究中。其中, 维克多和艾迪斯.特纳界定朝圣为一种阀限体验, 因为朝圣暗含着处于两种既有水平之间, 并且这种两种水平通过仪式促进了反思。从这个意义上说圣詹姆斯之路是一种有趣的阀限体验的研究领域, 因为它承载着当代意义。圣詹姆斯之路景观具有精神与治疗景观的特点, 在此景观之下自然与人造环境、社会条件与人类感知生成了一种有利于精神治疗的氛围。根据这些情感, 阀限是朝圣体验的本质, 不仅在朝圣之中甚至在朝圣之后。实际上, 这种精神旅程包含了追寻人类自身的归乡之旅, 因而体现于个人成人过程之中。基于改进旅游研究中景观认知途径的需要，为了凸显阈限对朝圣之前、之中以及之后之必需，我们自许从阈限角度凸显了朝圣景观。本研究工作是通过探索旅游游记作品中体现出来的感知与情感得以实现。这些描述性的文学作品不局限于描写了朝圣体验，相反为了放大他们的体验而把阈限塑造成一个文学主题。

RESUMEN

El término limen se introdujo en los estudios antropológicos a raíz de las teorías de Van Gennep (1960). Sucesivamente, Turner and Turner (1978) definieron la peregrinación como una experiencia liminal; que implica estar entre dos niveles existenciales que, a través de la ritualidad, favorecen la reflexión. En este sentido, el caso del Camino de Santiago (España) es un ámbito de estudio interesante, ya que está cargado de significados contemporáneos. Sus paisajes asumen valores espirituales y terapéuticos; en los mismos, el entorno físico y construido, las condiciones sociales y las percepciones humanas producen una atmósfera favorable a la curación espiritual. De este modo, la liminalidad es la esencia de esta experiencia de peregrinación, no solo durante la misma, sino especialmente después. El viaje espiritual implica la búsqueda de uno mismo incluso una vez a casa, actuando así en el proceso de formación del individuo. Partiendo de la necesidad de mejorar las investigaciones sobre el enfoque de la percepción del paisaje en los estudios turísticos, pretendemos singularizar el paisaje de peregrinación desde una perspectiva liminal para señalar el deseo de liminalidad antes, durante y después de la peregrinación. Esto se logra explorando las percepciones y las emociones expresadas en un cuerpo de producción literaria de viajes. Las narrativas que se han analizado no se limitan a describir las peregrinaciones, sino hacen de la liminalidad un tema literario para magnificar sus experiencias. Como resultado, el concepto de *paisaje literario liminal* se usa para referirse al deseo de los peregrinos de revivir la liminalidad a través de las páginas de narraciones de viajes y poder así seguir disfrutando de emociones y sentimientos. En definitiva, estas narrativas de viaje están produciendo nuevos modos literarios basados en la exploración geográfica de los paisajes del Camino en relación con los sentimientos humanos.

Introduction

Landscape and tourism pose a complex relationship that has led to different positions (Daugstad, 2008), according to the tourism-centred (Kolås, 2004; Saarinen, 2004; Terkenli, 2002; Urry, 1995) or landscape-centred propensity of the researcher (Castree, 2005; Stoffelen & Vanneste, 2015). In their work 'Gazing, Performing and Reading: A Landscape Approach to Understanding Meaning in Tourism Theory', Knudsen, Soper, and Metro-Roland (2007) assert that for a greater inclusion of landscape literature in tourism studies it is necessary to commit to the reading of the landscape. This means a deeper engagement with the landscape (in terms of performing and reading it) and an improved role of geography in the study of tourism. The scarcity of empirical research on the relationship between tourism and landscape makes it necessary to encourage this dialogue (Knudsen et al., 2008; Squire, 1994; Terkenli, 2004). Following this gap, the aim of this research is to enhance this desired dialogue through sources common to both recent lines of research: the history of tourism and literary geography (Alexander, 2015; Hones, 2011). In this way, the landscape of The Way of St. James is related to its contemporary travel literature, in order to focus on the liminal character of the pilgrimage landscape. This literary discourse demonstrates how liminality is a discovery, for both pilgrimage and religious tourism; in both cases, the observance of rites and practices 'initiates' a transitional state that accompanies the pilgrim, or the religious tourist, on his or her experience. It often coincides with the conventional experience of long nature walks (Redick, 2018; Shaffer, 1996), although the ritual of walking a historical route, and on a planned journey, introduces new and enriching elements to an already intense experience.

Writing journals is not a new practice, but has its roots in the past (MacCannell, 1976), when the first travellers contributed to the knowledge of the world through their stories, while living a process of self-discovery. At present, this is a relevant aspect and therefore more academics are devoting their research to investigate contemporary travel writers' lived experience (Hulme, 2002; Theroux, 2011). Through travel journals, a sense of self is expressed, so that contents and experiences are part of a process of self-discovery and self-transformation (Elsrud, 2001; Johnson, 2010; McWha, Frost, & Laing, 2018). In addition, they contribute to research in recreation and leisure studies concerned with finding out how place meanings come to be shared collectively within society (Stokowski, 2002). From these considerations, in a recent study, McWha, Frost and Laing (2018) pose the following question: "How do contemporary travel writers conceptualise their sense of self in their writing?" (2018, p. 15). A possible answer to this question is suggested, as the objective is to improve the understanding of the liminal status of the pilgrimage by providing its characterisation along The Way[1]. In so doing, we look deeper into the dynamics of travel writing as part of the process of construction of the 'self' (Cohen, 2010), and in its contents, referred to the power of the landscape perception. The ultimate objective is to propose an interpretation of the pilgrim *vs.* liminal landscape relationship through primary sources (travel narratives). In this regard, the pilgrimage should not simply be seen as an aesthetic contemplation of the landscape by the tourist (Redick, 2018). The pilgrim travels through the landscape and the different places on the route for days, and becomes involved in it. This process facilitates the liminal experience, where the landscape is the result of the visual conjunction of a series of natural elements and the emotions experienced during a slow and relatively long-lasting movement in time (Slavin, 2003). The case study refers to the pilgrimage of The Way, which has been chosen for being the major expression of medieval Christian pilgrimage and has survived until now (Figure 1). Together with the pilgrimages to Rome and Jerusalem, it was one of the major pilgrimages of the Christian religion. These three destinations were geospiritual centres of the Christian dominion (Lois, Castro, & Lopez, 2015). The Way was easily widespread all over Europe thanks to many Christian European passages influencing customs, legends, art and spiritual life (Lopez, Lois González, & Castro Fernández, 2017). As a consequence, legends and Jacobean traditions contributed to make The Way a route with consolidated religious and spiritual meanings. Its historical legacy makes The Way a proper space of memory, consisting of monumental wealth and rituals. Both factors have coexisted throughout these centuries reinforcing pilgrimage as an act rich in symbolic references laid down when travelling along The Way and respecting the necessary rituals (Coleman & Eade, 2004). During the twentieth century, The Way was subject to an intensive promotional campaign, which broadened its significance by turning it into a tourist product, and led to it being declared 'First European Cultural Route' by the Council of Europe, in 1987, and UNESCO 'World Heritage Site', in 1993 (Lois González, 2013; Lois González & Santos Solla, 2015; Lopez, Lois González, & Castro Fernández, 2017). The pilgrimage to St. James responds to the definition of liminality proposed by Turner (1973, 1974, 1979), as it relates to a state of existence within social experiences, with its rituals and performances that reinforce its spatial discourse. Also for Thomassen (2012): "the pilgrimage is an emblematic case of liminality because it so evidently represents both a spatial and temporal (and moral/social) separation from the ordinary" (p. 28).

The title 'Liminality Wanted' emphasises the will to stay on the search and experience liminality not only during The Way, but especially afterwards. Despite being a feature of the pilgrimage, Jacobean literature (born many centuries ago) has not been interested in the 'liminality in words'. This research is structured into four main sections. The literary review section is structured into three subsections; firstly, it sets the relationships between geography and literature; secondly, it introduces former studies concerned with landscape in literature, and thirdly it introduces the Liminal Pilgrimage Landscapes and Literary Spaces. The methodological section explains and sustains the operational process, based on an interpretative analysis of six travel narratives. In the Findings & Discussion section, the characterisation of the liminal literary landscape is supported by tracts of texts, with a more direct point of view. Finally, conclusions point out the main highlight of the research that inaugurates the literary exploration of landscapes of The Way. Limits are also indicated.

Tracing liminal landscapes in literary spaces

Geography & literature: Literary geographies

In the late 70 s, Salter and Lloyd (1977), Pocock (1978, 1979) and Tuan (1978, 1980) presented the first investigations of literary geography to expand the modalities of investigation of the lived space and the place of action of the human being. Literature was a new formula for understanding the lived spatial reality, capable of capturing human attention, creating, interpreting and exciting through its different representations. Since geography has opened its doors to literature, literary works have been considered geographical documentary sources (Noble & Dhussa 1990; Tuan, 1978). After their involvement in regional, historical and urban geography (Darby, 1948; Gilbert, 1960), they have also been useful fields of investigation for subjectivity, providing accounts of personal appreciation and experience of landscape (Brosseau, 1994).

Nowadays, the literary geographic tradition is re-emerging as a result of a growing 'spatialisation' of literary studies produced by the 'cultural turn' (Rossetto, 2014). Geohumanities are rediscovering new potentialities in the interaction between literary studies and geographical studies (Hones, 2008) and one them is literary geography, meant as a specific articulation of the cultural turn in human geography (Philo, 2000).

In other words, literature is the primary source of exploration of specific modes of geographical thought that cultural texts afford (Alexander, 2015). Growing reflection on the relationships between Geography and Literary Studies strive to broad their interdisciplinary connection (Ogborn, 2005 - 2006; Hones, 2008). Defining 'literature' is not easy, as scholars disagree on one single interpretation; while, on the one hand it is seen as an imaginative writing, on the other hand it has a more inclusive definition. In this sense, literary writing is a social process of creativity which is rich in its own norms of spatial organization and social interaction (Lefebvre, 1987; Saunders, 2010); in fact, for Brosseau (1994): "the literary text may constitute a 'geographer' in its own right as it generates norms, particular modes of readability, that produce a particular type of geography" (p. 349). For this reason, literary texts are being considered as part of the social world. Hones (2008) compares the literary text to a 'spatial event' produced "at the intersection of agents and situations scattered across time and space" (p. 1302). The transcription of extra-textual landmarks conveys subjective meanings produced by experiences of places and, in the case of the pilgrimage of St. James, this means sharing values and perceptions related to such an 'alchemical transmutation' produced by liminality: "as I was not able to make that internal change, my Higher Self led me to experience the necessary alchemical transmutation, walking The Way of St. James" (Villada, 2010, p.15).

Exploring travel narratives is a form of investigating the senses of places of outsiders, namely of pilgrims and tourists, who live the place from another perspective (Kaltenborn & Williams, 2002). The travel book is a genre of entertainment that contributes to transform the nature of travel but also to produce opinions of the historical process and representations of places (Laing & Crouch, 2011; McWha, Frost, & Laing, 2018). As Johnson (2010) points out: "these writings appear in a spatial and temporal context, and authors craft words to construct socio-cultural representations – geographical imaginings told from a particular viewpoint, in a particular time, to a particular audience" (p. 507). Final remarks justifying the reason of our choice regard the recent consideration of travel diaries as source of exploration of subjectivity and experiences (Brosseau, 1994), and the historical travelling profile of the pilgrim, whose narratives have facilitated the creation of a new reality (Petsalis-Diomidis, 2003). Already in the past, the pilgrim employed literature to share experiences, sensations and emotions and to keep alive the memory of The Way (Coleman & Elsner, 2003; Maniura, 2003).

Literary landscapes

In 1977, Salter and Lloyd pointed out the need to consider landscape in literature as a "supplemental and special source of landscape insight" (p. 1), underlying the potentialities in the realm of landscape in literature. Later studies illustrated the characteristics of landscapes and regions (Mallory & Simpson-Housley, 1987; Pocock, 1981), compared literary landscapes to metaphors and symbols (Porteous, 1986), or treated them as tourism resources (Pocock, 1987) and tools to study popular culture (Burgess & Golg, 1985). Cosgrove and Daniels (1988) compared landscape to: 'a flickering text displayed on the word-processor's screen, whose meaning can be created, extended, altered, elaborated and, finally, obliterated by the merest touch of a button' (p. 8). At present, the landscape is one of the most important fields of study in Geography, and is viewed from different perspectives (Daniels, De Lyser, Entrikin, & Richardson, 2011).

Landscape literature in geography addresses issues of meaning raised by the classic work of Urry's (1990) *The Tourist Gaze*. If landscape is committed to reading, tourism sees. Reading and interpreting the landscape, and in this case the pilgrimage land-scape, involves problems of mediation and construction of texts (Knudsen, Soper, & Metro-Roland, 2007). The arrival of landscape literature in tourism studies renews the role of meaning in tourism and clarifies the role of geography in tourism studies (Knudsen, Soper, & Metro-Roland, 2007). Recently, Ogborn (2002) pointed out the geo-graphical interest for understanding literary landscapes; indeed, they are endowed with: 'complex of production and reception spaces and practices, which irrevocably shape a text's geographies and meanings' (Saunders, 2010, p. 437). The perceptive re-construction of the landscape in literature is based on the use of the senses and is, therefore, means and a result of human perception and action (Terkenli, 2002). In this way, literary landscapes move through space and time, and thus operate as active media for the circulation of place (della Dora, 2009).

Liminal pilgrimage landscapes and literary spaces

The term 'Liminality' originates from the Latin concept of *limen* (subjective threshold); originally defined by van Gennep (1960) as a psychological limit, it indicated the con-dition of 'tradition between' two realities divided by an imaginary line. Turner (1979) developed this definition introducing the movement or transition from one stage of life to another or better 'a state which is betwixt-and-between the normal, day to day cultural and social states and processes of getting and spending, preserving law and order, and registering structural status' (Turner, 1979, p. 465). Recently, Andrews and Roberts (2012) worked on a collection of research that introduces new theoretical per-spectives and new insight into contemporary methodological approaches of liminality. They strengthen its importance to consider the liminal as: "the initial stage of a pro-cess. It therefore exhibits *temporal* qualities, marking a beginning as well as an end, but also duration in the unfolding of a spatio-temporal process: liminality as a genera-tive act, a psychosocial intentionality of being" (Andrews & Roberts, 2012, p. 1), and even state that landscapes are liminal as they are ontologically shaped.

Moving to the case-study, the expression 'Pilgrimage Landscape' was introduced by Alderman (2002), who considers it as a therapeutic, spiritual and religious landscape. In his opinion, the setting is relevant for the performance of pilgrimage.

In the case of The Way, it is a unique pilgrimage landscape due to: (1) culture and identity; (2) territoriality; (3) history and (4) power (Lois González & Lopez, 2012). The decision to travel on foot is strongly associated with a luminal experience that involves a change in one's life. In fact, the pilgrimage involves a long journey of days or weeks, crossing anything from mountains to valleys and plains. The movement dur-ing the days of walking combines the perception of nature with emotions and feel-ings. The landscape itself changes colours and textures throughout the day, with the change of seasons (Olwig, 2005), in the same way that the pilgrimage changes the narrative of existence, introducing liminality.

The very landscapes of The Way assume the nature of spiritual and therapeutic landscapes in which the physical and built environment, social conditions and human perceptions produce an atmosphere favourable to spiritual healing (Lopez, Lois González, & Castro Fernández, 2017). Assuming that landscape "constitutes a most significant geographical medium in the analysis of relationships that develop between tourist and visited location" (Terkenli, 2002, p. 232), it is understandable how on pilgrimage landscapes are also the interpreter of expectations of the pilgrim. Along this pilgrimage landscape, there is a continuous crossing of the threshold between pilgrimage life and real life, while maintaining a movement or passage which involves temporal and spatial dimensions of liminality, thus characterizing liminal landscapes as in-between spaces (Johnson, 2010; Thomassen, 2012).

As a consequence, one can speak of a 'liminal pilgrimage landscape', to refer to its effects. Therefore, liminality can be considered from a double perspective, that is, as a feature of the pilgrimage landscape, but also as a factor of attraction of the pilgrimage as far as it helps in achieving the feeling of introspection that leads to self-realisation. The liminal pilgrimage landscape is an individual and heterogeneous process because it holds the meanings and values that the pilgrims attribute to their personal and socio-cultural experience (Williams & Stewart, 1998; Wray et al., 2010). In the same way that the liminal space is personal and determined by previous knowledge, the experiential baggage that gives rise to a travel narrative presents a different understanding and description of the pilgrimage space.

Methods

Studies argue that landscape perception depends on the interaction between the human being and the landscape (Amsden, Stedman, & Luloff, 2011), the characteristics of both the landscape and the interpreter (Deng, 2006) and the cultural components (language, religion, values, and standards) (de Mooij & Hofstede, 2011; Hall, 1989). For example, perceived structural characteristics of a landscape (e.g., relatively open, occasional clumps of trees) and specific content and perceptual features (e.g., water, rock shapes, tree shapes) clearly influence landscape perceptions and preferences. Also, the style of the primary sources is different for several reasons, such as the available time, the time at which the text was written (during and after the pilgrimage), and the linguistic and creative abilities of the authors as well as their needs.

Former researchers claimed the need for a landscape perception approach in tourism studies (Jacobsen, 2007; Knudsen, Soper, & Metro-Roland, 2007; Mullins, 2009) and the necessity to provide a solid basis for future research on landscape-tourism interactions (Stoffelen & Vanneste, 2015). Although "textual analysis is a useful strategy for the exploration of geographical themes" (Hones, 2008, p. 1307), being a literary interpretation, there is ample freedom for the reader as there is no single system of landscape analysis that guarantees access to the 'truth', and the interpretations respond to standards and intentions of whoever interprets them (Salter & Lloyd, 1977), that is the researcher (Creswell, 2013). Thus, landscape perception and assessment follow the cognitive paradigm, according to which we look for meanings and symbols associated with landscapes or their properties (Fenton, 1985; Greenbie, 1982; Zube, Sell, & Taylor, 1982). Following previous qualitative research (McWha, Frost, & Laing, 2018), the Interpretive Phenomenological Analysis (IPA) is used to highlight and analyse the contents through a process of interpretation between two actors: the writer and the researcher (McWha, Frost, & Laing, 2018; Smith, 2008). The purpose of the analysis was to highlight an emerging theme common to the experience of pilgrimage and literary production, until it became the true meaning of the narrative (Creswell, 2013). IPA does not separate the description from the interpretation; instead it relies on the knowledge of the hermeneutic tradition, arguing that every description is a form of interpretation.

Sources are chosen according to the interest of the topic; dealing with six works of different authors writing about their pilgrimage along The Way (Fadel Rihan, 2014; Kerkeling, 2016[2]; MacLaine, 2000; Mallench, 2017; Rufin, 2013[3]; VV.AA., 2010). Among the authors, there are more well-known public figures (as is the case of Kerkeling, 2016; MacLaine, 2000), authors who have achieved popularity thanks to their travel narrative (Fadel Rihan, 2014; Rufin, 2013) and anonymous authors (Mallench, 2017; Rufin, 2013; VV.AA., 2010). All of them share the need and desire to write a travel narrative characterised by a deep self-reflective factor. This attempts to underline the subject-centred approach of liminal pilgrimage landscapes, considered as one of the relevant motivations and factors of attraction of The Way (Lopez, Lois González, & Castro Fernández, 2017). In their travel narratives, authors record a sense of appreciation of the landscape as "worth the effort for the landscape alone" (Mallench, 2017, p. 79). They walk or ride the French and the Northern Routes; their pilgrimages take place at different moments throughout the year; also, the year of realization of The Way is different.

The thematic essence is discussed in the following subsections; it attempts to analyse and set the literary liminal landscape of The Way following precepts of visual and aural aspects of landscape in literature. In fact, the slow pace of the pilgrimage is a determining factor for understanding and interacting with the environment, as the pilgrim becomes more attentive to the natural language, thus giving his or her own meaning to the landscape, as confirmed by one of the works analysed: "I was really, through my silence, my slow time and my pilgrimage, receiving what was mine, my learning, my harmonization and my understanding" (Fadel Rihan, 2014, p. 293).

To this purpose the landscape is "a way of seeing, a cultural image, a pictorial way of representing, structuring or symbolising surroundings" (Daniels & Cosgrove, 1988, p. 1), therefore the stories introduced show a strong and subjective component. For the present exercise of geographical interpretation, the texts are read in depth and the passages related to the liminal landscape are selected. The interpretation and discussion are structured in two axes of analysis: 'Liminal Landscape and Natural Elements' and 'Liminal Landscape and Emotional Movements', which communicate between them and converge in the Results section. The literary approach allows the use of textual citations as argumentative tools of the highlighted aspects (Chevalier, 2001; Lévy, 2006), but especially as direct testimonies of the liminal search and perception during the pilgrimage[4]. In so doing, the research contributes to the claim of Andrews and

Roberts (2012) in going beyond von Gennep and Turner's ideas of the liminal in rela-tion to ritual practices and the psychosocial processes, in order to consolidate an aca-demic concern with "the specific landscapes that give rise to practices of liminality, and what characterises these landscapes as liminal" (Andrews & Roberts, 2012, p. 6).

Findings and discussion: shaping the liminal literary landscape

As in the case of the tourist experience based on the production and consumption of symbols (Urry, 1990), the pilgrimage landscape experience can be compared to that of a polysemic landscape, enriched by personal meanings through the symbolisation of material elements and emotions. They lead to the creation of a setting (MacCannell, 1976), which the pilgrim-authors reproduce in their works.

Liminal landscape and natural elements

The liminality of a landscape is based on tangible objects (material and physical) and intangible (intangible and symbolic) (Sampson & Goodrich, 2009). It uses iconograph-ical methods of analysis, constructing, deconstructing, reading or experiencing place (Norton, 1996; Stefanou, 2000). In the descriptions of the liminal pilgrimage landscape, pilgrims manifest their feelings, open their emotional baggage and resort to meta-phors and symbols to empathise with their readers. Also, the passage from pilgrimage landscape to liminal pilgrimage landscape resides in the reinterpretation of physical and symbolic elements that give meaning to the landscape and are powerful in litera-ture (Isachenko, 2009; Sandberg & Marsh, 1988). The liminal landscapes are trans-formed into physical and symbolic products (Cunningham, 2009; Greider, & Garkovich, 1994) whose natural elements evoke romantic and nuanced scenarios (Butler, 1998; Daugstad, 2008; Jansen-Verbeke, 2008; Saarinen, 2004; Sharpley, 2004).

Along The Way, the natural landscape elements that the authors of the analysed travel narratives highlight are the water (in the form of river, rain or Ocean, for the pil-grims who continue to Finisterre) and the mountains, as it is the case of MacLaine (2000): "We walked though fields of silent cows, herd of sheep, pigs and horses. All stood as though in a water-soaked trance, not moving, not acknowledging us, some-how in a paradise of safety, knowing that all natural predators are in their own God-given moisturizing trance during the rain" (p. 48) or "as we headed toward Laredo, we were treated to typically spectacular mountains, with frequent breaks which would reveal the sea" (Mallench, 2017, pp. 91–92). Mallench (2017) pays attention to the Ocean "a good part of that day's walk was along the edge of the sea, which amazed us by the height and force of its waves as well as by its spectacular low tides" (p. 94).

Through the relaxed contemplation of the landscape and the enjoyment of nature, pilgrims and tourists live a powerful inner experience. Nature is a source of inspiration, as it brings the pilgrim back to a simple condition that favours the flow of emotions, stating:"The impression of belonging to the wild nature, of merging with it, of present-ing resistance to it, knowing that, if it were to insist, one would let it oneself be dragged by the waves or lead through the storms, it is a rare enjoyment" (Rufin, 2013, p. 77). The relationship between landscape and pilgrim is thus very strong: "when I

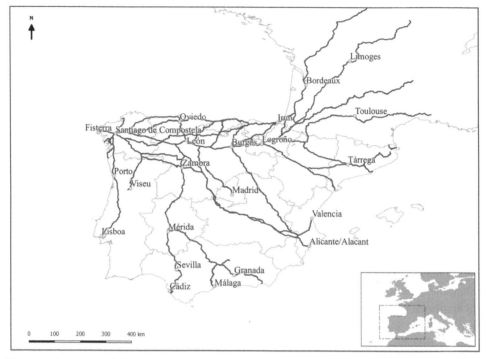

Figure 1. Itineraries of the way. Source: Authors.

rode my bike sometimes I had the feeling that the landscape carried me, framed me, pushed me with infinite benevolence, a strange sensation of forming a body with the earth, the sea, the cliffs along the coast of Cantabria, the seagulls playing with the breeze, the foam of the sea" (Bricard, 2010, p. 50). As Turner states, for this interpretation and exaltation of nature from the landscape it is not necessary to resort to pre-existing rites (such as those from the Catholic tradition), since the experience of the leisurely journey creates the images and sensations. This emotional movement is part of the pilgrimage's liminal experience because: "The Pilgrim knows in those moments of inclemency more emotion than before the colours of a sunny day" (Rufin, 2013, p. 77). Colours characterise the liminal landscape, since the nature of The Way appears alive and happy, as for example: "The green fields gave an air of immensity and greatness and the planting of tomatoes and peppers gave even more life to the place, adding colour where we passed" (Fadel Rihan, 2014, p. 95) and: "The sun was rising shy and beautiful. It was coming up behind the mountain, giving light with its strong rays, it turned out like a red ball and it gave a show that for a moment made you feel that the world was pink" (Fadel Rihan, 2014, p. 170). And also: "That the sky is actually sky-blue, in all the different shades anyone could imagine" (Medalla Cufí, 2010, p. 38).

As already mentioned, the liminality of the landscape is also interpreted by paying attention to the sound descriptions, as they reinforce the sense of nature and nourish an energy that exposes the spirituality of The Way: "the thunder timpani rumbled in rhythm to my turns until the cymbal lighting crash accepted my stop in mid-turn. I looked up and saw the sun shimmering above the storm. I felt warmth in my eyes. And when I gazed up at the reflection of the sun on the rain, I saw that there were two or more arched rainbows above the storms. Then the percussion of clouds cleared, the violin of breeze washed away the drama of the water music, and there was sheer silence" (MacLaine, 2000, pp. 147-148).

> Because despite the fatigue you can overcome anything, thanks to everything beautiful nature has, its landscapes, the smell of humidity, walking in the rain, stretches full of mud, hearing the birds sing, the sound of the wind and the rivers that we find along The Way (Ana Lilia in VV. AA., 2010, p. 133).

This and more examples show how the liminal landscapes are romantic landscapes (thanks to the poetry) and, together with the writer, they transport the reader, see Rufin (2013): "I enjoyed some of my most beautiful nights on the whipped promontories. I had the right to a few nimbus twilights of golden haze and to serene sunrises, purple violet like the lips of a newborn child" (p. 107). Other poetic descriptions are found in the work of Kerkeling (2016), according to which: "the one who goes on foot feels from a distance the telluric presences, the magical effluvia, the spiritual waves that emanate from a hidden source at the bottom of a valley or of a rocky peak that emerges from the cover of a forest" (Kerkeling, 2016, p. 130). These natural properties of liminal landscape are the result of interpretations and reflections that the pilgrim's writers agree upon. They recognise an inevitable relationship with the past, which encourages them to recover old symbolic interpretations of natural elements. In this search they learn to see the environment with different eyes and, above all, they move away from a religious gaze, approaching the spiritual gaze that triggers emotional movements.

Liminal landscape and emotional "movements"

The pilgrimage movement can be physical (moving from one place to another), metaphysical (emotional and internal) and temporal (connecting present with past or as life experience) (Coleman & Eade, 2004; Morinis, 1992; Stoddard & Morinis, 1997). In their travel narratives, pilgrims complete their landscape descriptions with their spatial and temporal interior movements, because in many cases the narrations look back in history or in their past lives: "on my journey westward along The Way, I felt I was travelling backwards in time to a place that began the experiences that made me and the human race what we have become today. Yes, I could say it was a mythological and imaginative experience" (MacLaine, 2000, p. 10). Other times they have the feeling of "running into the future" (Panayotou, 2010, p. 29). And it is through these 'confessions' that a liminal process, by which the 'I' is continually facing new challenges and self-discoveries, is decoded. This results in the emergence of a before and after, so the pilgrimage is a catharsis, which strengthens its charm and its aura of mystery that even today has a power of attraction, following the contemporary need to be reborn and renewed "the journey was for me an initiatory journey that opened the doors to a more complete life, gave me security and strength. I was dying in one kind of life to be reborn in another" (Martínez Silió, 2010, p. 97).

For this cathartic process, the Liminal Pilgrimage Landscape exerts an inspiring function, as it leads to a deeper reflection that resumes relations with its origins thanks to the simplicity of its elements. During the journey, pilgrims can reflect on their inner willingness. At a social level they free themselves from structures because all the individuals share the same intention, the same objective and the same status annulling any hierarchical differences:

> Because The Way is so much more than that: at best, it's hours and hours (and days and weeks) of walking in a series of stages so far you think time has stopped – and you find yourself with yourself again. Kilometres of reflection, helping the pilgrim to put his life in order, to identify remedy sources of unhappiness, to get rid of everything that fails to satisfy, to find the necessary strengths to make the changes so often imagined. On The Way, pilgrims frequently make life-changing decisions. They are assisted in this by companions who recount their own life experiences, offering such advice as they can (Mallench, 2017, p. 74).

This anti-structural experience (Turner & Turner, 1978) subverts the established order and makes pilgrimages inclusive experiences. The ease of these social relations reinforces the sense *of* communitas, within which habits, norms and rules (often not explicit) create: "this new state is not synonymous with loneliness, quite the opposite. The Santiago de Compostela pilgrim reached this stage of his or her evolution and is ready to welcome fellow men with the same ease and naturalness with which he or she communicates with nature" (Kerkeling, 2016, p. 147). Authors like, Fadel Rihan (2014), Kerkeling (2016), MacLaine (2000) and Mallench (2017) compare pilgrimage to a metaphor for life. The *climax* of the liminal movement of the pilgrimage is the feeling of renewal for which the pilgrim warns of a spiritual metamorphosis:

> My pilgrimage can be interpreted as a parable of the path of my life. It was a difficult delivery, which is true in my case. At the beginning of The Way and in my childhood I find it hard to find the pace. Up to the middle of The Way they accompany me, despite the positive experience that this implies, misunderstandings and confusion, and from time to time I lose the pace. But more or less towards the middle of The Way I begin to march bravely towards the goal. I feel as if The Way allows me to take a cautious look at my future. And happy serenity could be a real goal! (Kerkeling, 2016, p. 408).

The following Kerkeling quote (2016) shows the theoretical elements of liminality, emphasising the importance of initiation rites and limen experience to know themselves: "sadly, in our almost despiritualised western world there is a shortage of initiation rites that are indispensable for the human being. The Way offers you a real, almost forgotten possibility to face yourself. All men seek support, and the real support lies in detachment" (Kerkeling, 2016, pp. 408–409). These internal movements are attributed to an energy that can be translated into different forms, including spirituality: "something has changed in me since my spirituality had become a physical part of my life. I can feel 'energy 'now" (MacLaine, 2000, p. 41). The Way is still an interior *quest*, since: "when you start The Way of St. James and you reach the end, you find yourself" (Panayotou, 2010, p. 31) and it is "a path of self-discovery that is required to be respected and listened to before revealing its secrets" (Djeiji, 2010, p. 77).

Result

If at a general level, travelling and travel writing transform a person (Desforges, 2000; Haynie, 2014; McWha, Frost, & Laing, 2018), writing about the pilgrimage is also part of this cathartic process that changes people and views, making the travel diary a proof of self-transformation (McWha, Frost, & Laing, 2018):

> I was wondering what my return would look like. Would I be different than before? I asked myself these things. I cried a little. The emotions were very strong and The Way was silent. That was very good, wonderful. (…) Learning to live with time (…), The Way was teaching me this and I was an applied student (Fadel Rihan, 2014, p. 413).

The experience of liminality that authors share and translate in their work is recognised differently; first of all, it depends on the motivation and expectations that determine the pilgrimage experience. As a consequence, according to the pilgrim's inner willingness and the intensity of the moment, the landscape descriptions that inspire liminality desires resemble poetic literary compositions. It is especially in female writings that the natural wonders favour the inner encounter in the use of metaphors, highlighting how the landscapes of The Way inspire their artistic creativity. Although in most cases there are descriptions and digressions that highlight a solitary dimension in the landscape, in some cases the humanity of The Way itself is part of this landscape, and with it the liminal landscape (as exemplified by the previous passage Mallench, 2017, p.74).

On the one hand, writing travel diaries on their own are literal forms of self-therapy producing an equilibrium between themselves and the world that evokes the liminal pilgrimage experience (Bolton, 1999; Hiltunen, 2010). On the other hand, the same liminality contributes to the above mentioned therapeutic benefits that stay alive every time the pilgrim relives his or her experience; "remember the trail enables you to recall who you are. You are the repository of many experiences along the road of time. (…). In truth, you are seeking to travel forward to the beginning. *Ultreya*, (…) have courage, because all roads lead to the beginning (…) Thus, you must travel your road, out of time, until you make the symmetrical loop of understanding what went before. All lines loop back to the beginning" (MacLaine, 2000, p. 90). In any case, and this consideration is transversal, the liminal landscape of the pilgrimage is only one example of the numerous landscape and nature evocations that are present in the history of literature. The travel narratives are the literary spaces where they review and revive their escape from routine and the beginning and development of an 'adventure that I knew would change my life' (Panayotou, 2010, p. 25), both on a sociological as on a psychological level. The pilgrim leaves the *domi*, that is, the familiar space of the everyday, where everything is well structured, to enter the *foris*, the unknown space. They thus exceed the *limen* (the border between *domis* and *foris*) and experience this *liminality*, that is, an experience between two existential levels that they then transfer to their travel narratives:

> I had an insight: it was incredible how I walked the scenes and the passages of my life, I recognized people and attitudes and how I valued them right or wrong. I saw myself back and forth from all sides! I cried and I really recognised that I was there to take care of myself, to experience myself, to rediscover myself (Fadel Rihan, 2014, p. 105).

Attention to the theme of liminality in contemporary travel Jacobean literature is a form of exploration and consummation of the landscape through signs and the object of works (Terkenli, 2002), which adapt according to the pilgrim experiences. This means that 'landscape is thus no longer simply a 'way of seeing', but a 'way of being'" (della Dora, 2011). This landscape semantisation is another example of the Foucauldian 'power-knowledge' relationship (Foucault, 1980), being a process of appropriation and re-interpretation of meanings according to socio-political dynamics (Cloke & Perkins, 1998; Mitchell, 2001; Perkins & Thorns, 2001). The authors recognise the diversity of experiences: " ... my belief would create my reality, regardless of what has transpired down though the march of time in human history" (MacLaine, 2000, p. 49) and also: "The pilgrimage to Santiago has many peculiarities that sometimes when you are not on it you have no idea. It is a path with a thousand routes and a thousand possibilities and you can choose to make your way as you please in your own style" (Fadel Rihan, 2014, p. 288).

Following its *translatio* to the literature context, the Liminal Pilgrimage Landscape can be compared to an object (della Dora, 2009) to which current knowledge is paying more and more attention because of the state of division. As they continue their pilgrimage, pilgrims mature their possible editorial project, as Fadel Rihan (2014) writes, that 'I was thinking about writing a book about the trip, after all, I was about to set off on a great adventure that could yield a great text' (p. 43). However, it is above all in the words of Kerkeling (2016), that reveal the maturation of these projects, not planned but favoured by the status of pilgrim: time, contact with nature, return to the origins, to the essentials and self-reflection: "it could be vanity, but I have an instinctive feeling of writing a book that yearns to be published. And although I have never had the ambition to write books, here I am taking precise notes of everything as if it were an obligation, and my entries become more and more accurate. (...) Many people travel this Way animated by the books of Shirley MacLaine and Paulo Coelho. And no matter what you think about these two books, it's amazing how many people have started The Way thanks to them, because it works like a kind of stirrup" (Kerkeling, 2016, p. 235).

Conclusions

Recently, literary geography has focused its attention on a "more complex appreciation of the ways in which text and space, fiction and location, might be understood as inseparable and co-productive" (Hones, 2011, p. 686). The above-mentioned narrative works on The Way are not limited to describe the pilgrimage experiences; rather they make liminality a literary theme to magnify their experiences: "The book ... well, the book was written concomitantly to this movie. It is based on real facts, so I believe this will be an adventure book, about the beautiful and sweet adventure called life" (Fadel Rihan, 2014, p. 598). In this way, these travel narratives are producing new literary modes based on the geographical exploration of the landscapes of The Way in relation to human feelings.

The singularization of the liminal pilgrimage landscape makes it possible to compare it not only to a tourist landscape but also to a cultural landscape (O'Hare, 1997), as it attracts pilgrims who enrich it semantically. Following the definition of Knudsen, Soper and Metro-Roland (2007), the liminal pilgrimage landscape is also a text that is constructed over time by the action of a stroller who interprets it according to his or her memory and information (MacCannell's, 1976; Aden et al., 2009) The 'inbetweeness' felt along The Way and manifested in literary spaces is part of this cathartic and therapeutic process enhanced by liminal landscapes. This process continues in the resulting Literary Liminal Pilgrimage Landscapes, which is one of the possible discourses about "Pilgrimage Landscape"; it is one of the possible gazes into the pilgrimage landscape.

The characterisation of the literary liminal pilgrimage landscape of The Way is the result of a multilevel interpretation, first of the author/pilgrim and then of the geographer-researcher. This can be a limitation to the research. In addition, being a creative activity, the re-writing of the liminal pilgrimage landscape follows stylistic parameters, some limitations of form and a subjective perception that, in terms of truthfulness to the information, might raise some doubts. Many of the represented landscapes transmit this sensation, but we should ask ourselves if it is not a chain effect, for which this literature genre is being consolidated for being so powerful and captivating (Driver, 2001; Ogborn, 2002). Looking ahead, these limitations could be overcome by completing the literary exploration with interviews with the authors in order to confirm the perceptions and representations of their works.

At the same time, results contribute to answering former geographical demands (Lorimer, 2008; Porteous, 1984) about the need for more attention to creative activities. In fact, widespread access to cultural industries results in a proliferation of cultural products that interpret new forms of knowledge production, ranging from spatial characterization to significant geographical insights. Thus, the recent research field of literary geography might investigate unexplored potentialities of travel diaries (as therapeutic and cathartic tools) that contribute to the production of a subjective sense of place, but also as tools of power attending different social and cultural modes to shape the landscape. Future studies might address this issue in other pilgrimage landscapes, thus comparing the dynamics of the production of literary liminal spaces. Finally, The Way is taking part in the 'spatial and cultural turn', thus contemporary research into its narrative geographies should take into account creative industries, as they participate in its spatial meaning-making process.

Notes

1. The abbreviation "The Way" will be used henceforth to refer to The Way of Saint James
2. The first edition in the original German language was published in 2006. Its original title is *Ich bin dann mal weg*. For this study, an edition in Spanish language re-edited in 2016 is used.
3. The first edition in the original French language was published in 2013. Its original title is *Immortelle randonnée, Compostelle*. For this study, an edition in Spanish language re-edited in 2013 is used.
4. For a more comfortable and homogeneous reading, the translations of the selected passages are introduced.

Disclosure statement

No potential conflict of interest was reported by the authors.

References

Aa, V. V. (2010). *Peregrinas por el Camino de Santiago.* Madrid: Mujeres Viajeras, Casiopea Ediciones.

Aden, R. C., Wha Han, M., Norander, S., Pfahl, M. E., Pollock, T. P., & Young, S. L. (2009). Re-collection: A proposal for refining the study of collective memory and its places. *Communication Theory, 19*(3), 311–336. doi:10.1111/j.1468-2885.2009.01345.x

Alderman, D. H. (2002). Writing on the graceland wall: On the importance of authorship in pilgrimage landscapes. *Tourism Recreation Research, 27*(2), 27–33. doi:10.1080/02508281.2002.11081217

Alexander, N. (2015). On literary geography. *Literary Geographies, I,* (1), 3–6.

Amsden, B., Stedman, R. C., & Luloff, A. E. (2011). Exploring contexts of place: The role of setting and activity in a high-amenity tourism community. *Tourism Geographies, 13*(4), 531–548. doi:10.1080/14616688.2011.590518

Andrews, H., & Roberts, L. (2012). *Liminal Landscapes. Travel, experience and spaces in-between.* New York, NY: Routledge.

Bolton, G. (1999). *The therapeutic potential of creative writing: Writing myself.* London: Kingsley.

Bricard, M. C. (2010). Pedaleando el Camino. In A. Panayotu, M.M. Medalla Cufí, S. Peña, M.C. Bricard, A.L. Castillo Cuberos, M. Dojeji, E. Feinberg Aviva, T. Majeroni Sánchez, V. Martínez Silió, M. Vázquez, J.M.A.A. Arenas Aparicio, M. Mesenguer, Y. Barrientos, J. Petronela, Jazmín, Petronela, Mapi, Ana Lilia, Petronela & Verónica (Eds.), *Peregrinas por el Camino de Santiago* (pp. 47–56). Madrid: Mujeres Viajeras, Casiopea Ediciones.

Brosseau, M. (1994). Geography's literatura. *Progress in Human Geography, 18*(3), 333–353. doi:10.1177/030913259401800304

Burgess, J., & Golg, J. (Eds.) (1985). *Geography. The media and popular culture.* London: Croom Helm.

Butler, R. (1998). Tartan mythology – the traditional tourist image of Scotland. In G. Ringer (Ed.), *Destinations – cultural landscapes for tourism* (pp. 121–139). London: Routledge.

Castree, N. (2005). *Nature.* London: Routledge.

Chevalier, M. (2001). *Géographie et Littérature.* Paris: Société de Géographie de Paris.

Cloke, P., & Perkins, H. C. (1998). Cracking the canyon with the awesome foursome: Representations of adventure tourism in New Zealand. *Environment and Planning D: Society and Space, 16*(2), 185–218. doi:10.1068/d160185

Cohen, S. (2010). Chasing a myth? Searching for 'self' through. *Tourist Studies, 10*(2), 117–133. doi:10.1177/1468797611403040

Coleman, S., & Eade, J. (Eds.) (2004). *Reframing pilgrimage. Cultures in motion.* London: Routledge.

Coleman, S., & Elsner, J. (Eds.) (2003). *Pilgrim voices. Narrative and authorship in christian pilgrimage.* New York: Berghahan Books.

Cosgrove, D., & Daniels, S. (1988). *The iconography of landscape: Essays on the symbolic represen-tation, design and use of past environments.* Cambridge: Cambridge University Press.

Creswell, J. W. (2013). *Qualitative inquiry and research design: choosing among five approaches* (3rd ed.). Lincoln: Sage.

Cunningham, P. (2009). Exploring the cultural landscape of the Obeikei in Ogasawara. *Journal of Tourism and Cultural Change, 7*(3), 221–234. doi:10.1080/14766820903267371

Daniels, S., & Cosgrove, D. (1988). Introduction: the iconography of landscape. In D. Cosgrove, & S. Daniels (Eds.), *The iconography of landscape* (pp. 43–82). Cambridge: Cambridge University Press.

Daniels, S., De Lyser, D., Entrikin, N., & Richardson, D. (2011). *Introduction. Envisioning landscapes, making worlds. Geography and the humanities* (pp. xxvii–xxxii). New York: Routledge.

Darby, H. C. (1948). The regional geography of Thomas Hardy's Wessex. *Geographical Review, 38*(3), 426–443. doi:10.2307/210904

Daugstad, K. (2008). Negotiating landscape in rural tourism. *Annals of Tourism Research, 35*(2), 402–426. doi:10.1016/j.annals.2007.10.001

De Mooij, M., & Hofstede, G. (2011). Cross-cultural consumer behavior: A review of research find-ings. *Journal of International Consumer Marketing, 23*(3/4), 181–192.

Della Dora, V. (2009). Travelling landscape-objects. *Progress in Human Geography, 33*(3), 334–354. doi:10.1177/0309132508096348

Della Dora, V. (2011). *Inverting perspective: Icons' performative geographies. Envisioning landscapes, making worlds. Geography and the humanities* (pp. 239–246). New York, NY: Routledge.

Deng, J. (2006). Landscape perception: Towards landscape semiology. *World Architecture, 7*, 47–50.

Desforges, L. (2000). Traveling the world: Identity and travel biography. *Annals of Tourism Research, 27*(4), 926–945. doi:10.1016/S0160-7383(99)00125-5

Djeiji, M. (2010). El Camino de la Fuerza. In VV. AA. (Eds.), *Peregrinas por el Camino de Santiago* (pp. 75–79). Madrid: Mujeres Viajeras, Casiopea Ediciones.

Driver, F. (2001). *Geography Militant: Cultures of Exploration and Empire.* Oxford: Blackwell Publishers.

Elsrud, T. (2001). Risk creation in travelling: Backpacker adventure narration. *Annals of Tourism Research, 28*(3), 597–617. doi:10.1016/S0160-7383(00)00061-X

Fadel Rihan, T. (2014). *Uma viagem em um bloco de notas.* Di Rihan Bistrôe: Porto Alegre.

Fenton, D. M. (1985). Dimensions of meaning in the perception of natural settings and their rela-tionship to aesthetic response. *Australian Journal of Psychology, 37*(3), 325–339. doi:10.1080/00049538508256409

Foucault, M. (1980). edited by G, Colin). *Power/knowledge: Selected Interviews and Other Writings 1972–1977.* New York, NY: Pantheon Books.

Gilbert, E. W. (1960). The idea of region. *Geography, 45*, 157–175.

Greenbie, B. B. (1982). The landscape of social symbols. *Landscape Research, 7*(3), 2–6. doi:10.1080/01426398208706035

Greider, T., & Garkovich, L. (1994). Landscapes: The social construction of nature and the envir-onment. *Rural Sociology, 59*(1), 1–24. doi:10.1111/j.1549-0831.1994.tb00519.x

Hall, E. T. (1989). *Beyond Culture.* New York, NY: Random House LLC.

Haynie, A. (2014). Self-transformation through dangerous travel: Mary Morris's nothing to declare and Audrey Schulman's The Cage. In D. Ricci (Ed.), *Travel, discovery, transformation* (pp. 123–134). Piscataway, New Jersey: Transaction.

Hiltunen, S. M. S. (2010). Travel diaries as a therapeutic tool: My interior road to noh, waka, haiku, and renga. *Journal of Poetry Therapy, 23*(3), 157–170.

Hones, S. (2008). Text as it happens: Literary geography. *Geography Compass, 2*(5), 1301–1317. doi:10.1111/j.1749-8198.2008.00143.x

Hones, S. (2011). Literary geography: Setting and narrative space. *Social & Cultural Geography, 12*(7), 685–699. doi:10.1080/14649365.2011.610233

Hulme, P. (2002). Travelling to write (1940–2000). In P. Hulme, & T. Youngs (Eds.), *The Cambridge companion to Travel Writing* (pp. 1–13). Cambridge: Cambridge University Press.

Isachenko, T. (2009). Cultural landscape dynamics of transboundary areas: A case study of the Karelian Isthmus. *Journal of Borderlands Studies, 24*(2), 78–91. doi:10.1080/08865655.2009. 9695729

Jacobsen, J. K. S. (2007). Use of landscape perception methods in tourism studies: A review of photo-based research approaches. *Tourism Geographies, 9*(3), 234–253.

Jansen-Verbeke, M. (2008). Cultural landscapes and tourism dynamics: Explorative case studies. In M. Jansen-Verbeke, G. K. Priestley, & A. P. Russo (Eds.), *Cultural Resources for Tourism: Patterns, Processes and Policies* (pp. 125–145). Hauppauge, NY: Nova Science Publishers.

Johnson, P. (2010). Writing liminal landscapes: The cosmopolitical gaze. *Tourism Geographies, 12*(4), 505–524. doi:10.1080/14616688.2010.516397

Kaltenborn, B. P., & Williams, D. R. (2002). The meaning of place: Attachments to Femundsmarka National Park, Norway, among tourists and locals. *Norsk Geografisk Tidsskrift - Norwegian Journal of Geography, 56*(3), 189–198. doi:10.1080/00291950260293011

Kerkeling, H. (2016). *Bueno me largo*. Barcelona: Debolsillo.

Knudsen, D. C., Metro-Roland, M., Soper, A. K., & Greer, C. A. (Eds.) (2008). *Landscape, Tourism and Meaning*. Hampshire: Ashgate.

Knudsen, D. C., Soper, A. K., & Metro-Roland, M. (2007). Commentary: Gazing, Performing and Reading: A Landscape Approach to Understanding Meaning in Tourism Theory. *Tourism Geographies, 9*(3), 227–233. doi:10.1080/14616680701422681

Kolås, A. (2004). Tourism and the making of place in Shangri-La. *Tourism Geographies, 6*(3), 262–278. doi:10.1080/1461668042000249610

Laing, J., & Crouch, G. (2011). Frontier tourism: Retracing mythic journeys. *Annals of Tourism Research, 38*(4), 1516–1141. doi:10.1016/j.annals.2011.02.003

Lefebvre, K. (1987). *Invention as a social act*. Carbondale, IL: Southern Illinois University Press.

Lévy, B. (2006). Géographie et littérature. Une synthèse historique. *Le Globe. Revue Genevoise de Géographie, 146*(1), 25–52. doi:10.3406/globe.2006.1513

Lois González, R. C., & Lopez, L. (2012). El Camino de Santiago: Una aproximación a su carácter polisémico desde la geografía cultural y del turismo. *Documents D'anàlisi Geogràfica, 58*(3), 459–469.

Lois González, R. C. (2013). The Camino de Santiago and Its Contemporary Renewal: Pilgrims, Tourists and Territorial Identities. *Culture and Religion, 14*(1), 8–22. doi:10.1080/14755610.2012. 756406

Lois González, R. C., & Santos Solla, X. (2015). Tourists and pilgrims on their way to Santiago. Motives, Caminos and final destinations. *Journal of Tourism and Cultural Change, 13*(2), 149–164. doi:10.1080/14766825.2014.918985

Lopez, L., Lois González, R. C., & Castro Fernández, B. M. (2017). Spiritual Tourism on The Way of Saint James. The Current Situation. *Tourism Management Perspectives, 24*, 225–234. doi:10. 1016/j.tmp.2017.07.015

Lorimer, H. (2008). Poetry and place: The shape of words. *Geography, 93*(3), 181–182.

MacCannell, D. (1976). *The tourist: A new theory of the leisure class*. New York, NY: Schocken.

MacLaine, S. (2000). *The Camino. A pilgrimage of courage*. London: The International Best-Seller, Pocket Books.

Mallench, J. (2017). *The Camino de Santiago*. The Path to Understanding. Self-edition.

Mallory, W. E., & Simpson-Housley, P. (Eds.) (1987). *Geography and Literature: A Meeting of the Disciplines*. Syracuse: Syracuse University Press.

Maniura, R. (2003). Pilgrimage into Words and Images: The Miracles of Santa Maria delle Carceri in Renaissance Prato. In S. Coleman, & J. Elsener (Eds.), *Pilgrim Voices. Narrative and Authorship in Christian Pilgrimage* (pp. 40–60). New York, NY: Berghahan Books.

Martínez Silió, M. V. (2010). Camino Mágico. In VV. AA. (Eds.), *Peregrinas por el Camino de Santiago* (pp. 91–98). Madrid: Mujeres Viajeras, Casiopea Ediciones.

McWha, M., Frost, W., & Laing, J. (2018). Travel writers and the nature of self: Essentialism, transformation and (online) construction. *Annals of Tourism Research, 70*, 14–24. doi:10.1016/j. annals.2018.02.007

Medalla Cufí, M. M. (2010). Mi Proprio Camino. In VV. AA. (Eds.), *Peregrinas por el Camino de Santiago* (pp. 33–42). Madrid: Mujeres Viajeras, Casiopea Ediciones.

Mitchell, D. (2001). The lure of the local: Landscape studies at the end of a troubled century. *Progress in Human Geography*, *25*(2), 269–281. doi:10.1191/030913201678580520

Morinis, A. (Ed.) (1992). *Sacred journeys. The anthropology of pilgrimage*. Westport, CT: Greenwood Press.

Mullins, P. M. (2009). Living Stories of the Landscape: Perception of Place through Canoeing in Canada's North. *Tourism Geographies*, *11*(2), 233–255. doi:10.1080/14616680902827191

Noble, A. G., & Dhussa, R. (1990). Image and Substance: A Review of Literary Geography. *Journal of Cultural Geography*, *10*(2), 49–65. doi:10.1080/08873639009478447

Norton, A. (1996). Experiencing nature: The reproduction of environmental discourse through safari tourism in East Africa. *Geoforum*, *27*(3), 355–373. doi:10.1016/S0016-7185(96)00021-8

Ogborn, M. (2002). Writing travels: Power, knowledge and ritual on the English East India Company's early voyages. *Transactions of the Institute of British Geographers*, *27*(2), 155–171. doi:10.1111/1475-5661.00047

Ogborn, M. (2005). Mapping words. *57*, 145–149.

Olwig, K. R. (2005). Liminality, seasonality and landscape. *Landscape Research*, *30*(2), 259–271. doi:10.1080/01426390500044473

Panayotou, A. (2010). Corriendo el Camino. In VV. AA. (Eds.), *Peregrinas por el Camino de Santiago* (pp. 21–32). Madrid: Mujeres Viajeras, Casiopea Ediciones.

Perkins, H. C., & Thorns, D. C. (2001). Gazing or performing?. *International Sociology*, *16*(2), 185–205. doi:10.1177/0268580901016002004

Petsalis-Diomidis, A. (2003). Narratives of Transformations: Pilgrimage Patterns and Authorial Self-presentation in Three Pilgrimage Texts. In S. Coleman, & J. Elsner (Eds.), *Pilgrim Voices. Narrative and Authorship in Christian Pilgrimage* (pp. 84–109). New York: Berghahan Books.

Philo, C. (2000). More words, more worlds: Reflections on the "cultural turn" and human geography. In I. Cook, D. Crouch, S. Naylor, & J. R. Ryan (Eds.), *Cultural Turns/Geographical Turns: Perspectives on Cultural Geography* (pp. 26–53). Harlow: Prentice-Hall.

Pocock, D. (1978). The Novelist and the North. *Occasional Publications, New Series, 12. Department of Geography, University of Durham*

Pocock, D. (1979). The Novelist's Image of the North. *Transactions of the Institute of British Geographers*, *4*(1), 62–76. doi:10.2307/621924

Pocock, D. C. (Ed.) (1981). *Humanistic geography and literature*. London: Croom Helm. doi:10.1086/ahr/86.3.590-a

Pocock, D. C. (1987). Haworth: The experience of literary place. In W. E. Mallory, & P. Simpson-Housley (Eds.), *Geography and literature: A meeting of the disciplines* (pp. 137–144). Syracuse: Syracuse University Press.

Porteous, J. D. (1984). Putting Descartes before Dehors. *Transactions of the Institute of British Geographers*, *9*(3), 372–373. doi:10.2307/622241

Porteous, J. D. (1986). Inscape: Landscapes of the mind in the Canadian and Mexican novels of Malcolm Lowry. *The Canadian Geographer/Le Géographe Canadien*, *30*(2), 123–131. doi:10.1111/j.1541-0064.1986.tb01037.x

Redick, K. (2018). Interpreting contemporary pilgrimage as spiritual journey or aesthetic tourism along the appalachian trail. *International Journal of Religious Tourism and Pilgrimage*, *6*(2), 77–88.

Rossetto, T. (2014). Theorizing maps with literature. *Progress in Human Geography*, *38*(4), 513–530. doi:10.1177/0309132513510587

Rufin, J. (2013). *El Camino Inmortal*. Barcelona: Duomo Editorial.

Saarinen, J. (2004). Tourism and touristic representations of nature. In A. A. Lew, C. M. Hall, & A. M. Williams (Eds.), *A companion to tourism* (pp. 438–449). Oxford: Blackwell Publishing.

Salter, C., & Lloyd, W. (1977). *Landscape in literature*. Resource Paper, 76–73. Washington, DC: AAG, 28.

Sampson, K. A., & Goodrich, C. G. (2009). Making place: Identity construction and community formation through "Sense of Place" in Westland, New Zealand. *Society & Natural Resources*,
22(10), 901–915. doi:10.1080/08941920802178172

Sandberg, L. A., & Marsh, J. S. (1988). Focus: Literary Landscapes - Geography and Literature. *The
Canadian Geographer/Le Géographe Canadien*, *32*(3), 266–276. doi:10.1111/j.1541-0064.1988.
tb00879.x

Saunders, A. (2010). Literary Geography: Reforging the Connections. *Progress in Human
Geography*, *34*(4), 436–452. doi:10.1177/0309132509343612

Shaffer, E. (1996). *Walking with Spring*. Birmingham: Menasha Ridge Press.

Sharpley, R. (2004). Tourism and the countryside. In A. A. Lew, C. M. Hall, & A. M. Williams (Eds.),
A companion to tourism (pp. 374–386). Oxford: Blackwell Publishing.

Slavin, S. (2003). Walking as spiritual practice: The pilgrimage to Santiago de Compostela. *Body
& Society*, *9*(3), 1–18. doi:10.1177/1357034X030093001

Smith, J. (2008). *Qualitative psychology: A practical guide to research methods* (2nd ed.). London:
Sage.

Squire, S. J. (1994). Accounting for cultural meanings: The interface between geography and
tourism studies re-examined. *Progress in Human Geography*, *18*(1), 1–16. doi:10.1177/
030913259401800101

Stoddard, R. H., & Morinis, A. (Eds.) (1997). *Sacred Places, Sacred Spaces. The Geography of
Pilgrimage*. Baton Rouge (LA): Geoscience Publications.

Stefanou, J. (2000). The contribution of the analysis of the image of a place to the formulation
of tourism policy. In H. Briassoulis, & van der Straaten, J. (Eds.), *Tourism and the Environment:
Regional, Economic, Cultural and Policy Issues* (pp. 229–238). Dordrecht: Kluwer Academic
Publishers.

Stoffelen, A., & Vanneste, D. (2015). An integrative geotourism approach: Bridging conflicts in
tourism landscape research. *Tourism Geographies*, *17*(4), 544–560. doi:10.1080/14616688.2015.
1053973

Stokowski, P. A. (2002). Languages of place and discourses of power: Constructing new senses
of place. *Journal of Leisure Research*, *34*(4), 368–382. doi:10.1080/00222216.2002.11949977

Terkenli, T.S. (2004). Tourism and landscape. In   A.A. Lew, C.M. Hall, & A.M. Williams (Eds.),
Companion to Tourism (pp. 339-348). Oxford: Blackwell.

Terkenli, T. S. (2002). Landscapes of tourism: Towards a global cultural economy of space?.
Tourism Geographies, *4*(3), 227–254. doi:10.1080/14616680210147409

Theroux, P. (2011). *The Tao of Travel: Enlightenments from Lives on the Road*. London: Hamish.

Thomassen, B. (2012). Revisiting liminality: The danger of empty spaces. In H. Andrews, & L.
Roberts (Eds.), *Liminal landscapes. travel, experience and spaces in-between* (p. 21–35). New
York: Routledge.

Tuan, Y. F. (1978). Literature and geography: Implications for geographical research. In D. Ley, &
M. S. Samuels (Eds.), *Humanistic geography – prospects and problems* (pp. 194–206). Chicago:
Maaroufa Press.

Tuan, Y. F. (1980). *Landscapes of Fear*. Oxford: Basil Blackwell Publisher.

Turner, V. (1973). The center out there: The pilgrims goal. *History of Religions*, *12*(3), 191–230.
doi:10.1086/462677

Turner, V. (1974). Liminal to liminoid, in play, flow, and ritual: An essay in comparative symbology. *Rice Institute Pamphlet-Rice University Studies*, *60*(3), 53–92.

Turner, V. (1979). *Process, Performance and Pilgrimage: A Study in Comparative Symbology*. New
Delhi: Concept Publishing Company.

Turner, V., & Turner, E. (1978). *Image and pilgrimage in christian culture*. New York, NY: Colombia
University Press.

Urry, J. (1990). *The Tourist Gaze*. London: Sage.

Urry, J. (1995). *Consuming places*. London: Routledge.

Van Gennep, A. (1960). *The rites of passage*. Chicago: University of Chicago Press.

Villada, R. (2010). Prólogo. In VV. AA. (Eds.), *Peregrinas por el Camino de Santiago* (pp. 15–17).
Madrid: Mujeres Viajeras, Casiopea Ediciones: Madrid.

Williams, D. R., & Stewart, S. I. (1998). Sense of place: An elusive concept that is finding a home in ecosystem management. *Journal of Forestry*, *96*(5), 18–23.

Wray, K., Espiner, S., & Perkins, H. C. (2010). Cultural clash: Interpreting established use and new tourism activities in protected natural areas. *Scandinavian Journal of Hospitality and Tourism*, *10*(3), 272–290. doi:10.1080/15022250.2010.496570

Zube, E. H., Sell, J. L., & Taylor, J. G. (1982). Landscape perception: Research, application, and theory. *Landscape Planning*, *9*(1), 1–34. doi:10.1016/0304-3924(82)90009-0

Index

Note: Figures are indicated by *italics* and tables by **bold** type.

Abbott, W. 201
Abelsen, B. 113
Ackroyd, T. 86
adventure tourism 5, 7, 155–6, 165–8; activities 162; anthropologists 153; concept map 160–1, *161*; embodying the pregnancy 165–8; freedom, risk and the pregnant woman 163–5; interviewees 162; liminality and pregnancy 153, 154–6; liminal stage 168; Mexican context 153–4; Mexican women's participation 159; and Nepal's mountaineering 137, 138, 148; non-normative pregnancy 169; participants' demographics 159, **160**; physical challenge 169; record-setting achievements 142; rhizomatic body 156–8; semi-structured interviews 159; theoretical framework 161; tourist enterprises 169; traditions, cultural practices and symbolic constructions 168–9; women participants 161–2
A Festa do Boi (Spain): behavioural intentions 19; communitas dimension 18; Cronbach's Alpha 21; data collection and sample 17; festival consumption 23; festival experience 22–3; hedonism dimension 18–19; hedonism, satisfaction and behavioural intentions 15–16; host community 23; hypotheses 22; individual agency, festive social processes 25; liminal experience 12, 23; liminality 12; reliability and validity, measurement model **21**; research 16–17, 23, 24; rituals of passage, community and liminality 13–15; social restrictions 24; sociodemographic profile 19; Structural Equation Modelling 20; theoretical model 17–18; tourism experience 24
Aghoris 6, 63, *64*, 70, 71
alcotourism 176, 179–81, 183, 191; and party tourism 179–80
Alderman, D. H. 84, 220
Anderson, J. C. 20
Andrews, G. 157

Andrews, H. 2, 222–3
Antczak, O. 86
anti-fascist fighters 36
anxiety 62
apartheid 6, 121, 122, 124, 126, 129, 131
Appellplatz 37, 41
Arbeit macht frei (Work sets you free) 39
Argentina 65
Arnegger, J. 199
Aronsson, L. 48
Aslan, Reza 63
Auschwitz 48, 57
Australia 65
average variance extracted (AVE) 21, **21**

Babin, B. J. 18
Bagozzi, R. P. 18
Baker, D. A. 16
Baksi, A. 201
Bandura, A. 59, 62, 65, 66, 70, 72
Banerjee, S. 88
Bartlett's Test of Sphericity 110, 112
Beckstead, Z. 33
behavioural intentions (BI): hedonism and satisfaction 15–16; measurement 18–19, 194; reliability and validity, measurement model **21**; satisfaction 18, 22, **22**, 24
Belgium 44
Bell, D. 179
Bell, M. M. 91
Bengtsson, M. 161
Berger, R. 144
Bilu, Y. 113
Biran, A. 61
black spot tourism 81
Bonaire 6, 81, 89, 92–6; geopolitical relationship, Netherlands 88, 89; 'white slave' site 84–7
Bonhoeffer, Dietrich 41
Boorstin, D. J. 101
'booze cruises' 179
Bott, E. 142

Bourdieu, P. 14, 210
Bouwman, H. 200
Bridges, W. 198
Bristow, R. S. 6
Brosseau, M. 219
Buchenwald 33
Buckley, R. 199
The Burdened 36
Burning Ghats 63
Butcher, J. 175

Çakmak, E. 114
Canada 65
Cape Town 6, 124, 126
Cappellini, B. 200
Caquetío Indians 84–5
Caribbean 6, 81, 83–6, 178
Carnicelli-Filho, S. 143, 147
Catalani, A. 86
Caton, K. 56
"celestial phenomena" 105
Chambers, E. 13
Chancellor, C. H. 84
Chang, L. 109
Chen, C. M. 108
Cheung, L. 146
Chisholm, D. 157
Chua, A. Y. K. 88
Clair, J. A. 154
Clawson, M. 3, 7, 105
Climbing Sherpas 138, 142, 143, 145–7
Coelho, Paulo 228
Cole, T. 50
collective agency 147
Colombia 65
Comley, C. 157
communitas (COM) 3–5, 8, 124,
    131, 177, 178, 182, 187, 198; and
    authenticity 13; Cronbach Alpha 111–12; dark
    tourism 102, 107; death 102–3; DementedFX
    107, 109; dimension 18; family 110–11, 113;
    fear 105–7; fright tourism 105–7, 113, 114;
    gender 113; Human-Caused Disasters 109;
    Kaiser-Meyer-Olkin Measure of Sampling
    Adequacy 110; Kaiser Normalization 109;
    liminal experience 108; liminality 9, 13–15;
    literature review 103–4; pages, comments
    and followers 207–8; Principal Component
    Analysis 108, 111, **111**; recollection phase
    of experience 114; reliability and validity,
    measurement model **21**; sense of 25,
    71–2; social link 13; spokesperson 112–13;
    structural model results **22**; tourism 14, 102;
    travelers 101; travel phases 104–5
composite reliability (CR) 21, **21**
concept map 160–1, *161*
Cordes, K. A. 140
Corkern, W. 86
Cosgrove, D. 219

Creative Analytical Practice (CAP) 6–7
Crompton, J. L. 16
Cronbach Alpha 21, **21**, 109, 111–12
Crouch, D. 48, 187
Cruise Critic community 177, 182, 185
cruise tourism 7, 175–7, 179, 183
Cruz, L. 157
Czechoslovakia 35–6, 39

Daniels, S. 219
Darden, W. R. 18
dark attractions 6, 58, 102, 106
dark tourism 4, 5, 33, 72–3, 81–2, 96, 102–4,
    108, 114; advantageous comparison 70;
    Aghoris 63, *64*; Bandura's psychological
    theory 73; communitas 102, 107;
    definition 6, 105–6; dehumanization
    68–70; detrimental effects 65; diffusion
    of responsibility 71–2; displacement
    of responsibility 71; disregarding/
    misrepresenting consequences 70;
    euphemistic labelling 65–7; immorality 56;
    international tourist 63, 64; literature
    review 58–9; moral disengagement and
    moral agency 59–62, 73; morality 56;
    moral justification 67–8; reprehensible
    conduct 65; research 56, 106, 107;
    rhetoric of 74; sampling technique 64–5; in
    Scotland 106; social-cognitive theory 73;
    socio-cognitive approach 57; socio-cultural
    factors 74; tourists 56–7; tourist transgressive
    behavior 72; Varanasi 62–3, *63*, 64, 65;
    victims 65; "Yolocaust" 57
Das Cabinet des Dr. Caligari, 1919 102
death 33, 36, 40, 45–6, 49, 56–8, 61–7, 70–4, 81,
    83, 91, 102–6, 108, 114, 138–9, 146, 148, 155;
    communitas 102–3; and fear 142–5
debauchery tourism 7–8, 176, 190–2
deep self-reflective factor 222
dehumanization 68–70
deindividuation 72
Deleuzian 'rhizomatic' model 157
DementedFX 107, 109
detrimental effects 65
deviant leisure 56
Dholakia, U. 18
Díaz-Carrion, I. 7, 156
Dickinson, J. E. 196
difficult heritage 4, 6; Bonaire's slave
    huts 84–6, 95–6; dark tourism
    experiences 96; data and methods 86–8;
    English language reviews 89, 94; interpretive
    communities 94–5; and liminality 81–3; and
    the Netherlands 89; reviewers (*see* reviewers);
    reviewers' descriptions, experience 91–2;
    reviewers' descriptions, slave huts 90–1;
    reviewers' reflection on the experience
    92–3; scholars 96; slavery heritage
    tourism research 84; in tourism 93; tourist

experience 94; tourist spaces 81; TripAdvisor reviews 81, 95; UNESCO World Heritage Sites 93–4
Diken, B. 179
Dionysiac experiences 145
Displaced Persons (DP) camp 39–40
Doran, A. 156, 157
Dowling, R. K. 196
Downey, D. 2, 8, 33
Dunkley, R. A. 82, 95
Dwyer, O. 84

Eco, U. 106
Edensor, T. 178
Elsrud, T. 141–3
emotional movements 222, 225–6
Endlich Ruhe 34
Eschebach, I. 47
euphemistic labelling 65–7

Fadel Rihan, T. 226, 228
Fanon, F. 130
Fatanti, M. N. 201
fear 2, 4, 6, 103, 104, 110, 112–14, 139; characteristics of communitas 108; Cronbach's Alpha 109; and death 142–5; descriptive statistics 109; family, PCA **111**; friends, PCA **111**; and fright tourism 105–7, **110**; Human-Caused Disasters 109
festive ritual 14, 18, 20, 23–5; *A Festa do Boi* 16–17; reliability and validity, measurement model **21**
Filimonau, V. 196
Flossenbürg Concentration Camp 5, 39–43, *42*; redevelopment phases of *42*; site development *42*; visitor sign *43*
Flossenbürg Labour Camp 39
forgotten concentration camp 39
Forsdick, C. 82, 94
Foster, C. 86
Foucauldian 'power-knowledge' relationship 227–8
France 65
Fredman, P. 199
fright tourism 4, 6, 103, 105–8, 112–14; and fear 105–7; fear measurement **110**
Frohlick, S. 137
Frost, W. 217
Fry, R. W. 15
Fuhrerhaus 38
funerary workers 68
Furstenberg 35

Gambino, R. 66
Gazing, Performing and Reading: A Landscape Approach to Understanding Meaning in Tourism Theory 216
gender 73, 113, 126, 155–9, 165, 169, 188, 211
Gerbing, D. W. 20

German Democratic Republic (GDR) 35
German memorial sites: visitor experiences 33
Germany 5, 34–6, 41, 44, 49, 65, 91, 93
Gerritsen, R. 181, 191
Getz, D. 13
"ghoulish titillation" 106
Giddens, A. 144
Giordano, A. 50
Giovanardi et al. (2014) 15
Goodwin, H. 199
Graburn, N. 198
Graburn, N. H. H. 83, 153
Grappi, S. 18, 23
Great Cremation Ground 62
Greenberg, D. 154
Gretzel, U. 200
Griffin, M. 18
Group of Women 36
Grundén, A. 199
Guadeloupe's 'La route de l'esclave' 95–6
Gyimóthy, S. 196

Hall, G. S. 105
Hashtags 202, 205
Haslam, N. 69
Hebl, M. R. 155
hedonism (HED) 5, 23, 24, 140, 178, 179; academic disciplines 12; anti-structure and experimental behaviour 12; and behavioural intentions 15–16; dimension 18–19; liminality 12; reliability and validity, measurement model **21**; satisfaction and behavioural intentions 15–16; structural model results **22**; tourist experience 12
Heimtun, B. 113
Heintzman, P. 199
Heritage Walks 65
Hibbert, J. F. 196
Himalayan expeditions 137–8
hinduphobic 63
Hinton, S. 200
History and Memory of the Women's Concentration Camp 36–7
Hjorth, L. 200
Hochschild, A. R. 147
Hodalska, M. 57
Holocaust 41
Holst, T. 130
Holyoke 107
Horton, P. 157
Horvath, A. 124
Hottola, P. 179, 191
House on Haunted Hill, 1959 102
Hsieh, H. F. 161
human agency 59, 67, 74
Human-Caused Disasters 109

Ibrahim, H. 140
immorality 56

India 62, 63, 69–71, 139
individual changes 12, 18, 20, **21**, 23–5
information and communication technologies (ICTs) 159
Inglis, F. 179
Instagram 8, 197, 202–10; in tourism research 200–1
interpretive communities 94–5
Interpretive Phenomenological Analysis (IPA) 222
Isaac, R. K. 114
Italy 65

Jackson, M. A. 155
Jaimangal-Jones, D. 23, 198
Jencson, L. 145
Jesus im Kerker (Jesus in prison) 40
Job, H. 199
Johnson, C. E. 74
Johnson, P. 219

Kaiser-Meyer-Olkin Measure of Sampling Adequacy 110
Kaiser Normalization 109
Kay, J. 156–7
Keats, P. A. 46
Kelman, H. G. 69, 71
Kerkeling, H. 225, 226, 228
Kerstetter, D. 175, 176, 190
Kidron, C. A. 81, 91
Kim, J.-H. 15, 18
Kinane, I. 2, 33
kitchification 67
Kladou, S. 88
Kluger, R. 46
Knetsch, J. L. 3, 7, 105
Knigge, Volkhard 33, 43
Knijnik, J. 157, 165, 168
Knudsen, D. C. 216, 228
Kohler, R. 35
Kozinets, R. V. 181, 199, 201, 202
Kublböck, S. 43

Laberge, S. 156, 157
Ladge, J. J. 154
Laing, J. 217
Lammert, Will 36
Lança, M. 18
Laustsen, C. 179
Lehrer, E. 82
Lett, J. 18, 104
Light, D. 43, 47, 58, 106
limen 197
liminal experience (LIM) 3–5, 7, 8, 12–14, 18, 20, **21**, **22**, 23–5, 71, 81, 90, 91, 93, 94, 105–8, 114, 168, 179, 180, 186, 190, 192, 217, 224
liminality 12, 81–3
liminal landscapes 2, 5, 8, 33, 35, 137, 138, 140, 141, 147; deep self-reflective factor 222; and emotional movements

222, 225–6; Foucauldian 'power-knowledge' relationship 227–8; human being 221; literary geography 218–19, 229; literary landscapes 219–20; literary spaces 220–1; and natural elements 222, 223–5; pilgrimage landscape 220–1, 228, 229; pilgrims 228; thematic essence 222; tourism studies 221
liminal period 138
liminal places 136–7
liminal spaces 2, 4, 18, 24, 34, 56, 62, 72–4, 83, 123, 136–8, 141, 142, 147, *158*, 169, 197–9
liminoid 2, 4, 5, 8, 103, 107, 108, 114, 153, 157, *158*, 176–8, 180, 190
Lindberg, F. 199
Ling, R. 196
literary geography 218–19, 229
literary landscapes 219–20
literary spaces 220–1
Lloyd, W. 218, 219
Lofgren, O. 137
Lo, I. S. 201
Lois González, R. C. 8
Lopez, L. 8
Lopez-Nicoläs, C. 200
Louisiana's River Road region 95
Lovelock, B. 61
Løvlie, A. S. 196
Luque, T. 22
Lutheran Church 41

Macabre, 1958 102
MacLaine, S. 223, 226, 228
Madame Tussauds Wax Museum 106
Madge, C. 200, 206
Mahasmasana 66
Mahon-Daly, P. 157
Mair, Heather 7
Mälksoo, M. 146
malleability 2
Mallench, J. 223, 226
Malpass, J. 34
Manglam Travels and Groovy Tours 65
Manikarnika ghat, Varanasi *63*
Markula, P. 157
Martinique's 'La savane des esclaves' 95–6
masculinisation 156
Mason, M. C. 16
Massachusetts 106, 107
Mata, F. 164
Mavragani, E. 88
Mayer, M. 199
McCabe, S. 86
McColl-Kennedy, J. R. 146
McCormick, B. 15
McKercher, B. 82, 201
McWha, M. 217
Mecklenburger Seenplatte 34
9/11 Memorial 57

memorial sites 33–5, 43–50; Flossenburg 41, *42*;
  Ravensbruck 36–9
memory landscape 40
memoryscape 50
Merlin Entertainments Group 106
Metro-Roland, M. 216, 228
Mexico 7; adventure tourism, liminality and
  pregnancy 155–6; construction of concept
  map 160–1, *161*; cultural practices 168;
  embodying the pregnancy 165–8; freedom,
  risk and the pregnant woman 163–5; liminality
  and pregnancy 153, 154–5; non-normative
  liminality 169; participants' demographics **160**;
  physical activity 168; qualitative content
  analysis 159–60; rhizomatic body 156–8; semi-
  structured interviews 159; women 162–3
Microcosm of the Universe 62
Miller, Maggie C. 7
Milton, C. E. 82
Mkono, M. 200
Molina-Castillo, F. J. 200
Montanari, F. 18, 23
Moore, A. 3
Moore, R. 179
Moore, S. A. 196
moral agency 59–62, 69, 72
moral disengagement 57, 59–62; dark tourism
  (*see* dark tourism); and moral agency 59–62
Moral Foundations Theory 59
morality 56
moral justification 67–8
"moral panic" 59
Morgan, N. 83, 104, 198, 200
mountaineering: and adventure tourism
  137, 148; Climbing Sherpas 147; fear and
  death 142–5; Himalayan expeditions 137–8;
  liminal dimensions, mountainside 138–40;
  liminal landscapes 137; liminal places
  and spaces 136–7; moments of agency
  and potentiality 145–7; participants'
  demographics **160**; spaces of self-making and
  risk-taking 140–2
Mowatt, R. A. 84
Mt. Everest 137, 139, 141, 143, 144, 146
Mulcahy, D. 15, 24
Müller, M. 199
Mu, Y. 163

Nassivera, F. 16
natural elements 222
nature-based tourism 196, 197, 201, 202, 204,
  209, 211; and liminality 198–9
Nelson, V. 105
Nepal 4, 7, 137–43, 147, 148
Nepal, S. 163
Nepal's mountaineering 137, 138, 148
Netherlands 65, 85, 89
netnography 8–9, 176, 181, 190, 197, 201
Neuendorf, K. A. 161

Newman, M. 6
Newsome, D. 196
New York 57
Nightingale, V. 44
non-normative liminality 169
non-normative pregnancy 169
North America 6
North Bavaria 39
Nosferatu, 1921 102
Notteboom, T. 176
*Novelty emerges from unprecedented
  combinations of familiar elements*
  (Turner) 197

Oberpfalzer Wald region 38
O'Connor, H. 200, 206
Ogborn, M. 220
Oh Ship 183, 186–8
Oliver-Smith and Hoffman (1999) 145
Olsen, K. 114
Opotow (1990) 70
Oren, G. 61
Organisation for Economic Co-operation and
  Development (OECD) 159
Ortner, S. B. 139, 140
Oswalt, P. 37, *37*

Paladino, F. J. 18
palimpsest 34, 49, 50
Parker, E. 2, 33
party tourism 176, 179–81, 183, 191;
  alcotourism 179–80
passengers 189–90
Pereiro, X. 43
personal agency 61, 62, 71
Picard, D. 15
pilgrimage landscapes 217, 218, 220–1, 223,
  225, 228, 229
pilgrims 228
Plewe, J. T. 35
Pocock, D. C. 218
Podoshen, J. S. 108
Poland 35–6, 44
Pomfret, G. 157
Poria, Y. 61
post-liminal phase 103
post-liminal rites 13
pregnancy 153, 162–7; adventure tourism
  155–6, 165–8; cultural interpretations,
  liminality 154–5
pre-liminal phase 103, 107, 108
pre-liminal rites 13
Preston-Whyte, R. 82, 104, 137
Principal Component Analysis (PCA) 108,
  110–12, **111**
Prisoner of War (POW) camp 39
Pritchard, A. 83, 104, 198, 200
Prosise, T. O. 34
pseudo-events 113–14

Rachels, J. 61
Rachels, S. 61
Raine, R. 102
Rapson, J. 48
Ravensbruck Concentration Camp 5, 36–9;
    memorial site 35–9
recreation experience 105
'red slave' site 86
resistant bodies: liberation, animals and
    mythological creatures 204–6
reviewers: Bonaire and the Netherlands 89;
    English language 89; experience 91–2;
    place 90–1; reflecting on the experience 92–3;
    self-identified country of origin 89
Reynolds, D. 33
rhizomatic body 156–8, 165, 168
Ritchie, J. R. B. 15
Rites of passage 33, 103
Robb, E. 58
Roberts, L. 2, 222–3
Robinson, M. 15
Rodrigue, J. P. 176
Rodríguez-Campo, Lorena 5
Roobaroo Walks 65
Royal Air Force 38
Rufin, J. 225
Ruscher, J. B. 68
Russia 65

Sachsenhausen Concentration Camp 35, 46
Sadhus-India's Holy men, Varanasi, India 63
Salem Witch Trials 106
Salter, C. 218, 219
Samuels, J. 82
Sánchez Bringas, A. 168
The Santiago de Compostela pilgrim 226
Sather-Wagstaff, J. 82
satisfaction (SAT) 12, 14, 22, 23, 25, 175;
    hedonism and behavioural intentions
    15–16; reliability and validity, measurement
    model 21
Saxony 39
Scarles, C. 57
Schindler's List or The Boy in the Striped
    Pyjamas 47–8
Schutzstaffel 35
Scotland 106
Seaton, A. V. 102
Selänniemi, T. 175
self-sanctions 60
Shannon, S. E. 161
Sharpley, R. 102, 107
Sherpas 7, 137–9, 141–6, 148
Shields, R. 2, 123, 137, 200
Shiva 63, 66
Siegert, Toni 41
Silas, E. 196, 200
Silesia 35–6
Simon, R. I. 82

slave huts 6, 81, 84–7, 89–96
slavery heritage 81, 82, 84, 86, 87, 95
slum tourism 6, 7, 130
Smile all 80 s Cruise 183, 186, 187
social cognitive theory 61, 73
social media 5, 8, 9, 57, 72, 86, 181–3, 186,
    188, 191, 192, 196, 197, 199–201, 206, 208,
    209, 211; communitas: pages, comments,
    followers 207–8; data collection 202–3;
    geotag-based data 202; Instagram in tourism
    research 200–1; intersection, tourism
    and liminality 197; liminality 198–200;
    netnography 201; online communications
    of users 202; resistant bodies: liberation,
    animals and mythological creatures 204–6;
    surveillance and commercialization 208–9;
    #survival, dirtiness, poetry and zen 203–4; in
    tourism 196, 199–200; transitioning 206–7;
    Web 2.0-based technologies 196
socio-cultural factors 74
sociodemographic characteristics,
    respondents 19
Sonderblock 45
Sontag, S. 57
Soper, A. K. 216, 228
South Africa 6, 89, 121, 122, 124, 130, 131, 182,
    185, 186, 188, 189
Soviet Army 38
Spain 65
spokesperson 112–13
Sternberg, R. J. 73
Stone, P. R. 33, 58, 74, 102
Streetwise Varanasi Tours 65
Structural Equation Modelling (SEM) 20
Sudetendeutsche 40
Sudetenland 35–6, 40
Sumartojo, S. 44
Suyadnya, I. W. 201
Sweden 44
Switzerland 44, 65

techspressive 196
Tenkanen, H. 201
thanatourism 81
Theory of Moral Development 59
The Way of Saint James 8, 217–26
Thomas, S. 81
Thomassen, B. 2, 14, 104, 124, 140, 218
Thurnell-Read, T. 179, 185
Tipler, C. 68
Tischer, S. 37
tourism encounters 104, 124–5, 130–2
tourism experience 15, 17, 24, 33, 96, 110, 112,
    121, 159, 175, 178, 179, 183, 191, 197, 199,
    200, 202, 204, 209, 211
Tourism Geographies 4
tourism landscapes 4–5, 25, 41, 121
tourist agency 67, 71
The Tourist Gaze 3, 102, 220

tourists experiences 33
tourist spaces 81
tourist travel phases *107*
Townships 7, 121, 122, 124, 125–33
townships of South Africa: cast of
    (composite) characters 126; context
    of 124; discourse analysis 124–6; liminality
    122, 130; literature review 122–4; post-
    liminal stage 121; research participants 131;
    setting the scene 127–9; spaces of home 121;
    tourism 122; tourism scholarship 121; and
    tourist 131, 132, *132*, 133
*Tragical History of the Life and Death of Doctor
    Faustus* 102
transatlantic slave trade 84
transformative landscapes: Auschwitz 48;
    construction of liminality 49; dynamic multi-
    layered nature 34; emotional experiences
    of visitors 43–4; Flossenburg concentration
    camp 39–43; German memorial sites 33, 47;
    German visitor at Ravensbruck 45–6; Gusen
    subcamp memorial site 49–50; management,
    memorial sites 50; *Mecklenburger
    Seenplatte* 34; memoryscape 50; Ravensbruck
    concentration camp 35–9; *Rites of
    passage* 33; Sachsenhausen Concentration
    Camp memorial site 46; *Sonderblock* 45;
    tourist activities 45; 'traumatic memories' 34;
    US Infantry Division 48
transgressive behavior 6, 56–7, 59, 60, 69, 72–4
traumatic memories 34
travel narratives 8, 176, 181, 182, 190, 217–19,
    221–3, 225, 227, 228
Tribe, J. 200
TripAdvisor 6, 81, 84, 86–8, 93, 95
Tsai, T. H. 108
Tuan, Y. F. 218
Turkey 65
Turner, V. 2, 4, 12, 13, 18, 24, 33, 61, 83, 102–4,
    121, 122, 124, 131, 138, 153, 154, 158, 188,
    197, 220

UNESCO World Heritage Sites 93–4, 218
United Kingdom 44, 64, 101

United Nations Relief and Rehabilitation
    Administration (UNRRA) 39
United States 44, 64, 94
Urry, J. 3, 124, 131, 220

Van Gennep, A. 2, 4, 9, 14, 24, 33, 105, 121, 122,
    138, 153, 154, 197, 220
Varanasi 62–3, *63*, 64, 65
Varanasi Walks 65, *66*
Varley, P. J. 145
Vásquez, C. 86, 88
Vergangenheitsbewaltigung 46
Verkasalo, H. 200
Vespestad, M. K. 199
Violi, P. 46
visitor maps 35, 37–8, *39*, 41, 43, 48–9
visitor research 33, 43, 44, 46, 48, 49
Voase, R. 200

Wahlstrom, L. 48
Waitt, G. 124
Wall-Reinius, S. 199
Wang, D. 200
Weaver, A. 175, 190
Web 2.0-based technologies 196, 200
White, N. R. 198, 200
White, P. B. 198, 200
Whiteside, S. 210
white slave site 84–7
Wilhoit, E. D. 199
Woltering, M. 199
Wright, D. W. M. 114
Wydra, H. 124

Xan Arzua Association 24

Yankholmes, A. 82
Yarnal, C. M. 175, 176, 190
Yen, D. A. W. 200
"Yolocaust" 57
Youth Protection Camp Uckermark 36–7, 45

Zelizer, B. 48
Zembylas, M. 24